"*Firefall 2.0* is one of the most impc
about the most important thing we ne
from God's work in the past to prepare

MW00873598

John Avant, Pastor, First Baptist Church, Concord, Tennessee

"This compelling story of revival is almost unbelievable, except for the truth that God answers prayer and intervenes in history. *Firefall 2.0* will give you hope and change the focus of your prayers."

Mel Blackaby, Sr. Pastor, First Baptist Church, Jonesboro, Georgia

"Finally, a definitive book available to laity and pastors alike on the subject of revival and awakening. All of us are indebted to Malcolm McDow and Alvin Reid for putting this work together. This is more than history, it's page after page of hope that God can and will do it again. The crying need of our day is revival. This book will provide valuable insight and encouragement as you seek the Lord for a mighty move of His Spirit."

Michael Catt, Pastor, Sherwood Baptist Church, Albany, Georgia

"*Firefall 2.0* addresses the greatest need we have to accelerate the completion of the Great Commission. We need the fire to fall again! Do it again Lord!"

Ronnie Floyd, Pastor, Cross Church, Northwest Arkansas

"Saints across our nation are weary of 'Church Lite.' We need the same fire of God experienced by the First Century believers in the book of Acts to fall upon our lukewarm hearts and congregations. Then and only then will the Gospel of Jesus advance exponentially. Drs. McDow and Reid have blessed us by setting forth a fresh version of their timely work, *Firefall 2.0*."

Pastor Steve Gaines, Ph.D., Bellevue Baptist Church, Memphis

"This book both inspires and convicts, and I am happy to see it re-released in this new form. No one has taught me more about contemporary revival than Alvin Reid, and McDow's biblical insights from Old Testament stories of awakening only sharpen my focus and enlarge my expectations. Lord, send down your rain upon us!"

J.D. Greear, pastor of The Summit Church, Raleigh-Durham, and author of *Stop Asking Jesus Into Your Heart* and *Gospel*

"There are great books and there are important books. *Firefall 2.0* is both. This book tells the thrilling story of God at work through history. It leaves me with a longing to know God better and to follow Him more closely. Never has a generation needed the story of revival more than this generation. I urge you to read this book and ask the Lord to send revival once again!"

Doug Munton, Senior Pastor, First Baptist Church, O'Fallon, Illinois, and Adjunct Professor of Preaching and Evangelism, Liberty Baptist Theological Seminary

582-2290

"I have immersed myself in revival books for 20 years. *Firefall 2.0* contains the best biblical overview perhaps of all. This book has the rare quality of introducing an array of vital doctrine and is yet eminently readable. I found myself wanting to slow down, underline, meditate, pray, re-read and yearn for the heart of the book: revival. This book will be wonderful to use within a devotional time or for a group."

Rhys Stenner, Pastor, New Hope Baptist Church, Fayetteville, Georgia

"*Firefall* is a clear, convincing, and compelling account of what genuine revival is really about. Read this book, then get on your knees and ask God to do it again!"

Rick Warren, Pastor, Saddleback Community Church, Lake Forest, California

"This book provoked Repentance, Revitalization and Refreshment in me! It is a MUST READ for every blood bought born again believer that has been birthed in the Body of Christ! It will equip and encourage you to be the ocular demonstration and the pictorial illustration of incarnational truth manifesting the power of God in your person, which is a primary prerequisite for the ushering in of a Spiritual Awakening and Revival!!! Thank you Dr. McDow and Dr. Reid, for this word will revolutionize all relationships and realities with the Redeemer!!!"

K. Marshall Williams Sr., Nazarene Baptist Church, Philadelphia, Pennsylvania

"*Firefall* will bring hunger to your heart and definition to your prayers."

Tom Elliff, President, International Mission Board, SBC

"A. W. Tozer once famously advised, 'Listen to the man who listens to God.' As you read Firefall it becomes obvious quite early that McDow and Reid are worthy of a listen as their commentary on revival gives evidence of time spent in God's presence. This book is much more than a textbook on revival; it is a challenge to pursue it."

Gary Frost, Vice President of Midwest Region and Prayer, North American Mission Board, SBC

"The consequence of a life postured towards repentance and submission to God's Word is revival. *Firefall 2.0* captures a comprehensive look at what God did in the lives of saints, their communities, regions, and nations when repentance and submission to God's Word was normative. I believe God is priming our nation for a biblical revival and as we catch our cue's from Scripture regarding what this looks like, we can presently utilize Firefall 2.0 as a bridge between the Church's past and future."

D.A. Horton, Author, Pastor, Speaker, National Coordinator of Urban Student Missions, North American Missions Board

"The state of our world, our nation, our churches, our homes, and our hearts clearly indicates that the greatest need of our day is revival. In their revised edition

Firefall 2.0, Dr. Malcolm McDow and Dr. Alvin Reid remind us through thrilling biblical and historical accounts how the Lord God of heaven and earth has moved in revival in the past and changed the course of human history as a result of those spiritual movements. May this updated version of one of the most comprehensive works ever published on the subject of religious revival rekindle in your heart a yearning to see the Spirit of God move in spiritual renewal and awakening in the 21st century. After you read this book, get alone with the Father and plead with Him to send 'an old-fashioned, heaven-sent, sin-erasing, restoration, soul-saving, devil-chasing, Holy Ghost Revival' to this generation! May the fires of revival fall on us all before Jesus comes again!"

Preston L. Nix, Ph.D., Professor of Evangelism and Evangelistic Preaching and Roland Q. Leavell Chair of Evangelism, Director, Leavell Center for Evangelism and Church Health, and Chairman, Pastoral Ministries Division, New Orleans Baptist Theological Seminary

"Some books in my library require a stool to reach. A few, as with *Firefall 2.0*, are an arm's length away. Every believer needs to know the stories of sweeping revival from the biblical period to today. But I am drawn into the book for a special reason. My heart leaps when the story tells of young people who were at the tip of the spear of revival and awakening. Why? Because it's the longing of my heart to see that happen in our day. McDow and Reid have shown us how to raise the sails for that very thing to happen."

Richard Ross, Professor of Student Ministry, Southwestern Baptist Theological Seminary, www.RichardARoss.com

"Jonathan Edwards observed that hearing testimony about or reading about spiritual awakening is often a "spark" that God uses to kindle prayer, repentance, and a fresh movement of the Spirit. While there are many excellent historical studies on particular awakenings, there are few comprehensive works that seek to document spiritual awakening from biblical times to the present. *Firefall 2.0* helps fill that void, and it is my pleasure to commend it with the prayer that God will use it to kindle a spiritual awakening in our day."

Timothy K. Beougher, Ph.D.Associate Dean, Billy Graham School of Missions, Evangelism and Ministry; Billy Graham Professor of Evangelism and Church Growth, The Southern Baptist Theological Seminary

"Students of spiritual awakenings become the best teachers about them. In addition to studying and teaching these powerful movements of God, Malcolm McDow and Alvin Reid are both products of awakenings. In *Firefall 2.0*, McDow and Reid have updated their classic text, explaining how God shapes history through revivals. Anyone with an eye to learn about these events in the past or with a heart yearning for such events in the future will profit from this volume."

Matt Queen, Ph.D. L. R. Scarborough Chair of Evangelism, Assistant Professor of Evangelism, Associate Dean for Doctoral Programs, Roy Fish School of Evangelism and Missions, Southwestern Baptist Theological Seminary

FireFall 2.0

How God Has Shaped History Through Revivals

Malcolm McDow & Alvin L. Reid

Published by Gospel Advance Books, Wake Forest, North Carolina.

Original edition published by Broadman & Holman Publishers.

ISBN-13: 978-1499500561
ISBN-10: 1499500564

Table of Contents

Acknowledgements

Many people have helped in the writing of this book. John Landers of Broadman & Holman initiated the original project and offered numerous helpful suggestions along the way. A general survey of revival from the biblical period to today had not been published for many years, so we are thankful to B & H for recognizing the need for such a work. Our first discussions together about spiritual awakening came in 1983, with Malcolm as the professor and Alvin as the student in a course on the subject at Southwestern Baptist Theological Seminary. Now 30 years later, Malcolm is retired and Alvin has been following in his prof's footsteps, teaching at Southeastern Baptist Theological Seminary now for almost 20 years.

A special thanks goes to those who helped with this book. Connie Cox and Becky Harber at Southwestern typed most of Part 1. Dawn Jones, Nancy Cagle, Lisa Estes, and Debi Pruitt of Southeastern assisted with the original manuscript for Part 2. In the revised and updated edition, Peggy Loafman of Southeastern has helped immeasurably with the typing. Alvin's students Jared Johnson and Kevin Stone helped with reading, editing, and preparing the manuscript. Megan Lawrence proofread the new manuscript and offered helpful comments as well. Bailey Shoemaker of Southeastern helped with the newly designed cover. Finally, Alvin's son Josh added thoughtful questions for discussion at the end of each chapter for small group study.

Many colleagues, students, and friends gave helpful comments on the manuscript. The following read portions of the original or the revision, and many of the following also offered kind endorsements for the work: John Avant, the late Lewis Drummond, Jim Elliff, the late Roy Fish, Rod Gilbert, Frank Harber, Kevin Neece, Doug Munton, Steve Gaines, Tim Beougher, J.D. Greear, Gary Frost, Mel Blackaby, Michael Catt, D.A. Horton, K. Marshall Williams, Richard Ross, Preston Nix, Rick Warren, Tom Elliff, and Rhys Stenner.

Robert Coleman, one of the great men of God of our era, wrote a wonderful Foreword to the book. Pastor Ronnie Floyd, a man who has been leading in calling pastors together to pray for revival and has had revival on his heart a long time, wrote a concluding challenge at the book's end. We hope this update will be especially helpful to pastors who hunger to see God move in their churches.

Special appreciation is expressed to those who supported us in the writing of the original and revised versions, including our seminary Presidents Ken Hemphill, Paige Patterson, and Danny Akin; Academic Deans, the late Tommy Lea and the late L. Russ Bush III; and provost Bruce Ashford and Dean Chuck Lawless. Southwestern also granted a sabbatical leave for Malcolm to work on the original manuscript.

More than any other, we thank our families. When we wrote the original our children were obviously much younger! The McDow girls Melissa and Melody have made Malcolm a grandpa, while Alvin's kids Josh and Hannah have recently married as well. All serve the Lord and bring great joy to their Dads.

We especially thank our wives Melba McDow and Michelle Reid for their belief in us, in our ministries, and in our heart for revival. May our children and grandchildren see God move in revival.

Foreword

Sometimes heaven seems to come down to earth. Men and women with lives devastated by sin find in Jesus the grace to repent and the power to change. Wrongs are made right. Broken homes reunite. The church, made beautiful in holiness, reaches out in love to serve a hurting and lost world.

This is revival — coming alive to God. It is during these times of refreshing from the Presence of the Lord that the world of the Holy Spirit comes into bold relief.

Thankfully, in terms of personal spirituality, a revival undercurrent always flowers in the lives of those saints who never bow their knee to Baal. But there are seasons when this stream breaks forth in mighty power, affecting multitudes of people, and occasionally changing the courses of nations.

Studying these great epics of revival becomes a strong stimulant to faith. God is seen in His awesome Sovereignty, with uncompromising purpose, even seeking to make a people for His glory. By uncovering the spiritual principles inherent in these awakenings, we can learn what we must do to prepare the way for Him to act.

The authors of this book are eminently qualified to unfold these lessons. Dr. Malcolm McDow and Dr. Alvin L. Reid, both distinguished scholars and teachers, combine their gifts to trace in these pages the movement of revival from the biblical era to the present.

Giving the account an authentic flavor is their own experiences of divine fire. No mere theoreticians, these men write from the heart. You will sense the burden of their souls as they tell the story.

Never has their message been more timely. Civilization as we know it totters on the brink of self-destruction. One does not have to be a prophet to foresee the disintegration of our society unless revival comes.

Yet, as you will read, it is when the night closes in that we see the stars most clearly. This is happening today. While forces of evil are becoming more sinister and aggressive, a corresponding cry for spiritual awakening can be felt across the land.

As factual reporting, I believe this journey through history will give substance to your yearning for revival, even as it points the way. What is better, if you meet God's conditions for personal renewal, your life will help kindle the flame of revival in others. May the fire fall!

Robert E. Coleman

Preface

I am a product of revival. I received Jesus Christ as my personal Savior on October 24, 1951, in Waco, Texas, during the Mid-Century Revival. I was called to the ministry on August 11, 1954, during the same renewal. I was also greatly influenced by the Jesus Movement. In 1970, while serving as pastor in Memphis, Tennessee, I went through a time of spiritual crisis. This crisis started in June. Since I believed that prayer was God's answer for spiritual need, I prayed about the matter. However, the more I prayed the worse it got. Serving became drudgery; preaching became a duty. By October, I became desperate. I knew that I could not continue to serve in the midst of such a spiritual struggle. I was broken by God. Daily I prayed that God would do "something" in my life. He did!

On Novembers 30, 1970, I attended a conference at the Bellevue Baptist Church in Memphis. The speaker shared the testimonies of several people who had experienced personal revivals and the differences those spiritual encounters made in their lives. As I listened to the testimonies, I asked God to express His grace toward me through personal awakening. Immediately, I experienced a joy unspeakable, spiritual vitality, and submission to His lordship. On that night, I had a personal revival. The revival ignited in the church where I served on March 19, 1972

For years I wanted to write on the history of spiritual awakening. When I received the invitation from Broadman and Holman Publishers to write this book, it was an assignment that I wanted to do. We are happy to offer this revised and updated version both in print and electronic formats. I have had the privilege of writing the first seven chapters of this book. The principles of awakening in chapter 1 are based upon personal experiences, observations, and extensive studies. The Old Testament revivals are representative of the significant awakenings in Jewish history. Since awakenings never occur within vacuums, attempts are made to place each biblical revival within its historical context.

Moses at Sinai is selected because of its extraordinary impact upon Israel and because it was the first recorded national awakening. Elijah at Carmel is included because it was the only recorded revival in the Northern Kingdom. Jonah in Nineveh is selected because it was the only Old Testament revival among Gentiles. The revival under Asa is covered because it was the first revival after the division of the Davidic kingdom into North and South. The Josiah Revival is included because it was the last renewal before the exile. Ezra/Nehemiah is covered because it was the last awakening in the Old Testament, it prepared the Jews for the inter-biblical period, and it founded Judaism, which flourished in the New Testament era. The New Testament revivals are included because they were a part of the ministry of Jesus and the birth of the church, and because they are examples of the expansion of Christianity across the Roman Empire. The revivals in Christian history are selected because of their impact upon the spread of Christianity. The major reforms, although not revivals, are included because of their immeasurable influence upon Christian history. Even in the midst of reform, some of the Lollards and Anabaptists experienced renewals.

This book is offered with the desire that it might serve as a beacon to expand our understanding of spiritual awakening, enlighten us on God's movements in history, and inspire us to "wrestle with God" until the spiritual tidal waves of awakening move with heaven's force throughout the earth.

In 1966 I studied at the University of Edinburgh in Scotland. Standing in front of the pulpit in St. Giles Cathedral where John Knox thundered God's Word in the sixteenth century, I asked God to allow me to participate in a spiritual awakening. God has more than graciously granted that request. Awakenings teach that God's blessings in one generation are available for His children in any generation when His requirements in *2* Chronicles 7:14 are met.

Malcolm McDow
Fort Worth, Texas

I remember vividly the year 1970. A skinny and insecure eleven-year-old, I was too young to be one of the hippies so common at that time. I soon witnessed events like I have rarely seen. In a period of a few months, we received many of these so-called hippies into our fellowship at the Center Crest Baptist Church. The flood of young people caused a visible change in the life of our small congregation. Services concluded with index fingers stretched high into the air, "One way through Jesus!" was the cry. We began a "One Way Christian Night Club" to reach wayward teens. I didn't know it at the time, but our congregation was one example of the Jesus Movement that swept the country in the early 1970s. The unashamed love for Christ, the zeal for God's Word, the sincerity of these young people made an indelible impression on me. It played a vital role in my own conversion that year. *If Jesus can change some of these kids,* I remember thinking, *He can change me too.*

I have never gotten over what I saw and heard in those days. I have since had a growing hunger to see a mighty movement of God sweep our nation. A course with my coauthor on spiritual awakenings while in seminary deepened my longing to study such movements in history. A doctoral seminar with Roy Fish of Southwestern Baptist Theological Seminary on the subject of spiritual awakenings deepened my understanding of true revival. Then, in 1995, I was privileged to see the Lord move. He brought brokenness, confession, and cleansing in service after service. Churches and universities became islands of awakening like I had not seen as an adult.

In the eighteenth century, Jonathan Edwards said the thing that helped to promote the spirit of revival in his church at Northampton, Massachusetts, was to tell the people what God was doing elsewhere. I know how deeply reading accounts of past awakenings has influenced my life. Recent events illustrate to me the need to get the story of mighty revivals in history to the people.

For much of my life, I knew God moved mightily in Scripture. However, I somehow developed the idea that God was not as involved in history since the biblical days. My study of the great awakenings has demolished that myth. As I have shared the story of modem awakenings in classes and in churches, it has become apparent that a growing number of believers, including educators, ministers, and laity, long to know more about past accounts of great outpourings of the Spirit.

Firefall 2.0 is designed to be a general survey of some of the major movements in history. It makes no claim to be exhaustive in its treatment of history; it will hopefully provide a faithful narrative of more significant movements of revival. It represents out effort to inform believers in understanding what revival is and to inspire believers to pray with the prophet, "Oh, that thou wouldst rend the heavens and come down!" (Isa. 64:1)

In part 2, I examine the modern awakenings that have shaped the Christian faith, particularly in the West. May God once again visit His church with mighty revival.

Alvin L. Reid
Wake Forest, North Carolina

Introduction to Part One
Revival Movements from the Old Testament to the Reformation

In his book *The World Is Flat: A Brief History of the Twenty-First Century*, author Thomas Friedman surveys the dramatic changes brought about by new technologies like the Internet. From social media to smart phones, from bloggers to hackers, we live in arguably the most dramatic time of change in human history. News from anywhere on the earth can be accessed immediately, offering the possibility of spreading the gospel in ways never known before. But even as our digital age affords the opportunity to connect globally, there still resides in the heart of every person a hunger for God and a desire for more than a social network and a Google search.

People still want to know God and to see Him move. The question for us today is less, "How will He move in our time?" It is more, "Can we see Him at work today, and can we put ourselves in a position where God can use us for His glory?"

These questions can be answered in part by asking the question: "How has God moved in the past, and what can we learn from how He has moved previously to be ready for His fresh wind to blow in our time?" The study of the history of revivals can help us here. Understanding the work of God in the past can both inform and inspire us to seek a fresh wind from heaven, a fresh touch from the God Who is the Author of revival.

Today, discouraging signs abound. Stagnant growth, ineffective ministries, and a general malaise represent far too many churches in the West. At the same time, culture continues to marginalize Christian morality and advance a consumer mentality that has captivated most, including too many in the church. That we need a God-intervention in our time can hardly be debated. Still, encouraging signs give hope in a culture that increasingly dismisses biblical conviction. We can hope in a many in the younger generation weary of playing church — a mob of Millennials who have essentially said for the church either to live out the faith or leave them alone. A rising movement of gospel recovery gives testimony to the weariness with moralism and a hunger for the message of Christ, and an unprecedented vision for global evangelism exists. God is moving at places around the world and in pockets in the West.

Yes, the church in the West desperately needs a fresh wind of the Spirit to blow. He will not act in a way that is contrary to His Word and His ways. But if history tells us anything it tells us His ways are not our ways, and we may see the next great movement in recognizable but yet in unique fashion. A movement of revival today, like those in years gone by, will doubtless involve a significant number of young people.

In the pages that follow you will read the accounts of the work of God from the Old Testament to our day. You can read the book from start to finish, or you may want to study a particular awakening, like the First Great Awakening, individually. We have attempted to write this in such a way that you can do either.

For the past few centuries a typical Christian in the world would have been someone like each of us who wrote this book: a western, white man. But today a typical world Christian would more likely be a teenaged girl in Latin America or a young man in sub-Sahara Africa. Before long a typical world Christian may as likely be a Chinese as an American. For that reason the best person to write the next volume on more recent movements should probably be a person of color from a land other than the West. So much more could be and should be written. But for now the question remains, regardless of the color of our skin or the location on the globe: are we advancing the movement of the gospel in our time? For if we are, we put ourselves in a more likely place to see God at work.

Duncan Campbell, who saw God work in revival in the Hebrides Revival, tells of two angels having a conversation as they looked at an unsuspecting gathering of believers.

"Do you think God will send revival to those people?" One angel asked.

"The question," the other angel said in reply, "Is whether or not God can *trust* them with revival."

May we so live that God can trust us with a fresh measure of His Spirit. And may the stories you read in the pages that follow inspire you to become someone God might trust with a movement.

Part One:

Revival From the Old Testament Through the Reformation

Malcolm McDow

Chapter 1
Understanding Revival

"I will sing a new song to thee, O God"
Psalm 144:9

Across the years Christians have been fascinated, intrigued, and desirous of revival. Indeed, a unique and mysterious aura surrounds it. Christians ask questions:

What is revival?

What are the dynamics and characteristics of revival?

What is God's role in revival?

What part does the Christian play in revival?

These are serious questions demanding serious consideration.

God stands always as the grand architect of spiritual awakening. As we study spiritual movements in history, we also recognize that revivals are the products of the cooperative efforts between God and His people. Renewal requires both the supernatural and the natural. In the supernatural, God invades the lives of His people, exercises His sovereignty, releases His power, and fulfills His purposes. In the natural, the Christian fulfills the requirements of 2 Chronicles 7:14: humility, prayer, seeking God, and repentance. When Christians cooperate, God produces revival.

God's reasons for His divine interventions are preparation, proclamation, and preservation. In preparation, God rearranges the trajectory of His people, preparing them to fulfill their Kingdom mission. In proclamation, God empowers His people to proclaim prophetically and compassionately His divine reconciliation. In preservation, God intensifies discipleship, inspires evangelistic outreach, and conserves results.

What Is Revival?

The words *renewal, revival,* and *spiritual awakening* will be used synonymously in this book. We must distinguish them from an *evangelistic campaign.* An evangelistic campaign signifies the effort of the church to evangelize lost people in the community within a specified period of time. Revival is God's interaction with His people in order to energize them spiritually. Some writers distinguish the difference between revival and spiritual awakening. For some, revival means the spiritual resurgence of God's people, and spiritual awakening is the evangelistic ingathering as the result of God's people being revived.

In Jonathan Edwards's classic on the First Great Awakening we see that he held the view that spiritual awakening focuses upon conversions: *A Faithful Narrative of the Surprising Work of God in the Conversion of Many Hundred Souls in North Hampton and the Neighboring Towns and Villages.*[1] In addition, J. Edwin Orr distinguished between revival and spiritual awakening.[2] Frank Beardsley suggested a similar view when he stated, "Revivals of religion primarily are a means for the conversion of sinners."[3] Henry T. Blackaby and Claude King also favor this view.[4] However, for this book the terms revival and spiritual awakening are used interchangeably.

Old Testament Words for Revival

Three Old Testament[5] and three New Testament terms translated "renewal" or its equivalent help us to understand revival.

1. *Chalaph.* The Hebrew word *chalaph*[6] means to "change," "replace," "move from one place to another," or "substitute." It is a military term that depicts a person surrounded by hostile forces. The imagery is of a person who, although surrounded, has his situation altered through the resources of God. The word conveys the idea that the believer dwells in abject conditions until rescued by God from those conditions. Awakening is God's rescue of His people as He moves them out of the hostile surroundings of God's enemy into joyful, bountiful relationships with God. We see this term used in Isaiah 40:31. This word *chalaph* also means to "come over," "hover over," or "dwell over." From this perspective, revival occurs when God "hovers" or "dwells" over His people in order to alter or substitute the undesirable circumstances with God's desired conditions.[7]

2. Chayah. The second Hebrew word is *chayah.* This word has a variety of meanings. It can mean "life" or "live." This word includes the totality of existence. It conveys that God is the "Creator of life," "Possessor of life," "Preserver of life," or "Bestower of life." When applied to revival, it indicates that God provides a deeper spiritual quality of life, and awakening is the result of that experience.

Chayah can also mean "length of life." From this definition, revival means to come alive and enjoy a rich and full life. In simple terms, it means to "remain healthy."[8] This word can also mean to "keep God's commandments" (see Lev 18:5; Prov 4:4; 7:2). Interwoven in this idea is that revival is living in obedience to God. It can also mean, "cure from disease" (see *2* Kings 5:7). From this viewpoint, revival is the cure from spiritual disease.

From the plethora of meanings derived from the word chayah, awakening means that God restores to healthy relationships those who are spiritually strengthened by Him as they live in obedience to Him. This is the word used in the prayer for revival in Psalm 85:6.

3. *Chadhash.* This word means to "become new," "renew," "rejuvenate," or "restore a new song." Psalm 40:3a says, "He put a new song in my mouth, a song of praise to our God." Psalm 144:9a says, "I will sing a new song to thee, O God." These various images coalesce into the picture that revival produces "a new song," a symphony of praise to God.

In conclusion, these words convey that without awakening, God's people are surrounded by hostile forces; in awakening, they are delivered. Without awakening, they live in spiritual inertia; in awakening, they live in spiritual power. Without awakening, they are spiritually sick; in awakening, they are spiritually cured. Without awakening, they live in disobedience to God; in awakening, they live in obedience to

Him. Without awakening, their worship is impotent; in awakening, their worship is a new song, a symphony of praise to God. Indeed, awakening is a spiritual change that alters Christian living.

New Testament Words for Revival

1. *Anakainos*. One Greek word that serves as a mirror to reflect the beautiful picture of revival is *anakainos*.[9] In this word, the idea of "renewal of mind" emerges. The mind has become unfocused, has digressed from God's intended direction, and is cluttered with earthly desires. Revival is God's process by which He refocuses the mind upon Kingdom priorities. This idea is expressed in Romans 12:1-2.

2. *Egeiro*. The second word is *egeiro*. It means, "to awaken," "to raise," or "to rise." The basic meaning is "to awaken from sleep." When applied to revival, it projects the idea of cessation of the old lifestyle and the embrace of the new quality of living in God. It is the imagery of a Christian "lying down" or "sitting down." In this prone position, the Christian has ceased the performance of the primary activity in Kingdom living. He has stopped doing the tasks that he has been saved and commanded by God to do and needs to "wake up" or "stand up" to his responsibilities in Christ. From this idea, revival means to "arouse from sleep," or "change location." The Christian has gone to sleep on God, and God wakes up that believer; thus, spiritual awakening.

This is the word that is used in reference to the Resurrection of Jesus. In the physical sense, it means, "to raise from the dead." In the spiritual sense, it means "to awaken Christians from spiritual sleep" in order to focus them upon the things of God. In this definition, Christians are described as being mired in spiritual inertia, but through revival they are aroused by God to His claim upon their lives and empowered for Kingdom mission.

3. *Anastasis, anistemi.* The third word is *anastasis* and its derivative, *anistemi.* The word *anastasis* literally means "resurrection." *Anistemi* means "raise," "get up," or "rise," which suggests that spiritual awakening can be interpreted as a spiritual resurrection.

Anastasis unveils a kaleidoscopic meaning to revival. When applied to Christ's resurrection, it means restoration to resurrected life. When applied to salvation, *anastasis* means resurrection from spiritual death to spiritual life, which is the very essence of the new birth. When applied to revival, it means, among other things, that the children of God are raised from spiritual sleep to spiritual vitality.

The derivative, *anistemi*, means to "raise from the dead," "stand up," "get ready," "get prepared," and "appoint." From these ideas, revival conveys that the people of God in their unfocused conditions have strayed from God's intended plans, and He divinely invades their lives in order to restore and prepare them for the purposes that He has ordained for them.

Definitions of Revival

Now let us consider various definitions of revival, concluding with our own.

E. Earle Cairns: "I define revival or renewal as the work of the Holy Spirit in restoring the people of God to a more vital spiritual life, witness, and work by prayer and the Word after repentance in crisis for their spiritual decline. The permanent elements in revival are the Word, prayer, the Holy Spirit, and a sovereign God who uses man as His instrument."[10]

C. E. Autrey: "Revival is a reanimating of those who already possess life. Revival in the strict sense of the word has to do with God's people. It revives spiritual life that is in a state of declension. Revival is an instrument of evangelism."[11]

Richard Owen Roberts: Spiritual awakening is "an extraordinary movement of the Holy Spirit producing extraordinary results."[12]

Stephen Olford: Revival is that "strange and sovereign work of God in which He visits His own people, restoring, reanimating and releasing them into the fullness of His blessing."[13]

Edwin Orr: Awakening is a "movement of the Holy Spirit bringing about a revival of New Testament Christianity in the Church of Christ and in its related community."[14]

Malcolm McDow and Alvin Reid: "Revival is God's invasion into the lives of one or more of His people in order to awaken them spiritually for Kingdom ministry."

> Revival: "God invades the lives of His people, exercises His sovereignty, releases His power, and fulfills His purposes."

Six Types of Revival

Six classifications of spiritual awakening include personal, institutional, regional, specialized, national, and global. Revivals always start with personal encounters with God and travel through concentric circles to their conclusions. Although all revivals are personal, they seldom go through every circle of activity. They stop along the pathways within the divine intentions of God. Each type of revival reflects a legitimate renewal. Many speak of revival only when it has significant impact upon a nation, but not all revivals are so extensive. In the history of the United States, four national and two specialized revivals have had major national consequences.

Type 1: Personal Revival. Personal revival takes place within the life of the Christian. Before personal revival, the he misdirects priorities from the things of God to personal preferences and becomes desensitized to spiritual realities. Although he may be very active in the church, even a preacher in the pulpit, he lacks joy and excitement. Living the Christian life is performed more out of duty than out of privilege marked by praise. Worship becomes mechanical and formal instead of spontaneous and natural.

On the one hand, the believer lacks celebration in worship, is void of spiritual power, and lacks victory in living. On the other hand, he may know his spiritual condition yet rationalize that things are not as bad as they really are. In these circumstances, the Holy Spirit begins the work of conviction. As the believer begins to awaken, recognition of his need for revival progresses to desperation for it. He renounces sin, seeks the mind of God, and submits to God. The Holy Spirit becomes a fresh wind blowing across his soul, awakening the child of God from spiritual slumber.

As the Christian awakens, he enjoys fresh fellowship with God, a paring away of old agendas, redirection of his life's focus, the establishment of new priorities, a new surge of spiritual power, spiritual freedom, a new song in his heart,[15] a new thirst and hunger for the things of God, and a renewing of the covenant to serve God.

Delight replaces drudgery. Celebrative worship replaces cold orthodoxy. Renewed dedication replaces a sense of duty. The Christian awakens to a new morning of Kingdom citizenship and realizes that the wonder of knowing Christ offers yet more with each passing day. The response is often, "I thought something more might be available, but I did not know it was anything like this. Why did I wait so long?"

The Christian has just experienced personal revival. Renewal means more than rededication, which may last a few hours or a few days. Revival indicates chayah, an experience that is pinpointed in life and remembered forever. Occasionally, Christians whose salvation experiences were not dramatic may equate revival with conversion. Revival is not conversion; it is renewal. Revival does not produce sinless perfection; it is an experience with the Holy Spirit that produces a submission of life to the lordship of Jesus Christ. After the renewal occurs within the Christian's life, he still encounters problems and temptations; however, a new spiritual vitality energizes him to face the struggles.

Type 2: Institutional Revival. The second type of revival occurs in an institution, usually a church or a school. When one or a few Christians experience awakening and share their testimonies, the revival expands through the institutional family. One of the crucial, primary principles of revival is that it never starts with the masses. It always starts with one or a few whom the Holy Spirit ignites; then it spreads to many as a movement of God. If preachers and church leaders focus upon the entire congregation for the revival starting point, they will be disappointed. Revival always starts with that one or those few who are serious with God, are ignited by God, and who become flames from which others can be set afire.

An institutional revival can come even when some members are skeptical of God's movement within the body. When revival erupts, the tendency is to expect all to receive immediately what God is doing, but this is never the case. Skeptics are witnessing things beyond their experience. Because they have not experienced revival before, they seek to explain away the reality of the movement. These explanations often convey antagonistic attitudes toward revival. In addition, some Christians simply do not want to participate. You can be in the middle of the activity of God and miss Him.

When revival comes to an institution, believers are rejuvenated with spiritual vigor and establish Kingdom purposes as priorities. Changes often occur as old agendas are jettisoned and replaced with renewed biblical focus. In church revival movements, the worship services become exercises in celebration, preaching becomes focused upon God's intentions for the church, teachers are empowered with renewed commitments, and people attend church with rekindled expectations as they express their excitement for what God is doing. The end results in a church revival are: Jesus is Lord, the Holy

Spirit is unleashed, the Father is glorified, the church is edified, and lost people are evangelized.

Type 3: Regional Revival. Ordinarily, when revival ignites within the local church, it spreads to the community and to other churches in the area, crossing denominational lines and enhancing cooperation and fellowship among churches of different doctrinal persuasions. The revival may spread across the city, or it may be even more widespread.

In a regional revival, the entire area is impacted to some degree by the Holy Spirit. Changes are evidenced in race relationships, morality, economic enterprises, and ethical standards. There are always evangelistic results. Conversation in the marketplace is often focused on Jesus as the subject of rejuvenation, and excitement about spiritual matters is in the air.

Type 4: Specialized Revival. The specialized revival ordinarily focuses upon persons of a particular age group, usually youth. The Jesus Movement of the 1960s and 1970s was a specialized awakening. Although many older adults were participants, most of those involved were youth and younger adults. Specialized awakenings may occur on the institutional, area, national, or global levels.

Type 5: National Revival. The national awakening defines the ultimate spiritual movement within a country. In this renewal, the entire nation is impacted by God's invasion into the lives of His people. A revival of this magnitude will have impact to some degree in five primary areas: new church directions, economic adjustments, social reform, political corrections, and educational alterations.

When Christians think of revival, they tend to think of national awakenings. However, this type of renewal seldom occurs. In America, four revivals are classified according to these categories as national awakenings:

(1) First Great Awakening (1726-70). The dates of this revival range from Theodore Frelinghuysen in the Raritan Valley, New Jersey, in 1726, to the death of George Whitefield in 1770. In 1841, Albert Barnes suggested the revival lasted from 1730-50.[16]

(2) Second Great Awakening (1787-1843). In 1787, revival emerged at Hampden-Sydney that lasted in intervals until 1843. The Yale, Frontier, and Finney revivals are considered part of this spiritual movement. The modern mission movement, a result of the Haystack Prayer Meeting in 1806 in Williamstown, Massachusetts, was greatly impacted by this renewal.

(3) Layman's Prayer Revival (1857-59). Under the leadership of Jeremiah Lanphier, this revival ignited during a small noonday prayer meeting in September 1857 in the Old Dutch Reform Church on Fulton Street, Brooklyn, New York. Although the termination date is listed as 1859, revival fires continued in certain areas during the Civil War (1861-65), especially in Illinois and Virginia. Virtually all denominations were impacted by this revival. The great evangelist D. L. Moody spoke of the profound impact of this movement on his life. The conversion of Charlotte (Lottie) Moon in 1859 under the preaching of John A. Broadus ultimately changed the mission approach of the Southern Baptist denomination.

(4) Global Revival (1901-10).[17] The Mid-century Revival (1949-60) and the Jesus Movement of the 1960s and 1970s are considered to be specialized awakenings, although they had national impact.

In a national awakening, all segments of society are influenced to some degree. The tendency to discount any awakening that does not have nationwide impact is unwarranted.

Type 6: Global Revival.[18] In this type of movement, the entire world is impacted in some manner as the Holy Spirit invades the lives of God's people. Every continent and many nations, to some degree, benefit from a global revival. A revival is classified as global when enough strategically located countries around the world experience renewal.

The Revival of 1901-10 is considered a global revival. Although historians tend to date the revival with the emerging ministries of Evan Roberts (1878-1951) and Rhys Bevan Jones in Wales, the brushfires of revival were already burning. The Pentecostal movement in America was underway; the greatest impetus for the global revival was the Azusa Street revival. Preachers like Seth Joshua, used of God to ignite Evan Roberts when he was a 26-year-old ministerial student at Emlyn Academy in Wales, and Americans Wilbur Chapman and Billy Sunday exemplify some of the leaders in this movement. In this revival, every continent and many nations were impacted.

Qualities of Revival Leaders

Effective leaders are necessary for spiritual awakenings to have stability and enjoy longevity.[19] The pattern for national revivals typically includes one or a few leaders who emerge as the flag bearers on the national scene, and many others who provide leadership in smaller geographical areas. Revival leaders who are used mightily of God have discernible qualities. They are servants of God who interpret the renewal to the people, organize to conserve results, and direct activities under the leadership of the Holy Spirit. The effective leader hears God's voice when all other ears are deaf. He hears God's call, is unwavering in his commitment, and has a seemingly unexplainable power with people. God has touched him, and God uses him to touch others. The burden of revival is upon him; there is "fire in his bones," and he can do no other than to preach the message of renewal that God has laid upon his soul.

The revival leader has a keen awareness of the holiness of God and the sinfulness of man. He is not a copy machine to reproduce ideas, but God's spokesman to deliver God's message. He is a human being who has encountered God, experienced brokenness, and is on a mission for God. He is often misunderstood and frequently criticized. Yet, he is not easily deterred, derailed, or discouraged. Indeed, the effective revival leader is marked by certain indispensable qualities that make him useful in God's work.

Quality l: Prayer. The training for the effective revival leader is centered in the school of prayer. E. M. Bounds explains, "What the church needs today is not more machinery or better methods, not new organizations or more and novel methods, but men whom the Holy Ghost can use — men of prayer, men mighty in prayer. The Holy Ghost does not flow through methods, but through men. He does not come on machinery, but on men. He does not anoint plans, but men — men of prayer."[20]

Through prayer, the leader's voice ascends the heights of heaven and falls upon the ears of God. The leader knows that prayer for revival lives as long as God desires to bless His people. He knows that prayer is more than performance, posture, or petition; it is position. That position is in the center of God's will for his life.

In this position, God does not go around him to work, but goes through him and uses him as the conduit of grace. The effective leader knows that prayer is the track upon which people move toward the Holy God and their heavenly home. He knows that without prayer there is no power.

God's servants through history have been prayer warriors. Luther spent three hours a day in prayer. David Brainerd testified, "I poured out my soul before God that God should be known as God to the ends of the earth." He spent endless hours in prayer, at times on his knees in the snow. Andrew Murray testified that the effective leader knows that prayer is the indispensable armor in his arsenal; he dared not venture forth without it.

> Revival leaders are
> —Keenly aware of God's holiness
> —Frequently criticized
> —Not easily discouraged

Quality 2: Faith. The effective leader understands that "without faith it is impossible to please God" (Heb 11:6, NIV). A study of revival leaders in history illuminates the importance of faith. Whether it was Moses at Sinai, Elijah at Carmel, Peter at Pentecost, Luther at Wittenberg, Wesley at Bristol, Whitefield at Boston Common, or Finney at New York, revival leaders possess a deep conviction that God fulfills His promises.

Across the years, leaders who committed themselves to their task did not waver at the cost, but labored in triumphant faith. As in Acts 3-4, persecution was received as a blessing, and believers responded to injustices with attitudes of joy and privilege. Revival leaders may face opposition, but they are never ultimately defeated. They learn through experience that their faith aflame serves to ignite faith in others.

Quality 3: Focus. Effective revival leaders have passionate, single-minded obedience to God. They look upon their circumstances as windows of opportunity that must be opened. Wesley preached as a revival leader for 53 years, traveled 250,000 miles on horseback and foot, wrote more than 250 tracts and books, and preached approximately 40,000 sermons. Whitefield made seven trips to the American colonies and lived his motto: "I would rather burn out than rust out."

Leaders focus on the eternal, and their earthly conditions become stages upon which God demonstrates His sufficiency. Focus is indispensable, for it provides stability and longevity to the renewal. Every revival leader must be diligent in his efforts to safeguard against the promotion of self so that he does not become a stumbling block to renewal. He knows that no outside forces can halt God's work through his life; however, he is fully aware that the progress of revival can be stopped through his own deficient inner relationship with God.

With passionate zeal, the revival leader keeps the fires of renewal burning in his own life in order that fires might ignite in the lives of others. Because he has access to God, he indeed has power with men.

Quality 4: Vision. The revival messenger he serves with confidence in the omnipotent power, sovereign rule, and unfailing, glorious faithfulness of God. He exudes confidence in God's Word, which will "not return unto God void," but promises to return the trophies and treasures of human souls. He shuns compromise with the world as he rejoices in the privilege of serving God.

Whether it was Zinzendorf (leader of the European Pietistic movement that emerged at Herrnhut on August 13, 1727) or Francis of Assisi (revival leader 1209-26), God's marks His messenger with the strong conviction that God is triumphant and that the leader is merely participating in the victory already assured by God.

Quality 5: Industriousness. Whether we look at Moses in the Sinai desert, Wesley in England, Edwards in New England, or Finney in New York, revival leaders did not shun hard work, tedious tasks, or long hours. They are not concerned with leisure time, though they use retreats for rejuvenation.

The effective revival leader's major concern is to communicate Kingdom truths. The leader at times may exhibit endurance and physical strength that exceeds his own resources and cannot be explained with human rationale. He understands the importance of pacing his activity and possesses the ability to discern the differences between primary tasks and secondary causes.

In conclusion, the messenger chosen by God for leadership is an effective communicator with tireless energy who is committed both to Christ and to biblical theology. He makes himself available to God and exercises discipline to maintain his relationship with God. He is serious about his mission and would not trade his task for earth's greatest treasures. The leader is an ordinary human being who experiences the extraordinary hand of God upon his life, receives a message from God, establishes a vision that transcends earthly horizons, jettisons complacent mediocrity, and commits his life to the divine task laid upon him by God. He can do no more, and he dares to do no less.

Conditions in Society

Charles Finney said that revival "presupposes a declension."[21] Before every revival in history, deteriorating conditions have been evident in secular society and among God's people. In society, the secular man establishes himself as the ultimate authority for living. In this secular humanism, society deteriorates under inferior leadership, develops a lack of direction, flounders in a sense of helplessness, and turns to human resources for answers. It becomes mired in a cyclical pattern tending toward a downward spiral. Natural man looks at himself and rationalizes that he is not as alienated from God as some Christians proclaim. Through his human rationale, he convinces himself that his conclusions about himself are the realities of his nature and destination. He follows the imaginations of his heart, and these are always contrary to the mind of God. He relegates God to some antiquated past or considers that God is no longer relevant for today's sophisticated, advanced age of technology. Even if he acknowledges God, he believes that God exists to serve him instead of him to serve God. At best, he thinks that he chooses the option of how he is to respond to God. This reversal of divine authority leaves him alienated from God and in great need of spiritual life.

Conditions in the Church

Within the church, the decline is evident through her spiritual deadness. As spiritual lethargy permeates the church, skepticism toward God, biblical authority, Kingdom demands, the nature and mission of Jesus Christ, the condition of man, the purpose of the church, and the meaning of salvation emerge. Many churches are swept along with the tide of humanism. Church agendas become more important than the adoration of Jesus Christ. The church becomes spiritually impotent as it adapts its standards in order to be compatible with the world's standards. In these instances, worship services lose their power, Christians lose their vision, and spiritual inertia weaves its way into the very soul of the church. Changes within the church become more difficult. Church programs become the purpose of her existence as agendas consume people's time, talents, and treasure. In this weakened spiritual condition, the church's unwritten purpose becomes little more than to maintain ministry as it has always existed. The church drifts with the tides of society and the fads of human ingenuity. Indeed, the church desires to be served instead of acting as God's institution to serve.

The church substitutes ritual and form for biblical worship. In this climate, services often follow certain prescribed liturgies. Spontaneity and freedom of expression are discouraged.

God's people need a divine invasion to establish God's sovereignty and awaken His church in order to refocus its direction, redefine its ministry, and reclaim its purpose for existence. When the church is awakened, she is prepared to provide the answers that secular society is seeking.

Decline precedes awakening. James Burns observed, "The wave of spiritual progress recedes, but even in receding it is gathering in power and volume to return, and to rush further"[22] in its progress toward God. In the divine providence of God, the depth to which the church sinks has its limitations. Again Burns notes, "God has set a limit even to the defection of His church; when the night is at its darkest, the dawn is on its way."[23]

Four "Steps" to Begin Revival

How do revivals begin? Answers to that question vary widely. Jonathan Edwards believed Christians are passive beneficiaries in God's movement.[24] Charles G. Finney taught the opposite: revival is "a purely philosophical result of the right use of the constituted means."[25]

Both divine sovereignty and human free will are significant in initiating revival. God in His sovereignty exercises total freedom in His expression and movement. Yet, He has chosen to use spiritual awakening as a cooperative effort between Him and His people. Christians are not passive pawns on God's divine chessboard, waiting to be moved to the next position in God's divine plan. For far too long, Christians have been waiting in their "upper rooms" for the Holy Spirit to ignite revival. The wait ended at Pentecost. Christians need not wait for the Holy Spirit; He is waiting for Christians. Believers have not because we ask not.

> When a church is spiritually dead, worship services lose their power, Christians lose their vision, and spiritual inertia weaves its way into the very existence of the church.

Revival is a promise from God to the people of God. While no set formula exists to create revival, from the perspective of man, four steps consistently precede such movements: recognition of need, repentance from sin, obedience to God, and the exercise of faith.

Step l: Recognition of Need. Revivals begin when that one or more believes recognize the need for renewal and have become desperate enough to offer unqualified commitment instead of qualified compromise to God. Whether it was Patrick in Ireland, Columba at Iona, Francis of Assisi, or John Wesley in England, catalysts of renewal all had a sense of desperation. God is not reluctant to send revival, but He must arrange events in the lives of His people in order to prepare them for the experience. Desperation leads to conviction, repentance, cleansing, and revival.

Step 2: Repentance from Sin. In every awakening, repentance has been crucial. The Greek word for repentance is *metanoia,* which means, "change the mind" or "change the attitude." Ordinarily, Christians repent from the sins in life that cause misery. Since they do not want to experience misery, they quickly confess those overt sins. However, hidden sins and pet habits are the sins that block revival. In renewal, the Christian comes clean with God.

Step 3: Obedience to God. As Christians stand up to their responsibilities in Christ, they render obedience to Him. Obedience is the spiritual flag that unfurls within the Christian life when the King is in residence.

Step 4: Exercise of Faith. In spiritual interactions with God, the believer exercises faith, which is indispensable. The steps to revival are the same as the steps to salvation so that the way by which a person is spiritually converted is also the way by which a Christian is spiritually awakened. Both experiences are based on faith. The gospel that saves also revives. In this rejuvenated relationship with God, the believer is in the position to reach his highest potential, fulfill his loftiest purposes, and achieve his noblest goals.

Revival is God's idea, not ours. Since it is God's idea, it should be the Christian's deepest thought and his heart's most profound desire. James Burns writes:

> The times are ripe; the soul of man, weary of wandering, cries out to God, a spirit of intense expectation is abroad, of dissatisfaction with the past, of earnest longing regarding the future. Once more the long and bitter night has ended; the dawn is at hand, for the 'fullness of time' has come.[26]

Revival and Confession

Confession has been a crucial element in awakenings throughout history. When God confronts a Christian in His holiness, he does not claim any human right to be accepted by God. Rather, confession is the reaction of John on Patmos as he fell on his face before God. Ezekiel on the Chebar riverbank in Babylon bowed before God. Isaiah confessed, "Woe is me! For I am lost; for I am a man of unclean lips . . . " (Isa 6:5).

Encounters with God create an awesome sense of unworthiness that leads to the confession of those things that alienate us from God. Confession should be made within the circle of the healing. Hurt always precedes forgiveness. Where there is no injury, there is nothing to forgive. Where there is need for restitution, it must be offered according to the offense.

In the midst of awakening, Christians occasionally confess their sins in life to the entire congregation.[27] When this happens, church members must respond redemptively toward the one confessing sin. In a very real sense, the entire congregation becomes a mass counselor for the confessor. The confessor is seeking help, and the members of the congregation have the opportunity to respond in Christian love, compassion, and redemptive ministry. The church consistently advocates ministry; however, on some occasions when a Christian confesses, the confessor discovers that ministry does not include his particular area of hurt. Christians must remember that God does not place degrees of severity upon sin. In God's economy, every transgression is as serious to God as the worst act in the catalog of man.

In confession, the confessor must never share the faults of another or reduce the situation to a demonstration of human carnality. Confession presupposes the deep in working conviction of the Holy Spirit and must be offered only in keeping with His leadership.

Longevity of Revivals

Historical revivals of major significance always follow the patterns of the initial experiences within the small circles: When there is rapid spread to the masses, the spiritual work of God is achieved and sustained for a period of time before it declines. Each revival has its own characteristics and length. Ordinarily, at the outset, sparks of revival are detectable before the flame engulfs the masses. In addition, a revival usually does not maintain the same intensity throughout its existence. A revival may have one or more crests as God's spiritual tidal wave sweeps over people.

In the First Great Awakening in the colonies of America, revival started in 1726 with Theodore Frelinghuysen in the Raritan Valley, New Jersey. It then receded. But it reappeared in 1735 with Jonathan Edwards at Northampton. It receded again and returned with George Whitefield in 1740. In the Second Great Awakening, this pattern is evidenced at Hampden-Sydney in 1787, the Frontier Revival in 1800, Yale College in 1802, and with Charles Finney in the 1820s and 1830s. Sparks of renewal in the Jesus Movement were detectable in the mid-1960s, though the greatest impact was not experienced until 1970.

The length of a revival is determined within the mind of God, although Christians can hinder God's activity through nonbiblical responses. Sometimes Christians hinder revival by attempting to manufacture responses.

Examples of Revival Length

Revival	Dates	Length (Years)
First Great Awakening[28]	1726-70	44
Evangelical Awakening in Great Britain	1735-91	56
Second Great Awakening[29]	1787-1843	56
Layman's Prayer Revival	1857-59	2
Global Revival[30]	1901-10	9
Shantung Revival[31]	1925-39	14
Mid-Century Revival[32]	1949-60	11
Jesus Movement	1967-75	8

Some revivals have been short-lived while others have lasted for decades. James Burns wrote, "Luther set the limit to a revival at thirty years; Isaac Taylor at fifty years."[33] The length of a revival occasionally correlates with the lifetime of the leader.

Excesses in Revival

At times, abuses and excesses do occur, although they are most often exceptions. The normal response in the midst of a spiritual awakening is an awesome awareness of the presence of the Holy God. A holy hush literally permeates the atmosphere. However, overt emotional demonstrations have occasionally happened, as evidenced in the Kentucky Frontier Revival in the early 1800s and the Jesus Movement in the 1960s and 1970s.

These abuses sometimes cause opposition. Some question the genuineness of the revival, the reality of spiritual conversions, and the appropriateness of some of the confessional services. In response to these attitudes, one needs to remember that human nature still exists even though God has renewed believers. The revived Christian is not transported into some euphoric, Edenic existence that transcends human frailties. The ultimate result of awakening in the life of a believer is submission to the lordship of Jesus Christ. When Christ reigns, He impacts the total person, including emotions. W B. Sprague wrote, "It is admitted indeed that great excitement may attend a true revival; but it is not the necessary accompaniment of one."[34]

Revival is not a religious manipulation; it is God's activity among His people. As Christians respond to God in obedience, they relate to one another with patience, love, and compassion as they reach out redemptively to those who need New Testament conversion and discipleship.

The Impact of Revival on the Church

With each revival, there is an upward spiral of progress. James Burns wrote that revival is an "oscillating movement like that of a tide. Each wave is a revival; it rushes forward with . . . haste and . . . joy; it carries everything before it, and then, having spent its strength, recedes, only to be succeeded by another wave, and yet another. To the careless onlooker it seems as if nothing were gained, but behind the ebb and flow of the waves is the unconquerable power of the tide."[35] The rewards of revival are evidenced in the lives of renewed Christians, rejuvenated churches, evangelistic results, altered ethical standards, and improved human relationships.

Revival influences the church in its fellowship, worship, doctrine, and evangelism. Worship services become celebrative and exciting; vision is restored; expectancy returns; spiritual power replaces spiritual impotency; joy and victory are evident. When revival erupts, the church focuses on fellowship instead of formality, relationship instead of religion, praise in the midst of programs, and obedience in the midst of organization. The church turns outward to people as well as inward to the church body and upward to God instead of downward to self-centeredness. Revival returns the church to her ordained priorities and missionary priority as she undertakes the responsibilities of the Great Commission. Indeed, when the church is awakened, the community also becomes a beneficiary of her new spiritual vitality. In addition, young people respond in significantly larger numbers to the call of God to enter the ministry.

New Music

In the midst of revival, the Sunday services are influenced, especially music. Revivals in history change the music in the church services. Whether it was the Song of Moses; New Testament Christians who left services singing hymns and psalms; the Singing Troubadours under Francis of Assisi and their song "Canticles in the Sun;" Martin Luther, the "Nightingale of Wittenberg;" Charles Wesley; Thomas Hastings with Charles Finney; or Ira Sankey with D. L. Moody, music has been greatly impacted in the midst of awakening. Many great hymns have been written during revivals. A musical revolution took place during and after the Jesus Movement as youth musicals, praise choruses, and various musical instruments weaved their way into worship services. New terminology also emerged from the Jesus Movement, such as the term "seeker services."

Doctrinal Renewal

In the upward spiral of progress, the church experiences significant changes in doctrinal beliefs. Whereas in times without revival the church tends to move toward a humanistic philosophy, in revival the participants always make attempts to return to a simplified doctrine based on biblical teachings. A strong emphasis upon the deity of Christ, His atoning death on the Cross, His bodily Resurrection, biblical authority, the lostness of man, and the sufficiency of Christ to save emerges within the church. Without revival, church leaders tend to develop excessive ecclesiastical structure and alter doctrine. When they turn to Scripture, they seek those passages that support their conclusions, or they interpret passages specifically in order to justify their positions. The attitudes of revival leaders are juxtaposed to these attitudes. The First Great Awakening was used of God to bring salvation to unregenerate church members in New England as a result of the Half-Way Covenant of 1662.

Evangelistic Outreach

When the church experiences awakening, it becomes energized for evangelistic outreach. Every revival in history has produced significant numbers of conversions. At Pentecost, three thousand were added to the church. Almost the entire region of Lyons was evangelized under Irenaeus in the 180s as revival erupted following the severe persecution in A.D. 177. In the First Great Awakening, one out of every seven people in New England was converted.[36] In the first few months of the Welsh Revival, one hundred thousand conversions were reported. Phenomenal conversions were recorded in the Shantung and Hebrides Revivals. During the Prayer Revival of 1857-59, about one million Americans were converted. Whereas the church flounders and falters in her evangelistic responsibilities without revival, she pushes forward when she is refocused upon spiritual priorities.

The Impact of Revival Upon Society

Revival benefits society as people are lifted to new levels of achievement and productivity. James Burns calls this movement the "law of progress," for citizens experience economic, social, and spiritual uplift. The Pietistic Movement in Europe, the Wesleyan Revival in England, and the Awakenings in America served as catalysts for the Industrial Revolution of the nineteenth century.

Revival strengthens convictions, engenders courage, and promotes action among God's people. As a result, social changes are evidenced in ethical standards and moral values. Social justice emerges alongside evangelistic impact. As renewal conforms the minds of believers to God's purposes, society feels the impact of their obedience

In addition, awakenings on occasion prepare God's people for cataclysmic events. For example, the Prayer Revival of 1857-59 preceded the Civil War.

How to Sustain Revival

The way a revival originates is the way by which a revival is sustained. Prayer, confession, humility, and seeking God bring revival, and they also sustain revival. Biblical preaching is imperative. Revival leaders throughout history also maintained disciplined and powerful prayer lives. John Wesley had a prayer altar in his London home. New Testament Christians devoted themselves to prayer, even to the point that the place where they prayed shook. Without prayer, revival dies.

Maintaining Discipline

Revival refers to a movement of God among His people requiring discipline and sensitivity. Disobedience among God's people squelches revival. To perpetuate revival, Christians must keep their relationships with God up-to-date by confessing their transgressions and walking consistently with Him day by day.

Maintaining Balance

Another factor that essential to prolonging a revival is avoiding extremism. The extremes of James Davenport (see Chapter 10) in Boston during the First Great Awakening influenced Charles Chauncey and some Harvard professors to become strong opponents of the revival. This opposition brought the movement to a halt in that area. Since church leaders are responsible in maintaining renewal, they must exercise caution and follow biblical principles for providing leadership to keep the revival fires burning.

Conclusion

In a conference with his military leaders, Napoleon stood before a map of the world, pointed to China, and said, "There is a sleeping giant. Let her sleep." The church is God's giant, and the enemy of God wants her to remain in slumber. However, as the Holy Spirit awakens His church, she becomes the force by which God "turns the world upside down" (Acts 17:6). God gives revival so that His people can ignite others. The axiom of the Christian faith is that the church *gets* in order to *give.* When the church seeks to retain revival blessings, she loses the blessings that she seeks to keep. Spiritual awakenings teach that the greatest human relationship comes from new birth in Christ, and the greatest Christian existence is the daily revival experience with Christ.

Questions for Discussion

1. By way of examining your local church body, do you believe your church is in need of revival? Why or why not?

2. How often does your church experience revival of any kind (long, short, spontaneous, planned, etc.)?

3. What impact have revivals had previously in your church?

4. Do you daily beg God in prayer for the revival of your church and your city?

Chapter 2
Revivals in Israel to the Fall of the Northern Kingdom

And he said, I beseech thee, shew me thy glory.
Exodus 33:18, KJV

Like footprints in the snow, revivals trace God's tracks in the progress of human history. With each step, God discloses His glory to His people. From the revivals in Genesis to those in modern times, God has invaded the lives of His people with refreshing spiritual power in the midst of their spiritual need. One of the most significant renewals in history, the first recorded national revival, occurred at Sinai under the leadership of Moses. Few revivals in history have impacted a fledgling nation, and ultimately the human saga, as did this spiritual resurgence at Sinai.

Revival at Sinai

From the time of Joseph, the Hebrews had resided in Egypt, lived in relative freedom, and prospered. Then, a new pharaoh who did not know Joseph ascended to power. He viewed the Israelites as potential threats to Egypt. In his attempts to address the situation, the pharaoh subjected the children of Israel to forced labor and used them to build the cities of Pithom and Raamses (Exod 1:11). Into this atmosphere of slavery, Moses was born.

Moses in the Royal Family

Moses was the third child born to Amram and Jochebed of the Kohath clan and the tribe of Levi. Pharaoh issued an edict that the Hebrew male sons should be killed at birth. Because Aaron was not affected by this decree, the pharaonic orders were probably issued shortly before Moses was born.

For the first three years of Moses' life, Jochebed reared her biological son. After these brief years in his Hebrew home, he was taken to the Egyptian royal palace where he lived for the next thirty-seven years (see Exodus 2). As a member of the royal family, he was given every advantage. He received the finest education available in the Egyptian culture: mathematics; writing, including hieroglyphics and cuneiform; philosophy; military strategy; religious instruction; law; and engineering.[1] His years of preparation in the royal palace were invaluable in his subsequent leadership over Israel.

Moses in Midian

The life of Moses changed permanently after he killed an Egyptian. As Moses fled for his life in fear of punishment, he journeyed to the wilderness of Midian, where he encountered Reuel, the "friend of God." In Midian, Moses married Zipporah, the daughter of Reuel, and had two sons. For forty years he lived as a shepherd, a lifestyle opposite to his way of life in the royal palace of Pharaoh. Whereas the first stage of his life in the royal palace prepared him for leadership, the second stage in the Midian wilderness prepared him for survival, two indispensable skills for the third stage and the last forty years of his life.

Moses and the Exodus

Before a revival ignites a nation, it first ignites a leader. Few experiences have changed the direction of history, as did the episode at the burning bush when Moses experienced his personal revival and received his commission. Before this encounter with God, he was an ordinary man doing ordinary tasks in ordinary ways. After his encounter with God, he was an ordinary man awakened by the extraordinary God and charged with an extraordinary mission to be fulfilled in an extraordinary way.

As fire clothed a bush without consuming it, Moses was drawn to the unusual sight. The words of God came like hammer blows on an anvil: "Do not come near; take your sandals off your feet, for the place on which you are standing is holy ground" (Exod 3:5, ESV). In these words, God communicated the parameters of His sovereignty, holiness, demand for humility, and requirement of obedience. Whereas forty years earlier Moses was zealous in his attempt to deliver Israel, at the burning bush he offered excuses for why he was not the man to deliver God's people. However, when God decrees assignments to His servants, God does not accept excuses.

Moses offered his deficiencies in ability and speech as rationale to avoid the confrontation with Pharaoh. Moses said, "I am not eloquent . . . but I am slow of speech, and of a slow tongue" (Exod 4:10, KJV). Two views are expressed in explanation of Moses' excuse regarding speaking. The most popular interpretation of this verse is that Moses was not gifted in oratorical skills. It has been suggested that he may have had a speech impediment. However, this interpretation does not satisfy biblical teachings on this issue in the life of Moses.

The second interpretation focuses upon his linguistic skills and not upon his oratorical abilities. For forty years, Moses had lived among the Kenites in Midian who spoke the Semitic language. Thus, for forty years he had not consistently exercised his skills in speaking the Egyptian tongue; indeed, a language not used is a language easily forgotten. Moses did not tell God that he could not speak the language altogether; rather, he said that he was slow in its communication. Thus, his oratorical excuse was not a speech impediment but a language deficiency. The promise of God to provide Aaron as an interpreter strengthens this view.

Armed with a commission from God, Aaron at his side, and the transformed shepherd's rod in his hand, Moses confronted Pharaoh for the freedom of the Israelites.

God affected the release of the Israelites through ten devastating plagues, which were challenges to ten different pagan idols of the Egyptians. When Moses first encountered Pharaoh and requested permission to take the people three days' journey for religious worship, the ruler was not inclined to grant the request. Egypt was shackled with religious holidays, and another observance would simply further impact the economy and delay Pharaoh's plans of building cities in his empire.

Following the last of the ten plagues, the relinquishing of the Hebrews by Pharaoh, and the observance of the Passover meal, the Israelites collected gold, jewelry, and other possessions; departed from Rameses (Exod 12:37); and marched to the Red Sea. After the miracle of the parting of the waters and the destruction of the Egyptian army, the Hebrews followed God's instructions and turned southward to Sinai (Exod 3:12; 13:17-18). In the third month, the people of Israel were encamped at the base of the mountain. They were in the setting of one of the greatest revivals in history.

Moses at Sinai

The Revival at Sinai contained elements that characterize every awakening: spiritual declension, disobedience to God, impending judgment of God, prayer, a revival leader, changing of direction, and results. When God delivered the Ten Commandments, He gave not only political regulations to be followed but also spiritual guidelines to be lived. In these Ten Commandments, God gave instructions to the people that governed their relationships with God, others, and self. Because of the way God stated the commandments, He left no room for alternatives. One crucial law stated:

> Thou shalt not make unto thee any graven image, or any likeness of any thing that is in heaven above, or that is in the earth beneath, . . . Thou shalt not bow down thyself to them, nor serve them: for I the LORD thy God am a jealous God . . . (Exod 20:4-5, KJV)

In these words, God permanently expressed His position toward idols. Following the people's ratification of these commandments in Exodus 24:3, Moses left camp in the care of his brother, Aaron, and Hur, the husband of Miriam, and ventured once again up the mountain to commune with God. When God's revival leader was absent, spiritual declension was on the horizon. While Moses spent forty days in God's mountain conference room, spiritual rebellion developed in the camp. The prolonged absence of Moses, who dwelt in the cloud of the Shekinah glory of God on the mountain, caused them to wonder whether he was still alive. In their minds, it was time to select another leader and fashion a physical replica of the god they wanted to follow.

Since the people had witnessed the miracles of God and received the Ten Commandments, it is astonishing that they demonstrated such short memories and fashioned the golden calf. Attempts to identify this idol focus upon the Egyptian worship of either Mnevis or Apis. An ox represented Mnevis, and Apis was depicted as a bull. The calf was most likely the Egyptian god of Apis, which was a prominent religious entity in Memphis, one of the regions of Hebrew residence in Egypt. Both pagan religions centered on strength and fertility. In Canaan, such religious practice formed the heart of Baal worship. Whether a calf in their time or the idolatry of materialism in ours, false gods lure God's people from Him in every age.

In the construction of the calf, the Israelites were not explicitly rejecting God; in Exodus 32:5, Aaron announced a feast for Jehovah.[2] They sought to merge the Hebrew ancestral worship of God with the Egyptian's pagan worship. God totally rejected this effort, which represented their determination to worship God in the manner of their own choosing. This was an attempt at syncretism — the coalition of religions that places all religious persuasions on an equal basis. The heart of this view is that religious people, regardless of affiliation, are going to the same heaven; they are just taking different approaches to get there. Sincerity is substituted for Godly obedience, and religious inclusiveness replaces Christian exclusiveness. God had already decreed to the Hebrews His position toward syncretism; thus, they were without excuse. In the golden calf episode, the Israelites tried to lower God to the level of paganism. They had no idea how close they were to annihilation. Under those circumstances, only an awakening could save them.

The Intercession of Moses

While the people were engaged in revelry in the valley, the revival leader was in communion with God on the mountain. God abruptly interrupted the proceedings and informed Moses of the apostasy in the valley and His impending judgment upon the people. Moses, amazed and appalled at the circumstances, offered three prayers (Exod 32:11-14, 31-32; 33:12-16). In Moses' first prayer, three emphases of his intercession emerge that are vital when God sends revival: the people belonged to God, the glory of God was involved, and the promises of God hung in the balance.

When God shared His intentions to judge the Hebrews, He said to Moses, "Now leave me alone . . ." (Exod 32:10, NIV). This astonishing statement and the subsequent results unveiled the power of intercessory prayer. Moses' prayer was more than posture or petition; it was position. Moses' position was in the middle of God's will for his life. At the burning bush, in his own personal revival, he assumed the mediatorial role with God that transformed him into an instrument usable by God.

> Three aspects of Moses' intercession:
> 1. The people belong to God.
> 2. The glory of God is involved.
> 3. The promises of God are in the balance.

Revival at Sinai was the product of God using intercessory prayer to change the people. (The only time in Scripture where God expressed amazement is in Isaiah 59:16, and it occurred when He could not find intercessors.) Moses knew the difference between shallow petitionary prayer and life-surrendered intercession. He learned at the burning bush that life is the only currency that spends in the economy of God. His prayers at Sinai emphatically communicate that biblical prayer is first the life that is lived, and audible petitions follow as expressions of that life. Without intercession, there is no revival.

God responded with the offer to Moses that He would make him the father of a new nation. Moses refused and responded with the assessment that such action on God's part would not glorify God but tarnish His Holy name. Personal pride, human agendas, fame, and fortune had no appeal, for only God had any value in this revival leader's life.

The power of Moses' prayers and the product of every revival are evidenced in the words, "And the LORD repented" (Exod 32:14a). When man repents, it presupposes wrong. Since God can do no wrong, God cannot repent as man does. So, what does this phrase mean? The Hebrew word for "repent" is *naham.* It means, among other things, a "show of compassion." It literally means "and the Lord showed compassion." This is the heart of revival, and at that moment on Sinai, renewal was emerging.

In this episode, the dynamics of revival surface. When a person repents, the person's will is changed. When God "repents" or "shows compassion," He wills a change in events. Thus, events are changed, not God. At Sinai the people were about to receive the wrath of God, but through His compassion, events were changed and the people experienced revival instead of judgment. This revival altered the people's situation from disaster to blessings.

The Excuse of Aaron

Even though God had informed Moses, he was not prepared for the scene that he witnessed when he returned to camp. In response to the debauchery, he immediately rebuked Aaron and established court at the "gate of the camp" (Exod 32:36), which in Old Testament culture was the place where legal matters were transacted. When Aaron responded to Moses' charges, he attributed the calf to a miracle produced by the fire. In his mind, he had done no wrong. He believed that he was truly worshiping God through the golden calf in spite of what God said about idols. In reality, he was indicating that, since it was a creation by miracle, God had produced the calf, for only God performs miracles. This accused God of violating His commandment and equated Him with idolatry, which only intensified the sin of Aaron.

Moses demonstrated his leadership, the seriousness of spiritual disobedience, and the extent of revival results. While the Levites, Moses' tribe, responded immediately to his challenge to serve God, some chose not to participate in the spiritual awakening that was permeating the camp. The judgment that was rendered toward the three thousand seems harsh and unwarranted to modern people; however, those who died were engaged in lustful orgies that, if left unchecked, would have brought disaster upon this fledgling nation. This awakening was designed, among other things, to correct morality and worship practices.

Repentance

Repentance is a part of every revival, and the evidence of it is expressed through various methods, including confession and restitution. In the renewal at Sinai, repentance was evidenced through the drinking of the water that contained the residue of the melted calf. For the Egyptians, this was an abomination, for it was the consumption of their god. For the Israelites, it signified total repudiation of syncretism, genuine repentance, acknowledgement of God's sovereignty, and acceptance of the parameters by which God is worshiped. This event took place in the peak of the awakening.

A phenomenal aspect of this event was that the people obeyed and drank, which was another evidence of revival. Not even Moses, as a mere human being, could have forced a population of that magnitude to do that which was so abhorrent. The Isrealites' obedience was a disclosure of Moses' remarkable standing with God, his astounding leadership with the people, the extent of restitution, which signifies repentance, and the correction of idolatrous worship practices. Under normal circumstances, the people would have ridiculed, criticized, and rejected Moses' demands altogether. However, Moses had awesome power from God that he enabled him to have incredible power with the people.

Withdrawal of God

Within hours, the revival returned the camp to spiritual sanity (Greek *eknepho).* As Moses ministered to the needs of the people, many of them became keenly aware that his reactions were merely the extension of God's responses to spiritual rebellion. In an amazing message to Moses, God told him that He would no longer dwell among the people as He had previously done. This withdrawal did not mean that God totally removed Himself, for this would have challenged His attribute of omnipresence. This revelation indicated, at least in part, God's displeasure toward the Israelites' actions and was a demonstration of His grace to withhold judgment upon them. Martyn Lloyd-Jones indicated that the withdrawal signified that God would not dwell in visible ways among the Hebrews as He had previously done.[3]

This message from God led to the second prayer of Moses, which is recorded in Exodus 32:31-32. This prayer pulsated with identification and compassion, marks of every revival leader. As he boldly interceded for the people, Moses offered his life as a substitute. The height, depth, breadth, and length of intercessory prayer are evidenced in this great moment as a servant mediated with God on behalf of people. He did not ask for personal privileges or benefits. His deepest desire was that God be glorified and the people be blessed. Moses was so shaken by the divine announcement of God's withdrawal that he had to have assurance of God's presence. His third prayer summarized the essence of revival, "I pray Thee, show me thy glory" (Exod 33:18).

In response to this plea, God placed Moses in the cleft of the rock, covered his face as He passed, and allowed him to have just a glimpse of the afterglow of His glory. What Moses saw, a privilege that the committed of God's people long to have, was a mere shadow of God's character, and it transformed his countenance. When he returned to camp, the revival glow on his face served as visible evidence of the glory of God in the awakening at Sinai. In every revival, the participants receive a touch from God that they never forget.

Results of the Sinai Revival

This revival intensified Moses' position of leadership, eliminated the practice of syncretism, prepared the people for the wilderness wanderings, established the parameters of the Judaistic religion, and laid the foundations for the ultimate structure of the nation's government. In a very real sense, the nation of Israel was birthed in this revival. It must be left to conjecture what would have happened to Israel and to the ultimate direction of human history if this spiritual awakening at Sinai had not occurred. In this spiritual movement, God altered the destiny of the people as He manifested His power, exercised His grace, disclosed His claims, and revealed His purposes. The human race since Sinai has been a beneficiary of this awakening.

This renewal corrected false worship practices, purified doctrine that was known at that time, and communicated the seriousness with which God interacts with His people. Seldom have revivals accomplished so much, and this was in the midst of a nation without a country; when circumstances seemed insurmountable, they merely became stages upon which God unleashed the sufficiency of His mighty power. As He manifested His awesome glory, the people of God were renewed, directions were altered, and He was glorified. The revival at Sinai demonstrated that the preservation of God's purposes is more certain than today's sunset.

> As God manifested His awesome glory, the desirous people of God were renewed, trajectories were altered, and He was glorified.

Revival at Carmel

The awakening at Mt. Carmel under the leadership of Elijah marks the only recorded spiritual awakening in the history of the Northern Kingdom. The extraordinary difference between this revival and most other awakenings was God's miraculous intervention. Few revivals are ignited with a miracle of the magnitude of God's invasion at Carmel.

Conditions in Israel Before Revival

Under the leadership of Jeroboam after the death of Solomon, Israel was divided into the Northern Kingdom, which included the ten tribes of Israel, and the Southern Kingdom, made up of the two tribes of Judah and Benjamin. Immediately upon his ascension to the throne of Israel, Jeroboam established two golden calves in Bethel and Dan (1 Kings 12:28-32). During the fifty-eight years from Jeroboam to Elijah, eight incompetent leaders headed the nation of Israel.[4]

Omri,[5] the father of Ahab, purchased a hillside upon which he built the city of Samaria. In the sixth year of his reign, he moved Israel's capital from Tirzah to Samaria. After his twelve-year reign, his son Ahab succeeded to the throne in about 872 B.C. and reigned for twenty-two years (1 Kings 16:29). Ahab's total focus was on the economic prosperity and political safety of the nation. In an effort to strengthen these areas, he married Jezebel, the daughter of Ethbaal, king of Phoenicia (1 Kings 16:30-31). Ethbaal, which means "Baal exists," served as priest to Baal. He usurped the throne of Phoenicia through the assassination of his brother Pheles[6] and reigned from 887-856 B.C.[7]

Jezebel

Jezebel first appears in Scripture in about 871 B.C. (1 Kings 16:31). After her marriage to Ahab, she used her tireless energy, her position of power, and her cunning in order to establish Baal worship as the state religion in Israel. Baal, which means, "husband," was inseparably associated with the female idol of Asherah, which means "lady of the sea."[8] Baal, whom the Greeks called the Hercules of Tyre, was worshiped as the sun god who controlled the seasons, provided rains, and sustained the basic elements of life.

Whereas Ahab had little interest in religion and even less interest in Jehovah, Jezebel was consumed with the worship of Baal. Altars to God were dismantled, and shrines to Baal and Asherah were erected throughout the nation. Four hundred and fifty prophets of Baal and four hundred prophets of Asherah not only led pagan rituals but also gave counsel to the national government leaders. As a part of Jezebel's religious interest, Ahab built a temple to Baal in Samaria along dimensions similar to the temple in Tyre, the headquarters of Baal worship.

Jezebel knew that in order to fulfill her plan to convert Israel to Baal worship, she must silence the prophets of God. These prophets felt the sword of persecution as Jezebel systematically martyred all that she could locate (1 Kings 18:4). A few survived only because Obadiah, a court official, spared them and provided for them. Jezebel made it blasphemous to worship God; thus, the prophets of the Lord were considered traitors to the nation. When God told Elijah that only seven thousand had not bowed their knees to Baal, it communicated the overwhelming success of Jezebel in directing Israel away from Jehovah worship. However, it also revealed that even in the midst of violent persecution, God maintained a remnant that remained true to Him. The glory of Israel could be described in the word "Ichabod – the glory has departed." The country was mired in moral and spiritual decay within and threatened by invaders without.

While Jezebel was establishing Baal worship as the state religion, Ahab continued his efforts to build cities, reinforce his military strength, and increase economic prosperity. The nation was so prosperous that Ahab built an ivory palace, which was an incredible display of wealth. In addition, he established ties with Judah through the marriage of his daughter, Athaliah, with Jehoram, the son of Jehoshaphat (2 Chron 21:1-6). During his turbulent reign, Ahab engaged in several military campaigns, primarily against the Assyrians. Assyrian monuments that depict the achievements of Shalmaneser III, king of Assyria (859-824 B.C.), contain references to Ahab, especially in regard to the Battle of Karkar in 853 B.C.[9] Into this moral and spiritual decline, God sent His prophet Elijah.

Elijah, Revival Leader

When Elijah emerged on the scene, he was identified as Elijah the Tishbite. As he progressed in his ministry, he was called Elijah, the man of God. Later in his ministry, he was simply called the man of God. His life and ministry were so associated with the Lord that he was known through his standing with God. Elijah means, "My God is Jehovah," and few men have lived their names more completely than this man from Tishbe.

Elijah's appearance in Scripture is as abrupt as his departure in a chariot of fire. The first time that he is mentioned in Scripture is in 1 Kings 17:1 as he appears before Ahab. On eight occasions, Elijah is identified as a native of a village called Tishbe in the region of Gilead, which was located in the high, rocky hill country east of the Sea of Galilee. Elijah was truly a "balm from Gilead" for the nation of Israel. Like a torch that suddenly flares into a flame, Elijah appeared onstage in Israel in a direct confrontation with Ahab.

When Elijah appeared in Israel, the hills and groves were aflame with the sacrifices to the pagan gods of Jezebel. This highlander from Gilead stood before Ahab and delivered God's message of judgment. He left no doubt as to whom he was and the purpose of his mission. Elijah uncompromisingly told Ahab, "As the LORD God of Israel lives, before whom I stand, there shall be neither dew nor rain these years, except by my word" (1 Kings 17:1). Elijah was not only establishing his position as a prophet of God but also warning Ahab of God's impending judgment.

As Elijah announced the coming famine, he challenged two crucial areas of Israel's national life: Baal's authority over rain and the certain economic prosperity of the nation. One challenge was a direct confrontation with Baal. Since Jezebel's pagan idol was promoted as the provider of rain and the basic elements of life, Elijah challenged this claim through the famine. The other challenge confronted the economic prosperity of the country. Since agriculture was at the heart of the material wealth of the land, a famine would utterly destroy the economy, the very element upon which Ahab focused his life.

Elijah's appearance was astonishing within itself, but it is intensified when it is understood that Elijah, as a prophet of God, was considered a traitor who lived under Jezebel's death sentence. Following Elijah's message to Ahab, he took refuge at the brook Cherith in obedience to God. Although his personal revival is not recorded in Scripture, his solitude at Cherith served as a preparation chamber for Carmel. While he resided at the brook, he was fed in the morning and evening by God's ravens.

Even though Elijah was right in the center of God's will for his life, the brook dried up shortly after his arrival. As he sat by the side of the dry creek, he was the recipient of God's exhaustless provisions. In that position, he was aware that his resources were totally inadequate, but God's resources were more than sufficient. Elijah learned to focus, not on the blessings of God, but on the God who provides the blessings. God allowed those provisions to vanish in order to position His messenger for greater ministry. Elijah's days in the cloistered shelter of Cherith were over. It was time for him to move to the next phase of God's purpose for his life.

Even as the brook began to falter in its provisions for Elijah, God was already at work in Zarephath. Elijah's association with the widow and her son at Zarephath lasted for almost three years (see I Kings 17). At Zarephath, which means "place of the crucible," Elijah was thrust into the marketplace of ordinary people in order to render ministry in the name of God.

After about three years, Elijah obeyed the call of God to confront Ahab once again (1 Kings 18:1). After a conversation with Obadiah, Elijah and Ahab met face to face. Even though the famine had destroyed the economy of Israel, Ahab did not repent. He immediately called Elijah, "[Y]ou troubler of Israel" (1 Kings 18:17). In this accusation, he used much stronger language than mere "troubler." He asserted that Elijah had joined dark supernatural forces to bring destruction on Israel. This only compounded the sins of Ahab, because he equated God as the enemy of Israel. It is astonishing that he remembered the words of Elijah in regard to material matters but was not interested in the spiritual message.

This episode involved two major tests between God and Baal. The result of the first test, which was the initial famine, should have been sufficient for Ahab to recognize God's supremacy over Israel. However, this was not the case. Although God removed the very things in which Ahab placed his trust, his mind was still obsessed with material possessions. Ahab rejected God's reminder of inward spiritual deficiencies and refused to accept personal responsibility for his actions.

Elijah was quick in his response to Ahab. He reminded the king who the real enemy of Israel was. This confrontation was an incredible display of boldness on Elijah's part. Even though he was under the death sentence issued by Jezebel, he addressed the king as one who was in total control. With incredible boldness and remarkable courage, the prophet informed the king of the second challenge to Baal and gave instructions to gather all Israel at Carmel for a contest by fire between God and Baal. There is no evidence that Ahab argued with Elijah. Instead, he immediately obeyed.

Revival Fires

Four groups gathered at Carmel: Elijah, representing Jehovah; the king and his entourage; the people of Israel; and the 450 prophets of Baal. Even though the 400 prophets of Asherah were invited, Keil and Delitzch indicate that they were not present.[10] Conspicuously absent was Jezebel, who was residing in her summer home at Jezreel.

Carmel, which means "plentiful field," is a twelve-mile-long mountain range located on the shores of the Mediterranean Sea in the upper territory of Asher, and it rises up to eighteen hundred feet. Although many attempts have been made to locate it, the exact location of the contest by fire is unknown. The event probably occurred at El-Mahrakah, which means "place of burning," or "sacrifice."[11]

In a remarkable demonstration of total control, Elijah established the parameters of the trial by fire. Since Baal was the sun god, surely he could vindicate himself with fire. The prophet allowed the servants of Baal to select the sacrifice of their choice and to go first.

Prior to the beginning of the duel by fire, Elijah addressed the people. His message is the heart of every revival. As Moses challenged the Israelites at Sinai, Elijah issued a similar challenge at Carmel, "How long *will* you hesitate between two opinions? If the LORD is God, follow Him; but if Baal, follow him" (1 Kings 18:21, NASB). In this message, Elijah accused the people of being double-minded; they could not decide on who was the true God of Israel.

In James 1:8, the Bible says that a double-minded person is unstable in all of his ways. The Israelites demonstrated their instability in their inability to choose whom they would serve. The people were pagan in religion, vacillating in opinions, without convictions, and floundering in spiritual ineptness. Elijah, like Joshua (Josh 24:15), called for decision. The condition of the people and their vacillating attitudes is a classic paradigm prior to awakening.

The Baal devotees could not complain about the rules. In human rationale, they had every advantage. Because Elijah believed in the God of miracles, he had no doubts about the miracles of God and allowed the pagans to go first. Arrayed in their white linen priestly garments and their pointed hats, they started their ritual. From 6:00 A.M. until 3:00 P.M., the 450 functionaries of the pagan cult used every means at their disposal to evoke Baal's response. Approximately at noon, Elijah chastised them for their ineptness and futility of their actions by accusing Baal of being indisposed. An Ugarit tablet described Baal as taking journeys and as often unavailable.[12] On Carmel; all human religious endeavors were exposed as being mere figments of human imagination to give license to engage in carnal behavior. The priests were in total exhaustion, frustration, and defeat when they ceased their ritual contortions.

Elijah assumed the stage at 3:00 P.M., the scheduled time for the initial stages of the evening offering. He called the people of Israel to get as close as they could. Elijah not only desired to show that there were no tricks involved, but also it seems that he wanted the people to get as close to the revival flames as they could get. Systematically, the prophet rebuilt the dismantled altar. Suggestions about the broken altar place its original erection from the days of the Judges to sometime during the reign of Jeroboam. However, during the reign of terror under the leadership of Jezebel, the altar was no longer in service.

Upon this site of an abandoned altar that was once used for the glory of God, Elijah proceeded to restore the altar to its former purpose. He not only put the wood and sacrifice in place but also did the extraordinary: he dug a huge ditch around the altar, stacked twelve stones, and poured twelve jars of water, symbolic of the twelve tribes (not just the ten of Israel). Water was poured over the entire altar to the point that the ditch was full of water. When the man of God finished preparation, he knelt in prayer.

This awesome scene — where heaven touched earth and the holy invaded the unholy — was a marvelous display of the true elements of revival. In this event, the areas of prayer, faith, and cooperation were evident. Only God could send fire, but He required Elijah to prepare the altar. Whereas the Baal devotees took nine hours, Elijah prayed for less than one minute. Elijah demonstrated that a revival leader can do more in a few minutes than a carnal leader can do in years. The essence of his prayer was that God glorify His name. It seems that Elijah never did finish the prayer. He never requested God to answer by fire. He did not suggest to God how to produce the revival. He merely built the altar, prayed, and left the results to God.

In the middle of Elijah's intercession, the fire fell. In His response, God eternally declared His longing to send revival to His people by consuming not only the sacrifice but also the wood, altar, stones, water, and dirt around the altar. It was total consumption. This demonstration of power through fire was God's symbol of acceptance of the sacrifice, the affirmation that Elijah was His prophet, an expression of His desire to reconcile His people, and evidence of His delight in producing revival. Previously, God used fire as a symbol of His approval at the tabernacle in the wilderness (Lev 9:24), at the dedication of the altar on the future site of the temple (1 Chron 21:26), and at Solomon's dedication of the Temple (2 Chron 7:1). On each occasion and at Carmel, God communicated the parameters by which He is to be worshiped.

When fire consumed the sacrifice, it was also symbolic of God's willingness to forgive sin. The swiftness with which God worked shows that He is not reluctant to send revival, forgive transgressions, and reconcile people to fellowship with Himself. This visible display created such a response that the people could not contain themselves as they confessed. When Elijah had issued the challenge to serve the LORD as God, there was silence. The people in the presence of the Holy One shouted, "The LORD, he is God; The LORD, he is God" (1 Kings 18:39b, NASB). Indeed, the confessions of the people flowed as the fires from heaven fell. The language used indicates that this resounding chorus of confession was continually repeated. From the slopes of Carmel to the plains of Esdraelon, the shouts of the people were heard.

Israel had not heard such confessions in years. Like an ignited firebrand placed upon dried kindling, God ignited the spiritual fires — long extinguished — once again in human hearts. It was indeed a spiritual homecoming for the prodigal people, and they found that the waiting Father yearned for their return. Seldom has there been a spiritual reversal so swift and complete as evidenced at Carmel.

Results of the Carmel Revival

The first immediate result of the revival was the restoration of the revival participants to Jehovah worship. Their confession included repentance for past neglect, disobedience, and rejection of God. The second immediate result was the validation of Elijah's stature as a prophet of God. The event at Carmel was the greatest act in Elijah's prophetic ministry. He was a revival leader and is remembered for this event more than all his other deeds combined. The third immediate result was the execution of the 450 prophets of Baal.

To the modern mind, this action might appear to be extreme. However, these Baal promoters were in violation of the Mosaic Law. Their crimes against God and the nation of Israel were punishable by death (Deut 13:1-5; 17:1-5). Elijah simply carried out the requirements of the law. If these priests had not been executed, Elijah would have been breaking the Mosaic Law himself. He had the legal and spiritual authority to carry out the sentence for the crimes of these priests. Their execution greatly crippled Baal worship in Israel, for the cult had no priests immediately available to perform the rituals. The fact that Ahab was present at the executions and made no attempt to stop the proceedings only intensified the impact of this revival upon Israel.

The fourth immediate result of the revival was rain. After Ahab dined and Elijah prayed for rain, the showers soaked the land. Once again, God demonstrated that He is the provider of the essentials for life. Whereas the three and one-half year famine was evidence of the nonexistence of Baal, the rain was evidence of God's marvelous provision. The duration of this revival is not recorded in Scripture. However, when Elijah went to Jezreel and heard the threats of Jezebel, he retreated to Beersheba and ultimately to Sinai.

As the Mosaic Law required execution of Baal's prophets, so Jezebel's law required execution of God's prophets. Elijah learned that when revival erupts, revival leaders encounter severe opposition. Indeed, when God produced this revival, Elijah faced the strongest opposition that he ever encountered. However, as Elijah received God's word at Sinai, he received comforting, sustaining words in the crucible of opposition.

This revival at Carmel communicates that God longingly seeks to disclose Himself, glorify His name, and bless His people. Without revival, the Israelites were floundering in physical and spiritual need. In revival, they were the recipients of God's abundant blessings.

Revival at Nineveh

The revival at Nineveh was unique in its leadership and locale. There has never been another renewal with a revival leader who matched the obstinate reluctance of Jonah. In addition, this is the only Old Testament revival that occurred outside of the Hebrew nation. While the awakening at Sinai was on foreign soil, the recipients were Israelites. However, the Ninevite Revival was on gentile soil and among gentile people. Nonetheless, this revival had significant impact upon the nation of Israel.

The Assyrian Empire

During the ninth century B.C., the Assyrian Empire — under Tukulti-Ninurta (890-885 B.C.), Ashur-nasirpal II (883-859 B.C.), and Shalmaneser III (859-824 B.C.) — was established as the dominant power on earth. At the Battle of Karkar in 853 B.C. on the Orontes River in Syria, Shalmanezeer III defeated the coalition of Ben-Hadad I of Syria (880-842 B.C.), Ahab of Israel, and Irhuleni of Hamuth. Shalmaneser III declared himself as the mighty king of the universe, the powerful ruler of the four regions of the earth. Upon his death, his son Shamshiadad V (824-811 B.C.) succeeded him. He was not the leader and administrator his father was and spent most of his reign responding to the revolts throughout his realm. Upon his death, his wife Semiramis ruled as regent until their son, Adadnirari III (805-783 B.C.), was old enough to become king. It was probably this king who ruled in Nineveh during the revival under Jonah. In the line of succession, through weaker kings Ashurdan III (772-755 B.C.) and Ashur-nirari V (754-745 B.C.), the Assyrian Empire waned in power. However, when the strong, aggressive leader Tiglath-Pileser III usurped the throne in 745 B.C., he systematically began to restore Assyria to her former glory. In 2 Kings 15:19-20, Menahem of Israel paid tribute to "Pul'' due to Israel's military loss to Assyria in 738 B.C. When Tiglath-Pileser died in 727 B.C., he was succeeded by his son Shalmaneser V (727-722 B.C.) who conquered Samaria in 722 B.C. However, it was Sargon II (722-705 B.C.) who claimed credit for the destruction of Samaria and boasted about the deportation of 27,290 Israelites. It was also Sargon who imported foreigners as settlers in Samaria, an event that ultimately developed the Samaritan people.[13]

This brief history is significant in order to understand the importance of the revival at Nineveh under Jonah. The entire empire pivoted around this "great city." God announced to Jonah that He was going to destroy Nineveh unless the city repented. If the revival had not occurred and God had ultimately destroyed the metropolis, the Assyrian Empire would have been reduced to a mediocre nation. Because of the revival, Nineveh and the Assyrian Empire were spared and maintained their position as the world power. This nation ultimately conquered Jonah's beloved land of Israel. Thus, in a very real sense, the revival at Nineveh had a significant impact upon the ultimate downfall of Israel.

The City of Nineveh

The city of Nineveh was founded by Nimrod about 2400 B.C. (Gen 10:9-11). It was named Nineveh after the pagan god "Nin." It was not only one of the oldest cities in the world during the time of Jonah but it was also the largest city on earth. The city of Nineveh was located about 250 miles north of Babylon in the fork of the rivers of Khosr on the northwest, Tigris on the west, and Gazr on the southwest, and mountains rose on its eastern side. In the first century after Christ, Diodorus Seculus described Nineveh as an oblong city about sixty miles in circumference.[14] Since the book of Jonah states that it took a three-day journey to traverse Nineveh, the distance included the entire metropolis encompassing the cities of Asshur, Calah, and Arbella. The city of Nineveh proper covered about eight miles.[15]

Although the total population of Nineveh cannot be determined with certainty, the book of Jonah mentions 120,000.[16] The most accepted explanation of the 120,000 residents is that this number only included the infants; therefore, the total population was probably substantially higher than this figure. Strabo stated that it was much larger in population than Babylon.[17] The estimates go up to two million.[18] The population figure that is most often adopted is six hundred thousand. Although this great city appeared invincible, Nineveh eventually fell as a coalition of Medes, Babylonians, and Scythians conquered the city after a three-month siege in 612 B.C., bringing to fruition the prophecies of Nahum 3:7 and Zephaniah 2:13.

Throughout the world, the Assyrians were known for cruel and inhumane treatment. Nahum said the corruption included fraud, crime, violence, idolatry, and sensuousness. The Assyrians had often exercised barbarous cruelty against Israel. It is remarkable that God used an Israelite, a recipient of that cruel force, in Nineveh as the revival leader. In the mind of Jonah, God should have exercised judgment instead of mercy upon the foes of His people.

Jonah, the Revival Leader

Like Elijah, Jonah appeared suddenly and disappeared with equal abruptness in Scripture. Apart from the book that bears his name, the only other place in the Old Testament where his name appears is 2 Kings 14:25. This verse indicates that he was from Gath-hepher, which means "winepress of the well," located north of Nazareth in the tribe of Zebulon near the Syrian border. He also prophesied to Jeroboam II (793-753 B.C.) that the king would expand the borders of Israel that later occurred.

Attempts have been made to link this prophet with other events in the Old Testament. Jerome identified Jonah as the son of the widow of Zarephath whom Elijah raised from the dead.[19] In addition, the theory is proposed that he was the young prophet sent by Elisha to anoint Jehu as king of Israel.[20]

When God commissioned Jonah, son of Amittai (which means "truth") of Gath-hepher, to go to Nineveh and "cry against" the city (Jonah 1:2), the prophet refused to do so.[21] His flight from God was not a rash decision, but the product of deliberate action. As he became a fugitive from God, he fled to Joppa, caught a ship that was, according to the Hebrew language, readily available, and embarked for Tarshish. Attempts have been made to locate this ancient city. Josephus identified Tarshish with Tarsus of Cilicia, the birthplace of the Apostle Paul.[22] John Calvin noted that it was not a city at all; rather, it was the country of Cilicia.[23] The traditional views are that Tarshish was located on either the northwestern coast of Africa or the southern tip of Spain.

After Jonah positioned himself in the lower regions of the ship, he was soon asleep. The Hebrew word that is used for "deep sleep" in Jonah 1:5 suggests almost a supernatural sleep.[24] When God "hurled" a great storm upon the sea, the "sea of calamity met the sea of crime."[25] Even in the midst of a storm that approached hurricane force, Jonah remained in his sleep, oblivious of the peril around him. As long as he was fleeing from God, danger threatened not only him and the Ninevites but also the sailors. Because the task of going to Nineveh was so distasteful and repulsive and because he would rather flee from God in disobedience than serve Him in obedience, Jonah was creating calamitous conditions for others. Whereas Jerome said he slept because he had such peace of mind, Keil and Delitzch said he slept because he had a guilty conscience.[26]

When Jonah was awakened and questioned and when the lots fell on him, he was asked four vital questions that also form the foundation of every revival:

Who are you?
Where do you come from?
To whom do you belong?
What are you doing here?

Like branding irons, these questions must have seared the conscience of Jonah. When he used the term *Hebrew* for clarification, he was following the Hebrew custom of using the term in national identification to foreigners. His self-inflicted verdict was "guilty, throw me into the sea." For various reasons, the sailors tried to save the rebellious prophet as they dug their oars into the tempestuous waters. After everything failed, they reminded God of their innocence and cast Jonah overboard. The cessation of the storm was so sudden that the experienced mariners knew that the miraculous was involved, or they would not have offered sacrifices. God literally muzzled the storm.

In the stomach of the fish prepared by God,[27] Jonah prayed. His prayer described his situation, acknowledged the sovereignty of God, and expressed confidence in God for deliverance from his undesirable conditions as he sought restoration to fellowship with God. After three days of Jonah's incarceration, the fish jettisoned him onto land.

When Jonah was safely on shore, God issued His commission for the second time. Three commands given by God to Jonah in Jonah 3:2 depict the urgency of revival: "arise," "go," and "proclaim." Whereas he was going "down" when he was fleeing from God, he was going "up" when he was living in obedience to God. Since Jonah was probably advanced in years and in the latter stages of his ministry, he had never received an assignment that was so distasteful to him.

Jonah in Nineveh

When Jonah arrived in Nineveh, he went a day's journey into the city. Interpretations include: (1) He started preaching immediately upon entrance into the city and preached for the entire day as he walked the streets of Nineveh. (2) He journeyed an entire day before he started preaching. (3) The day's journey was the distance, about twenty miles; he traveled from Nineveh to Calah, the location of the king's palace, before he started preaching. Regardless, Jonah delivered the message given to him by God, "Forty days, and Nineveh shall be overthrown."[28] It was a message of "repent of else." The people of Nineveh placed their carnality on display as they substituted the corruptible for the incorruptible, creature for the Creator, physical for the spiritual, and temporal for the eternal. As a result, they languished in the ineptitude of their own resources and under the judgment of God.

Three commands given by God to Jonah depict the urgency of revival:
1. Arise.
2. Go.
3. Cry.

As Jonah walked through the streets or stood on corners, he repeatedly proclaimed God's message of impending judgment. Never in the history of Nineveh had a message of this nature been heard. It is remarkable that a foreign enemy could walk the streets proclaiming a message of destruction and receive an audience for that message. Only God could create a situation like that. The Bible is clear that practically every person in Nineveh heard the news as the message resounded throughout the city. This city that was not only great in her size but also great in her wickedness heard God's protest against her spiritual depravity. Jonah did not whisper the message in alleys but shouted it abroad. Although he could have literally lost his life if they had rejected the message, he fulfilled his commission from God.

When the news reached the king, he gave immediate orders to fast and dress in sackcloth. The conditions given in 2 Chronicles 7:14 — humility, prayer, seeking God's face, and turning from wicked ways — were met in Nineveh. Immediately, the king's instructions were implemented. Across the entire metropolitan area, revival emerged. Seldom in history has an entire city responded to revival as Nineveh did. The slumbering conscience of Nineveh was awakened to the awesome power of God. What the armies of nations could not do, the message of God did as the entire city was brought to repentance. Again this was an incredible demonstration of the power of one godly man over the multitudes of ungodly people.

This revival reached the city because it touched the city leaders. As the king became paralyzed in his convictions, he became an instrument of God to spread the spiritual movement. Even though the Ninevites were not practitioners of Jehovah worship, they were quickly introduced to the God who demands worship from His creation. Jonah proclaimed, "Salvation is from the LORD" (Jonah 2:9, NASB). The Ninevites were exposed to the fact that God's salvation is not an emotional state, a ceremonial ritual to Ishtar, a cultural association, or an educational process. They learned that salvation is the divine act of God in the life of a responsive person for the purpose of reconciliation. Indeed, revival was aflame in Nineveh.

Results of the Nineveh Revival

Although Assyrian writings do not contain any mention of this awakening, that is not evidence that the awakening did not have significant impact upon the city and area. Whereas the length of the revival is uncertain, many of the results are discernible. One immediate impact was the alteration of Nineveh's position before God from utter destruction to preservation as an empire (Jonah 3:10). The preservation of the Assyrian Empire ultimately led to the destruction of Israel. Another result was the staggering number of lost people who were reconciled unto God. Although the Bible does not record the moral and spiritual reforms, it does say (Jonah 3:5) that they believed God; thus, the city was transformed, to a degree, in its moral standards.

The results also impacted Jonah, although adversely. It is incredible that Jonah had just participated in one of the greatest spiritual awakenings in the Old Testament but chose neither to participate in its benefits nor to rejoice in the results. Whether he left in the midst of the revival or at the end of the forty days in order to take his retreat at the hut and under the gourd or palmcrist tree is uncertain. It is possible that he went outside of the city to await the fate of Nineveh. When he concluded that God indeed had spared Nineveh and was not going to destroy the city, he became furious. The Hebrew language suggests that he was livid. He then disclosed why he had refused to come to Nineveh originally as he confessed to God that he feared God would do as He had done in the sparing of the city. Jonah did not want mercy for Nineveh; he wanted destruction.

There are no human explanations as to why God used a leader who was so reluctant and obstinate. There are no other revival accounts in history where a revival leader compares with Jonah's response to God and attitude toward people. The only conclusion is that since God used Jonah, God can use anybody. Former president of Southeastern Baptist Theological Seminary Lewis Drummond described Jonah: "He loved God, but not quite fully. He served God, but not completely. Some love, some service, some surrender, but not what really matters: absolute surrender."[29]

> Jonah reminds us that our love for God and for people should rise above our love for our country.

Jonah's myopic vision so focused on Israel that his nationalistic spiritual blinders prevented him from seeing the complete picture of God's purpose for humanity. In his mind, he was simply being an Israelite patriot in his reluctant attitude toward Nineveh. His racial and cultural bias delayed revival in Nineveh and robbed him of joy. God reminded Jonah that the prophet had demonstrated more compassion for gourds than for people. He chastised Jonah for his misplaced affections as He reminded the recalcitrant prophet that Nineveh was not a plant on a hillside but a city full of people. In this revival, God conveyed that He transcends national boundaries and racial groups. Under the revelation of God's abounding love and outreaching grace, Jonah's national isolationism was dwarfed into insignificance.

The book of Jonah was not written to relate a fish story; rather, it was written to describe God's infinite love and grace. In revival, whether in the wilderness as with Moses, on a mountaintop as with Elijah, or in a metropolitan city like Nineveh, God graciously allows His creation to experience the true meaning of forgiveness and restoration to His indescribable fellowship.

Questions for Discussion

1. Who is the Moses in your local church, the one who has no hesitation in calling for the need of revival? How does that person profess that? Biblically?

2. What are some excuses your church has used to shy away from revival?

3. What would revival look like in your church in comparison to Moses' day? To the 1700s? The 1970s?

Chapter 3
Revivals in the Southern Kingdom and the Post-exilic Period

"The LORD is with you, while you are with him. If you seek him, he will be found by you . . ."
2 Chronicles 15:2b

Revival Under Asa

Revival often signifies God's "yes" in response to the petitions for mercy from His people. This axiom is evident in the awakening that occurred under the leadership of Asa, king of Judah. This renewal ignited in the midst of religious reform. Although there are many similarities between reform and revival, there are also many differences.

Reform focuses upon practices; revival focuses on people. Reform denotes the correction of abuses through systematic change over a period of time; revival shows the instantaneous response of God's people to His divine invasion. Reform may or may not lead to revival; revival always leads to reform. Reform may not spiritually energize the inner person; revival always does. Reform is the correction of methods; revival is restoration to fellowship with God. Both revival and reform are essential in Christian progress.

Revivals never occur in vacuums and cannot be understood apart from their historical contexts. In the revival under Asa, God responded in order to correct the worldly conditions that caused alienation from Him.

Conditions Before Revival

The revival under Asa occurred thirty-five years after the death of Solomon and the division of the kingdom into north and south.[1] During the last years of Solomon's reign, thc nation's spiritual resolve drastically declined. Solomon amassed wives and concubines as readily as he amassed wealth. In attempts to appease these women, he defected from the worship of God and implemented pagan practices throughout the land. He started his reign so rightly and ended it so wrongly. He started it with deep spiritual commitment and ended it in worldly compromise. Solomon had the wisdom to astound the world, but he did not have the wisdom to control his life. The nation of Israel paid an enormous price for Solomon's lack of resolve and discipline. At the time of his death, Israel was languishing in economic, moral, and spiritual bankruptcy.

The Reign of Rehoboam

Upon the death of Solomon, Rehoboam, the son of Solomon through Naamah (1 Kings 14:21), ascended to the throne. Rehoboam succeeded Solomon with no apparent opposition from any member of the royal family.[2] At his coronation in Jerusalem, only the tribes of Judah and Benjamin were represented (2 Chron 9:31). In order to receive coronation from the ten tribes of the north, he journeyed to Shechem, located on Mt. Gerizim in the mountain range of Ephraim. Shechem held a prominent place in the life of Israel. At this site, Joshua and the representatives of Israel ratified the covenant (Josh 24:1, 25). In a very real sense, Shechem was the first capital of Israel as they settled in the new land. It was also at Shechem that the Israelites buried Joseph (Josh 24:32). The northern residents were prepared to accept Rehoboam as king if certain stipulations were met. The mere fact that they were not formally represented at the Jerusalem ceremony should have communicated a powerful message to the new king; however, this was not the case. Solomon could pass the crown to Rehoboam, but he could not impart wisdom.

When the ten tribes of the north presented their grievances to Rehoboam, the new king faced his first major decision. In response to their petition for less taxation, Rehoboam, after conferring with both older and younger national advisors, accepted the advice of the younger counselors and replied with a terse response.

The three days that Rehoboam took to review the petition of the northern tribes proved to be among the most critical days in Israel's history. In this event, Rehoboam demonstrated a despotic attitude and serious leadership deficiencies. When he announced his decision for even heavier taxes, the northern tribes immediately rebelled. When Adoram was sent by Rehoboam to suppress the rebellion, the emissary was stoned to death. The new king retreated to Jerusalem, amassed an army of 180,000, and marched against the insurrectionists. He cancelled the effort when Shemaiah, God's prophet, delivered God's message that Rehoboam was not to retaliate with military action. He went to Shechem to receive a crown, but he returned to Jerusalem with his kingdom no longer intact.

Upon his return to Jerusalem, Rehoboam began to fortify cities[3] and strengthen his control over the Southern Kingdom. His efforts were greatly assisted when many of the Levite priests and Jehovah worshipers, due to the erection of the golden calves in Bethel and Dan by Jeroboam, left their ancestral possessions and migrated to Judah. For the first three years of his reign, Rehoboam promoted the worship of God throughout his realm. However, upon completion of the project to fortify the cities, he defected from his commitment to God (1 Kings 14:21-22).

In the fifth year of Rehoboam reign, Shishak, king of Egypt, invaded Judah (1 Kings 14:25-28). When Rehoboam and the leaders of Judah humbled themselves, Judah was spared from total destruction. However, five years after Solomon's death, the vast treasures stored in the temple and in his palace became the spoils of war for Shishak. In this event, God disclosed how temporal earthly possessions really are.

After the Egyptian ruler completed the conquest of Jerusalem, he turned his attention toward Jeroboam and Israel. Since Jeroboam and Shishak were brothers-in-law, having married sisters, the Israelite king probably felt secure from an Egyptian attack. This was not the case as Shishak unleashed his military might against Jeroboam. In the midst of the campaign against Israel, the Egyptian ruler abruptly ceased military operations and returned to Egypt in order to address problems within his kingdom.[4]

During the last twelve years of Rehoboam's reign, he contributed significantly to the spiritual and moral decline of Judah as he promoted the worship of pagan cults. The nation was desperately in need of revival. During the early years of the history of the kings of Israel and Judah, a principle of God's judgment upon a nation emerges. Ordinarily, one thinks of judgment as it relates to ultimate destruction. However, God's judgment was exercised in stages. One crucial element of His judgment was the provision of inept and incapable leaders. This principle is especially seen in the reigns of Rehoboam and his successor, Abijah.

The Reign of Abijah

Following the death of Rehoboam, who ruled for seventeen years, Abijah, the son of Rehoboam through Micaiah became king and reigned for almost three years (2 Chron 13:2).[5] His major contribution to the nation of Judah was his military victory over Jeroboam, king of Israel, at Zemaraim located in the hill country of Ephraim (2 Chron 13:4). Because of this conquest, Jeroboam never recovered politically, and Judah lived in peace for several years. In addition, Judah added several cities of Israel to her territory.

Abijah, like his father, promoted pagan cults (1 Kings 15:1-3). When Abijah died, pagan poles, shrines, groves, and stones dominated the landscape of Judah. In the sixty years since the death of David, the Davidic kingdom had divided and digressed into paganism.

The Reign of Asa

Since Asa ruled for forty-one years, he was probably a boy king, ten to twelve years of age when he ascended to the throne.[6] In that case, he would have been under the tutelage of the high priest, which might provide one reason why he had such a strong inclination toward God. For the first ten years of his reign, the kingdom enjoyed peace, due in large part to Abijah's victory over Jeroboam (2 Chron 14:1). During those ten years he built new cities, fortified existing ones, and developed an army of 580,000 soldiers. His most important contribution was the implementation of vigorous religious reform.

The progressive spiritual decline under Solomon, Rehoboam, and Abijah positioned Judah in precarious standing with God. Because of God's faithfulness in keeping His promises to David, Judah was preserved. Throughout their history, the Hebrews were so closely linked with God that prosperity or decline was recorded according to their relationship with God. When the nation obeyed God, she prospered. When the nation disobeyed God, she dwelt in calamitous conditions.

Reform Under Asa

When Asa became king, Judah was floundering in its carnal condition. The young king began systematic abolition of paganism throughout the land. He removed the altars erected to foreign gods, dismantled the poles, destroyed the groves, and tore down the piles of stone. Indeed, he inaugurated an aggressive promotion of Jehovah worship among the people. As a part of his reform, however, he did not eliminate the high places.[7] A distinction existed between altars to the pagan gods and the high places left in place by Asa. The altars in high places were sacrificial sites of the people in their worship of God. The temple was approximately fifty years old when Asa became king, and the practice of sacrifice only at the temple was not fully established. Thus, many of the people continued their ancient traditions of sacrificing in various locales throughout the kingdom. Since before Abraham, this method of sacrifice was practiced, and the priests who sought to limit offerings to the temple only discovered that tradition was hard to break.

Because of peace in the land, an aggressive economy, and religious reform, Asa strengthened his position as king of Judah. However, the ten years of peace were interrupted when Zerah, king of Egypt, marched against Judah. Asa marshaled his army of 580,000 men and confronted Zerah's army of one million soldiers at Mareshah in the valley of Zephathah, located about thirty miles southwest of Jerusalem. Whereas Rehoboam was defeated by Shishak in this same location, the fortunes of Asa were just the opposite.

When Asa saw the vast army of Zerah,[8] he knew that his military force was no match physically against the enemy. In this time of great need, he turned to God in prayer, asking for divine intervention. In his prayer, he acknowledged the covenant relationship between Israel and the LORD, the size of the enemy army, which the war was more than theirs, which God alone could gain the victory, and the dishonor that God would sustain in defeat. Asa assessed that Zerah was on a campaign against God as much as he was against Judah. With God as their sword for attack and their shield for protection, Asa's army launched an assault against Zerah that scattered the invading forces. As the Egyptians fled, the Judaites chased them as far as Gerar, a major city of the Philistines. The victory was so decisive that Egypt did not wage war against Judah for almost three hundred years.[9]

As Asa and his army returned to Jerusalem, they were met by Azariah, heard God's message, and experienced a magnificent spiritual awakening. Some confusion surrounds the chronology of the war and revival. The Bible indicates that the peace was interrupted ten years after Asa became king but the revival at the festival ignited in the fifteenth year of his reign. Attempts have been made to reconcile the dates of the two events. One view is that the war lasted four years. Another view is that Asa remained in the southwest region of the kingdom in order to restore the area due to the damages of war. Another view is that there was simply a four-year span between the encounter with Azariah and the revival festival in the fifteenth year of Asa's regime.[10]

Regardless, Asa encountered Azariah, God's prophet, as he returned to Jerusalem. In this meeting, God's messenger reminded the king and the soldiers that

God provided the victory and challenged them in their responsibilities to God. The crescendo of the message, a foundation for awakenings, was "The LORD is with you, while you are with him. If you seek him, he will be found by you, but if you forsake him, he will forsake you" (2 Chron 15:2b).

The Coming of Revival

As Azariah addressed Asa and his army, he did not offer words of flattery or praise or compliment the splendid military victory over Zerah. The prophet recited the history of Israel's relationship with God. He reminded the king that more calamitous to a nation than foreign foes is the neglect of the Lord God. He reminded them of God's miraculous provisions of strength and protection. He challenged them to seek the Lord God with total commitment. Azariah did not preach what they *wanted* to hear, but what they *needed* to hear.

A cornerstone of revival is people seeking after God, which is the theme of Azariah's message. On nine occasions in Scripture, Asa is described as seeking God. The search for God involved more than audible petitions. It involved voluntary and complete turning to God, an attitude of adoration, a devotion to serve Him, a decision to turn from sin, a commitment to fulfill His will, and determination to persevere in prayer. Through diligently seeking God, temptation is conquered, humility sustained, and fellowship with Him is experienced.[11] Kaiser wrote, "All true repentance, communion with God, service to Him, prayer to Him, and spiritual growth in Him revolves around truly seeking God."[12]

Azariah's message was used of God as a spiritual sword to cut asunder personal attitudes and to arouse spiritual resolve in Asa to make whatever sacrifices necessary in order that God should rule in sovereignty over Judah. Somewhere on the road to Jerusalem, Asa had a spiritual experience that changed reform into revival. In his attempts at reform, he had not been thorough in his abolition of paganism from the land. His own grandmother, Micaiah, wife of Rehoboam, maintained her idolatrous devotion to Asherah. Asa's greatest challenges were not on the battlefield but within his own household. Whereas in reform he did not confront his grandmother, in revival he removed the queen mother from her royal position, pulverized her idol, and cast the remains into the Kidron valley.

Initially, revival started on the return trip to Jerusalem. Whereas Asa and the army enjoyed a new spiritual vitality, the people of Judah had not experienced spiritual renewal. It needed to spread to the nation. During the Pentecost festival in the third month of the fifteenth year of his reign, Asa summoned the people of Judah to Jerusalem for a great celebration. The crest of the revival and its spread to the nation occurred during the feast. As Asa gave freely from the spoils of war, sacrifices were offered to the Lord. The aroma of the offerings and shouts of joy mingled to fill Jerusalem with worship of the Lord God. It had been several years since the city had heard the glad sounds of celebration, worship, and spiritual rejoicing. Whereas reform caused change with little celebration, revival brought change with great rejoicing.

There were two keys to this revival: seeking God and obedience -- elements of every renewal.

Across the years, God had served His people; in this revival, they renewed their commitment to serve Him. God had heard their petitions; in this revival, they had the privilege of hearing the voice of God. God had not abandoned the disobedient people; in this revival, they returned to God and experienced His indescribable fellowship and unspeakable joy. In this renewal, God altered the pagan conditions developed under Solomon, Rehoboam, and Abijah and restored the people to His glorious and bountiful fellowship. And the people rejoiced.

Results of the Revival

This movement brought monumental results for the nation of Judah. In addition to the completion of religious reform, the people renewed the covenant with God to seek Him with heart and soul (2 Chron 15:12). They also vowed that anyone who would not seek the Lord God would be put to death. For the modern mind, this is not religious freedom, but coercion. However, the national laws of Judah as well as God's eternal law for humanity did not permit the neglect of the Lord. Under the Mosaic Law, rebellion against God was tantamount to treason, a crime that was punishable by death. When the people affirmed that rejection of God would lead to execution, they were renewing the Mosaic covenant, submitting to God, and pledging to keep Judah under the sovereign rule of God. The people sealed their vows with shouts of approval, trumpets, and horns (2 Chron 15:14).

Because of the revival, the nation enjoyed relative peace for the next twenty-one years. In comparison to Judah, Israel had only one revival in her history — Elijah at Carmel — while Judah had several. Judah had less internal strife, fewer external attacks, and a longer existence. It is not a coincidence that revivals and God's protection are linked.

Another result of the renewal under Asa was joy and restoration to God's fellowship. Unfortunately, as in all revivals, all revivals, not every citizen of Judah chose to participate, as evidenced by Micaiah. However, the nation of Judah was bathed in a national awakening that corrected pagan practices and completed religious reform. The results were tantamount to the preservation of the nation.

The Bible does not record the length of this revival; however, religious decline followed within a few years. As Asa defected from God, he committed three major mistakes. First, he made an alliance with Ben-Hadad, king of Syria. Although political alliances in our contemporary culture are desirable, in Asa's culture they were signs of rejection of God. The second mistake he made occurred when he imprisoned Hanani, the prophet of God. Instead of responding to God's message as he did with Azariah, he arrested Hanani. The third mistake was that he went to "physicians" to find a cure for his physical illness. These "physicians," who were forbidden by God, were sorcerers who engaged in incantations and witchcraft.

In these three events, Asa revealed that the spiritual vitality he had during revival was no longer present in his life. Asa needed to remember that he could not live permanently on one renewal experience, even if it was an encounter with God. He neglected the daily seeking and consistent obedience to God needed to maintain spiritual power, joy, and fellowship. Because Asa faltered in this area, he faltered in every area. Due to his lack of daily discipline to obey God and to walk with Him, he and the nation of Judah paid an enormous price.

Revival Under Josiah

The revival under Josiah was the last renewal in Judah prior to the Babylonian exile. When Josiah became king, Judah was writhing in the worst moral and spiritual condition in her history. What had caused Judah to digress to such depths of spiritual depravity? What influences contributed to the revival under Josiah? This revival cannot be understood without a brief overview of the reigns of Manasseh and Amon, the influence of Assyria upon Judah, the rise of the Babylonian Empire, and the reign of Josiah. Indeed, during the seventh century B.C., the history of Judah cannot be understood apart from her relationship with Assyria. From Hezekiah to Josiah, the nation of Judah was under the domination of the Assyrian Empire.

The Reign of Hezekiah

Judah was spared the destruction that was imposed upon Israel by the Assyrian kings Tiglath-Pileser (745-727 B.C.), Shalmaneser V (727-722 B.C.), and Sargon II (722-705 B.C.). Although Judah was subjugated to Assyrian control when Hezekiah was forced to pay tribute to Sargon in 715 B.C., it was not until Sennacherib (705-681) became king that Judah became a vassal state within the Assyrian Empire. After Sennacherib's victory over Marduk-apla-iddina and his Elamite and Arab allies at Cutha and Kish in 702 B.C., the Assyrian king turned his attention to the rebels in the west. He defeated the Egyptian army at Elltekeh; and marched against Judah.

Hezekiah, realizing that Judah was no match for the Assyrian military machine, offered tribute to Sennacherib in 701 B.C., which he accepted at Lachish (2 Kings 18:14-15). During this campaign, 185,000 Assyrians died from a plague. The Bible says that God intervened; however, Herodotus wrote that a hoard of mice invaded the Assyrian camp and produced the illness.[13] Following this campaign, Sennacherib made an inscription saying that he conquered forty-six major cities, numerous towns and villages, and deported 200,150 people from Judah.[14] Judah was under Assyrian control.

The Reign of Manasseh

Upon the death of Hezekiah, his son through Hephzibah, Manasseh (697-642 B.C.), became king at the age of twelve and ruled for fifty-five years (2 Kings 21:1). This included a co-regency with Hezekiah for the first ten years of his reign. The Bible is explicit in the description of the spiritual corruption Manasseh inflicted upon Judah. Indeed, Manasseh was considered the primary reason for the downfall of Judah (2

Kings 21:11-15). His reign has been called "the heyday of Judean idolatry."[15] He restored the pagan altars, groves, shrines, poles, and stones that were demolished by Hezekiah during the revival that occurred under his leadership. Manasseh transformed the house of God into a temple for paganism; sacrificed his own son to Moloch; and was addicted to sorcery, witchcraft, magic, and other types of superstitions. He aggressively promoted the worship of Baal and Asherah as he led Judah into idolatrous worship that surpassed the cultic practices of the surrounding heathen nations. In addition, he executed those who opposed his efforts.

The pagan practices of Manasseh were interrupted when he was taken captive to Babylon (2 Chron 33:11). The Bible is silent regarding the date and length of Manasseh's captivity. As a captive in Babylon, he repented and sought God. Upon Manasseh's return to Jerusalem, he began to correct some of the pagan practices he had instituted. However, his reform attempts appeared less than enthusiastic. What he had done in his earlier years could not be eradicated in his later years as the Judean monarch. Judah was mired in paganism.

The Reign of Amon

After the lengthy reign of Manasseh, his son through Meshullemeth, Amon (642-640), became king at the age of twenty-two and ruled for two years (2 Kings 21:19). His reign was characterized by evil: "He did evil in the sight of the LORD, as Manasseh his father had done" (2 Kings 21:20, NASB). Although his reign was brief, he vigorously promoted cultic worship practices throughout Judah as he attempted to reverse some of the reforms of Manasseh. His regime was cut short when some of his servants assassinated him within his own palace. By the end of Amon's reign, Judah was saturated with idolatry. In fact, nothing could save her from ultimate destruction. The revival under Josiah simply delayed the inevitable.

The Reign of Josiah

Josiah (648-609), the son of Amon through Jedidah, became king of Judah in 640 B.C. at age eight and reigned for thirty-one years (2 Kings 22:1). Four strategic events marked his reign: his religious experience at sixteen (632 B.C.), the reform movement that he launched at the age of twenty (628 B.C.), the revival (622 B.C.), and his death in the battle with Pharaoh Neco at Megiddo (609 B.C.). Without the prolonged distraction of the Assyrians, Josiah could not have implemented reform; the Assyrians would not have allowed it.

When Josiah became king, the Assyrian Empire was riddled with strife, disputes, and dynastic struggles. Because of the constant conflict within various regions of Assyrian domain, Josiah had freedom to institute reform, which led to revival.

The Reforms

At the age of sixteen, Josiah had a deep experience with God. Four years after his spiritual transformation, Josiah launched religious reform that focused on three areas: abolition of idolatry, cleansing of the temple, and desecration of pagan places. He systematically abolished idolatry not only in Judah but also in Israel. His reform went as far north as the tribes of Manasseh, Ephraim, Simeon, and Naphtali (2 Chron 34:6-7). Josiah destroyed the altars to Baal and the golden calves erected by Jeroboam at Bethel and Dan, demolished the Asherah obelisks, removed all of the vessels used in cultic worship, leveled the groves, and pulverized the stone piles. The child sacrifices to Moloch were abolished. He destroyed the altars to God in the high places. He exhumed the bones of the dead cultic priests and scattered them upon the pagan altars in fulfillment of the prophecy to Jeroboam (1 Kings 13:1-2). In addition, he deposed the non-Levitical priests from religious practices. Moreover, the Levitical priests who engaged in pagan rituals were brought to Jerusalem and declared ineligible for religious office, although they were not deprived of their means of livelihood. Throughout Judah and Israel, Josiah synchronized the reform efforts.

This reform was even more remarkable considering Josiah's circumstances. He was not reared in a Godly home, no sacrifices were offered at the temple to God, the scrolls that contained the Mosaic Law were lost, and paganism was rampant. Since the Northern tribes were under the control of Assyria, his reform efforts in the Northern Kingdom were considered acts of aggression against the Assyrians. Indeed, because the worship of Yahweh was so intertwined with Israelite nationalism, the entire reform movement was an act of rebellion not only against the Assyrian gods but also against Assyrian control. Josiah, in his efforts to reform Israel, was seemingly attempting to resurrect the Davidic kingdom.[16]

As Josiah turned his attention to the temple, he reclaimed and sanctified it for Jehovah. As he began a vigorous renovation program, he appealed for funds to the people across the land, commissioned two priests from the Merari clan and two from the Kohath family as managers of the project (2 Chron 34:12), and gave instructions for a quick completion of the temple restoration.

In the midst of the renovation, Hilkiah, the high priest, discovered the lost scrolls that contained the Mosaic Law. Whether the scrolls contained the entire Pentateuch or only the book of Deuteronomy must be left to conjecture. Ernest Baker suggested that it took about three to four hours to read Deuteronomy and approximately twelve to fourteen hours to read the entire Pentateuch.[17] Josiah was not concerned about the length of time that it took to read the law; rather, he mourned the neglect on the part of the people toward it. The law was tantamount to the constitution of the nation. The misplacement of the Mosaic Law was equivalent to the nation operating without the principles upon which it was founded.

The Bible does not indicate when or where the law was lost or where it was found. It was probably lost during the reign of Manasseh. Three views are proposed as to its location when it was found. One view suggests that it was found in the Ark of the Covenant, which had been stored when the temple was converted to a pagan shrine.

The second view is that it was discovered in the cornerstone of the temple. The third view is that it was found in some storage area of the temple.[18]

When Hilkiah found the law, he gave the scrolls to Shaphan, the royal scribe, who in turn gave the scrolls to Josiah. As the law was read to the king, he tore his robes as he responded in anguish and consternation. He was greatly distraught that Judah had been so negligent toward God's commandments. In the reading of the law, reform was about to be transformed into revival.

The Revival Under Josiah

God uses various methods to produce revival. Under Asa, it was Azariah's message and the religious festival that ignited the movement. In Nineveh, it was the preaching of Jonah. With Elijah, it was the miracle of fire. Through Josiah, it was the return to God's Word. Although it was the first time Josiah had ever heard God's law read, he responded immediately to its message. From this episode, as with all revivals in history, the place of God's Word in renewal is discerned. Spiritual decline occurs when God's Word is denied or neglected; revival occurs when His Word is heard, understood, and applied. The Bible and spiritual vitality are inseparable. When Josiah heard the law, he accepted its claims upon his life and applied its teachings within the nation. The sacred scrolls may have been located in God's house, but revival ignited when God's Word was stored in human hearts. For approximately one hundred years, Judah had languished in spiritual ineptitude, but that was about to change. Kaiser wrote, "[God] will not let his fallen children roam about in spiritual fatigue forever."[19]

When Josiah heard the reading of the law, he became terrified and sought an interpretation. Instead of going to Jeremiah, who started his prophetic ministry in 627 B.C. (Jer 1:1-2), or to Zephaniah, a descendant of King Hezekiah and a relative of Josiah who started his ministry about the same year as Jeremiah, the king's emissaries went to Huldah, the prophetess and wife of Shallum who was keeper of the royal wardrobe. She assured the king that God's instructions recorded in the law were valid and that judgment was impending, but not in his lifetime.

> Although it was the first time that he had ever heard God's Law read, Josiah responded immediately to its message.

Josiah summoned the people to Jerusalem to hear the reading of the law. As the law was read, conviction pierced the hearts of the people. The king led a public commitment that Judah would be obedient to God, ratified anew the covenant, and observed the instructions recorded in the law. Revival began to ignite in the lives of the people. Josiah gave instructions to the priests to make preparations for the sacrifices. From his own herds, Josiah provided thirty thousand sacrificial animals, plus three thousand bulls. Others in the nation gave liberally for the occasion. As the priests fulfilled their functions, the musicians led in praise and worship. For seven days the festival resounded with joyful psalms, and sacrificial aromas saturated the Jerusalem atmosphere. What a transformation! Under Manasseh and Amon, the nation toiled in spiritual depravity. In April of 622 B.C., the nation of Judah had an encounter with God that restored its spiritual vitality, released it from spiritual oppression, and produced a symphony of praise to God.

Revival was aflame in Judah, and the people celebrated with joy, thanksgiving, and gladness. In the midst of the revival, the people were awakened from their slumber, assumed their responsibilities before God, reaffirmed their commitments to God, and joyfully celebrated their restored fellowship with God. It is astonishing that God's people had become so negligent toward Him that they regressed to such depths of spiritual bankruptcy. However, God's mercy and grace were extended one more time to an undeserving people in order that God might be glorified and the people experience the awesome power of God. The catalysts that God used to produce this revival were a dedicated servant in Josiah, God's Word, the message of Huldah, humility of the leaders, a reform movement under the leadership of the king, and the worship of the people.

Results of the Revival

In a study of the revivals in the Old Testament, no king in the Northern Kingdom served as a revival leader; in the Southern Kingdom, six kings were used of God to ignite renewal. This was the thirteenth significant revival from Sinai to Josiah.

The first result of this revival was the ratification of the covenant. Every period of spiritual decline in Israelite and Judaic history was marked by the violation of the covenant with God. In every revival, the covenant was ratified anew. This ratification was symbolic of the people's commitment to God and restoration to fellowship with Him.

Other results included the observance of the Passover, which for years had been neglected; reclamation of the temple for God; abolition of paganism wrought through the reform Josiah had started; restoration of the Levitical priesthood; the return of the Ark of the Covenant to its rightful place in the temple; joy and gladness; restoration of the worship of the Lord; and the prolongation of the nation of Judah (although thirty-five years after this revival, Judah was destroyed). For Judah, this awakening created serious inner spiritual reflection and produced unreserved obedience to God. It started with a youthful king who dedicated himself to God at the age of sixteen, implemented reform at twenty, and became a revival leader at twenty-six. Although the people had a limited knowledge of God, they acted upon the knowledge they had, and God responded with revival. It is not the amount of knowledge that matters, but the application of the knowledge one has.

This renewal also demonstrated the patience, grace, love, and mercy of God. Under Manasseh and Amon, the people had forsaken God and broken their covenant with Him. God tenderly and graciously turned the people back to Himself. This revival communicated that sin cannot take people beyond the boundaries of His loving kindness. When the people of Judah responded to God, they discovered that God was there all the time.

The effects of this revival lasted for thirteen years — the rest of Josiah's life. In the message of Huldah, the prophetess declared that the impending judgment would not occur during Josiah's life. His death occurred in 609 B.C. Once again, Assyria was involved. In 614 B.C. Cyaraxes, king of the Medes, and Nabopolassar, king of Babylon, formed a coalition in order to attack Nineveh. In a three-month siege during the summer of 612 B.C., Nineveh fell. The Assyrian king, Sin-shar-ishkim, was killed and was replaced with Asshur-uballit II. The new king fled to Haran for safety. However, in 610 B.C., the coalition forces successively captured Haran. Before the defeat, Asshur-uballit sent an appeal to Psamtik I (664-609 B.C.), Pharaoh of Egypt, for assistance. By the time the message arrived in Egypt, it was too late for Psamtik to respond.

The Pharaoh died and was succeeded by his son, Neco II (609-594 B.C.). The new Pharaoh marshaled his forces and marched to Haran to assist the Assyrian king. Neco probably thought that a weak Assyrian Empire was much better than a powerful, aggressive, and ambitious coalition of Babylonians and Medes. When Neco reached Megiddo, Josiah confronted him. In the battle with Neco, Josiah was killed. When Neco arrived in Haran, Assyria had fallen, an event that permanently ended the Assyrian Empire. When Josiah was returned to Jerusalem for burial, Jeremiah offered a lament that communicated the attitude of the people of Judah. He was revered as the most righteous king, including David, to ever rule over Judah or Israel.

Conclusion

The cycle often seen in revival movements is discerned in this renewal. First, the nation faltered in her allegiance to God. The Word of God was neglected and ultimately lost. The nation digressed into idolatry. The judgments of God were upon the nation. A servant of God became concerned about the spiritual climate of the land. He experienced revival and became usable by God to ignite others. Revival spread to the masses. Restoration to God's fellowship was accomplished. Indeed, those who "seek Him, He shall be found" by them (Jer 29:13). Baker wrote, "History shows that God does not give up on men. . . . Faith will never become extinct. God will visit and revive. . . [his people] before such a catastrophe occurs."[20] However, in spite of the revival under Josiah, God's judgment was ultimately exercised upon Judah through the military power of Nebuchadnezzar.

Revival Under Ezra and Nehemiah

Whereas the Assyrians destroyed Israel and the Babylonians demolished Judah, the Persians, through Cyrus's policy of tolerance, served as the catalyst in the restoration of the Jewish nation. After the exiles returned to Jerusalem, they experienced four recorded revival movements, the most significant of which was the renewal under the leadership of Ezra and Nehemiah in 444 B.C.

The Persian Empire and Judea

The Persian Empire began to emerge in 559 B.C. when Cyrus (599-530 B.C.), son of Cambyses, became king of Anshan, a vassal state of the Medians. In 550 B.C. he revolted against the Medians, and by 546 B.C. he had subjected to his rule both the Median Empire and the kingdom of Lydia. By 539, he had taken the city of Babylon, and the whole region came under his dominion.

Cyrus adopted remarkably humane policies toward captured nations. He allowed exiles to return to their homelands, appointed native leaders, and promoted the religions of each country. In 538 B.C., he issued the decree (which is contained in its entirety in the Cyrus Cylinder) that the Jews could return to Jerusalem.[21] He appointed Sheshbazzar, Zerubbabel, and Joshua as the leaders of the expedition, instructed Mithridates to return the Jewish temple treasures[22] that were stored at the Babylonian temple in Esagila, donated funds from the Persian treasury, and provided documents of instructions to government leaders in the west.[23] With these possessions in hand, the three men led some fifty thousand Jews on the journey to Jerusalem. Although some Jews returned to Jerusalem, most remained in Babylon. Fortunately for the Jews, the policies of Cyrus were followed by his successors.

Ezra

Ezra was a Levite and a descendent of Hilkiah, the high priest under Josiah. In 458 B.C., he received permission from Artaxerxes I to return to Jerusalem. In his letter of introduction to the leaders in Jerusalem, Artaxerxes identified Ezra as a scribe. This was a high position in the Persian court, possibly equivalent to "Secretary of State for Jewish Affairs."[24] Because of this status, Ezra went to Jerusalem as an official of the Persian crown. Without this royal authority, he could not have achieved his objective. Before his departure for Judea, he received significant funds from the Persian treasury, additional temple treasures taken by Nebuchadnezzar, and freewill offerings from the Jews. He assembled a contingency of Jews on the banks of the Ahava River and spent three days organizing the group. When he discovered that there were no Levites among the immigrants, he sent a deputation to Casiphia. Thirty-eight priests and 220 temple attendants were enlisted for the journey.

After the completion of the organization, the decision not to request an armed guard (due to Ezra's insistence to Artaxerxes that God's protection was sufficient), and the spiritual preparation, the caravan departed on the eight-hundred-mile trip to Jerusalem on the twelfth day of the first month. After four months of travel, Ezra arrived in Jerusalem, distributed the treasures, delivered the documents, and assumed the responsibilities of chief judge over religious matters. As he surveyed Jerusalem, he was horrified at the conditions that existed, especially the mixed marriages. He was so stunned that he was speechless for a day. At the end of the day, he offered prayer to God that was akin to the intercession of Moses at Sinai. In contrition, he interceded for the people, acknowledged their unworthiness, and petitioned for mercy. An assembly was convened on the twentieth day of the ninth month in the midst of a great rainstorm and cold weather in order to resolve the matter of mixed marriages. The people determined to remedy the situation by dissolving the mixed marriages by the first of the new year.[25]

Ezra began to implement reform that was still in progress when Nehemiah arrived in 444 B.C. As a part of that reform, he, with the help of Shechamiah, took a census to determine the number of mixed marriages, led in the dissolution of some of those marriages, read the law, observed the Feast of the Tabernacles,[26] established a day of mourning, confessed sins, and ratified the covenant. Like a choral refrain, the ratification of the covenant was a part of every revival in the Southern Kingdom.

The covenant was the foundation of the relationship between God and His people. When they neglected their commitments to God, they placed themselves under His condemnation. In revival, the people renewed their pledges with solemn vows to keep the covenant with God that was embodied in the law. The cyclical pattern of the Israelites mirrors the pathway taken by every generation. Among the Israelites, spiritual declension was interrupted by revival. However, because God's instructions for revival were not obeyed, the revival ceased and the downward spiral returned. The Jews in every generation needed to learn that relationship with God is a daily journey. In the midst of this renewal, the people made a commitment to keep the Sabbath, observe sabbatical years in agriculture, pay the temple tax, and supply the temple with the necessary provisions for sacrificial celebrations.

Ezra ranks among the greatest leaders in the history of the Israelites. Under his leadership, Judaism according to rabbinical tradition was born. He has been called the "Second Moses." Indeed, Ezra "would have been worthy of receiving the Torah had Moses not preceded him."[27] In addition, he was recognized as the founder of the guild of scribes who were so prominent during the New Testament era. The Talmud identified him as Malachi.[28] Josephus identified him as Esdras.[29] He was recognized as the author of Chronicles, restorer of Jewish literature, and author of Ezra-Nehemiah.[30] Ezra and Nehemiah have been called the creators of the Jewish community in Palestine and two of the greatest leaders in Jewish history.[31] They have been compared to Aaron and Moses, Zadok and David. The place and date of Ezra's death are not known. Josephus wrote that he died about the time that Eliashib was the high priest and was buried in Jerusalem.[32]

A teacher, reformer, revival leader of two awakenings, interpreter of the law, administrator, and author of biblical literature, Ezra was deeply spiritual, uncompromising in his convictions, and impervious to public opinion. These are always marks of effective revival leaders. The phrase "hand of the Lord was upon" Ezra is found often in the biblical book that bears his name. This phrase includes divine leadership, guidance, protection, provision, and power. The revival and reform that occurred under Ezra during the Feast of the Tabernacles were preludes to the revival and reform in 444 B.C. under the combined leadership of Ezra and Nehemiah.

Ezra was deeply spiritual, uncompromising in his convictions, and oblivious to public opinion. All marks of effective revival leaders.

Nehemiah

Nehemiah served as a cupbearer for Artaxerxes I.[33] Herodotus wrote that the office was "one of no trifling honor."[34] His office as cupbearer included palace administration and protection of the king, who lived in Susa. In 445 B.C. Nehemiah heard distressing news from Hanani about the existing conditions in Jerusalem. For years, the walls and gates had remained in shambles. However, apparently in 446 B.C., further damages were done to the city.[35] Following four months of spiritual preparation, Nehemiah secured permission from Artaxerxes to return to Jerusalem in order to restore the city. The king appointed him the *Tirshatha,* or governor, over the territory that included, among other territories, Palestine, Syria, and Arabia. Then he was given letters of introduction to government leaders, especially Asaph, keeper of the forest, who was instructed to supply the building needs of Nehemiah. Because of his appointment as governor over the territories in which Jerusalem was the capital, he had authority over Sanballat, governor of Samaria, and Geshem of Arabia. He assembled a caravan of immigrants and departed for Jerusalem. He left the comfortable lifestyle of the royal palace for the stressful life as the Persian satrap in the west.

After he arrived in Jerusalem, he made a midnight inspection of the city, summoned the leaders, shared his assessments, and proposed solutions, which included reconstruction of the walls and gates. The repairs were probably along the same lines as the city perimeters prior to the exile. If this was the case, the city, according to archeologist K. M. Kenyon, would be 3,750 feet long and 900 feet wide at the greatest extent, tapering to about 540 feet at the southern end.[36] It took fifty-two days to complete the restoration of the walls and no less than ten gates.

During construction, Nehemiah was threatened, taunted, attacked, ridiculed, and tempted as opposition came from Tobiah, Sanballat, and Geshem. In addition, he was delayed in the restoration due to injustices inflicted upon the poor by rich noblemen. The government leaders of the area were exacting heavy taxes, and the wealthy lenders were charging 12 percent interest on money borrowed to pay the taxes. Many of the Jews were losing all of their possessions, including their families, because of the unethical practices. Nehemiah responded in anger with physical violence and strong language as he severely rebuked the noblemen. He demanded and received full restoration of property and families.

In addition, when Sanballat and Tobiah asked Nehemiah on four different occasions to meet them at Ono, located at the southern end of Sharon Valley (Neh 6:1-4), Nehemiah detected a plot to discredit him. When he undertook the divine assignment to restore Jerusalem, he certainly anticipated opposition. However, the temptations of Nehemiah appeared innocent and appealed to human pride. They were allurements that required meticulous discernment. He saw the trickery involved and prudently rejected their overtures. When their attempts failed, Sanballat solicited the help of Shemaiah and the prophetess, Noadiah, to offer false accusations that were tantamount to treason against the Persian government. When Nehemiah was advised to take refuge in the temple, he rejected the offer.

Following the restoration of the walls and gates,[37] Nehemiah assembled the people for a celebration. Since he considered the renovation effort a monument to God's provision, the opponents were not invited to the event. The celebration occurred during the Feast of the Tabernacles in 444 B.C., fourteen years after the renewal under Ezra.

Nehemiah was a spiritual leader, reformer, administrator, and government official. Few leaders among the Jews had the impact of this official in the Persian court. Josephus wrote, "He was a man of good and righteous character . . . and he hath left the walls of Jerusalem as an eternal monument of himself." [38]

The Revival Comes

Like all revivals in the Southern Kingdom, this one occurred during the celebration of an annual festival. There are no recorded revivals in the history of the Northern Kingdom during festivals. There were two major reasons for this lack: (l) they did not follow God's instructions in festival observances; and (2) they included the golden calves of Apis from Bethel and Dan in the celebrations that they did observe. There is biblical evidence that they did not observe the feasts on an annual basis. In the Southern Kingdom, every national revival occurred during one of the three required feasts: Passover, Pentecost, or the Feast of the Tabernacles. One explanation for this association was that the festivals allowed the people to assemble as a nation. It is interesting to note that the revival at Pentecost in Acts 2 ignited during this festival.

When Nehemiah assembled the nation for the Feast of the Tabernacles, the focus was upon the reading of the law.[39] For seven days — three hours each day — Ezra and his associates read the Old Testament Pentateuch. As the law was read, priests were in the midst of the people to explain the meaning of God's instruction.

As the people heard God's Word, they came under such conviction that they mourned and wept over their sins. They were reminded of the holiness of God, the requirements of the covenant, and their own neglect in obedience to God. In the light of God's commands, they realized their own failures and were challenged with their responsibilities to God. In their spiritual remorse, they made no demands for human rights nor extolled their own human virtues. They were engulfed by the awesome holiness of God and their own unrighteousness. They were deeply convicted that God deserved priority in their lives and in the nation. In response, they wept over their transgressions.

Nehemiah challenged them not to weep, but to respond to God in great rejoicing, for God's mercy had provided restoration. Since God had forgiven their transgressions, they were not to focus on what they had done in the past, but rather on what God was doing in the present. Without revival, they were comfortable in their spiritual complacency and mediocrity. In the presence of the glory of God, they were reminded that God does not compromise with His people or accommodate them to journey unchecked in their spiritual spiral of decline.

They were God's chosen people, but they had not chosen God. He made them special, but they had not made Him special. God kept the covenant with them, but they had not kept the covenant with Him. They were the beneficiaries of God's blessings and provisions, but they had responded with presumption, neglect, and complacency. Those conditions were changed in the midst of this revival.

The priests counseled and prayed with the multitudes. Their prayers included confessions of sin; praise to God; thanksgiving for His longsuffering, grace, and forgiveness; and petitions for His blessing. The prayers ended with a pledge to be obedient to the covenant, which they ratified.

In their oath to keep the covenant, the people pledged their loyalty to keep the Sabbath, abstain from mixed marriages, be faithful in giving in order to provide for the priests and the temple, and correct unethical business practices. When restitution was necessary, they committed themselves to fulfill the demands. Because of prior disobedience, they had positioned themselves in opposition to God. In this revival, they were confronted with the enormous price of disobedience and the requirements of restoration to His unhindered fellowship.

As they responded in brokenness, humility, and obedience, they discovered that restoration to fellowship with God is more desirous than any earthly possession. This feast had not been celebrated in this manner since the days of Joshua (Neh 8:17).[40] Every detail of the law was followed. The events included seven days of celebration, followed by the days of festival observance.

Results of the Revival

This revival was the product of prayer, obedient revival leaders, reading God's Word, and confession of sin. This renewal contributed significantly either directly or indirectly to the future of the Jews. It helped to solidify the post-exilic Palestinian community as it established permanently Jewish monotheism. Many of the Jewish institutions were impacted to some degree by this revival, including temple worship, synagogues, scribes, Pharisees, and Judaic traditions.

For the next 470 years, there was no major spiritual awakening in Palestine.[41] In the absence of revival, Judaism crystallized into a cold, rigid orthodoxy with an exclusive religious structure. By the first century, instead of offering the people freedom to worship God, they offered oppression that shackled their spiritual lives. Instead of godly relationships, they offered rules. Instead of spiritual vitality, they offered structured liturgies. Instead of joyous celebration, they offered cold formality Instead of fellowship with God based on grace and faith, they offered religion based on works.

This renewal intensified reform. New leaders were appointed. A program for the resettlement of Jerusalem was implemented. One out of every ten Judean citizens outside of Jerusalem was required to settle in the city. Social reform and domestic changes occurred, especially in regard to mixed marriages. For the modern mind, this domestic situation seems inconceivable. However, the stringent requirements were in fulfillment of Mosaic Law.

Marriages involving other nationalities threatened to compromise religious priorities. In mixed Jewish homes, wives were overwhelming influences upon their husbands to embrace syncretistic views toward God. In addition, mothers controlled their children's education. As a part of the curriculum, pagan mothers taught the religions of their ancestors. Ezra and Nehemiah concluded that mixed marriages contributed to the first exile, and they did not want another. If the marriages were left unchecked, they concluded that the results would be disastrous. Moreover, mixed marriages would have ended the Jewish nation. Their heritage, position before God, and destiny as a nation were hanging in the balance.

Out of this awakening, patriotism intensified, moral corrections were implemented, ethical standards were altered, domestic patterns were established, and religious reforms were achieved. In many ways, the revival under Ezra and Nehemiah was similar to the one at Sinai under Moses. Whereas the Sinai revival helped to establish the foundations of the Hebrew nation, the renewal at Jerusalem helped to establish the foundations for Judaism. Both movements corrected religious syncretism and established religious practices. The Sinai renewal helped to prepare the Hebrew nation for the wilderness wanderings; the Jerusalem revival helped to prepare the people for the inter-biblical period. Both revivals focused upon the ratification and pledge of allegiance to the law.

Conclusion

The length of the revival intensity is unknown. When Nehemiah returned to Jerusalem in 430 B.C., he had to correct some situations that had developed. However, the lingering influence can be measured only within the mind of God. Certainly, the future of the Jewish nation was impacted. Only the revival at Sinai could be placed by this renewal in regard to its importance to the Israelite nation.

Questions for Discussion

1. Discuss the difference between a spontaneous revival and a planned annual revival. Give the pros and cons of each.

2. Think of a time that you have experienced revival, church-wide or personal. What kind of changes occurred within your church and/or personal life?

Significant Revivals in the Old Testament

Revival	Scripture	Classification
Pre-Flood (Enoch and Noah)	Genesis 5:21-24; 6:8-10	Personal
Abraham[42]	Genesis 22:1-19	Personal
Jacob at Bethel I	Genesis 28:10-22	Personal
Jacob at Bethel II	Genesis 32:22-32	Personal
Revival at Sinai	Exodus 32-34	National
Othniel[43]	Judges 3:7-11	National
Ehud	Judges 3:12-30	National
Deborah and Barak	Judges 4:1-5:31	National
Jephthah	Judges 10:6-12:7	National
Samuel	2 Samuel 7:2-12	National
Solomon's Dedication of the Temple	2 Chronicles 5:1-7:10	National
Asa	2 Chronicles 15:1-18	National
Elijah at Carmel	1 Kings 18:1-46	Specialized
Jonah	Jonah 1:1-4:11	Regional (Nineveh)
Isaiah	Isaiah 6:1-13	Personal
Hezekiah	2 Kings 18:3-7 2 Chronicles 29:1-36	National
Josiah	2 Kings 22:8-23:3	National
Ezekiel[44]	Ezekiel	Personal
Zerubbabel	Ezra 3:1-6	Regional
Zerubbabel II (Haggai and Zechariah)	Ezra 6:13-22	National
Ezra	Ezra 9:1-10:17	Regional
Ezra and Nehemiah	Nehemiah 8:1-11:2	National

Chapter 4
Revival in the New Testament

Thomas said to him, "My Lord and my God!"
John 20:28, NIV

The New Testament narrates the biblical account of one long spiritual awakening that had many revivals within the larger movement. Just as the First Great Awakening (1726-70) and the Second Great Awakening (1787-1843) in America were long revivals with many crests, so the New Testament renewal, the first awakening in history that followed this pattern, experienced many revival movements.

The revival started in A.D. 26 with John the Baptist in the Jordan region. It intensified under Jesus; crested at Pentecost; spread to Samaria, Damascus, Cornelius' house, Antioch, Cyprus, Pisidia, Philippi, Thessalonica, Ephesus, and other places; and ended with John the Apostle on the Island of Patmos. During those 70 years, the ministries of John the Baptist and Jesus and the advent of the Holy Spirit at Pentecost transpired. The church was birthed and expanded from the Upper Room to the outer borders of the Roman Empire and even beyond. The penning of the 27 books of the New Testament and many other accomplishments occurred. Indeed, this renewal established the pattern for all subsequent biblical awakenings and is a magnificent example of the true meaning of revival.

Jesus came in "the fullness of time" (Gal 4:4, NRSV). Before His coming, God was at work preparing the world for His royal arrival. As a vital part of the preparation, God united the Mediterranean world under one Roman government and prepared the Jewish nation with a Messianic hope. The New Testament revival occurred within the Roman world, Hellenistic culture, and Jewish religious context.

Religious Life of the Jews

The New Testament awakening began within the context of first century Judaism. When John the Baptist appeared in the Jordan region, Judaism was mired in a lifeless, hopeless system of rigid religious structure that produced spiritual oppression. Indeed, the religious life of the Jews had been transformed from a spiritual relationship with God in 444 B.C. to an enslaving religion of traditions and regulations by the first century.

High Priests

During the first century, the religious life of the Jews was primarily directed by the high priest and the Sanhedrin. From the time of Aaron to the time of Antiochus IV, the office of high priest was passed through the Aaronic line. When Antiochus IV replaced Onias III with Jason, the office became a position of government appointment.

From the time Herod appointed Ananel as high priest in 37 B.C. until the last high priest, Phannias (A.D. 67-68), twenty-eight men filled the office.[1]

The two high priests who exercised the most influence during the New Testament revival were Annas and Joseph Caiaphas. Annas, who is mentioned often in the New Testament, was appointed by Quirinius in A.D. 6 and served until A.D. 15. Joseph Caiaphas, moderator at the trial of Jesus, was appointed by procurator Valerius Gratus (A.D. 15-26)[2] in A.D. 18 and served until A.D. 36. Within the tenure of his office, the New Testament awakening ignited and greatly expanded. He had every opportunity to respond positively. Yet he was the strongest opponent.

Along with the high priests, religious authority resided within the *Sanhedrin*. From the time of Salome Alexandra (76-67 B.C.), the place of the Sanhedrin was firmly secured within the national life. This court not only determined religious policy but also served as the judicial system. Although the rabbinical tradition traces the origin of this council back to the seventy elders appointed by Moses as his advisors, (Num 11:16ff), the name first appeared in history in a letter written by Antiochus III to the Coelesyrian governor shortly after the battle of Paneas in 198 B.C.[3] In the New Testament, the Sanhedrin represented a constant nemesis to Jesus and other revival leaders. They were responsible, humanly speaking, for Christ's crucifixion and the persecution of the early revival leaders.

Hasidim

Within Judaism, several religious groups developed. Among the most prominent were the Hasidim, Sadducees, Pharisees, Essenes, scribes, and Zealots. The Hasidim, which means "Godly people," began to emerge during the time of Ezra and Nehemiah. As the group developed, they became solidified in their zeal toward the Mosaic Law. Out of this group came the oral laws and Jewish traditions that so dominated the religious life of the Jews in the first century. Against the backdrop of these traditions, Jesus countered with His message of the Kingdom.

Sadducees

The Sadducees were composed of a few wealthy families and high priests. In spite of their challenges to Jesus and His disciples, the spiritual awakening continued, even to the point that believers counted it all joy to suffer for His name. The origin of the Sadducees is obscure. During the reign of John Hyrcanus (134-104 B.C.), they emerged as a strong political force. However, it was during the regime of Alexander Jannaeus (103-76 B.C.) that they established their place in Judaism. Their staunchest opponents were the Pharisees.

During the Jewish revolt against Jannaeus in 94-88 B.C., the Sadducees supported the king while the Pharisees rallied behind the insurgents under the leadership of Demetrius. Once the king repelled the rebellion, he turned on the insurrectionists with a vengeance, including the Pharisees. In retaliation, he crucified eight hundred rebels, which included some Pharisees.

Inevitably, this event only intensified the animosity between the two parties. It is well documented that the Sadducees differed from the Pharisees in the areas of politics and religious doctrine, especially in the interpretations of the Mosaic Law and oral traditions and the idea of the resurrection of the human soul. It is interesting to note that their common cause, the elimination of Christ, served to create cooperation between the two groups.

The Sadducees, under the leadership of Caiaphas, controlled the trial of Jesus. Although they were successful in their demands to crucify Jesus, they could not destroy the fires of revival. The actions that they thought would extinguish the movement only served as fuel to spread the fires. Christ's crucifixion and Resurrection were followed by the advent of the Holy Spirit at Pentecost, which carried the renewal to new heights.

Pharisees

The Pharisees were strict adherents of the law and more conservative in doctrine than the Sadducees. According to Josephus, they numbered about six thousand at the close of the reign of Herod the Great.[5] Although the party was small in membership, the Jewish population overall was more sympathetic to their views than those of the Sadducees. Their doctrinal views included belief in the oral laws, Jewish traditions, exclusivity among the Jews, Mosaic Law, and the soul's resurrection.

The origin of the Pharisees is uncertain; however, they predated the Sadducees and probably originated during the time immediately following the return of the exiles from Babylon. In the first century, they were the religious power with which Christians had to contend. Some of the Pharisees and many of their sympathizers became converts to the Christian faith and leaders of spiritual awakening. Of course, Saul of Tarsus, the Pharisee among the Pharisees, was the greatest of these.

Essenes

The party of the Essenes provides great interest and importance to the first-century revival. Very similar to the Hasidim in their emphases on piety and religious adherence, they differed from the Hasidim in their insistence upon communal living. Pliny, in his *Natural History,* stated that they lived in celibacy, poverty, and asceticism on the west side of the Dead Sea near Engedi. [6] Philo estimated the number of Essenes at "about four thousand, and describes them as living in villages, working hard at agriculture, devoting much time . . . to the communal study of moral and religious questions."[7] Like the early Christians described in Acts 4-5, the Essenes held their properties in common.

The Essenes made a strong impression upon the Jews. Their disciplined lives, communal living, and mutual support were attractive to people who were struggling for economic security and religious stability.[8] Although Philo wrote that the Essene sect was started by Moses, the earliest references to them emerged during the reign of Jonathan Maccabees (160-143 B.C.). Many, though not all, scholars believe that John the Baptist was an Essene.

Scribes

From the time of Ezra, the scribes were the professionals charged with guarding the law and teaching that law to the people. By the first century, the group was fully developed and exercised a strong influence in Judaism. The scribes challenged Jesus and His teachings on several occasions. Their misinterpretations of God's law and fanaticism for Jewish tradition served to imprison the souls of the people. Their offerings of hope were empty. Their teachings on access to God were meaningless. Instead of providing joyful fellowship with God, they created an empty vacuum. Into that vacuum Jesus came preaching, "[A]nd you will know the truth, and the truth will make you free" (John 8:32).

Zealots

The word *zealot* means "someone who has zeal for the honor and glory of God."[9] In the first century, the Zealots were primarily those who zealously dedicated themselves to the cause of God and the liberation of Israel. In their minds, it was inconceivable that any foreign nation should have dominion over God's people. Within this group, some rabid fanatics emerged called the *sicarii.* This group originated with Judas the Galilean in A.D. 6. Because of their fanaticism against Roman rule, the Jewish War started and the termination of Judaism as known through the temple worship occurred in A.D. 70.

Out of this group came a revival leader in Simon the Zealot (Luke 6:15; Acts 1:13).[10] In his conversion, Simon exchanged his blind zeal for Judaism for a commission in the apostolic circle of Jesus Christ. He was convicted under Jesus' preaching, learned from His teachings, and marveled at His miracles; but most of all, he lived daily in His fellowship, the very essence of awakening.

The Revival Under John the Baptist

Within the context of the Roman Empire and Judaism, the New Testament revival ignited in A.D. 26 with John the Baptist in the Jordan region. Over the next seventy years, Christianity — without the benefits of buildings, finances, and other modern resources — spread across the Roman Empire. Serving in the midst of revival, the disciples developed strategies to evangelize the multitudes and wrote the literature of the New Testament. The accomplishments of the first-century church are prime examples of the awesome power unleashed by God in a true biblical revival. The modern church that seeks to pattern itself after the New Testament church must remember that the first believers thrived on the movement of the Holy Spirit.

John's Call to Revival

After his birth in about 5 B.C., very little is known of John's life before his appearance in the Jordan region. Luke wrote, "And the child grew and became strong in spirit, and he was in the wilderness till the day of his manifestation to Israel" (Luke 1:80). Although his association with the Essenes and the Qumran community is not certain, his message on holy living, helping the poor, and relationships with others was in agreement with Essene teachings.[11] When John appeared in the Jordan region, the dawn of the New Testament revival was on the horizon.

John started preaching in the wilderness, but he was not isolated. Bethany, located on the eastern side of the Jordan, was the crossover point of the Jordan River for travelers coming from the east and for Jews in Galilee traveling to Jerusalem. Since the Samaritans prohibited the Jews in Galilee to pass through their land on the way to Jerusalem (although passage was permissible leaving the city), they had to travel down the eastern side of the Jordan and cross at Jericho. Consequently, many of those from Galilee, where Jesus conducted so much of His ministry, were revival participants.

With the force of heaven, John preached the theme of the revival: "Repent, for the kingdom of heaven is at hand" (Matt 3:2). John did not offer pious platitudes or trite clichés. He did not recite the oral laws or Jewish traditions of the Hasidim. His message was not enslaved with the religious structure of the Sanhedrin, but was a voice from heaven announcing spiritual freedom. Like a fresh wind blowing across arid wasteland, his messages were saturated with the hope of glory.

Repentance

John called for personal accountability to God and set forth God's requirements for access to Himself. He shared that the people had to get serious with God, for God was most assuredly serious with them. Uncompromisingly, he thundered that there is no access to God apart from repentance. This is more than mental assent, regret for sin, and audible expression of sorrow; it is a reversal of life from focus on sin and self to a cross-centered life. The person who repents agrees with God and takes God's position against self in regard to sin. As the revival in the Jordan region intensified, the evangelistic results were enormous. In deep conviction, the hearers asked John, "What must we do?'' John stressed two things: baptism and righteous living.

Baptism

Baptism was not new with John's ministry. It was a common practice among many religions. The Jews required the ceremonial washing, or baptism, of proselytes as a part of their initiation into Judaism. The Essenes required baptism as a part of the ceremonial induction into the sect. However, John's baptism contained a new meaning. John instructed the people to be baptized as the outward evidence of the inward change that occurred through repentance.[12] For John, works did not produce repentance; rather, repentance produced works. Baptism was not administered in order to repent; rather, baptism occurred because repentance had effected inward change. With this shift, John's definition for baptism inaugurated a new theological meaning that was fulfilled in the ministry of Jesus Christ.

Righteous Living

John counseled his listeners to live according to God's instructions. To the crowd in general, he called them to show mercy to the poor. To the tax collector specifically, he stressed honesty and integrity. To the soldier, he emphasized kindness, contentment, and avoidance of the abuse of power. John challenged the status quo as he gave instructions that elevated conduct to new heights in human relationships. His preaching was revolutionary in the midst of a spiritual revolution that altered history

Eschatological hope

The revival ignited and flourished on the theme, "[T]he kingdom of heaven is at hand" (Matt 3:2b). This message communicated that the people's hope did not rest with Caesar or in Judaism, but in the Messianic hope of God's Kingdom. From Adam in the Garden of Eden, God's people had held to a Messianic hope that God would provide a deliverer (Gen 3:15). Isaiah prophesied that a "voice of one crying in the wilderness" (Isa 40:3, NKJV) would prepare the way for the Coming One. Malachi announced that a forerunner would precede the Messiah. In John, the Old Testament prophecies were fulfilled. His eschatological message contained two elements: the announcement that the Kingdom of heaven was at hand and the testimony that the Messiah had arrived.

Like a herald announcing the arrival of an earthly king, John proclaimed the arrival of the heavenly King and His Kingdom. He warned that the Day of Judgment was dawning and that preparation must be made. In his message, he stressed the eternality of the Coming One, His worthiness to save, the spirituality of His Kingdom, and His lordship over life. The crowning sermon of his ministry was delivered when he saw Jesus and exclaimed, "Behold, the Lamb of God, who takes away the sin of the world!" (John 1:29) The totality of the Christian message is contained in this statement. John on this occasion was the first to introduce Jesus to the world as both Savior and Lord.

Doctrinal Corrections

In his revival ministry, John challenged many doctrinal views of Judaism. He confronted the oral traditions of the Hasidim, Jewish ancestral pride in the children of Abraham, and the sacrificial system of temple worship. He informed the religious leaders that the Abrahamic covenant with God was not based upon heritage, culture, or earthly accomplishments, but upon spiritual relationships. When the religious leaders asked for his credentials, he asked, "Who warned you to flee from the wrath to come?"

(Matt 3:7). This question challenged their views on access to God. Judaism taught a relationship through works and temple sacrifices, regardless of the condition of the heart. John proclaimed that fruitage for God was based upon rootage of the heart in God.

Humility

After Jesus started His ministry, His immediate rise in popularity caused some of John's misguided disciples to ask John's opinion about the ministry of the next revival leader in Palestine. When John assessed his position against the background of Jesus Christ, he responded, "He must increase, but I must decrease" (John 3:30). If he never said another word, these words were enough to reveal his character.

John became a nationally recognized personality. The multitudes traveled up to one hundred miles to hear him preach. His meteoric rise was unparalleled, for his entire ministry lasted just over a year. However, when Jesus appeared, the forerunner recognized the primary personality in God's strategy of redemption. He declared that his position was nothing; Christ's position is everything. He was fully aware that his days of introduction were coming to a close, and it did not matter. The One he introduced was on the scene. John demonstrated heroism in self-effacement for revival leaders to emulate.

The Results of the Revival

Although John's public ministry lasted a little more than a year, his contributions to Christian history are impossible to evaluate. However, several elements readily surface.

God used John's mission and message to ignite the New Testament revival and arouse the spiritual conscience of the nation in preparation for the ministry of Jesus Christ. As John declared the emergence of God's Kingdom, Messianic hope was intensified throughout the nation, even to the point that the religious leaders in Jerusalem sent emissaries to inquire of him if he were the Promised One.

Although baptism was not new with John, his baptism of Jesus inaugurated this rite as a part of the Christian heritage.

John challenged the moral and spiritual positions of the secular and religious leaders. He confronted their conduct and erroneous doctrines and offered alternatives that were liberating to the human soul.

John established the example of revival preaching. His focus was upon God's Kingdom, Messianic hope, God's expectations, and answers to life's most profound questions. He fulfilled his mission humbly, uncompromisingly, and authoritatively. Although Thomas confessed, "My Lord and my God" in John 20:28, John lived this affirmation. Jesus assessed his ministry when He said that John was the greatest servant born of woman (Luke 7:24-28).

John closed the age of the Law and the Prophets and announced the coming age of Jesus Christ. In Jesus, the age of Christianity dawned.

In John, the Old Testament was summarized and the Messianic prophecy was echoed once again. In Jesus, the Old Testament was fulfilled, as the prophecies became realities. Both were revivalists of the highest magnitude, and the people heard them not as echoes of men but as voices from heaven.

The Revival Under Jesus

Where Jesus is, revival is; Jesus is revival. The spiritual movement that started under John the Baptist intensified and spread under Jesus. Serving within the Roman Empire and Jewish culture, Jesus fulfilled His mission in the midst of spiritual awakening. Since His life is so well chronicled, no attempts are made here to give a historical account of His ministry. Instead, miniature snapshots of revival principles that surface within His ministry are developed.

Where Jesus is, revival is; Jesus is revival.

John was approximately six months into his ministry when Jesus left Nazareth for the Jordan region to be baptized by John in A.D. 26. As Jesus was baptized, He was confirmed in His mission by the descent of the Holy Spirit and through the *Bath Kol* ("voice of God): "This is my beloved Son, with whom I am well pleased" (Matt 3:17). Jesus' baptism, among other things, identified Him with humanity, whom He came to save; set an example for His disciples to follow; and established an ordinance for His church. Following His baptism, He was driven into the wilderness by the Holy Spirit to encounter Satan.

Temptation

In Jesus' encounter with Satan, His victory over temptation and Satan's strategies are discerned. Satan's methods are always the same with every person. He used the same method on Jesus that he used on Eve in the Garden of Eden. He attacked Jesus at all points, which are the three basic points in life: body, soul, and spirit (1 Thess 5:23). As Satan tempted Jesus, he started outwardly with the physical appetite, moved to the soul, and progressed to the spirit. His suggestions to Jesus were satisfying to human need, attractive to the senses, and convenient for life's goals. However, Jesus demonstrated that His Kingdom is not based upon the satisfaction of physical appetites, actions to gain popularity, or following the pathways of least resistance.

In each temptation, Jesus communicated the method of victory. Jesus responded with spiritual resolve and with Scripture. He revealed that His mission would not be reduced to physical gratification, sensationalism, or compromise. In words and action, Jesus preached the most powerful message in history on how to deal with temptation. Revival lives or dies in one's ability to handle temptation. Satan did not tempt Jesus to do what He could not do, but what He could do. Enticements beyond one's abilities are not temptations at all.

Indeed, victory over temptation determines the existence, progress, intensity, impact, and longevity of revival. No Christian dwells in revival for long without victory in this area. As the Christian uses Scripture, exercises faith, and uses spiritual determination, victory is achieved and revival is maintained. Because Christ conquered, the believer can conquer.

The Teachings of Jesus

Conversion

Following His temptation, Jesus fanned the flames of awakening with winds that contained the force of a spiritual hurricane. He became a national personality almost immediately. As He preached, the multitudes heard Him gladly, Messianic hope intensified, and human needs were met. Jesus, like John before Him, countered the oral laws and Jewish traditions of the Hasidim. He also challenged the religious authority and teachings of the Sanhedrin, high priests, Sadducees, scribes, and Pharisees. His message revealed the Father and explained His mission. From one end of the nation to the other, huge crowds gathered to hear Him preach. Within the context of the Roman Empire and Judaism, Jesus served as the greatest revival leader in history.

As He attracted the attention of the religious leaders in Jerusalem, Jesus initially received mixed reviews. The vast majority of the leaders responded with instant opposition. However, a scattered few desired to investigate this Nazarene who was assuming center stage in the religious life of Palestine. On one occasion when Jesus was in Jerusalem, Nicodemus, a religious teacher of the Jews, came to Jesus at night for a dialogue on theological matters. In the course of conversation, the subject focused on how one has access to God. In this episode, Jesus taught that God wants relationship and not religion.

Nicodemus knew the traditions and followed the rules of Judaism; however, he was still searching for intimate fellowship with God. In this dialogue with Nicodemus, Jesus taught that a person prior to conversion is not simply away from God but is dead to God and under God's condemnation. Within the confines of this death, a person is incapable of earning eternal life, but must receive the indwelling One who is capable of raising the spiritually dead. Jesus explained that His mission is for this purpose (John 3:16). He called this spiritual resurrection being "born again" or salvation (John 3:3, 5, 17). Jesus taught that conversion is not cultural, inherited, or earned; it is a gift from God through faith in Him. Conversion is effected when Jesus takes up residence in the life of the believer. This experience ushers the believer into the Kingdom and makes the person a child of God. The two basic elements in conversion are repentance and faith.

In every revival, persons who are already converted are awakened from their spiritual slumber, and lost persons are initially saved. Following conversion, Christians often redirect their priorities from Kingdom matters to personal preferences. In their efforts to satisfy human appetites, they neglect the things of God and focus upon earthly objectives. As they do so, they go to sleep on God, and God must wake them up; thus, we have the term spiritual awakening.

When the Holy Spirit invades the life of a Christian, the result is tantamount to God's command to "be filled with the Spirit" (Eph 5:18). Indeed, awakening is simply living the spirit-filled life. Since God issued the command for believers to be submissive to the leadership of the Holy Spirit, revival is God's demand for His people. Jesus taught that conversion is the first step that leads to the Christian life that is lived in renewal.

Holiness

As Jesus' popularity grew, thousands gathered in open fields, on seashores, and on mountainsides to hear Him. His messages focused on living in righteousness, or holiness. Jesus did not teach that holiness is enlightenment, profession, works, zeal, or morality; it is, rather, conformity to the mind of God and the application of God's instructions in daily living. From the life of Christ and His teachings, especially the Sermon on the Mount, several principles on holiness surface.

Holiness is "right being" that produces "right doing." Holiness is not a divine suggestion; it is God's demand. Christ imputes this condition to the believer through faith.

In the Gospel of John, Jesus often talked about union with the believer. From these references, the Christian is assured that God does not issue a command without providing the resources needed to obey. Within our human resources, the command to be holy is impossible to keep. However, the Father through the Son accepts the believer. This is the good news. Salvation is not earned; it is a gift.

The focus of the Christian message is the conformity of the believer into the likeness of Christ. Although God is concerned about His people's physical comforts, His primary purpose in human life is to create and develop holy character. Revival is one method God uses to achieve His objectives. Indeed, holiness in Christ is the "prize of the upward call of God in Christ Jesus" (Phil 3:14). The life of Christ was characterized by holiness. Righteousness requires two things: faith in Christ and consistent living in the power of Christ's Resurrection. This daily living is the essence of biblical revival.

Prayer

As Jesus progressed in His ministry, He enlisted twelve men to form an apostolic band. As these men observed Jesus, they were awed by His preaching, miracles, and lifestyle. However, the one element they observed that they wanted to emulate more than any other was His ability to pray. From the beginning, the disciples sensed that they were on a mission that was extraordinary. If they were going to be effective, they knew that they must have the kind of power that Jesus was demonstrating. It didn't take long for them to discover that prayer and spiritual power are inseparable. When the disciples asked Jesus to teach them to pray, He offered the "Model Prayer." In this event, He taught several principles about prayer.

First, Jesus affirmed that prayer is an acquired discipline. Indeed, the more one prays, the more one wants to pray. Intimacy with God in prayer produces maturity in praying. Prayer is not getting what the Christian wants, but what God wants. The believer who earnestly prays knows that prayer is not getting things from God; it is getting to know God.

Second, Jesus taught the disciples that the Father's answers to prayer are not based upon activity alone, but upon position with God. In the term "Our Father," Jesus communicated that positionally the believer is a child of God. Prayer does not start with what a person *says,* but who a person *is* in Christ. With this understanding, Jesus proceeded to teach that prayer impacts the believer's relationships in three ways: acknowledgment of God's sovereignty, forgiveness toward others, and personal daily needs.

Third, Jesus taught that prayer is not designed to get God to act, but to get the believer in the position to receive God's answers. As the Christian persists in prayer, God breaks down the walls of pride, attitudes of self-sufficiency, and personal agendas. The person schooled in God's academy of prayer learns that God takes the believer's inadequacies and applies His sufficiency in order to fulfill His mission. Through prayer, the Holy Spirit invades the Christian's slumber, awakens, and equips him for new dimensions in Christian living.

Prayer is the track on which revival travels. Prayer is the food on which revival exists, the very breath of awakening. P. T. Forsyth wrote, "The worst sin is prayerlessness."[13] He also said, "Not to want to pray, then, is sin behind sin. And its end is not being able to pray. That is its punishment."[14] God produces, intensifies, spreads, and maintains revival through this spiritual communication. As the Lord unleashes His power within the believer's life, He ignites the fires of revival and expands His Kingdom through His revived servants. Where there is no earnest prayer, there is no revival.

Prayer is the track on which revival travels.

Faith

Across Palestine and to the outer limits of the nation, Jesus fulfilled His mission. He consistently utilized opportunities to drive home crucial spiritual lessons to the crowds and to His chosen twelve. The closer He came to the close of His earthly ministry, the more He intensified His instructions. Among the crowds, on retreats, or on journeys, He used many means to clarify Kingdom realities. On one occasion, He used a fig tree to clarify the incredible power that is contained within faith.

As Jesus talked about fig trees and moving mountains, He discussed two kinds of faith: big faith and little faith. From the inferences of His teachings, big faith is faith that is exercised. Little faith is faith that is not exercised.

No revival in history has occurred apart from faith. New Testament faith contains two crucial elements: hearing and applying. Hearing is auditory reception of God's instructions; applying is the Christian's application in daily living. Faith that ignites revival is more than shallow expressions and mental assent; it is life commitment. It receives the Word of God, incorporates its truths, multiplies its teachings, produces revival, and shares its product. When faith is exercised, God produces revival.

Worship

According to the synoptic Gospels, two days before the Passover, Jesus was in the home of Simon in Bethany, a village about two miles east of Jerusalem. Mary, the sister of Lazarus — whom Jesus raised from the dead — entered the room and anointed Jesus with expensive ointment. Out of this event, some principles of adoration emerge that are crucial in the Christian's response in the midst of revival.

Four basic elements of worship characterized Mary's actions: gratitude, natural response, privilege, and evidence of an inward change.

First, she was not in the room to make requisitions of Jesus, but to offer her gratitude to Jesus for what He had done in her life. In her expression of gratitude, she selected an expensive gift; her gratitude would not let her do less. Second, in her natural response, her adoration was heartfelt, personal, and freely given. It was not something that she had to do, but something she wanted to do. Third, she considered the action her privilege, not a duty, as she gave freely and joyfully. Fourth, this act was not for public show; it was outward evidence of an inward spiritual change. When worship in revival is measured by these characteristics, excesses are eliminated.

Jesus accepted her worship, gave it a spiritual meaning, and established it as a paradigm for biblical adoration. Because some of the disciples had not worshiped, they criticized, a natural reaction for those who are deficient in worship. Another principle surfaces at this point. When Mary poured the ointment on Jesus, He was the center of attention. When criticism was expressed, attention was diverted from Jesus to the broken box of ointment. At that moment, the conditions among the disciples were changed from unity in worship to division of fellowship. In response, Jesus rebuked the criticism.

He also used this event to teach the urgency of worship. Jesus implied that Mary did what she could, when she could do it. In a matter of a few hours, Jesus was crucified. When Mary went to the tomb to anoint the body of Jesus, Jesus was not there. Therefore, the occasion at Simon's house was the only time Mary had to anoint Jesus. Indeed, she worshiped when she could. Since revivals are not perennial, participation must occur when they ignite. Just as Mary did not tarry, delay, or sleep through her opportunity to respond to Jesus, Christians must not delay in revival participation. One of the primary purposes of revival is worship. However, worship is not an end in itself; it equips God's servants for Kingdom living and service.

Restitution

As Jesus passed through Jericho and met Zacchaeus (Luke 19), the dynamics of biblical restitution surfaced. Even though Zacchaeus was reconciled in his vertical relationship with God and his inward relationship with himself, God's forgiveness demanded that his horizontal relationships with his fellowmen be restored. Because he was a tax collector, he had dealt dishonestly with some people. He did not rationalize that his actions were common practice among men of his profession or promise to deal justly with people in the future. He knew that restitution for past actions was necessary. He did not confess the faults of others, but assumed personal responsibility for his past deeds and resolved to correct the wrongs he had done. Zacchaeus committed himself to restore up to fourfold that which he had taken dishonestly

In response to Zaccheaus' pledge, Jesus declared that forgiveness was at work in his life and that salvation had come to his house. If Zacchaeus had refused to restore broken relationships, his spiritual decision would have been less than God's demands. Zacchaeus did not seek to make restitution in general areas; rather, he specified the area that needed his attention and made restitution according to his offenses. The impact and the longevity of revival often depend somewhat upon the participants' willingness to make restitution and right past offenses.

Jesus' Death and Resurrection

For approximately four years, the fires of awakening were ablaze in Palestine. Multitudes of people participated in the revival blessings of God. They witnessed miracles, heard preaching, and enjoyed the presence of Jesus. However, the religious leaders and Roman legates chose not to participate. The criticism of the religious leaders turned from animosity to an absorbing passion to rid Palestine of the revival leader. Since they could not control Him, they decided to eliminate Him.

> You can be in the middle of the activity of God and miss His work.

Following Jesus' arrest, the trial before Caiaphas and the Sanhedrin, His appearances before Pilate and Herod Antipas, His scourging, ridicule, and the journey to Calvary, Jesus was crucified. In the plan of God, He decreed that reconciliation for mankind would come through the death of Christ on the Cross. The Cross not only provides freedom from sin in salvation; it also provides freedom from sin in the Christian's life that produces awakening. Sin prevents revival, and Christ's death on the Cross atones for sin. Consequently, the Cross is central for revival.

Although the religious leaders thought they were putting an end to Jesus, they actually released the power of heaven in human lives. When conditions appeared hopeless and His people were floundering, Jesus in His infinite mercy, majestic glory, and awesome power, provided atonement in order to rescue His people from the downward spiral of spiritual declension and restore them to His fellowship. Indeed, at the heart of every revival is the Cross of Jesus Christ. The Cross communicates that revival calls for sacrifice. Renewal begins and is sustained through the denial of self and the establishment of Christ as Lord in life. Jesus called this cross bearing (Luke 9:23). Paul called it the crucified life (Gal 2:20).

In spite of the fact that Jesus repeatedly shared with His disciples during the last several months of His ministry that He was going to be crucified, there were no disciples at the tomb to witness the Resurrection. In their minds, when Rome crucified someone, the person remained dead. If the disciples believed Jesus, it seems logical that they would have formed a Resurrection committee to maintain a vigil to watch the event. Mary went to the tomb to anoint a dead body, not to observe the Resurrection. Because of unbelief, the disciples missed the greatest event in history: the Resurrection of Jesus Christ.

Christianity centers in the Cross and the Resurrection. Through the Cross, salvation is provided; through the Resurrection, salvation is validated, received, and lived. The Resurrection not only validated His atoning work on the cross but it also validated the availability of resurrection power for His people.[15] Revival is Christ's resurrected life appropriated in daily living. To the degree that this is achieved, awakening is experienced. Revival is simply living in the warmth, victory, and power of the Resurrection. Life is not made by God for us to live in defeat, frustration, and discouragement; it is made to live in the resurrection power of Jesus Christ. Indeed, this is spiritual awakening.

The revivals in history that have followed the patterns established by Jesus have enjoyed incredible results and remarkable longevity. When His principles have not been applied, the renewals have experienced excesses and abbreviated durations. As Jesus ascended from the Mount of Olives, His last instructions to His followers were to wait until they received the power of the Holy Spirit and then to evangelize the lost to the ends of the earth. Quite often, the last words of a person demonstrate the priorities of that person. Indeed, this was the case with Jesus. Before the message could be proclaimed effectively, the messengers needed the Holy Spirit.

Revival at Pentecost

At the Crucifixion, in spite of their affirmation of undying loyalty, the disciples fled. Peter, who vowed death before desertion, denied that he ever knew Jesus. Previously, Jesus declared that He would build His Kingdom upon the kind of faith that Peter demonstrated at Caesarea Philippi. If Jesus intended to build His Kingdom on these men, radical transformations in their lives had to occur. Only the Holy Spirit could produce those changes.

Preparation for Revival

The term *Pentecost* means "fiftieth," and it was observed fifty days after the Passover. The festival had been a part of Jewish heritage since Moses and the revival at Sinai. It was a joyful celebration of thanksgiving to God for His provision during the times of harvest. Just as Jesus transformed the Passover in His provision for spiritual deliverance, so the Holy Spirit changed Pentecost into His provision for spiritual harvest. Luke recorded that 120 believers were gathered in the Upper Room in one accord. Howard Marshall suggested that the number was mentioned because "in Jewish law a minimum of 120 Jewish men were required to establish a community with its own council."[16] Since the church was a new community of believers, this number was significant.

As they met, they maintained orthodoxy in their theology, worshiped Jesus, transacted business, shared experiences, pondered the teachings of Jesus, and engaged in prayer. Although it is not specifically stated, they must have reviewed some of the Old Testament Messianic passages and applied them to Jesus. This was the topic of Peter's sermon to the people. Surely some of the materials in his message were topics of discussion in the Upper Room. They had the excitement, faith, patience, obedience, and expectancy; yet the crucial Source was lacking: the Holy Spirit. Since Jesus commanded them to wait for power from the Holy Spirit, they gathered in the Upper Room in obedience to His instructions. The revival at Pentecost followed the principle of starting with a few and spreading to the masses.

The Advent of the Holy Spirit

With indescribable force, the Holy Spirit entered the Upper Room. Luke lists three things that accompanied the event: wind, fire, and speech. The first element was a sudden roar like a mighty rushing wind as the Holy Spirit came. It was not wind, but it was *like* wind. The description indicates that the Holy Spirit manifests His presence; reveals His identity, for the disciples had no doubts about who was present; and provides incredible power. Even though Jesus had promised power, those present never imagined, even in their wildest dreams, the power that was evident in the Upper Room. The disciples were not the only ones in Jerusalem who heard the roar, for others in Jerusalem heard the sound as well.

The second element was divided tongues that were like fire. The tongues were not fire; they were *like* fire. Since fire is symbolic of purity, the disciples experienced the righteousness of God as each person was touched by the tongues of fire. Out of this event, the Holy Spirit revealed that He is personal, is openly known, provides power, and spiritually purifies.

The third characteristic was that each person was filled with the Holy Spirit and spoke in tongues. When a person is filled with the Spirit, it means that he is in right relationship with God, others, and self. The evidence of right relationship to God is gratitude demonstrated through obedience, worship, and service. The evidence of right relationship with one's fellowman is the desire to render the best good to that neighbor. The highest good for any human being is reconciliation to God. Thus, the revived Christian is used of God for that purpose. The evidence of right relationship to self is evidenced in joyful, victorious living. This is the very essence of revival.

Luke says that the disciples spoke in tongues. The Greek word used in verse four for "tongues" is *glossias.* The word *glossary* comes from this word, which means, among other things, a collection of words. The word for "tongues" that is used in verse six is *dialecto,* or dialect. The theological question is: "Was the miracle in the speaking or in the hearing?" The view that the miracle was in the speaking stresses the term *glossolalia.* This view interprets the speech as "unknown tongues" or a "heavenly language." The view that the miracle was in the hearing stresses the term *dialecto*. This interpretation advocates that the people were able to understand each other in their own dialects without the benefit of studies in a language school. Luke proceeds to list fifteen dialects that were represented among the people. Since this festival was one of three that the Jews were required to attend (Deut 16:16), the Jews came from various parts of the Roman Empire.

In the Upper Room, the disciples received the fulfillment of Jesus' promise that they would be empowered by the Holy Spirit. How long they remained in the Upper Room must be left to conjecture. However, they did not remain long, for they were on the streets of Jerusalem by 9:00 A.M. Prior to the advent of the Holy Spirit, the disciples were in the Upper Room behind locked doors for fear of the Jews. After the advent, they were on the streets evangelizing the lost. Before His coming, they were doing church business. After His coming, they were doing God's business. Before His coming, they anticipated His mission in wonder. After His coming, they participated in His mission with power.

On the weekend of the Crucifixion, the disciples floundered in their devastated dreams and shattered hopes. In the Upper Room, their experiences transcended their fondest expectations. They experienced revival through the Holy Spirit, and they knew it. The spiritual table was set for the heavenly banquet; it was just a matter of inviting the guests. The wait was over! Locked doors, fears, and uncertainties disappeared in the presence of the Holy Spirit. The church was equipped for the mission, and it was time to get started. From that point in time, God's people have not waited for the Holy Spirit; He has waited for His people. Without revival, the church waits for the Holy Spirit. In revival, the church is on assignment for Jesus Christ.

The Preaching of Peter

Because they had contact with heaven, the apostles were prepared to make contact with people. The Jewish leaders had lost their uniqueness. Their "orthodoxy" had stifled the people's spirits and demolished their hopes. On the day of Pentecost, the light of heaven penetrated their spiritual darkness. The believers spoke of the mighty acts of God (Acts 2:10-11), and a crowd gathered. Peter preached the first sermon following the advent of the Holy Spirit. In the message, he stressed the elements of revival preaching: Jesus as the promised Messiah and His eternal existence, death, resurrection, ascension, exaltation, eschatology, salvation, and lordship. No less than fifteen basic doctrines of the Christian faith are contained in this message. As Peter preached a simple, powerful, convicting message, the spiritual waves of revival swept across the crowd. The responses of the people were examples of reactions to every awakening.

Reactions of the Crowd

There are three reactions to every renewal: opposition, indifference, and obedience. The opposition at Pentecost started immediately as the believers witnessed. Because some of the Jews could not explain the event, they criticized. It takes no intelligence to criticize; anyone can do it. Their first accusation was that the disciples were intoxicated. Two Greek words are used in the New Testament that are translated "wine." The Greek word that is used here is *gleukas,* which means "sweet wine" or "new wine." This word is transliterated into English as *glucose.* The other Greek word is *oinos*. This word literally means "fruit of the vine." [17] The opponents at Pentecost accused the disciples of being intoxicated on *gleukas.* The incredible aspect of these criticisms is that the criticizers never waited for an explanation. They had already formed rigid opinions, and anything beyond the parameters of their already formed conclusions was not acceptable. Their motto was: "Do not confuse us with the facts." Their reactions included disbelief, intolerance, ridicule, and disrespect. Because they were not open to God, they missed the fellowship of His presence and the joy of revival.

Although it is not stated specifically, there must have been those who heard, but responded with indifference. They were not vocal opponents or active participants; they simply chose to delay their decisions. Since they did not decide for themselves, they allowed time to decide for them, and time decided against them. In their indifference, they were as spiritually destitute as the opponents.

The participators were also represented. When they heard the message of Peter, they asked, "What shall we do?" Those honest seekers sought honest answers to life's greatest question. An honest inquiry for spiritual counsel was met with an honest answer from Peter. No greater question could be asked and no greater answer could be given: "Repent, and be baptized" (Acts 2:38). Luke relates that three thousand people responded to Christ in faith. As evidence of their conversion experiences, they were baptized. Since there were several public pools in Jerusalem, it was not difficult to baptize that number. The baptismal services were public testimonies to the inward changes in their lives.

At Pentecost we see the three common responses to revival:

1. Opposition.
2. Indifference.
3. Obedience.

Results of Pentecost

The results of Pentecost remain impossible to measure fully, for the final chapter has not been written. However, some of the immediate results are discernible. In His promise to send the Holy Spirit, Jesus said that the Spirit would convict of sin, righteousness, and judgment. Apart from the convicting work of the Holy Spirit, there is no salvation. Although the Holy Spirit is the eternal Third Person of the Godhead, He was revealed at Pentecost in a way that He was not previously known. Christians need to thank God that they live on this side of Calvary and Pentecost and can look backward to God's redemption. In addition, the Holy Spirit officially constituted the church.

Because the Pentecost event was the advent of the Holy Spirit, just as the Bethlehem event was the advent of Jesus, Pentecost is not repeatable. However, the spiritual power that was manifested at Pentecost is available for all believers in all generations for the purpose of evangelizing all people in all the ages. As the Christians experienced the power of the Holy Spirit, they were transformed into courageous messengers. The three thousand converts were not solely due to Peter's preaching; rather, they were the products of spiritually awakened Christians sharing their experiences with Jesus Christ in the power of the Holy Spirit. This is still the combination that revival produces in the lives of God's people.

The revival at Pentecost completed the third stage of the New Testament revival. From the time awakening ignited with John, the revival pointed to the ultimate crest in the atoning work of Christ and the coming of the Holy Spirit. The provision for salvation was complete; it is now a matter of announcing that reconciliation with God is available. In a matter of a few years, the Christians — without the benefit of modern resources — turned the world upside down. This was achieved as the revival spread from the Upper Room to the borders of the Roman Empire, and even beyond. The disciples knew that there were no outside forces that could stop the movement. From their experiences, they were convicted that they could be stopped only through inner deficiencies in their relationships with God. Those early disciples did not consider earthly possessions of great value. They had heaven's greatest treasure and were armed with the commission to share it.

The awakening at Pentecost is the paradigm for revival. It teaches that the church did not start with power; she started with life, and out of that life came power. A desire for revival is the desire for spiritual life. When spiritual life is present, that life produces power. The Holy Spirit does not give power; He gives Himself. Where the Holy Spirit is, power is. At Pentecost, the Holy Spirit produced renewal in the lives of a small group of people who, although unattractive to the world, were open and available to Him. This was the basis for revival then, and it is still God's requirement for renewal today.

Revival at Samaria

Within a short time, the criticism of the revival turned into persecution of the believers. This fierce opposition was intensified when many priests were converted. The remarkable success and attention that the early disciples received were more than the religious leaders could handle. They took measures that they thought would stop the church. Their opposition progressed from criticism to arrests to floggings to the martyrdom of Stephen. The church was in her infancy when Stephen, one of the seven mentioned in Acts 6, was martyred. Because the religious leaders could not match Stephen in intellect, they resorted to force, the normal pattern under such circumstances. In attendance at Stephen's death was a young Jewish scholar from Tarsus by the name of Saul. The heroic faith of Stephen made a deep impression upon this future revival leader: Paul the apostle.

Following the death of Stephen, intense persecution continued against the believers. Luke records in Acts 8 that their actions against the Christians were akin to a wild boar on a rampage. No Christian was safe. In response to this opposition, many of the believers left Jerusalem. God used that which the opponents thought would curb the movement to spread the fires of revival. When Philip, another one of the seven mentioned in Acts 6, left Jerusalem, he went to Samaria, and revival ignited.

Philip in Samaria

When Jesus delivered His last instructions to His disciples prior to His ascension from the Mount of Olives, He mentioned four geographical areas: Jerusalem, Judea, Samaria, and the end of the earth (Acts 1:8). The book of Acts is the historical account of the church evangelizing those four geographical regions. The Jerusalem church evangelized the first two areas. The third area was evangelized when Philip left Jerusalem and went to Samaria. Paul and others evangelized the fourth area.

Philip transcended racial barriers between the Jews and the Samaritans and preached the gospel in Samaria. This was not the initial encounter of these people with the gospel. Approximately five years earlier, Jesus encountered a Samaritan woman at the well (John 4). The three days of preaching by Jesus and the resulting revival on that occasion served as preparation for the awakening under Philip. As Philip preached and performed miracles, the people were astounded. His message was similar to Peter's sermon at Pentecost: the kingdom of God and its fulfillment in Christ. Multitudes responded to the gospel. The whole city was filled with joy. When news of the revival in Samaria reached the church in Jerusalem, a committee composed of Peter and John was sent to investigate and validate the renewal.

Since John wanted Jesus to call down fire from heaven to destroy the Samaritans, it seems appropriate that the Jerusalem church selected him to go to Samaria. When the apostles arrived, they prayed for the people and laid their hands on them to receive the Holy Spirit. Confusion has surfaced in regard to this event. Although many interpretations have been offered, the most plausible one appears to be that the actions of the apostles were affirmation of the work that had been achieved under the ministry of Philip. The incredible results of the revival caused such a response that the whole city was aroused. Indeed, the second recorded revival in Acts was underway.

Results of the Samaritan Revival

The Samaritan revival crossed racial barriers between Jews and Samaritans. In addition, the evangelistic results were incredible. In spite of the desirable results, however, the first theological problem and revival abuse within the early church occurred. Although the church encountered internal difficulties over the widows' needs

(Acts 6) and the incident with Ananias and Sapphira (Acts 5), it was free of doctrinal controversies until the Samaritan revival.

A man named Simon had a reputation as "the power of God which is called Great" (Acts 8:10). While the revival was not the catalyst for the beginning of Simon's work, he used the renewal to attach his work to Christianity. When the miracles under Philip occurred, he coveted the power to duplicate such phenomena. He associated himself with the believers and was baptized, although subsequent events in his life indicate that he was never saved. When Peter arrived in Samaria, Simon offered money to the apostle to receive the power of the Holy Spirit. After Peter rebuked him, Simon intensified his teachings among his followers. Christian writers in the second century identified Simon as the founder of the Gnostic heresy.[18]

Regardless of the role of Simon Magus, the revival at Samaria was one of the great spiritual movements of the New Testament. This renewal furthered the expansion of the church as multitudes were added to God's kingdom. Luke ceases to record the events of the Samaritan revival after the Spirit led Philip to the Gaza region, where he encountered the Ethiopian eunuch. By this time, the Samaritan church was aflame with revival in order to fulfill her purpose for existence in the region.

The New Testament revival in its initial stages was centered in Judaic culture. When those at Pentecost returned to their respective regions, it seems logical that revivals ignited in some of those places. However, since the book of Acts records only the ministries of a select few, especially Paul, the works of the witnesses at Pentecost who returned to their homes in gentile cities are not recorded. Following the initial revivals that are recorded in Acts, the Antioch church launched missionary enterprises that included the labors of such men as Paul, Barnabas, and Silas. As these served, awakenings ignited in such places as Pisidia, Philippi, Thessalonica, and other places. One of the crucial revivals occurred in Ephesus.

Revival at Ephesus

On Paul's third missionary journey, he spent about three years in Ephesus. This city was the commercial gateway to Asia Minor. Ephesus was cosmopolitan in makeup, commercial in operations, and pagan in religion. In the minds of the Ephesians, they had all the religion that they needed, and Christianity was not on the agenda for consideration. However, when Paul arrived, rays of revival were about to break upon this pagan city that would change her spiritual climate dramatically

Paul encountered about twelve of the followers of John the Baptist. The dialogue centered upon Jesus as the fulfillment of the message of John the Baptist in Ephesus. When Paul asked them if they had received the Holy Spirit, their response was that they had not heard of the Holy Spirit. Did this confession mean that they had never heard of the name of the Holy Spirit or that they had never experienced Him? Since John mentioned the Spirit in his sermons, it is logical that these followers heard the initial revival leader talk about the Holy Spirit. If they had any knowledge of the Old Testament at all, they must have been familiar with the passages that discussed Him. In reality, their confession was that they did not know anything about His coming at Pentecost. Because of this, they were not Christians. After they confessed Christ as Savior, they received the Holy Spirit and were baptized. The laying on of hands by Paul, like the episode at Samaria, was an affirmation that their experiences with Christ were valid.

When Paul arrived in Ephesus, he followed the missionary strategy that was his pattern in every city: he went to the synagogue. In the synagogues, three groups of people gathered: Jews, proselytes (Gentiles who met all the requirements to enter Judaism), and God-fearers (those who were in agreement with Jewish monotheism but who had not submitted to the rituals in order to become proselytes). Paul's strategy was to go to the synagogues and preach the Messianic message of Christ. The most productive evangelistic results came from the God-fearers.

Awakening fires began to ignite and the results were more than the Jewish leaders could take. Following three months of work in the synagogue, the opposition became so fierce that Paul had to move to the hall of Tyrannus. This facility was probably used by Tyrannus, which means "tyrant," for classes in the morning and by the apostle in the afternoon or evening. For two years, Paul used the hall as his base of operation. The spiritual awakening spread across the city and throughout the surrounding area. The evangelistic results were enormous. The revival fires were saturating the very warp and woof of the entire city. The Ephesians knew that a new religion was in town. Boldly and courageously, Paul proclaimed the message that Jesus is the Christ.

As the awakening spread, miracles began to occur. The extraordinary aspects of these events were that aprons and clothes that the apostle handled were used as instruments of healing. Modern Christians should not look upon this episode of Paul's ministry as a pattern for the church to follow today. In Acts 19:11, the Greek word *tuchous* means "special" or "extraordinary." John Stott noted that those were unusual events for those special occasions, not paradigms for all generations.[19]

As the miracles occurred, the seven sons of Sceva sought to duplicate them. Since these were the sons of the priest who expelled Paul from the synagogue, their efforts were attempts to stop his ministry and to introduce abuses into the Ephesian awakening. As the seven sons of the Jewish priest sought to exorcize a demon, the possessed man overpowered the imposters. One vital principle of awakening emerges from this episode. When renewal ignites, the spiritual work is so extraordinary that those who do not understand the revival seek to manufacture experiences that are similar to the work of God. However, God's work cannot be duplicated; all efforts are proven counterfeit. These attempts prove to be futile and disastrous to those who make the attempts. On occasion, those who are not revival participants equate the counterfeit efforts with the real work of God, and these conclusions hinder the renewal.

As word about the event involving Sceva's sons spread across Ephesus, believers responded in holy awe to the incident. They knew that God was operating in His sovereignty. Even after many of the Ephesians became Christians, they kept items from their practices in paganism. They sought to hang on to God and to the things of this world at the same time. This event caused such conviction that they brought the pagan materials and burned them. These acts signified repentance and restitution. Luke records that the value of the books and other materials was estimated at fifty thousand drachma. A drachma was equivalent to a day's wage. This was an incredible amount of money at that time. From this event God communicates that He does not share His rightful place in the lives of His children with the things of this world. This revival corrected their carnal behavior.

The entire city of Ephesus took notice of the actions of these Christians. Demetrius, the silversmith who manufactured replicas of the goddess Artemis, responded with a vengeance. It was not that Demetrius was concerned about the temple; he was concerned about his own financial future. He knew that if this action was not challenged, his already suffering business due to the revival would be damaged even more.

Demetrius rallied the pagan worshipers for a demonstration in the stadium. It didn't take much to work the mob into frenzy. The silversmith did not announce what a problem the awakening was causing his business; rather, he diverted attention to what it would do to the worship of Artemis. The people of the Mediterranean world were aware of the magnificent temple that the Ephesians had erected to Diana. It was considered one of the Seven Wonders of the World.

Maule described the edifice as a building that "was a work of 220 years; built of shining marble; 342 feet long and 164 broad; supported by a forest of columns, each fifty-six feet high . . . At the center, hidden by curtains, within a gorgeous shrine, stood the very ancient image of the goddess . . . reputed to have fallen from the sky . . . The temple, as Paul saw it, existed until A.D. 262, when it was ruined by the Goths."[20]

As the mob gathered in the stadium, they cried, "Great is Artemis of the Ephesians!" (Acts 19:28) For two hours they screamed the refrain. Paul tried to enter, but was stopped by other Christians and the city officials. They knew that his presence would increase the already uncontrollable tensions. However, Gaius and Aristarchus were brought into the arena. As they tried to explain the circumstances, they were shouted down by the mob. There was no latitude for discussion and negotiations. The mob stood on the verge of a riot that could have inflicted great damage upon the city.

The tempers were brought under control when the city magistrate reminded the rebels that the worship of Artemis was worldwide and that the headquarters of the pagan temple was in Ephesus. He jogged their memories that Rome took an extremely dim view toward any area within her borders that rioted. Further progress in their rebellious direction could only have disastrous consequences for them and for Ephesus. Only after the city clerk reminded them of the precarious situation that they were making for themselves were they willing to disperse.

The actions of the pagans were evidence of the powerful influence the revival was having on the city. Following this event, Paul knew that the circumstances were not conducive for his continued ministry in the Ephesian church and he soon departed for Macedonia.

This revival in Ephesus contained several characteristics of awakening: the worldly conditions, a revival leader, start of the revival, rapid spread, enormous evangelistic results, and moral corrections. It also contained abuses and strong opposition. However, it is also a biblical example of the awesome power that God unleashes upon an area through servants who are committed to Him. The Ephesian church, once renewal reached its crest, made such an impact upon the entire area that the non-Christians took notice.

The church did not adapt her standards in order to be compatible to the world's standards. It did not offer what the people wanted to hear, but what they *needed* to hear: the message of Jesus Christ. Because Paul was faithful in preaching the gospel, God responded with a spiritual awakening that was used to evangelize much of Asia Minor.

Even though the Ephesian church started in revival, it did not continue to serve in renewal. Somewhere along the way, it neglected to nourish the flames of awakening and her spiritual vitality waned. Jesus delivered a message to this congregation through the apostle John in the book of Revelation. Within approximately forty years, the spiritual zeal was gone, and Jesus accused them of leaving their first love.

In the commendation, Jesus noted that they were orthodox in their theology, discerning in their ability to determine doctrinal truth, and dedicated in their works. Indeed, according to the standards of man, this church was still a great church. It was still the flagship congregation for missions.

The church had all the right external signs of a strong congregation, but the church had lost spiritual power and received a stern rebuke from the Lord. Jesus reminded the Ephesians that He does not look upon the outward appearance but upon the heart.

Jesus challenged the church to serve with the same kind of spiritual resolve that it had when it was founded. He issued four elements of every revival: remember the beginning, repent of all transgressions, return to Jesus Christ, and renew the proper relationship. The Ephesian church had forgotten the purpose of her existence. The Ephesian church was busy doing church work but was not doing the work of the church. Jesus reminded His people that the priority of the church is to live in the midst of spiritual awakening. When the Ephesian church served in spiritual power, it glorified God, exalted Jesus Christ, obeyed the Holy Spirit, edified the people, and expanded God's kingdom. When the spiritual waves of revival no longer swept through the congregation, the church resorted to activities. This is a powerful lesson for the modern church.

Before Pentecost, Rome simply heard rumors of the Palestinian revival. Within thirty years of Pentecost, Christianity saturated the Roman Empire. This phenomenal success was the result of the Holy Spirit working through believers who were serving in the midst of awakening. The ultimate results of this renewal are determined within the context of the eternal redemptive work of Christ, the convicting and illuminating ministry of the Holy Spirit, the birth and continual expansion of the church, and the lasting influence of the New Testament literature. Indeed, as the church grew in the midst of awakening and faced hostilities, the need for literature arose. In response to those needs, God used certain revival leaders to write the books of the New Testament.

Questions for Discussion

1. In the New Testament, various leaders encouraged their followers in support of revival. Would you say your church leaders would be in support of revival? What brings you to your conclusion?

2. John the Baptist had a clear message when he felt revival happening. If you had one clear message for your church, what would that be?

3. Jesus welcomed conversations with anyone from all walks of life. Is your church open to ministering to anyone who walks through those doors?

4. In light of revival and the pursuit of holiness, how can you lead your church in that pursuit of holiness?

Significant New Testament Revivals

Revival	Scripture
John the Baptist	Matthew 3:1-18; 14:1-12 Mark 1:2-14; 6:14-29 Luke 1:5-24, 39-45, 57-80; 3:1-22; 7:18-39 John 1:15-36; 3:22-36
Jesus	The Four Gospels Acts 1:1-11 (specifically) Entire New Testament (generally)
Pentecost	Acts 1:12-2:47 The book of Acts (specifically) The New Testament (generally)
Samaria	Acts 8:1-25
Damascus	Acts 9:1-31
Cornelius' House	Acts 10:1-11:18
Antioch	Acts 11:19-30
Cyprus	Acts 13:1-12
Pisidia	Acts 13:13
Iconium	Acts 14:1-5
Lystra	Acts 14:8-21
Philippi	Acts 16:1-40
Thessalonica	Acts 17:1-9
Berea	Acts 17:10-15
Corinth	Acts 18:1-17
Ephesus	Acts 18:19-21; 19:1-20:1, 17-36
John of Patmos	Revelation 1-22

Chapter 5
The Spread of Christianity Through Revivals, A.D. 100-1100

"The world is still sleeping its 'sleep of death.' It has been a slumber of many generations—sometimes deeper, sometimes lighter—yet still a slumber like that of a tomb, as if destined to continue till the last trumpet sound; and then there shall be no more sleep. Yet God has not left it to sleep or unwarned. He has spoken in a voice that might reach the dullest ears and quicken the coldest heart. Ten thousand times has He spoken and still speaks. But the world refuses to hear. Its myriads slumber on, as if this sleep of death were the very blessedness of its being."
John Gillies[i]

Revivals reveal the accounts of the awakened few and not of the sleeping multitudes. The advances of the church throughout history have been closely associated with the ministries of those servants who served in the midst of spiritual awakenings. The growth of the church has always been cyclical. In awakenings, the church has been spiritually aroused to fulfill her divine mandate. Without awakening, she relies heavily upon ecclesiastical structure and human ingenuity. In awakening, she relies upon God, proclamation of His Word, witness to Christ, and prayer. Without awakening, she relies upon form and ritual. These differences are evident in the church during the several centuries following the close of the New Testament era. By the end of the second century, Christianity was entrenched throughout the Roman Empire, due in large part to the spiritual awakening of the first century, Tertullian wrote: "Christians . . . filled all places of their [Roman] dominions, their cities, islands, castles, corporations, councils, armies, tribes, the palace, senate, and courts of judicature; only they had left to the heathens their temples."[2]

In the spread of the church, some may conclude that the spiritual movements were not revivals; rather, they were simply phenomenal evangelistic responses. However, a revival often occurs when one or a few experience renewal and are used of God to produce evangelistic results, the pattern that the awakenings in the Patristic period and the Middle Ages followed. While life in the early church and Middle Ages was quite dismal, both culturally and spiritually, God did not forget His creation. In the midst of the difficult times, God punched spiritual holes in the darkness of human circumstances.

Revival Under Irenaeus

Some of the revivals in the early church ignited as the result of persecution. The heroism demonstrated by martyrs deeply impressed those who were responsible for the atrocities inflicted against the Christians. This was evident in the awakening under Irenaeus at Lyons.

Irenaeus

Irenaeus was born in or near Smyrna in Asia Minor about A.D. 130. Only brief sketches of his life exist. In a letter to his childhood friend, Florinus, who had lapsed into Valentinian Gnosticism,[3] Irenaeus testified that he was a third generation Christian and a disciple of Polycarp:

> For, when I was still a boy, I knew you in lower Asia, in Polycarp's house . . . speak of the place in which the blessed Polycarp sat and disputed, how he came in and went out, the character of his life, the appearance of his body, the discourses which he made to the people, how he reported his discourse with John and the others who had seen the Lord, how he remembered their words, and what were the things concerning the Lord which he had heard from them, and about their miracles, and about their teachings, and how Polycarp had received them from eye-witnesses of the Word of Life, . . . I listened eagerly even then to these things through the mercy of God which was given to me, and made notes of them, not on paper, but in my heart.[4]

As an adult, Irenaeus moved from Asia Minor to Rome and then to Gaul. After his arrival in Gaul, Irenaeus served as presbyter of the church at Lugdunum, near Lyons. In A.D. 177 Eleutherus, who was sympathetic toward Montanism, was appointed bishop of Rome. Irenaeus was sent by Bishop Pothinus of Lyons, who was in Lyons because of Polycarp, as a part of a deposition to Rome to meet with Bishop Eleutherus, possibly over the Montanist controversy. While Irenaeus was in Rome, the persecution of A.D. 177 in Lyons occurred. After the ninety-year-old Pothinus was martyred, Irenaeus became the bishop of Lyons in about A.D. 178. He served in that capacity until his death. Although the events of his death are uncertain, Jerome wrote that he was martyred during the persecution of Septimus Severus in A.D. 202.[5]

Irenaeus was a pastor, churchman, theologian, writer, peacemaker, preserver of tradition, and revival leader. He was one of the most capable theologians of the second century. His monumental work entitled *Against Heresies* was written from 182 to 187 and is one the most important documents of the early church. In those five books, he refuted Gnosticism, listing fifteen existing sects of this heresy during his time; gave an account of New Testament history, which included how several of the books were written; provided his own list of acceptable books; and shared insights into early church tradition. His accounts of Gnosticism served as the most valuable resources on this heresy until thirteen codices of the Gnostic works contained within the Nag Hammadi Library were discovered in 1945 near the site of the fourth-century monastery at Chenoboskion, Egypt.

The Revival at Lyons

While Irenaeus was in Rome, persecution against Christians broke out in Lyons. Forty-eight names of those who lost their lives have been preserved. Among the most notable were Pothinus; Ponticus, a fifteen-year-old boy; Vettius Epagathos, a leading businessman of Lyons; and Blandina. The most heroic martyrdom was that of Blandina, a woman of phenomenal courage and unwavering faith. Following the persecution, the churches at Lyons and Vienne wrote a letter to the Christians in Asia Minor with a description of the atrocities:

> To begin with, they heroically endured whatever the surging crowd heaped on them, noise, abuse, blows, dragging along the ground, plundering, stoning, imprisonment, and everything that an infuriated mob normally does to hated enemies. Then they were marched into the forum and interrogated. . . . They made full confession of their faith in Christ with eagerness. Blandina was filled with such power that those who took it in turns to subject her to every kind of torture from morning to night were exhausted by their efforts and confessed themselves beaten — they could think of nothing else to do to her. They were amazed that she was still breathing for her whole body was mangled and her wounds gaped . . . [yet] she proclaimed her faith . . . . "I am a Christian." Following days of intense persecution, she was taken to the arena, tied to a post in the form of a cross, and wild beasts were turned loose upon her. However, not a beast touched her. She was taken back to the jail and suffered again and again at the hands of her adversaries. On the last day, Blandina was returned to the arena, along with Ponticus, a fifteen year old Christian. . . . After whips, after the beast, after the griddle [red hot copper metal applied to the body], she was finally dropped into a basket and thrown to a bull. Time and again the animal tossed her. Then she, too, was sacrificed, while the heathen themselves admitted that never yet had they known a woman to suffer so much or so long.[8]

One of the Christians at Lyons (probably Irenaeus) wrote that, as the martyrs went to their martyrdom, "their faces [were] aglow with nobility and grace so that they wore the chains clasped to them like lovely ornaments, like the bride adorned in embroidered apparel of gold."[9] Before the persecution, the Christians at Lyons testified to their faith in Christ. During the persecution, they sealed their testimonies with their lives. They testified by their actions that death did not make them martyrs; rather, they were already martyrs living the crucified life in Christ (Luke 9:23; Gal 2:20). Indeed, death does not make a martyr; death reveals a martyr. At Lyons, the martyrs demonstrated that they were already dead to self and alive in Christ. Their martyrdom simply revealed it.

When the pagan citizens of Lyons observed the incredible courage demonstrated by the martyrs, they saw a quality of life that they knew they did not have. After Irenaeus became bishop, a spiritual tidal wave swept Lyons and the surrounding areas. Within a short time, Lyons, which was the "Little Rome" of Gaul, was declared a Christian city.[10] As the church labored in the power of awakening, the pagans were no match for them. Multitudes accepted Jesus Christ as Savior. Previously the pagans were fierce opponents to Christianity; however, in the midst of revival, many were brought into the Kingdom of God through the efforts of believers who were, like those at Pentecost, courageous in the faith. The Christians were not temporary or haphazard in their commitments. They surrendered all to Jesus Christ.

The early believers demonstrated that Christianity is not fundamentally an adaptation to a standard of ethics or adherence to a set of teachings, nor is it the acknowledgement of philosophical views. They heard the call: "Come . . .deny . . . take up your cross" (Luke 9:23). Their conviction was that cross bearing is not a ritual; rather, it is a call to deny self. They possessed an unwavering certainty that their destinies were in Christ, and all else paled in the glow of His effulgent glory shed abroad in their souls. The Christians at Lyons demonstrated that through Christ they were more than conquerors. A few years later, Tertullian wrote: "the blood of the martyrs is the seed of the church." Undoubtedly, he had these martyrs in mind as he wrote those words, for this proved to be true at Lyons.

Following the evangelization of Lyons and the surrounding areas, Irenaeus sent missionaries to other parts of Gaul. It is possible that some of those missionaries served even in Britain. Above all else, Irenaeus was a revival leader. Through his leadership, the church in the midst of awakening established a Christian foundation in Lyons and other places. The citizens of Besancon and Valence claimed that Irenaeus was the first to preach the gospel to them. What occurred under Irenaeus was an inspiration for those Christians who followed.

Revival Under Gregory Thaumaturgus

Gregory was born about A.D. 205 in Neo-Caesarea, Pontus, to wealthy pagan parents.[11] His name at birth was Theodore, but he probably received the name of Gregory at his baptism. When Gregory was fourteen, his father died. Following his education in his hometown, Gregory pursued studies in law at Alexandria and Athens. In about A.D. 233, he and his brother Athenodorus, who also served as a bishop in Pontus, left Neo-Caesarea for law school in Berytus, or Beirut — the place that Emperor Justinian called the "mother and nurse of civil law."[12] They stopped in Caesarea and stayed with their sister, who was married to the governor of Palestine. About the same time, Origen arrived in Caesarea following his excommunication from the church in Alexandria. Gregory came under the teaching of Origen in about 234, was soon converted to Christianity, and spent five years with him. Origen detected unusual abilities in Gregory and urged him to consider the ministry. In about 238, Phaedimus, bishop of Amasea, sought to ordain him as bishop of Neo-Caesarea. Since he wanted no part of the ministry, he retired to a place of solitude to reflect upon his future and to escape from Phaedimus. After the Amasean bishop was unsuccessful in locating Gregory, he proceeded to ordain Gregory in his absence. Ultimately, in 240, Gregory reached the decision that God had called him to serve as bishop of Neo-Caesarea.

It is said that when Gregory became bishop, there were seventeen Christians in the city; when he died, there were only seventeen pagans in the city. Converts included Macrina, who was the grandmother of Basil the Great, Gregory of Nyssa, Peter of Sebaste, and their sister, Macrina.[13] As Gregory began to serve, an unusual spiritual movement swept across the area. Much of this movement was due to the miracles that he performed. His ministry was so marked by miracles that he received the name Thaumaturgus, or "miracle worker." It is impossible to sort out fact from fiction in the miraculous aspects of his ministry. It is said that he could move large stones with a word, heal the sick, exorcise demons, dry up lakes, and stop overflowing rivers.[14] At least it is certain that he was a miracle worker in reconciling people to Jesus Christ. Gregory was foremost a servant of Christ, and he was used of the Holy Spirit to turn an entire area to God. Following his death in about A.D. 270, as often happens in situations like Gregory's, cultic groups arose and attached their work to the miraculous aspect of his ministry However, the achievements of his ministry indicate that he was the foremost revival leader of the third century.

Other Revivals

Revivals often accompanied persecution. This was evident in Smyrna at the martyrdom of Polycarp, which some date on February 22, 156. The incredible faith and the physical torture endured by this eighty-six-year-old bishop were used of God to produce unusual spiritual responses in Smyma.[15] At the martyrdom of Justin in Rome in 166 under the Roman prefect Rusticus, the courage that Justin demonstrated caused many to turn to God. The heroism demonstrated by Leonides, father of Origen; Felicitas; Perpetua; and others who gave their lives for the Christian faith in Egypt during the persecution of Septimus Severus in 202 produced significant spiritual responses. During this persecution, Origen sought martyrdom but was spared when his mother hid his clothes. His father had been condemned to die for his faith, and the young man Origen sought to join his father in dying. By hiding his clothes Origen's mother kept the lad at home. Much like the martyrs at Lyons, the Christians in Egypt marched to their deaths with such heroic courage that their persecutors were deeply impressed with their faith. Many were converted to Christianity as a result.

In 379, the Nicene group in Constantinople invited Gregory of Nazianzus to serve as the presbyter of a new congregation called "Church of the Resurrection." During the Pentecost season in 380, Gregory preached a series of five sermons on the Trinity. His sermon on the Holy Spirit is still considered one of the greatest messages ever preached on the Third Person of the Godhead. A significant spiritual response accompanied this message. This awakening influenced Emperor Theodosius to convene the Council of Constantinople in 381, which clarified the equality of the Holy Spirit within the Godhead. Thus, in a very real sense, this revival solidified the doctrine of the Trinity in orthodox Christianity. In 387 in Antioch, John Chrysostom preached the famous "Sermons on the Statues" in response to the people's destruction of the image that Emperor Theodosius erected to himself. An unusual spiritual response occurred as people came under conviction and sought reconciliation.

Patrick and the Revival in Ireland

The Christianization of Ireland is closely associated with the name of Patrick.[16] Before Patrick's arrival, the Irish people were mired in deep superstitions. Although attempts to spread the gospel in the area were made as early as the second century, it was not until Patrick arrived that Christianity was firmly planted. The accounts of Patrick's ministry among the Irish unfortunately consist of a mixture of fact and fiction.[17] Therefore, it is difficult to construct an accurate account of his ministry in Ireland. Nevertheless, Patrick serves as a dramatic example of what God can do with a life committed to Him.

Introduction to Patrick

Patrick was born about 389 in the village of Bonnavem Tabernine to wealthy and prominent parents. His name at birth was Magonus Sucatus Patricius. His father, Calpornius, served as a deacon, and his grandfather, Potitus, served as a presbyter in the village. His Godly parents taught him Christianity; however, he testified that his younger days were not lived in an exemplary Christian manner. The subsequent sharp pains of humiliation, isolation, and injustice served as the crucibles that molded Patrick into the spiritual leader of the Irish.

At the age of sixteen, Irish pirates took Patrick captive. He was sold into slavery and served as a shepherd in Northern Ireland. Although the exact location is uncertain, Gallico identified Patrick's owner as Miliucc and the place of his captivity as Mount Slemish, Dalaradia, north of present-day Belfast.[18] Although he was reared in a Christian home, Patrick wrote in his *Confessions,* "I did not know the true God."[19] As he endured the suffering of working and sleeping in the cold, harsh outdoor environment, he recalled the Scriptures his mother taught him. He testified that as he remembered her prayers and teachings, he was converted.

After he converted to Christianity, Patrick devoted himself to prayer. He wrote, "In a single day I would say as many as a hundred prayers, and almost as many in the night."[20] During the six years he spent in slavery, God planted a love "in his heart for the people of Ireland."[21] At the age of twenty-two, he managed to escape. He traveled through Gaul and possibly Italy and ultimately returned to Scotland. Ireland, however, was indelibly etched upon his heart and he could not escape his version of a Macedonian call. In a vision, he saw a man whom he called Victoricus presenting a letter to him. The opening words read, "The voice of the Irish," and the invitation said, "We ask thee, boy, come and walk among us once more."[22]

Revival Fires

In the spring of 432, Patrick arrived in Tara, Ireland, during the time of the pagan Druid festival.[23] According to Druid customs, no fires burned on the eve of the great spring festival until the king ignited the ceremonial fire within the sacred enclosure. To light a fire during this portion of the festival was a crime punishable by death. Patrick mounted the hill called Slane in Meath, about ten miles across the valley of Berg from Tara, and built a huge fire in direct violation of the Druid custom. King Loaghaire could easily see the light piercing the darkness and was furious. When he consulted his Druid priests, he was told, "Oh, High King, unless this fire which you see be quenched this same night, it will never be quenched; and the kindler thereof will overcome . . . all the folk of your realm."[24]

Immediately, nine chariots were prepared, and the king and his entourage raced ten miles to the scene. As the legend goes, the king stopped short of going all the way to the fire. In a rage, he challenged Patrick's actions. Lochru, a Druid magician, cursed the Lord God. Patrick prayed that God would pick him up and slam him to the ground. Instantly, Lochru was lifted into the air and violently thrown to his death. In response, the king gave orders to his guards to kill Patrick. When Patrick prayed, "Let God arise and his enemies be scattered," the guards fought among themselves. After the commotion was over, only the king, his wife, and two other companions were alive. The queen requested of Patrick, "O man, righteous and mighty, do not destroy the king; for the king will come and kneel and worship thy Lord." After the king bowed before Patrick, he and his party returned to Tara in humiliation.

However, the king was still not convinced. He hosted a banquet the next day for the top leaders of the nation. When Patrick appeared in the banquet hall, Lucetmael, a Druid priest, challenged Patrick to a contest. After several confrontations, which Patrick decidedly won, a contest that included fire was scheduled. Two huts were built: one of green wood and the other of dry wood. The Druid priest, wearing Patrick's coat, entered the one with green wood. Benen, a disciple of Patrick entered the hut of dry wood wearing the Druid's cloak. The two huts were set on fire. Only Patrick's coat remained from the Druid's hut and only the Druid's coat was destroyed in Benen's hut. Furious over the loss of his priest, the king rushed Patrick, only to encounter interference from God. After several of the pagan guests at the banquet were killed, the king admitted defeat and submitted to baptism. This legend, although probably containing some truth, differs from other accounts of early Irish Christian history.[25] Nevertheless, the words of the Druid priests at the spring festival proved prophetic.

A spiritual movement spread throughout the area. As the awakening expanded, Patrick performed miracles,[26] preached, introduced Latin to the people, started schools for the clergy, developed training programs for new Christians, wrote hymns, and organized churches. The ordination and training of native clergymen contributed significantly to the success of his labors. For the next thirty years, Northern Ireland lived in the midst of a spiritual awakening. Taylor wrote that approximately 120,000 people were saved and 365 churches were started.[27] Patrick mentioned in his *Confessions* that thousands were saved. From his base in Armagh, Ireland, he served the people with such distinction that he is known as the "Patron Saint of Ireland." He was a revival leader of deep piety, humility, simplicity, and unselfish devotion. Through his administrative skills, he established the necessary organization to sustain the results of the awakening. In the centuries that followed, Ireland became a mission base to evangelize much of Europe.

Revival on Iona Under Columba

As believers left Ireland to serve in other lands, one of the most prominent was Columba, or Columcille, who is given credit for winning certain pagan regions of Scotland for Christ. Columba was the sixth-century representative of evangelistic Christianity in Great Britain.[28] According to Ian Finlay, Columba was born on December 7, 521, at Gartan, near Lough Swilley, Ireland,[29] to Fedilmith and Eithne. His father was the chieftain of the area and a direct descendant of the king of Ireland. His mother belonged to the ruling house of Leinster, and his grandmother, Erca, was the daughter of King Ere. Columba was in line to become king of Ireland, but God had grander designs for his life. Still, his royal heritage established relationships with nobility and opened doors as he served in Scotland.

At the age of twenty-one, Columba had a spiritual experience that changed his life. Out of that experience, he decided he belonged to Jesus Christ and chose the monastic form of living. He was given the best education available in Ireland. He especially devoted himself to the study and memorization of Scripture. Following his education, he was ordained to the priesthood in about 551. His initial ministry was done in his homeland as he tirelessly preached, established numerous monasteries, and founded churches. However, his revival ministry occurred in Scotland.

In May 563, Columba and twelve priests, following the gospel tradition, left Ireland for Scotland. Conall, king of the Scots, provided him a small island off the coast of Scotland called Iona. They spent the first two years at Iona erecting a monastery and establishing a church. This setting became the springboard for Columba's ministry until his death in 597.

Almost immediately, the spiritual response was phenomenal. As the gospel spread, he encountered opposition from Druids who lived in the area. As a result, Columba met their challenges with numerous miracles.[30] Like Patrick, his miracles have mingled with legend to the point that it is impossible to determine the difference between fact and fiction. It is recorded that his servant Diormid was at the point of death. Columba prayed that he would be healed. This request was answered and Diormid later was the one to close Columba's eyes in death.[31]

As a revival leader, Columba reached the masses for Christ, conserved the results, recruited laborers, developed strategies that lasted for centuries, and used Iona as a base to train and equip those who were sent forth to share the gospel. Within a short time, some 150 men moved to Iona for training. Columba did not allow the island to become a cloistered monastery for recluses; rather, it became the departure point for those who spread the gospel abroad. In addition, his program included preaching, teaching, establishing churches, building monasteries, studying, and copying the Scriptures. The most powerful aspect of his ministry was his holy living, which deeply impressed those he sought to win to Christ.

> Columba reached the masses for Christ, conserved the results, recruited laborers, and developed strategies that lasted for centuries.

On one occasion, Columba and his fellow monks traveled to Inverness in order to share the gospel with King Brude. Adamnan's account of Columba's reception by the king is an interesting story. When Columba and his entourage arrived in Inverness, the gates were barred to them. Columba approached the gates, marked them with the sign of the cross. When he laid hands on the doors, they opened automatically, "the bolts having been violently driven back."[32] The king and his court were astounded at the event and went out "to meet the blessed man and with reverence address him with the most respectful and conciliatory words; and from that day ever afterwards that sane ruler as long as he lived, honoured the holy and venerable man with the greatest honour."[33] King Brude was soon converted, which opened the entire area for the proclamation of the gospel. From Inverness on the northeast coast to the middle of Scotland, Columba tirelessly traveled and shared the Christian message. Bede wrote that he "converted that nation to the faith of Christ by his preaching and example."[34] The influence of Columba and the work at Iona were felt for centuries. By the time of his death, Scotland was evangelized. In later years, those who were sent forth from Iona introduced much of Europe to Christianity.

Revival at Canterbury Under Augustine

The revival at Canterbury, England, under the leadership of Augustine[35] served as the catalyst for the Christianization of southern England. Prior to Augustine's arrival, England was mired in the rank paganism of the Angles and Saxons, invading clans who remained on the island following their conquests. The Christian church largely neglected the country even though feeble attempts had been made to reach the nation for Christ. However, a series of divinely guided events led to a spiritual awakening that redirected its history. Bede, who wrote as early as 731, recorded, "God in his goodness did not utterly abandon the people whom he had chosen; for he remembered them, and sent this nation more worthy preachers of truth to bring them to the faith."[36] The leader of those preachers was Augustine.

Augustine was born about 545. In his youthful years, he felt the leadership of God to enter the ministry of the Roman Church. In 596, while serving as prior of Saint Andrew's monastery in Rome, he was commissioned by Pope Gregory I (590-604) to lead a group of forty missionaries to evangelize the Angles. While traveling through Aix, Gaul, on their way to Britain, they received discouraging news about the barbaric nature of the Angles. Augustine returned to Rome to ask the pope to allow them to return to the safe confines of Saint Andrews monastery. In a letter from Gregory dated July 23, 596, the pope encouraged them to proceed to Canterbury as commissioned. [37]

Arrival in Canterbury

The group arrived on the island of Thanet near Canterbury in the kingdom of Kent in 597. Although King Ethelbert was a pagan, he was married to a Gallic Christian by the name of Bertha, who had her own monk, Luidhard. At first the king was cautious and unreceptive, but he allowed Augustine to share Christ with the people of Kent. Ethelbert said:

> Your words and promises are very fair; but as they are new to us, and of uncertain import, I cannot approve of them so far as to forsake that which I have so long followed with the whole English nation. But because you have come from far into my kingdom, and, as I conceive, are desirous to impart to us those things you believe to be true, and most beneficial, we will not molest you, but give you favorable entertainment, and take care to supply you with your necessary sustenance; nor do we forbid you to preach, and gain as many as you can to your religion.[38]

Awakening Ignites

After establishing their base at the Saint Martin of Tours Church, the missionaries launched their ministry among the people. Living simple, holy lives, these monks made deep impressions upon the pagans. In a short time, several of the people were converted. However, it was not until the king was converted that a phenomenal awakening swept the land. The king was deeply impressed by the spiritual sincerity of Augustine and his companions and by the miracles, as with Patrick and Columba, that frequently occurred. Gregory, in a letter to Augustine, wrote, "I hear that Almighty God has worked great wonders through you for the nation which he has chosen."[39] He explained that the power to perform miracles was for the salvation of the people.

After the awakening ignited, the king assembled the people daily to hear the preaching of the gospel. Unlike in other parts of Europe, the king did not use physical coercion in his efforts to evangelize the people. Bede wrote, "He would not compel anyone to accept Christianity; for he had learned from his instructions and guides to salvation that the service of Christ must be accepted freely and not under compulsion."[40] In less than a year, ten thousand people were awaiting baptism.

After Augustine returned from Arles in Gaul, where he was ordained to the office of bishop, he led the baptisms of over ten thousand people on Christmas day in 597. The revival spread rapidly among the people. As the awakening ignited in Canterbury and the spiritual flames spread abroad in England, churches were built to conserve the results. In 601, Augustine was appointed by Gregory as Archbishop of Canterbury, the first to hold this office. He continued to serve in the midst of renewal until his death in 605.

This revival established Christianity permanently in England. From this country, the gospel spread to the continents of Europe, Asia, Africa, and ultimately North America. Christianity was firmly planted in Ireland under the revival of Patrick, in Scotland under the revival of Columba, and in southern England under the revival of Augustine. The Christian heritage of the English-speaking world evolved from these three spiritual movements.

Revival Under Aidan in Northumbria

In spite of the labors of Patrick, Columba, and Augustine, pockets of paganism still existed in Britain. One region relatively untouched by the gospel was Northumbria, an Anglo-Saxon kingdom in the northern part of England. The first Christian penetration occurred when Ethelberga, daughter of King Ethelbert and Bertha, married King Edwin in June 625.[41] As a part of the marital arrangement, the queen was permitted to exercise Christianity. She, like her mother before her, had her own priest, Paulinus, who was consecrated bishop by Justus of Canterbury

Edwin was converted to Christianity and was baptized on June 8, 626.[42] He was followed in baptism on Easter 627 by the pagan religious leader, Coifi, and many of the citizens of his kingdom. However, when Edwin was defeated in 633 by the coalition of the pagan king Penda of Mercia and the Welsh king Cadwallon, who professed Christianity,[43] the entire region was once again influenced by paganism. Following the defeat, the royal family went into exile.

The prince who rose to claim Northumbria permanently for Christ was Oswald, the son of Edwin's predecessor, Ethelfrith. While Oswald was in exile, he traveled among the Christians at Iona and in Scotland. While at Iona, he was converted and baptized. When he became king of Northumbria in 634, he was already burdened for the spirituality of the citizens of his kingdom. In response to his request, the mission at Iona sent a missionary named Corman, who proved to be ineffective, concluded that the task was impossible, and left Northumbria in frustration. When he gave his report to the mission at Iona, he described the people as "untamable men, of a hard and barbarian mentality."[44] A voice was heard from the audience, "It seems to me, brother, that you have been too severe with your unlearned hearers, in that you did not, conformably to the apostolic discipline, give them the milk of more gentle doctrine, till, having been gradually nourished by the word of God, they should be able to receive more advanced teachings, and to practice God's sublimer concepts."[45] The voice belonged to Aidan, who was then sent by Iona to Northumbria.

In 635, King Oswald gave Aidan the island of Lindisfarne, off the east coast, to serve as the mission's headquarters. As the king served as the interpreter for Aidan, a spiritual awakening ignited. Bede wrote, "It was most delightful to see the king himself interpreting the word of God."[46]

Through the revival efforts of Aidan, paganism was eliminated and Christianity was embraced in Northumbria. For seventeen years, Aidan preached throughout the land. This revival resulted in the "conversion of the multitudes and the establishment of monastic seminaries."[47]

Christianity spread so rapidly that Aidan requested and received help from Scotland and Ireland. He labored faithfully as he established churches and trained indigenous clergy. In addition, many of the surrounding areas were also reached for Christ. Aidan was deeply humble and always the servant of the people. When Oswin, king of Deira, gave him a horse, Aidan in turn gave it to a poor beggar. When Oswin rebuked him for his generosity, Aidan told the king. "Is that son of a mare more precious in Your Majesty's eyes than the son of God?"[48] Cairns wrote, "When he died in 651, Celtic Christianity had been firmly established in northern England."[49]

Revival Under Boniface in Germany

The leading revivalist of the eighth century was Winfrith, or Boniface. He was born about 680, probably near Crediton in Devonshire, of noble parents.[50] Even in his early years he had a strong desire for spiritual things. When he shared that he felt the call from God to enter the ministry, his father, who wanted his son to follow in his footsteps, opposed him. In spite of opposition from his father, Winfrith embarked upon the monastic life. In 710, he took a vow of poverty, renounced all future rights to own property, and was ordained. In 715, he launched the two-fold mission that consumed the rest of his life: awaken the Christians and evangelize the pagans.

Early Ministry

By 715, Boniface served with Willibrord in Utrecht, Holland. However, a conflict between Radbod, king of Holland, and Charles Martel, king of France, hindered any Christian advance, and he returned to England. In 718 he returned to the continent. He first went to Rome and received permission from Pope Gregory II (715-31) to go into Germany and evangelize the Germanic people. On December 29, 718, his name was changed from Winfrith, which means "war and peace," to Boniface, which means "benefactor." Gregory named him Boniface after Boniface I (418-22), for the date marked the three hundredth anniversary of the appointment of Boniface as bishop in Rome. On May 15, 719, he was commissioned to go north to Germany. Before assuming his permanent duties in Germany, he went back to Utrecht where he served for three years with Willibrord.

Awakening in Germany

In 722, Boniface left for Germany, where he had the most productive ministry among eighth-century preachers. At first, he established his base at Amoneburg. As he and his companions preached, thousands were reached for Christ and many in the area who were already Christians renewed their commitments. His success was so phenomenal that his methods and theology were questioned. No one was supposed to have the kind of response he was having. He was summoned to appear before the pope in Rome to explain himself. After validating his orthodoxy, the pope ordained him bishop.

The previous events were mere preludes of things to come. In 725, an event occurred that changed the spiritual map of Europe. At Geismar, the people worshiped a huge sacred oak dedicated to Thor, the Scandinavian god of thunder. The superstition, much like the Druids' toward fire during the time of Patrick, was that anyone who laid an axe to the tree would die. In defiance of the pagan view, Boniface began chopping the tree down. The huge crowd of pagans awaited punishment to be inflicted.

However, before the tree was leveled, a strong gust of wind blew the tree over, and it broke into four pieces. The people were astonished. Boniface took the wood from the tree and built a small chapel to St. Peter. Out of that event, a powerful spiritual movement swept the land. The conversions were so numerous that it was virtually impossible for the missionaries to keep up with discipleship. Towns and villages turned to Christ as the entire area was permeated with the gospel.

Seldom has a population been evangelized so swiftly and completely as the region where Boniface served. What the revival under Patrick meant to Ireland, the revival under Boniface meant to the Germans. The major result of this awakening was the establishment of the Roman Church in Germany that lasted until Martin Luther.

As Boniface served, he did so under the protection of the Frankish kings. In a letter to leaders in his kingdom, Charles Martel wrote concerning Boniface, "Wheresoever he goes, no matter where it shall be, he shall with our love and protection remain unmolested and undisturbed."[51] Laboring under royal protection, Boniface established churches throughout the land; preached tirelessly; trained the clergy; enlisted help from England; destroyed pagan shrines; baptized thousands; implemented a new strategy for spreading the gospel by using women in his work, especially his cousin Leoba; and performed miracles.

Like others who did miracles, legends developed surrounding his miraculous works. Supposedly, at the sight of his martyrdom a fountain of crystal clear, sweet water sprang up when the hoof of a horse of King Pippin's army sank into the mound heaped over the site.[52] Regardless, many miracles of healing were a part of his ministry.

In 731 Boniface was made archbishop of Mainz. Shortly before his death, he turned the duties of archbishop of Mainz over to his associate, Lull, and made one final round in his province in order to confirm recent converts. On June 5, 754, he met with a group of new Christians for this purpose. When some pagans heard about it, they went to the tent that was erected for the confirmation and attacked Boniface. On that morning, he and fifty members of his party were martyred for the Christian faith.[53] Latourette wrote, "Humble, a man of prayer, self-sacrificing, courageous, steeped in Scriptures, a born leader of men, affectionate, a superb organizer and administrator, he was at once a great Christian, a great missionary, and a great bishop. The Church in Germany owed him an incalculable debt."[54]

Following the revival under Boniface, no significant awakenings occurred in Europe for four centuries. The spiritual clouds of darkness hovered over Europe like a black cloak. Although Christianity spread, the methods used were coercive. Kings felt that they honored Christ by forcing pagans to embrace Christianity or die. Under the coercion of such emperors as Charlemagne, entire tribes confessed Christianity, not Christ, in order to stay alive.

As the spiritual dynamism of the church receded, the people floundered in the spiritual dust. Without the spiritual power of the New Testament church, the Roman Church focused upon ritual and doctrinal development in order to perpetuate its views and maintain power over the people. As it expanded its power and amassed wealth, it no longer fulfilled its biblical mandate to evangelize the lost.

Questions for Discussion

1. Revivals sometimes start in the midst of persecution. What persecution have you seen surrounding your local church, understanding that it may not be on the same level as persecution of that day?

2. How widespread is the Christian faith in your town or city? How do you think you could more effectively reach your location to spread Christianity?

3. Throughout various revivals, one can see bold evangelism. Discuss the last time your church purposely went outside of the church together with the goal of simply sharing Christ with the lost.

Chapter 6
Revivals on the Eve of the Reformation, 1100-1500

We must obey God rather than men.
Acts 5:29b

After the year 1000, the religious life of Europe began to change. Scholasticism, which was influenced by the Irish neoplatonic philosopher John Scotus Eirgina (c. 815-877), gained force as a theological movement. The Roman Catholic Church formalized its theology at a number of points. The crusades increased the temporal power of the Roman Church. Corruption increased within the church, but so did attempts to bring reform. Among the most notable efforts were those by Peter de Bruys and his followers, called Petrobrusians; Henry of Lausanne and his followers, called Henricians; and Arnold of Brescia and his followers, called Arnoldists. The response of the Roman Church toward those groups was suppression and excommunication. Yet in spite of opposition from Roman leaders, nothing could stop those set free from the slavery of spiritual oppression. Such men as Peter Waldo heard the voice of a higher call, responded unreservedly, and became catalysts for revival.

Revival Under Peter Waldo

The premiere revival in the twelfth century came under the leadership of Peter Waldo of Lyon, France, whose followers became known as the Waldensians. The date of Waldo's birth is uncertain.[1] The first time that he appears in history is 1170. About this time, he had a spiritual encounter with Christ that changed his life. Many accounts are offered in regard to his Christian conversion. One story relates how he heard a minstrel sing a ballad about the life of St. Alexis. In this ballad, Alexis divested himself of his possessions and lived an austere life as he traveled in the name of Christ, even to the Holy Land, and ultimately died under a stair step.

As the story goes, Waldo invited the minstrel home to hear more. On the next day, he was troubled and sought counsel from a priest at the local cathedral who quoted to him Matthew 19:21, the words of Jesus to the rich young ruler. Out of that experience, Waldo made the decision to sell his considerable possessions and serve Christ through a life of poverty.[2]

When he shared his decision with his wife, she was distraught. Waldo told her she had to choose between him and material wealth; she chose material wealth. Waldo provided for her; placed his two daughters in the Abbey of Fonterault; restored, like Zacchaeus, any money wrongfully gained; and distributed the remainder to the poor. From June until August 1173, he systematically distributed his wealth among the poor who were suffering through a famine at that time. As he donated his last possessions, he addressed the crowd of scoffers, "This act I do for myself and for you: for me, so that if from now on I possess anything you may indeed call me a fool; for you, in order that you, too, may be led to put your hope in God and not in riches."[3]

Peter's zeal for spiritual knowledge led him to pay two monks, Bernard Ydros and Stephen of Ansa, to translate the Scriptures from Latin into French. As he absorbed the truths of God's Word, he began to share verses with other people. He became a walking Bible. The admonition of the Lord, "Go . . . and preach the gospel to the whole creation" (Mark 16:15), was indelibly engraved upon his soul.

A vow of poverty often meant residence in a monastery, but not to Waldo. He was led to share the message of Christ with the people. As he shared, he immediately attracted a small community of followers who became known as the "Poor Men of Lyons." This group patterned themselves after the New Testament disciples as they went out two-by-two and preached.

From the beginning, Waldo and his group of preachers encountered opposition from Bishop Guichard of Lyons. In 1177, Waldo was called before the synod of the diocese at Lyons to give an account for his actions. At the meeting, Guichard ordered, "You are prohibited from meddling with preaching, even if it is for explaining the Scriptures as you say. You have nothing to do but to obey."[4]

Waldo responded, "Judge ye whether it be lawful before God to obey you rather than God: for we cannot refuse to obey him who hath said, 'Go ye into all the world and preach the Gospel to every creature.'"[5] This biblical admonition became the motto of the Waldensians. Waldo was immediately banished from the diocese.

At the Third Lateran Council in 1179, under the leadership of Pope Alexander III, Waldo's group was questioned by Walter Map from Britain and was ridiculed by the delegates at the council. They were told that they could not preach without the permission of the local bishop. Waldo and the members of his party retreated and reflected upon the teachings of God's Word. The words of Acts 5:29, "We must obey God rather than men," were seared in their minds, and revival leaders emerged.

As they preached in the native languages and shared Scripture, Waldo's followers experienced a spiritual surge that challenged the masses. Revival broke out. As Waldo sent his followers out two-by-two, the area around Lyons resounded with the gospel. Thousands of people were reached. The success of the "poor preachers" intensified the opposition.

In November 1183, Pope Lucian III at the Council of Verona issued the edict, "And as some with a certain appearance of piety, . . . arrogate to themselves the right of preaching, . . . we include under the same perpetual anathema all those who, in spite of our interdiction and without being sent by us, shall dare to preach whether in private or in public."[6] They were condemned in 1184 at the same council simply for "the crime of preaching the gospel" and were expelled from Lyons. Comba estimates that about eight thousand were expelled.[7] The accusers thought that they were eliminating them; instead, they scattered spiritual ideas across Europe that could not be stopped.

The Waldensians continued to spread and to preach the gospel. Some journeyed to Toulouse where dissenters such as the Cathari, the Petrobrusians, and the Henricians had established a stronghold. Others traveled north into Germany, east as far as Austria, and south into Lombardy. By the time of Waldo's death around 1217, the movement had penetrated most of Europe. It was not that Waldo left the Roman Church; rather, the Roman Church expelled him on the grounds that he and his followers wanted to share the gospel with those who were lost. Their views on preaching and attitudes toward the clergy were tantamount to believing in the priesthood of the believer. Doctrinal differences emerged later, especially in the areas of baptism and the Lord's Supper. Waldo's followers believed that they were under divine orders to share Jesus Christ with others. Although dissenters preceded them, the movement was a significant catalyst that ultimately produced the Reformation. Walker wrote that the Waldensians could be called the first Protestants.[8] In 1532, they officially joined the reform movement in Europe.

The Waldensians faced persecution by the Roman Church. In 1211, some eighty of the Waldensians were martyred at Strasbourg.[9] Because this was a lay movement, the Roman Church could not suppress their views. Three characteristics of awakenings stand out in this movement: deep spiritual convictions that transcended worldly standards, preaching of God's Word, and the prominence of Scripture in their faith. Two hundred years before Wycliffe, Waldo was responsible for the translation of portions of the Bible into the vernacular. He used memorization of Scripture as the rule of faith and practice for all members of his group. In addition, he used women in significant roles.

> Waldo's followers were expelled from Lyons, which scattered spiritual ideas across Europe.

The uncompromising views of the Waldensians could not be confined to a stale ecclesiastical structure. An eternal principle of revival emerges from this conviction: once a believer commits his life to Christ, the Christian cannot help but respond in obedience to the Lord. In the Waldensian Council of Bergamo in 1218, an organization was established that assured the perpetuation of the movement started by a Christian in Lyons who simply wanted to share his faith.

Revival Under Francis of Assisi

Francis of Assisi was born to Pietro and Giovanna de Pica Bernardone, probably in 1182.[10] He died in his forty-fifth year, on October 3, 1226. A Franciscan monk at Erfurt in the middle of the thirteenth century placed Francis' birth in 1182. His father, a cloth merchant of some means, was on a business trip to France when he was born. When his mother presented him at the Santa Maria Maggiore Church in San Rufino for baptism, he was given the name of John, or Giovanni. However, after his father returned from his business trip, he renamed him Francis.

Francis' early education was received from the priests of San Giorgio Church in Assisi. Because he never distinguished himself in the art of writing, he used a secretary, Leo, to record that which he later wrote. He spent his youthful years in pursuit of worldly pleasures and often surrounded himself with less than desirable companions.

In 1202, when the forces of Assisi were defeated by Perugia at the Battle of Collestrada near the Bridge of San Giovanni on the Tiber River, Francis was captured and spent a year in prison in Perugia. After his release in November 1203, he returned to Assisi and resumed his worldly lifestyle. However, in the spring of 1204 he contracted tuberculosis that affected him for the rest of his life and ultimately caused his death. This illness started a conviction process that led to his Christian conversion.

Spiritual Influences

Francis went through several stages of spiritual growth. His first spiritual encounter occurred in August 1205 as he was on his way to join the pontific military forces under the command of Walter de Brienne at Apulia. As he spent the night in Spoleto, he had a dream that refocused his priorities. In response, Francis asked, "Lord, what wilt Thou that I should do?" The answer came, "Return to the place of thy birth, for thy vision shall through Me have a spiritual fulfillment."[11] Troubled by the experience, he spent the rest of the night in meditation on this message.

The next day, he returned to Assisi with an inner resolve to seek the things of God. As his old friends sought to include him in their worldly activities, they detected a change in him. They asked, "What is the matter with you that you do not come with us? Are you dreaming of getting married?"

"You are right," replied Francis, "I dream indeed of taking a wife, and she to whom I shall give my troth is so noble, so rich and so wise that not one of you has ever seen her like."[12] That "wife" was poverty.

With a thirst for spiritual things, Francis and a friend journeyed to a grotto near Assisi where he had his second significant spiritual encounter. When Francis went aside for prayer, God gave him inner peace and direction for ministry. The next significant spiritual encounter occurred on February 24, 1206, as he visited the chapel of Saint Damian for worship. In his prayer, he said, "Great and glorious God, . . . I pray ye shed abroad your light in the darkness of my mind."[13] He received an impression from Christ that he was to repair the chapel. For the next three years, he restored churches. Among them was the chapel of Portiuncula, which became his headquarters.

On one occasion, Francis took clothes from his father's store without his father's knowledge and sold them. His father was furious. He brought Francis home, beat him, and chained him. While his father was on a business trip, his mother released him. Enraged by the chain of events, his father enlisted the help of Bishop Guido and a council to intervene in his attempts to retrieve his money

When Francis appeared before his father and the council, he not only returned the money from the sale of the clothes but also gave his father the clothes he was wearing. In his public confession, Francis said, "Listen, all of you, and understand it well: Until this time I have called Peter Bernardone my father; but now I wish to obey God. I return him the money about which he is so anxious, and my garments, and all that he has given me. From this moment I will say nothing but 'Our Father in Heaven.'"[14] This act severed his relationship with his father that apparently was never restored.

On February 24, 1209, Francis had a final encounter that established the direction of his ministry. In a time of worship at Portiuncula, he received the deep impression from Jesus, "Go preach, saying that the Kingdom of heaven is at hand" (see Matt 10:7-42). With great joy, he responded with the commitment, "This is what I want, what I have been waiting for; this shall be from henceforth my daily and hourly practice."[15]

Flames of Revival

The next day at San Giorgio church, as Francis preached his first sermon impromptu and from the heart, a spiritual tidal wave swept across the congregation. There was such convicting power that his listeners were pierced in their hearts and awakening ignited. Englebert wrote that it was "like an awakening, a new beginning."[16] Burns wrote, "From that day the Reformation began, a reformation wider than that even which Francis longed to see, a reformation which was to give back to men the open Bible, and to free them from every vestige of ecclesiastical tyranny."[17]

The direction was established; the course was set; the commitment was made; and there was no retreat. For the next seventeen years, Francis traveled, even to Egypt and the Holy Land; preached; organized his followers into an order that became known as the "Franciscan Order of Monks;" wrote; ministered to the poor; reached out to the sick, especially lepers; and sent forth preachers to share the message of Christ.

What Waldo wanted to do in Lyons before Bishop Guichard expelled him, Francis did in Assisi with the blessing of Bishop Guido. His acceptance of Francis was symbolized when the money and clothes were returned to Francis' father and the bishop draped his cape around Francis' unclad body on that cold, wintry day. Only God knows the results if Guichard had embraced Waldo as Guido accepted Francis. What did happen was that Waldo, in his expulsion, started the Protestant Waldensians while Francis, in his acceptance, started the Catholic Franciscans.

In a matter of months, Francis gathered twelve men as his disciples, trained them, and sent them out to preach. The first two followers, Bernardo de Quintivale and Pietro Cattini, joined him on April 16, 1209. Bernardo joined Francis after he spent a night with him. Feigning sleep, he saw Francis arise from his bed and spend most of the night in prayer. Bernardo felt that anyone who would do that deserved serious consideration. Francis and his disciples not only experienced results immediately, they also encountered opposition. They responded to the ridicule and scorn in ways similar to the disciples in the New Testament.

Francis organized the small group into the *Frati Minores,* or Brothers Minor. With this title, Francis communicated that they were the "least of the saints." The rules that governed their lives were poverty, chastity, and obedience. Their objectives were to preach the gospel and win as many converts as possible.

Instead of earthly possessions, they possessed joy of soul, gladness of heart, peace of mind, freedom from physical cares, and the power of the Holy Spirit. The people felt the impact. Through the help of Bishop Guido and Cardinal John of Saint

Paul Church in Rome, Francis received sanction from Pope Innocent III for his order in 1210.

He expanded the movement on Palm Sunday, March 18, 1212, by including Clare Sciffi, the pious sixteen-year-old daughter of a leading businessman in Assisi.[18] Francis established a base for her at Saint Damian. As women began to join the group, they became known as the Clarisses, or the Order of Clare. Clare served faithfully until her death on August 11, 1253.

Since Francis was never ordained as a priest, the two movements were first and foremost lay-oriented. Because of this, an aura of freshness, innocence, purity, sincerity, and honesty surrounded this ministry; it had a magnetic appeal among other lay people. The members of the order served because they wanted to serve, not because they had to serve or for personal profit.

Francis was always preaching, whether his famous sermons to the birds or the proclamation of the gospel to the crowds. He preached up to five times a day, and his sermons were described as "penetrating the heart like fire."[19] In response, thousands of people gathered at Portiuncula to join with Francis; others he counseled to stay where they lived and not to join his group. The ones who joined did not gather for fellowship, to seek refuge from the world, or to discuss current issues. They gathered to receive mutual encouragement, training, and assignments for preaching the gospel. As they traveled and shared, the revival spread among the people.

> For Francis, the direction was established; the course was set; the commitment was made; and there was no retreat.

Francis was constantly singing, and he encouraged his followers to sing. The messengers became known as the "Singing Troubadours." Toward the close of Francis' ministry, their theme song became "Canticles of the Sun,"[20] written by Francis in 1225 following a severe illness that produced virtual blindness. In the English hymnal, the song is musically rearranged under the title of "All Creatures of Our God and King." Francis was used of God to break the shackles of spiritual slavery. What Scholasticism did to open the mind, Francis did to open the soul. Burns said he "was the real precursor of the Renaissance,"[21] and in him the "age of dogmatism ended."[22]

Francis' life was a living sanctuary of the Holy Spirit. The account of the stigmata of a cross on his body testifies to the spiritual life of the man. Doyle noted that the sign of the cross was seared on his body miraculously on September 24, 1224.[23] In a vision, Francis saw:

> A man standing above him, like a seraph with six wings, his hands extended and his feet joined together and fixed to a cross. Two of the wings were extended above his head, two were extended as if for flight, and two were wrapped around the whole body. When the blessed servant of the Most High saw these things, he was filled with the greatest wonder, but he still could not understand what this vision should mean. Still he was filled with happiness and he rejoiced very greatly because of the kind and gracious look with which he saw himself regarded by the

> seraph, whose beauty was beyond estimation. . . . And while he was thus unable to come to any understanding of it and the strangeness of the vision perplexed his heart, the marks of the nails began to appear in his hands and feet. . . . Furthermore, his right side was as though it had been pierced by a lance.[24]

Francis heard the higher call from God, and he reserved nothing for himself. Because of Francis' devotion to Christ, God used him as a revival leader to plant seeds of the gospel that could not be stopped from germinating. The results of this revival under Francis can be measured only within the mind of God.

Francis summarized his ministry:

> One grace leads to another; and one vice leads to another. Grace asks not to be praised, and vice cannot endure to be despised. . . . Holy purity of heart sees God, and true devotion enjoys Him. If you love, you shall be loved. If you serve, you will be served. If you fear, you will be feared. If you do good to others, others will do good to you. Blessed is he who truly loves, and desires not to be loved again. Blessed is he who serves, and desires not to be served. Blessed is he who fears, and desires not to be feared. Blessed is he who does good to others, and desires not that others should do good to him.[25]

The austerity with which Francis served was more than some of the followers could handle. Even Dominic, who visited Portiuncula in 1218, was appalled at the lack of provisions. Cardinal Ugolino — who eventually became Pope Gregory IX — as began to assume control and made alterations in the order, especially with regard to the rule of poverty. At that time, the order took on a new direction. The revival intensity in which the movement started had basically run its course. Francis impacted his generation with such influence that Pope Gregory IX canonized him on July 16, 1228, less than two years after his death at sundown on Saturday, October 3, 1226.[26]

Revival Under John Tauler

The fourteenth century witnessed the golden age of mysticism. In England, such mystics as Richard Rolle, Walter Hilton, and Lady Julian made important contributions to the spirituality of the times.[27] However, the significant revivals that emerged from mysticism occurred on the continent, especially in Germany. The father of fourteenth-century German mysticism was Meister Eckhart, who was condemned by Pope John XXII in 1329 due to his teachings in the area of mysticism. As Eckhart taught his views in such places as Cologne and Paris, he emphasized the importance of a personal relationship between God and man. One of his most prominent students was John Tauler.

Preparation for Revival

John Tauler was born in Strasbourg in about 1300.[28] Very little is known of his early life except he was from a wealthy family. He later said, "If, as my father's son, I had once known what I know now, I would have lived from my paternal inheritance instead of resorting to alms."[29] The family was deeply religious. John joined the Dominican Order of Preachers and his sister entered the Dominican convent of St. Nikolas in Strasbourg.

By 1314, John was a novice in the Strasbourg monastery and was introduced to Prior Eckhart for the first time. He later continued his studies in Cologne and possibly in Paris.[30] Following his education, he lectured at Strasbourg and preached in the surrounding area.

The conflicts between King Ludwig of Bavaria and Pope John XXII led to the king's excommunication in 1325, and ultimately caused a schism between the two in 1329. This feud between the pope and the king greatly impacted preaching in Ludwig's realm, where Tauler served. At first, the Dominican friars in Strasbourg were allowed to preach and to offer mass. However, when the king's edicts against papal supporters were enforced in 1339, Tauler was forced into exile and went to Basel. While in Basel, he was introduced to the mystic Henry of Nordlingen, who was a leader of the group called "The Friends of God." In about 1347, Tauler returned to Strasbourg. In 1348, the Black Plague ravaged the nations, destroying approximately one-fourth to one-third of the population of Europe.[31] In the midst of this devastation, Tauler labored incessantly.

Spiritual Fires

At the age of fifty, Tauler had an experience that changed his life. He was a popular preacher who exercised unusual persuasion over a congregation. People traveled great distances to hear him preach. His sermons were filled with Scripture, illustrations, relevant application, and practical counsel for daily living.

On one occasion, as the story goes, Nicolas of Basel traveled some 150 miles in order to hear Tauler preach.[32] After hearing him for twelve weeks, Nicolas asked Tauler to preach a sermon on how to attain holiness. Tauler announced to the congregation that in three days he was going to preach on that topic. The huge crowd heard twenty-four steps on how a person becomes holy. Nicolas took notes on the message and in a later conference with Tauler read the notes back to the preacher. Nicolas told Tauler that he ought to practice what he preached and accused Tauler of being a Pharisee. Nicolas told Tauler that he lacked spiritual power in his preaching. After the conversation with Nicolas, Tauler stopped preaching for two years and spent the time in meditation and reflection. Out of this event, he experienced a personal revival as he committed his life anew to Christ.

His first attempt at preaching following the two-year absence was a trying ordeal. As he stood in the pulpit, Tauler could not speak as he wept uncontrollably. The other friars were so embarrassed that they refused to let him preach after that event. However, in time, he received an invitation from his sister to preach at the convent for the nuns. His text was Matthew 25:6: "Behold, the bridegroom! Come out to meet him." As he preached, fifty of the listeners fell to the floor as if they were dead.[33] An awakening ignited in Strasbourg. As the revival leader, Tauler often said, "No one can teach what he has not himself lived through." [34]

As Tauler's fame spread, people came from great distances to hear him. Before his personal revival, he was a popular preacher. After his renewal, he became God's spokesman. Before his personal revival, people responded to him as an orator. After revival, they responded to him in deep conviction of sin. As the Holy Spirit worked, entire communities experienced revival. Features of his preaching included the Holy Spirit, conversion, and holy living. In a sermon on holy living, he said:

> A pure heart is more precious in the sight of God than aught else on earth. A pure heart is a fair, fitly-adorned chamber, the dwelling of the Holy Ghost; a golden temple of the Godhead; a sanctuary of the only-begotten Son, in which he worships the Heavenly Father; an altar of the grand, divine sacrifice, . . . a treasury of divine riches; a storehouse of divine sweetness; the reward of all the life and sufferings of Christ.[35]

He said "works of love are more acceptable to God than lofty contemplation."[36]

On another occasion, Tauler said:

> Wisdom is not studied in Paris, but in the sufferings of the Lord. . . . The great masters of Paris read large books, and that is well. But the people who dwell in the inner kingdom of the soul read the true Book of Life. A pure heart is the throne of the Supreme Judge, a lamp bearing the eternal light, a treasure of divine riches, a storehouse of heavenly sweetness, a sanctuary of the only begotten Son.[37]

By the time John Tauler died on June 16, 1361, Germany had been exposed to a theology and a pattern of preaching that helped to lay the foundations for the Reformation. His *Theological Germanica* influenced many of the reformers. The seeds of the doctrine of justification by faith, which was the heart of Martin Luther's theology, were found in Tauler.[38] Luther said that Tauler's theology was the most wholesome expression of truth in the Latin and German languages.[39]

In regard to Tauler's preaching, Andrew Weeks wrote: "Tauler's sermons became the classic standard of a reflective spirituality. Their popularity survived in Pietistic circles into the nineteenth century."[40] Tauler was a revival leader who majored on expounding Scripture and on a person's personal relationship with Christ through faith. The impact of this revival is evidenced in its influence upon the people who heard him, the reformers who followed him, and the Pietists who studied him.

Revival Under John Wycliffe

John Wycliffe has been called "The Morning Star of the Reformation."[41] He was born in about 1324 on the Wycliffe estate in Spresswell, near Old Richmond, Yorkshire, England, and was of noble heritage. He enrolled at Oxford and studied at Queen's, Merton, and Balliol Colleges. In 1353 his studies were interrupted by his father's death and his return home to settle family affairs. He returned to Oxford in 1355. In 1356 he started studies toward a master's degree in philosophy at Balliol. He quickly distinguished himself as a scholar, gaining a reputation "as second to none in philosophy, and in scholastic discipline altogether incomparable."[42] After he received his master's degree in 1361, he became rector of the Fillingham church, but he seldom visited the parish.

The Making of a Reformer

When he was appointed as warden of Canterbury Hall in 1365, a struggle between the monks and the secular priests caused Wycliffe to develop some opinions about the papacy that greatly influenced his reform ministry. This dispute was over the distinctions that the church placed upon the two offices. Since the monks were considered the more elite group, animosity existed between the two orders. Under Bishop Islip, Canterbury Hall was combined as a residence for both monks and parish priests. However, Simon Langham (1310-76), Islip's successor, rescinded the practice. Wycliffe preferred Islip's approach and appealed to Pope Urban V to revert to this pattern, but he lost the appeal. Out of this experience with clerical pride and later disappointing encounters with the pope, Wycliffe's attitudes changed toward the papacy and the ideas of reform were planted.

Because the Bible received his most diligent attention in his academic pursuits, Wycliffe acquired the title of "Evangelic, or Gospel, Doctor" when he received his doctor's degree in 1372. This knowledge of Scripture provided the foundation for his ministry of reform. In an academic environment where the *Sentences* of Peter Lombard were viewed as having more authority than Scripture, Wycliffe's devotion to the Bible was unique. Roger Bacon wrote that he who reads "the text of Scripture is compelled to give way to the reader of the *Sentences,* who everywhere enjoys honor and precedence."[43] John of Salisbury, a scholar of the twelfth century, said that scriptural teachers were "not only rejected as philosophers, but unwillingly endured as clergymen — nay, were scarcely acknowledged to be men. They became objects of derision."[44]

In this spiritually depraved climate, Wycliffe demonstrated the courage to be the voice of God, a translator of the Bible, and an expositor of Scripture. For his theological views and his determination to appeal to Scripture as the highest authority instead of the papacy, he was labeled as a heretic and was ultimately condemned by the faculty at Oxford and by Archbishop Courtenay of Canterbury in a convocation at the Black Friars Convent in 1382.[45]

Although Wycliffe received the appointment as parish priest at Lutterworth from King Edward III in 1374, he did not arrive on the church field until 1382. On December 28, 1384, while observing mass in his parish church at Lutterworth, he suffered a massive stroke. He died on December 31, 1384.[46]

The Council of Constance in 1415 instructed Bishop Shepingdon to exhume the body of Wycliffe and burn the remains. However, since Shepingdon had served as a leader of the Lollards before he was forced to recant, he refused to obey the order. On December 16, 1427, Wycliffe's remains were removed from St. Mary's Church cemetery, burned, and scattered upon the Swift River.[47]

The Ministry of Wycliffe

Wycliffe was a reformer, not a classical revival leader. Like Luther and Calvin who followed him, his movement was one of reform, or a renewal of Christianity. Spiritual awakening is different from reform. Awakening brings immediate change, energizes Christians, and produces unusual evangelistic results. Reform brings a gradual alteration of the church's doctrine and practice. God directs both, and both receive strong opposition.

Because of the spiritual declension of the Roman Church for more than one thousand years, she no longer fulfilled her divine mandate. Previous attempts at reform were suppressed with a vengeance by Rome. However, under such leaders as Wycliffe, Huss, and the sixteenth-century reformers, the Roman Church encountered resolve that she could not control, and Christian history was permanently altered. Early flames for reform were ignited in England through the labors of Wycliffe and the Lollards.

In his ministry of reform, Wycliffe majored primarily on clerical corruption, church wealth, civil authority over papal authority, scriptural authority as the ultimate source for faith and practice, Lordship of Christ as the head of the church, and the repudiation of the Roman position on the Eucharist. His attack on the doctrine of transubstantiation in 1381 cost him the support of some of his followers.

For Wycliffe, if the priests no longer controlled the spiritual destinies of the people through the mass, their powers to control the people would also be reduced.[48] In his views toward the Eucharist, Wycliffe taught that salvation did not come through the elements of the mass but was received by faith in Christ alone.[49]

Wycliffe and the Lollards

The work of Wycliffe was expanded through his followers, who were called the Lollards or "Poor Priests."[50] Hague defined the term "Lollard" as a singer of sacred songs. A Lollard "denotes a person who is continually praising God with a song or singing hymns to His honor."[51] Like Francis of Assisi approximately 150 years before him, Wycliffe taught his followers to sing the songs of the faith and to preach the message of Christ. Unlike Francis, however, Wycliffe challenged some of the teachings of Rome and the authority of the papacy.

In 1382, while serving at Lutterworth, Wycliffe organized the small group of followers called the Lollards. This group grew with such "amazing vitality that it became a proverb that every second man you met in England was a Lollard."[52] More realistically, about a fourth of the nation was supposed to be in sympathy with Wycliffe.

The source of the sermons of the Lollards was Scripture. Under the leadership of Nicholas Hereford, the Latin Vulgate was translated into the English language. Known as the Wycliffe translation, it was the version used by many of the reformers in the sixteenth century. For the first time, the Bible was available in the English language.

As the Lollards traveled, they preached in open fields, marketplaces, churchyards, and churches that were open to them. Because they did not have approval from the bishops to preach, they were often persecuted. When William Thorpe was on trial before Archbishop Arundel for preaching without permission, the Lollard said, "Though we have not your letter, sir, nor letters of any bishops, written with ink upon parchment, we dare not therefore leave the office of preaching; . . . for God commands us"[53] to preach.

Multitudes responded to their message as the people were able to hear the gospel in terms that they understood. The Lollards did not rely upon religious formulas or prescribed liturgies; they depended upon Scripture and preached the message of salvation in Christ. They served under the leadership of God and only "after the moving of the Holy Spirit."[54]

By the time of Wycliffe's death, the Lollards had traveled throughout England, preached to the multitudes, and incurred persecution. Although Wycliffe was not a revival leader, some of the Lollards experienced renewal as they preached. Entire communities were spiritually energized. Thousands were saved. A spiritual hope, long suppressed, arose from the ashes of despair and throbbed within the hearts of the multitudes. Across England, people lifted their voices in praise to God once again. Many churches came alive. As many of the Lollards served in awakening, England felt the impact.

By 1395 the Lollards were represented in Parliament, and their *Twelve Conclusions* were presented for legislative enactment. As long as King Richard II (reigned 1377-99) ruled over England, they were not hindered by the government in preaching. However, when King Henry IV (reigned 1399-1413) ascended to the throne, the fate of the Lollards was sealed. In 1401 the *De haeretico comburendo,* or *On the Burning of a Heretic,* was passed and the Lollards became the targets of persecution and martyrdom.[55] As they were persecuted, many recanted, went underground, or were martyred. However, their ideas could not be stopped as they were unleashed upon England and Europe. When King Richard II married Anne, the daughter of King Wenceslas of Bohemia,[56] in 1382, the political alliance ultimately made a passageway for Wycliffe's ideas to spread to that nation and influence a young scholar by the name of John Huss.

Revival Under John Huss

John Huss was born about 1372 in Husinec, Bohemia. From this town, he assumed the name of Huss. Although nothing is known of his parents or early childhood, he apparently was reared in a godly home. In 1390 he entered the University of Prague. He received his bachelor's degree in 1394 and master's in 1396. Also in 1396, he joined the faculty at Prague. By 1401 he was the dean of the school. In 1404, he received his degree in theology. Although he concentrated on Peter Lombard's *Sentences* in pursuit of his doctorate, he never earned the degree.[57]

In 1402, Huss was appointed preacher at the Church of the Holy Innocents of Bethlehem in Prague and immediately attracted large crowds. His preaching was marked by earnestness and a compassion that were seldom seen in preachers. He quickly became the most popular preacher in the country. The queen enlisted him as her private confessor and frequently, along with her court, heard him preach.

From the beginning, Huss was open to reform ideas as a result of his exposure to the writings of Wycliffe. In 1406, Jerome of Prague returned from Oxford with additional works of Wycliffe and shared the writings with Huss. Because of the alliance between England and Bohemia, the writings of Wycliffe were widely read at the university, and the fires of reform began to spread.

On May 15, 1408, the German members of the university faculty filed charges of heresy against Huss because of his reform views. However, Huss had the support of the Czech king, Wenceslas, who altered the rules of the university to give the Czech faculty the majority of the votes, even though the Germans outnumbered the Czechs on the faculty three to one.[58]

In 1409 the tensions resulted in the departure of the Germans from the University of Prague, which virtually left Huss as the champion of reform. In 1410 Archbishop Zbynek of Prague, a sympathizer of Huss until the heresy charges were filed, ordered that all writings of Wycliffe be surrendered for burning. Although Huss refused to submit to the demands, about two hundred copies of Wycliffe's writings were seized and destroyed.

At the center of the reform was the Eucharist. Huss adopted the views of Wycliffe that the elements remained the same after the priestly formula was pronounced. In 1411 Huss was excommunicated from the Roman Church by the archbishop. In 1412, in order to avoid serious problems for the people of Prague, he left the city and conducted an itinerant ministry. The king and most of the rank and file among the people supported his labors.

When King Wenceslas' brother, King Sigismund, who later became emperor of the Holy Roman Empire, convened the Council of Constance on November 1, 1414, he urged Huss to appear before the Council and present his case. Huss agreed to do so when Sigismund gave him letters of safe conduct. When he appeared in Constance, he was immediately arrested. The members of the Council said that they did not have to honor a promise given to a heretic. On July 6, 1415, he was condemned as a heretic as thirty articles of heresy were read against him. The Council sentenced him to death on the same day. As the Council committed his soul to Satan, Huss lifted his head toward heaven and said, "I commit myself to the most gracious Lord Jesus."

Under the guard of one thousand armed men, Huss was escorted at midday to the place of execution. When he was offered the opportunity to recant and live, Huss replied, "I shall die with joy today in the faith of the Gospel that I have preached." As the flames rose to take his life, he sang of his faith and commended his soul to Christ. The ashes of the martyr were gathered and scattered upon the waters of the Rhine River.

> As the Council of Constance committed his soul to Satan, Huss lifted his head toward heaven and said, "I commit myself to the most gracious Lord Jesus."

Results of the Reform Under Huss

Like Wycliffe, Huss was a reformer, not a revival leader. When he was martyred, the reform movement began to spread. Huss became a national figure and a rallying point for those who were interested in change. Several groups were influenced by his teachings, including the Taborites, Utraquists, and Bohemian Brethren. Through these groups, the flames of reform continued to burn within the religious scene in Europe.

Revival Under Savonarola

The fifteenth century was a time of transition and expansion. Constantinople, which had served as the capital in the east since May 11, 330, fell in 1453, and many of the refuges migrated to Italy. With their immigration, they brought scholarship and leadership that contributed significantly to the golden age of the Italian Renaissance.

Johannes Gutenberg (1400-1468) invented the printing press in Mainz, Germany, in 1451. Medieval Scholasticism, for all practical purposes, was dead. The Renaissance enjoyed front stage. Art, literature, and science captured the minds of many scholars. Exploration for new territories occupied the dreams of several adventurous explorers, including Christopher Columbus. Appetites for material possessions dominated society, and the morality of the times was deplorable.

The papacy was once again united after the schism of the Avignon papacy, yet the reunited Roman Church did not turn to God and serve as a spiritual force. Instead, the papacy, especially under the leadership of Paul II (1464-71), Sixtus IV (1471-84), Innocent VIII (1484-92), and Alexander VI (1492-1503), was characterized by corruption, greed, and sensuality that paralleled the pagan conditions that existed during the days of the Roman Empire. Under these circumstances, Girolamo Savonarola appeared in Florence as a voice from God.

Savonarola's Life

Girolamo, or Jerome, Savonarola was born in Ferrara, Italy, on September 21, 1452, the third of seven children in the family of Niccolo and Elena Savonarola. His mother was from the illustrious family of Bonaccorsi of Mantua.[59] His grandfather, Michele Savonarola, moved from Padua to Ferrara in 1440 and served as the noted physician to the court of the royal family of Este and lecturer at the university until his death in 1462. He was awarded the distinguished honor of the Knights of Jerusalem by Pope Nicholas V (1447-55).

Since his father was deficient as a proper motivator for his son, most of Savonarola's early training came from his grandfather and mother. His progress in academic pursuits was "so marvelous that he very soon outstripped all of his fellow students."[60] Even in his youthful years, he had a desire for spiritual realities. He preferred solitude for spiritual meditation and reflection to the worldly revelry of his peers. In his time of seclusion, he often played the lute or composed poetry. As he viewed the worldly pomp of the wealthy and the religious insensitivity of the church toward the multitudes, he responded with mental indignation and emotional grief.

In 1472, he began a courtship with Laodamia Strozzi, daughter of Roberto Strozzi, who lived next door. This relationship led to a one-sided romance. As he fell deeply in love with her, hopes for a lasting love and a family arose within his heart. Thinking that she felt toward him the way he did toward her, he shared his love with Laodamia. In ridicule, she informed him that, as a Florentine, Strozzi could never marry a Savonarola. Her rejection of his love devastated his dreams and shattered his hopes, and never again would he love another woman.[61]

Following this event, his thoughts turned toward God and His purpose for life. In 1474, he heard a friar preach a sermon in Faenza that changed his life. On that occasion, he was converted and returned to Ferrara with a new purpose for living. Following several months of meditation and reflection, he heard from God. On April 24, 1475, while his parents attended the festival of St. George, he left home for the Dominican monastery at Bologna, where he immediately took the vows of a novice. In remorse over the manner in which he left home, on April 25 he wrote a letter to his family. He shared that he had entered the monastery due to the corruption of the world and only after serious meditation.[62] At the age of twenty-two, he was committed to the calling of God that charted the rest of his life.

While Savonarola was driven to the monastery by the political corruption of his age, he viewed the spiritual conditions of the church as just as deplorable. In despair, he spent time in the study of the Bible, which became the source of his authority. As he preached at the monastery, he referred often to Scripture, which frequently brought rebuke from his instructor, Giovanni Garzoni. Scriptural references in sermons were, according to the custom of the times, simply not acceptable in preaching. In 1481 he was sent to his hometown of Ferrara to preach. Following scant results, he was transferred to Florence in 1482. In the same year, he preached his first sermon at the San Lorenzo Church during the Easter season to a congregation of about twenty-five people. The popular preacher in Florence was an eloquent preacher at the Church of Santo Spirito by the name of Mariano da Genazzano.

Savonarola was void of the rhetorical eloquence of his counterpart at Santo Spirito. Misciattelli cited Cerretani, a contemporary of the two preachers, who gave a description of his preaching: "Savonarola introduced what might be called a new way of preaching the Word of God; an apostolic way; not dividing his sermons into parts, or embellishing them with high sounding words of elegance, but having as his sole aim the explaining of Scripture, and the return to the simplicity of the primitive church."[63]

His preaching was met with disdain from the people in Florence. When Savonarola's friend, Benivieni, spoke to him about the poor response, Benivieni said, "It cannot be denied that your doctrine is true, useful, and necessary, but your manner of delivery lacks grace, especially when compared with the elegance of Fra Mariano."[64]

Savonarola replied, "Elegance of language must give way to the simplicity of the preaching of sound doctrine."[65] Due to the lack of response, he was sent to Sangimignano during the Lenten seasons of 1484 and 1485. In this rustic mountain village of common people, the revival leader emerged.

Revival Fires in Florence

Savonarola did not start with great spiritual power, but he soon received it. As he meditated and reflected upon God, a new spiritual vitality arose within him. From visions and dreams that he received from God, he concluded that God had a special purpose for his preaching. Out of this experience, Savonarola experienced a personal revival that changed his life.

As he preached with new spiritual power, the listeners were struck with the awesome holiness of God. Lives and habits were changed. The entire town responded to the moving of the Holy Spirit. In this mountain village, the greatest revival of the fifteenth century ignited. It quickly spread to other villages, and ultimately the news reached Florence that an awakening was in progress at Sangimignano. During the Lenten season of 1486, Savonarola preached at Brescia. As he spoke, some of the hearers testified that they saw a holy halo over his head.[66]

Savonarola preached with such spiritual power that people responded either with life commitments or vigorous rejections. He remained in northern Italy until January 1489. During his ministry in the north, he developed a deep and lasting friendship with a brilliant young philosopher by the name of Giovanni Pica della Mirandola (1463-94).

Through the influence of Pica, Savonarola was invited back to Florence. His first assignment upon his arrival at San Marco was to teach a group of friars. His subject was the Apocalypse. His lectures were received with such popularity that he was invited to preach in the church. Christian history has not forgotten the event.

On August 1, 1489, Savonarola stood in the pulpit of the Church of San Marco in Florence to preach his first sermon after his return to the city. The church was filled with people from all classes of society. Some people came out of curiosity. Some came because they knew him from his first tour of service in Florence. Some came because of a heart-felt hunger for spiritual truths. As the people gathered, the spiritual atmosphere was intensely electric. Whereas few people heard him during his first tenure of service in Florence, the masses heard him on this occasion.

As Savonarola mounted the pulpit on that day, any past struggles with uncertainty and mediocrity were over. The greatest revival leader of the fifteenth century stood among the people. His sermon was based upon the Second Coming, the focus of so much of his revival preaching. As Savonarola preached with uncompromising conviction and spiritual unction, the people were deeply moved. God opened their hearts and minds to the gospel, and revival ignited. The news of the revival spread across Florence. The reactions were characteristic of all revivals. William Crawford said:

> Opinions were divided. Some declared that the preacher was only a fanatic, who by his rare voice and power as an orator swayed the people; others went so far as to say that he had no eloquence at all, the effect on the crowd being brought about by a combination of loud words and striking imagery; the men of the academy inclined to the view that the preacher, though a man of remarkable natural ability, was after all unlearned in the language and thought of the schools, and that therefore his influence would only be transitory.[67]

Revival Preaching

As incredible results occurred, Savonarola's popularity grew. He became the topic of conversation in Florence and the surrounding areas. The San Marco Church no longer could hold the people who came to hear him preach. The only building that was large enough was the Duomo Cathedral. The days of popularity for Mariano were over; a new voice, void of rhetorical genius and homiletical refinements but filled with divine power, was being heard. James Burns described his preaching:

> First, he would begin in measured and tranquil tones, taking up the subject, turning it quietly around, suggesting some scholarly exposition, advancing some interpretation, dealing with it casually, critically, suggestively; then, suddenly, often without warning, he would change; the meditative style was flung aside as the mantle of the prophet fell upon him; fire flashed from his eyes, the thunder came from his voice; now in passionate entreaty, now in scorching indignation, the sentences rushed out, never halting, never losing intensity or volume, but growing and growing until his voice became as the voice of God Himself, and all the building rocked and swayed as if it moved to the mighty passion of his words. And what of the hearers? They were as clay in his hands. Tears gushed from their eyes, they beat their breasts, they cried unto God for mercy, the church echoed and re-echoed with their sobs.[68]

Savonarola's Popularity

The citizens of Florence knew they indeed had a prophet in their midst. His straightforward, uncompromising sermons were well received by the people. Misciattelli described their responses:

> The people got up at midnight so as to be in time to hear the sermon. They went as far as the Duomo, where they waited patiently in the Piazza until the doors opened. And nobody complained of cold or any other discomfort. Then they would stand on the cold marble pavement even in the winter, young and old, women and children of every condition, with so much jubilation and enjoyment that it made one marvel. They went to sermons as if going to a wedding. Then in church — how silent it was! Every person went to his place with a little light in their hands, . . . and prayed. Although there were many hundreds of people present, not even a whisper could be heard. Then would come in the children singing hymns and praises with such sweetness that Paradise seemed to have opened. They would thus wait patiently three to four hours until the Friar entered the pulpit. Then how admirable the attention that was paid to his words — no feeling of tiredness, no longing for him to finish, every eye and every ear on the alert so as not to miss a single word. And when the end came it seemed as if the sermon had only begun. His words were like keen darts which entering the hearts of his hearers ignited in them a blaze of emotion and faith.[69]

The reporter who recorded his messages often testified, "I burst into tears and could not write further."[70] Savonarola was the spiritual voice of Florence and the nation of Italy. His preaching was so uncompromising that many influential citizens of Florence sought to tone down his messages, including Lorenzo di Medici, the patriarch of the city. Lorenzo was irate when Savonarola was unwilling to listen to him. In a plan of action to silence the revival leader, Lorenzo enlisted the help of the willing Mariano. In May 1491 Mariano preached a sermon against Savonarola. The revival leader responded with a message that silenced Mariano's arguments. Henceforth, Mariano was a bitter enemy of Savonarola.

San Marco Church

In July 1491, Savonarola became the prior of San Marcos Church. For the next seven years, he served as a voice from God to challenge the corruption of the papacy and clergy, the greed of government, the worldliness of the laity, and the lack of concern on the part of all for the things of God.

As revival flourished in Florence, his preaching and ability to predict events earned him the reputation of a prophet. He often received visions from God, even to the point of prophesying future events. Among his many prophecies, he predicted the deaths of Lorenzo de Medici, Pope Innocent VIII, and Fico Mirandola. [71] He even predicted that he would live eight more years and die.[72]

Government Leader

An event happened in 1492 that greatly expanded Savonarola's influence. Charles VIII, king of France, launched a military campaign against Italy. On September 21, 1492, Savonarola preached a sermon on the coming judgment. In the midst of the message, he suddenly, unexpectedly, and forcefully proclaimed, "Behold! I bring a flood of waters upon the earth!"[73] Like a thunderbolt, this statement startled not only the congregation but also the preacher.

As the French army marched against Florence, Pietro de Medici, the son and successor of Lorenzo, met with Charles to negotiate a truce. The citizens of Florence were so irate that they exiled Pietro from the city, thus ending, for all practical purposes, the rule of the Medici family. With the government leader gone, the people turned to Savonarola for leadership. When he met with Charles, he requested that the French king depart from Florence and the king agreed to do so. Following this event, the revival leader became the unofficial political leader not only of Florence but also of the commonwealth of Naples. Under his leadership, the entire city became virtually monastic in lifestyle. Before the revival ignited, the city was mired in immorality and carnality. He tried to enact legislation against immorality, but was overruled by the city council. What he could not achieve through legislation, God achieved through the power of the Holy Spirit.

Tempered with Compassion

An encounter with his friend Fra Antonio Benivieni changed the direction of Savonarola's ministry. Benivieni confronted him about the harsh and condemnatory remarks that he consistently made in his preaching: "Are you aware that since you began to hurl your imprecations to left and right men and women run for cover when they see a man in the Dominican habit coming their way? Would they run if our Lord Jesus Christ came into their hutches and hovels? Are we not Christ's messengers and should the people not see and hear us gladly as they once saw and heard the Lord?"[74]

Savonarola was so convicted that he refused to appear in public for several weeks. He remained in his cell at San Marco meditating, fasting, and praying. When he appeared in public again, his revival ministry was on a new course. Although he was uncompromising in his relentless campaign against vices, he refocused his ministry on those who were victims of those vices.

A tenderness and love emerged in Savonarola's relationships and preaching. Children and youth became his preoccupation. Whereas they once feared him, they now gladly crowded about him. He organized church services for them. At the first service, two thousand attended. The theme of the message was that Christianity was not church attendance but the way of life in Christ. In reaction to the overwhelming response, he appointed friars as the directors of programs designed to get youth involved in the cause of Christ.

Revival Spreads

The response was outstanding as street gangs were reached and became involved in the youth assignments. Among the projects was the cleaning of the streets and statues of the city. Young female converts, aided by some of the prominent women of the city, formed groups to reach the women of brothels. In two months, one of the districts was deserted.

A converted member of a street gang was asked to testify before the city council about the work that was being done among the gangs:

> Christ, the King of Florence, has freed our city from the bondage of sin. A prophet has arisen amongst us who has kindled hearts and minds with the pure light of the Spirit . . . Fifteen thousand boys and girls are organized to form a new Christian militia. We have sworn an oath not to rest till we have spoken to every youth and maiden wherever they be of the love of Christ, and God's willingness to forgive sin.[75]

One sensational conversion was that of Bettucio, a cavalier of Florence. He attended church for the purpose of mocking and ridiculing the preacher. As Savonarola preached, he fell under such conviction that he was dramatically converted, distributed his wealth to the poor, and became a monk. Florence underwent such a transformation that visitors who were familiar with Florence prior to revival did not recognize the city.

Van Passen observed: "The cabarets, baginos (brothels), and gambling houses had gone out of existence, not by signorial or ecclesiastical decree, but by the former customers staying away. Instead of lewd songs, spiritual songs were heard. No blasphemies were heard in the smithies, at times the entire marketplace broke into a religious song festival. Churches were crowded, the poor were taken care of."[76]

Clash of Wills

Savonarola consistently preached against the worldliness of the clergy. On one occasion he said, "In the early church, it was the chalices that were made of wood and the prelates were made of gold; today it is the prelates who are made of wood, and their chalices rich in gold."[77]

When Roderigo Borgia became Pope Alexandria VI on August 10, 1492, the ministry of Savonarola was greatly impacted. The worldly lifestyle of the new pope was included in Savonarola's messages against worldly living. The pomp of Alexander was more than he could take. In 1495, Pope Alexander forbade him to preach, and out of respect for the church and the office of the pope, he obeyed.

However, Savonarola began a campaign to have the pope removed from office. In an attempt to curtail the activities of Savonarola, the pope offered him a cardinal's hat if he would modify the tone of his sermons. In his next sermon, he preached, "I will have no hat but one dyed with my blood."[78] His sermons against the lavish lifestyle of the papacy brought ultimate response from the pontiff. Upon charges of heresy, the pope issued a brief for Savonarola's excommunication on May 13, 1497.

On May 22, Savonarola, without knowing of the brief, sought reconciliation with the pontiff. The charges of heresy against him were totally unfounded, and he assured the pope of his loyalty and support. However, on June 18, the excommunication was read publicly in Florence. The pope threatened that supporters of Savonarola would be excommunicated and their property seized. The papal threat altered the position of the city council, and protection for Savonarola was gone.

When the edict was made, vice and corruption were once again at work in Florence.[79] Whereas Florence thrived in the midst of a decent moral climate in the revival, the city quickly returned to carnality when Savonarola was silenced by the corrupt pope. Attempts to get the ban lifted were made by friends, even suggesting payment of a bribe by Savonarola of five thousand scudi to the pope.[80] He refused to be part of any such action.

Contest by Fire

As the end of Savonarola's life approached, he had been excommunicated and labeled as a heretic. Then, bizarre and tragic events began to occur. One of the most unfortunate events happened when the Franciscan friar Francesco de Puglia challenged Savonarola, in response to his claim to sound doctrine, to a test of orthodoxy through a contest by fire. The duel stipulated that the two would walk between rows of burning logs that would be hot enough to kill. The survivor would be declared orthodox in his doctrine.

Savonarola considered the proposal ridiculous, but his close friend, the impetuous Fra Domenico, accepted the challenge on Savonarola's behalf. On April 7, 1498, the day set aside for the contest, multitudes of people gathered in the plaza. "A platform eighty-feet long by ten-feet wide, paved with brick and four feet off the ground was constructed. It was heaped with masses of fagots, saturated with oil. There were two feet of space between the wood and when the men entered the entrance was to be closed off. No one could survive the contest."[81]

Although several members of his congregation volunteered to stand in for him, Savonarola refused their offers. When Puglia backed out, some of the people demanded that Savonarola go ahead with the contest and enter the fire alone. He was in a losing situation. First, his refusal would cause some to label him a coward. Second, if he entered and died, that would have supported the claim that he was a heretic. Third, he believed the challenge was tempting God and beyond the teachings of Scripture. When he refused to enter the fire alone, a mob stormed San Marco Church, the convent was set on fire, and more than a hundred members were either killed or wounded.[82]

The Close of His Ministry

The mob demanded the surrender of Savonarola. In order to avoid harm to the people he loved so deeply, he gave himself over to the mob. He was not allowed to attend his own trial. Five days before his trial, the torture began. His shoulders, elbows, knees, and hips were dislocated. The torture was beyond human endurance.

On one occasion, with his mind dulled from the excruciating pain, he recanted and confessed to whatever they demanded. As soon as he regained his senses, he recanted his confessions. Convicted of crimes that he did not commit, he was sentenced to death.

When the legate of the pope, Benedetto Paganotti, read the decision of conviction, he pompously and arrogantly said, "I separate you from the Church militant and the Church triumphant."[83] Savonarola replied, "Only from the Church militant; the other is beyond your power."[84]

On May 23, 1498, at the age of forty-five, Savonarola was led to the crowded Piazza della Signora along with his two associates, Fra Domenico and Fra Silvestro, and was hung. As the hangman placed the noose around his neck, he spoke his last words, "The Lord has suffered as much for me."[85] His body was burned, and the ashes were scattered upon the Arno River.

Revival Results

Savonarola's voice was silenced but not the flames for reform. A convert of his ministry was John Colet, a professor of Greek who taught Erasmus. It was Erasmus's Greek translation of the Bible that was used widely among the reformers. Savonarola also influenced Luther: "Whereas Antichrist has condemned Savonarola, God has canonized him in our hearts."[86]

In the awakening under Savonarola, every characteristic of revival is discerned: the place of Scripture; the difference a personal revival makes in ministry; the suddenness with which revival ignites among the people; rapid spread to the masses; the prominent place of spiritual leadership attained by the revival leader; the phenomenal changes within society; incredible changes in human lives; inexplicable responses within human rationale to the preaching of the revival leader; and intense opposition by the non-participants.

This awakening was the last piece in the puzzle that set the stage for the Reformation. The Reformation was not the tragedy; the tragedy was that there was a need for the Reformation. The Church in Rome, which had not had an awakening in over a thousand years, discouraged, suppressed, and persecuted those whose heartbeats were for the gospel and the glory of Jesus Christ, especially Girolamo Savonarola. However, a fire was burning in Europe that no force on earth could extinguish.

Questions for Discussion

1. St. Francis of Assisi sacrificed much to follow Christ. What are some things you need to sacrifice in order to experience true revival in Christ?

2. Savonarola demonstrated a tremendous resolve in the cause of revival, ultimately being burned at the stake. What cost would you pay to see a movement of God?

3. What experience have you had that changed your life? Many revivals have started as a result of a significant experience in a person's life.

Chapter 7
The Reformation and Revival

"My conscience is captive to the Word of God."
Martin Luther[1]

Martin Luther's famous confession before the Diet of Worms on April 18, 1521, characterized sixteenth-century reform and revival leaders. It is hard for modern Christians to understand the circumstances of Reformation times. Many of the things that are taken for granted today, especially religious liberty, were nonexistent just five hundred years ago. Those brave few who dared to dream, to think new thoughts, and to challenge the status quo paid the supreme price of persecution and even martyrdom. Those heroes of the faith did not consider personal agendas or entertain compromise. They put everything on the line for their faith.

Revivals are often overlooked as significant contributors to the Reformation. However, the revivals under Waldo, Francis, Tauler, Savonarola, and others created spiritual hunger in human hearts that the Roman Church could not satisfy. Indeed, revivals laid the foundation for the upward spiral of human progress that found its fruition in the Reformation.

Whereas revivals were indispensable contributors to the Reformation, the Reformation in turn provided the atmosphere for subsequent revivals in Christian history. Much like the reform movements under some of the kings in the Old Testament preceded awakenings during the history of Judah, the Reformation set the table for all renewals since Martin Luther. This continental divide in Christian history not only altered church practices and changed doctrinal beliefs but also created hunger in human hearts that became depositories for spiritual awakening.

Some crucial doctrinal understandings and church practices were altered during the Reformation. People's ideas about faith, Scripture, salvation, preaching, God's sovereignty, and music were all influenced. Because these changes impacted later revivals, this chapter focuses primarily on the contributions of the Reformation to revivals. The few revivals that occurred in the sixteenth century ignited primarily through the ministries of the Anabaptists.

The Reformation and Politics

Revivals never occur in vacuums. Political, moral, and religious conditions always impact awakenings. This was certainly true in the sixteenth century. In the political arena, it would have been virtually impossible for the Reformation to have occurred without the political crises that diverted the attentions of the government leaders, especially Charles V, Emperor of the Holy Roman Empire, away from the efforts of the reformers.

Continental Europe

The four political powers in Europe during this time were France, Spain, England, and the Holy Roman Empire, which included Germany. King Charles I of Spain was also Emperor Charles V of the Holy Roman Empire. The combination of these two thrones made Spain the most powerful nation in Europe during the Reformation. Spain maintained this position until its defeat in the naval war of 1588. Spain's rise to power began when Ferdinand of Aragon (reigned 1479-1516) married Isabella of Castile (reigned 1474-1504) in 1469. Through this marriage, the nation was solidified politically and began to expand her borders.

When King Charles I (1500-1558) of Spain became Emperor Charles V of the Holy Roman Empire in 1519, he took control of a large portion of Europe. He inherited Spain and its territories through his mother, Joanna, the daughter of Ferdinand and Isabella. He inherited the Holy Roman Empire through his father, Philip, the son of Maximilian I (King, 1493-1519) of Germany and Mary, the daughter of Charles the Bold of Burgundy.

Charles was a staunch Catholic, but he was unable to prevent the Reformation. The Muslims were a constant threat to the eastern borders of his empire. For example, on August 29, 1526, King Louis II of Hungary, a part of the Holy Roman Empire, suffered a smashing defeat at the hands of the Turks at Mohacs. When Charles' brother, Ferdinand, was crowned king of Hungary on November 3, 1527, Charles was forced into an even greater involvement with the Muslims.

In addition, the imperial forces of Charles were engaged in a fierce struggle with the papacy and Rome. The conflict resulted in the capture of Pope Clement VII and Rome on May 6, 1527. Although Charles made brief attempts to stop the work of the reformers, especially at the Second Diet of Speyers in 1529, he was unsuccessful due to these crises.

England

Although no significant revivals ignited in England in the sixteenth century, the events that occurred were monumental in laying the foundations for future awakenings. Toward the end of the fifteenth century, bitter conflicts ended. The Hundred Years' War was over. The War of the Roses (1455-85) between the lords of York and Lancaster was instrumental in the destruction of the power of regional nobility and the centralization of power in the hands of the kings. Henry VII (reigned 1485-1509) of the House of Tudor was victorious in the war. Through his marriage to the heiress of the House of York, he united England under his rule. Under his leadership, the English monarchy enjoyed the greatest power in the nation's history up until that time. Capitalizing upon his authority, Henry VIII (reigned 1509-47) centralized the government, implemented a schism from the Roman Church, and founded the Church of England.

The schism involved England, the papacy, and Spain. The ties between England and Spain were established through Henry's marriage to Catherine, the youngest of the three daughters of Ferdinand and Isabella. Although Catherine was married to Arthur, older brother of Henry, the union ended with the death of Arthur on April 2, 1502. Henry was forced to marry Catherine on June 11, 1509. This was not an event that Henry cherished. Mary Tudor (reigned 1553-58) was the only child who survived from this union. Henry's efforts to get Pope Clement VII (1523-34) to dissolve his marriage with Catherine were blocked by Emperor Charles V, the nephew of Catherine. When Henry's attempts failed, he led Parliament in May 1534 to separate from the Roman Church and establish the Church of England. On November 3, 1534, Parliament passed the Supremacy Act, which made Henry and his successors the heads of the English church.[3] By the time of Henry's death on January 28, 1547,[4] England was entrenched in its separation from Rome. The efforts of Queen Mary Tudor to revert England to Catholicism could not derail the nation's intent to maintain sovereignty over her choice of churches.

Luther, Reform, and Revival

A spiritual vacuum, persecution, clerical insensitivity toward the people, and the sale of indulgences, among other things, provided the conditions for the rise of Martin Luther in Saxony. Like a bugle in the night, Luther sounded the wake-up call across Europe. The religious abuse that aroused Luther past the point of no return was the sale of indulgences.

The Indulgence Controversy

Controversy began when Albrecht of Brandenburg borrowed money from Fugger's Bank in order to buy the archbishoprics of Mainz and Madgeburg in 1517. He decided to sell indulgences to raise the money to pay back the loan. Indulgences were not new. Pope Julius II (1503-13) used this method to raise money in 1506 to construct St. Peter's Cathedral in Rome. Indulgences actually dated back to the bull *Unigenitus* of Clement VI in 1343. The practice was expanded by Pope Sixtus IV in his bull, *Salvator Noster,* in 1476.[5] The Romans' view of salvation at this time was that a person could earn righteousness before God through good works and through the purchase of indulgences. McGrath wrote that for "a sum of three marks, a sinner could be released from all punishments that he would otherwise face in purgatory."[6]

Albrecht commissioned John Tetzel as the collector of the indulgence funds. Luther took particular exception to the message of Tetzel: "As soon as a coin in the coffers ring, a soul from purgatory springs." This was more than Luther could take. He was convinced that this practice was unscriptural and provided false hopes for the people. After preaching a series of sermons against indulgences, he devised and posted his famous Ninety-Five Theses on the cathedral door at Wittenberg on October 31, 1517.[7]

Luther could not have anticipated Rome's reaction. He had no desire to create a church schism but merely to engage in an academic debate over the validity of indulgences. However, the pope and church leaders were in no mood to debate the issue. Immediately, John of Eck, professor of theology at Ingolstadt, charged Luther with heresy. The Reformation lay on the horizon of human history, and no force on earth could stop it.

Contributions to Revival

For centuries, both the medieval and the Renaissance Roman Church had failed in her spiritual duties. Instead of standing against oppression, it oppressed; instead of providing protection, it used coercion; instead of offering mercy, it condemned; instead of showing love, it persecuted; instead of displaying understanding, it practiced intolerance; instead of bringing hope, it taught hopelessness; instead of teaching salvation by grace, it created constraints that shackled the spirit; instead of pointing people to Christ, it pointed people to itself; instead of extending compassion, it exercised control. Luther offered an attractive alternative that was challenging to the mind, appealing to the imagination, and moving to the heart. Indeed, the Christian church was at a crossroads: reform and revival or self-destruction. Luther's major contributions that impacted the revivals of the sixteenth century and beyond included his emphases upon saving faith, Scripture, preaching, and music. [8]

Saving Faith

If the Reformation for Luther could be reduced to one question, it would be: "How is a person saved?" Through years of diligent study and the crucible of experience, he concluded that a person is justified before God through faith. He related the futility of his own efforts to reach God through works:

> I was a monk, and kept my rule so strictly that I could say that if ever a monk could get to heaven through monastic discipline, I was that monk. All my companions in the monastery would confirm this. And yet my conscience would not give me certainty, but I always doubted and said, "You didn't do that right. You weren't contrite enough. You left that out of your confession." The more I tried to remedy an uncertain, weak and troubled conscience with human traditions, the more I daily found it more uncertain, weaker and more troubled.[9]

For Luther, a person is saved by faith alone. Nothing is added to or subtracted from this indispensable element in one's relationship to Jesus Christ. Since it is impossible to have revival without faith, this emphasis became the cornerstone for the spiritual awakenings in subsequent Christian history.

The Scriptures

Luther's contributions to the revivals through the translation of God's Word into German are immeasurable. While at the Wartburg Castle, he began translation of the New Testament in 1521 and published it in September 21, 1522. The complete

Bible was available in 1534. The primary translation of the Bible in use at the time was the 1226 "Paris Version" of Jerome's Latin Vulgate, which Jerome finished in A.D. 404.[10]

While Luther was certainly not the first to offer a translation of the Bible in German (eighteen German translations were already in existence),[11] Luther's labors made the Bible more readily available. The Roman Church discouraged the people from reading Scripture. One Catholic leader stated, "It is not according to the mind of God or of canonical scriptures that ignorant people should read holy scripture, but is reserved to priests and doctors alone."[12] Luther countered this attitude with a vigorous campaign to get the Bible into the hands of the laity. He believed that an informed laity was a powerful asset in his struggles against the Roman Church.

Copies of the Bible were rare and expensive. For example, in 1309, the nuns of the convent at Wasserler, Germany, sold a four-volume Bible to a nobleman for sixteen pieces of silver. Three years later, the same nuns bought 180 acres of land — including woods, a complete farm, and two farmhouses — or five pieces of silver.[13]

Three thousand copies of Luther's New Testament were printed and sold within the first three months. The price was one and one-half guilders per copy, the cost of living for two months for the average university student.[14] Copies printed after 1550 included user-friendly features such as chapter and verse divisions. These innovations to Scripture helped Christians check references and memorize biblical passages.

By the time of Luther's death, the Bible was more accessible to the populace than at any previous time in history. Luther stressed the importance of Scripture in a sermon that he preached in 1522: "I simply taught, preached, wrote God's Word; otherwise I did nothing . . . . the Word so greatly weakened the papacy that never a prince or emperor did such damage to it. I did nothing. The Word did it all."[15]

When the message of Scripture was unleashed upon human hearts, fire from heaven fell. The Bible was heaven's manna for the hungry soul; it was heaven's water for the parched spirit. Indeed, when the Word of God was read, understood, and applied to life, spiritual resolve rose to new levels, and God's people became an unconquerable force.

Preaching

The focus of medieval worship was the celebration of the sacraments. Although some preachers preached, they were the exceptions and not the rule. With Luther, the sermon returned to the central place in the worship service. Luther took seriously the command of Christ to preach the gospel and the teachings of Paul that faith comes through the hearing of the Word of God. From the legacy of Martin Luther, the term "preacher" became a common name for the clergy among reformers, replacing the name "priest.'[16] The major reformers and revival leaders of the era were first and foremost preachers. Once again, the importance of preaching God's Word was evidenced in the works of the sixteenth century Protestant leaders.

Church Music

With Martin Luther, music returned, and the church sang once again. Schaff wrote, "The most valuable contribution which German Protestantism made to Christian worship is its rich treasury of hymns."[17] Because Martin Luther was a gifted soloist and an accomplished flutist, he was called the "Nightingale of Wittenberg." He was not only an ardent collector of hymns and the publisher of four hymnals,[18] but he also was a songwriter of thirty-seven hymns. The most famous was the Lutheran battle hymn of the Reformation that he wrote on November 1, 1527, as a result of some turbulent experiences in his life the previous summer. It appeared in public for the first time in February 1528 under the title "A Mighty Fortress Is Our God."[19]

Luther said, "Music is one of the finest and most magnificent of God's gifts."[20] In a letter he wrote on October 4, 1530, he remarked, "after theology, no art can be compared with music."[21] Estep noted that some have given Luther the title "Father of Protestant Hymnody."[22] With the heart's release from spiritual bondage, songs of joy and victory were heard across Europe. Wherever revival leaders have served, music has been an integral part of the spiritual movements. The contributions of Luther to revivals through music can be weighed only on the scales of eternity.

By the time of Luther's death on February 18, 1546, Europe was ablaze with reform. The old church structure was not disposed to accept the new views that were rapidly capturing the attention of the people. The explosion of these new ideas on the European scene created a hunger that only the spiritual resources of heaven could meet.

Zwingli, Reform, and Revival

Uldrich Zwingli made several key contributions to spiritual awakenings through theological and church reforms. It was also out of the reform efforts of Zwingli in Zurich that the rise of the Anabaptists occurred.

The Reform of Zurich

Several experiences greatly impacted Zwingli, who was born on January 1, 1484, in the small village of Wildhaus, located high in the Toggenburg Mountains of Switzerland. By 1522, the reform in Switzerland was heating up. It burst into flames in March 1522 due to the desecration of the Roman practice of fasting during the Lenten season. Instead of fish, sausage was served at a dinner hosted by Christopher Froschauer for his employees and the local priests. Using Zwingli's sermons on the sole authority of Scripture as their source, they contended that it was not necessary to observe fasts. Immediately, the city council put the offenders in jail.

Instead of being conciliatory, Zwingli made a public issue of the matter when he preached a sermon on March 29, 1522, entitled "On the Choice and Freedom of Foods." The sermon was printed and distributed on April 16, 1522. He strongly advocated that the Bible does not require fasting. The city council ultimately agreed with Zwingli that fasting is a voluntary spiritual exercise.[23] However, the damage to the relationship with the Roman Church was done. Hugo von Hohenlandberg, Bishop of Constance, immediately launched an investigation of Zwingli.

The gap widened between the Zurich clergy and the Roman Church. On July 21, 1522, the city council approved Zwingli's practice of expository preaching, a vital step in effecting reform. In addition, Zwingli resigned as the priest of the Great Minster Church on October 10, 1522, and the city council promptly appointed him the preacher of Zurich. In this position, he was in place to lead the reform.[24] Tensions intensified when Leo Jud challenged the traditional use of the Mass and images in worship. A series of debates was arranged to discuss the issue.

Because the papacy was dependent upon Swiss mercenaries to fight papal military struggles, Pope Adrian VI wanted to avoid problems in Switzerland. When he received word of the impending debates, he wrote a conciliatory letter to Zwingli on January 23, 1523. However, it was too late. The sixty-seven articles of Zwingli were already published, and a debate was scheduled before the Zurich city council for January 29, 1523.

The debate drew over six hundred people. Zwingli and Jud easily defeated the Roman representatives, who were under the leadership of Johann Faber. Meeting Zwingli on his own turf and before a hostile assembly placed the opponents at an insurmountable disadvantage.

When Faber addressed the council, he shared that his mission was not one of debate but reconciliation. He sought a change of venue and challenged the competency of the gathered panel to judge such church matters. He also reminded the council that the recent Diet at Nuremberg promised an investigation into the matter. Faber said, "For, as I think, such matters are to be settled by a general Christian assembly of all nations, or by a council of bishops and other scholars as are found at universities."[25] Faber suggested the universities of Paris, Louvain, or Cologne, all strongholds of Roman orthodoxy, as the sites for the debate.

In ridicule, Zwingli suggested Erfurt or Wittenberg. As Zwingli addressed the council, he appealed to Scripture as the only source to judge the practices and doctrines of the church. At the end of the debate, the city council ruled in favor of Zwingli.

After the first debate, tensions in Zurich became even more intense, especially over the Roman view of the Mass, images used in worship, and the doctrine of purgatory. In an attempt to settle the issues, Zwingli, Jud, and the city council proposed another debate scheduled for October 26-28, 1523. Before an audience of some nine hundred people, Zwingli and Jud vigorously challenged Roman views. Although Zwingli and Jud insisted upon using the vernacular in the celebration of the Mass, the city council voted to retain Latin in its observance. The council adopted a policy of gradual change in its decision involving the use of icons. They appointed a committee of fourteen, including Zwingli and Jud, to resolve the matter.

After some reflection, Zwingli was pleased with the decision to approach the issue cautiously. However, a small group of Zwinglian followers, including Conrad Grebel, Felix Manz, and Simon Stumpf, wanted faster change and became disenchanted with Zwingli's leadership. These men were among the first leaders of the Anabaptist movement.

The final break of Zurich from Rome came in 1524-25. As a result of Zwingli's influence, the city council removed the icons from the seven churches in Zurich in the summer of 1524. In December 1524, the monasteries were dissolved. During holy week of 1525, the Mass was terminated, and the observance of the Lord's Supper in the vernacular as a memorial was implemented.

Ecclesiastical and doctrinal changes came in rapid succession. The sermon became the focal point of worship. The language of the people replaced Latin in worship services. Changes in the ecclesiastical structure of the clergy were implemented. During the spring of 1525, Zurich had completed the changes in reform. By the time of Zwingli's death on October 11, 1531, during the Second Kappel War, Switzerland was grounded in reform and would not be derailed in this spiritual resolve.

Theological Contributions to Revival

Revivals impact theology, and theology impacts revivals. Four basic areas of theology in the Zwinglian reform impacted subsequent revivals: predestination, because of its stress upon God's sovereignty; the Lord's Supper and baptism, because of their relationships to salvation; and Scripture, because of its centrality in awakenings.

Predestination. The debate over the doctrine of predestination is not new. It was a theological battleground in the sixteenth and seventeenth centuries. Even before Calvin, Zwingli, following the Augustinian tradition, advocated God's total sovereignty in all spiritual matters. Zwingli's views on predestination were expressed in two documents entitled *On True and False Religion* (1525) and *On the Providence of God* (1530), which was a revision of a sermon that he preached in October 1529 at the Marburg meeting with Luther. Timothy George writes:

> Zwingli, like Luther, saw predestination as a bulwark against works of righteousness. Since people do not elect God, but God chooses and singles them out, believers cannot claim any of the credit for their own salvation. . . . According to Zwingli, "election" should be attributed only to those whom God has destined for salvation. The reprobate are not "elected" to damnation, although, as a matter of fact, God "rejects, expels, and repudiates" them nonetheless. Zwingli did teach a doctrine of double predestination in both "election and rejection are the works of God's free will."[26]

Zwingli, like Calvin, viewed God's predestination as the source of all of His dealings with man. Thus, for Zwingli, revivals would be within the total discretion of God.

The Lord's Supper

During the Reformation, theological debate centered on how one has access to God. Crucial questions were crying out for answers:

What produces the right relationship with God?
Is a person reconciled to God through partaking in physical elements?
Is spiritual life the product of works?
Is spiritual life the result of an inward relationship with Christ?
What role does the priesthood of the believer play in one's relationship to God?

Since the Roman Church taught that salvation was obtained through the sacraments, spiritual power carne through the church. Thus, the Roman Church did not see the importance of revival. For Christians to have personal relationships with Christ, a shift in the theological meaning of the Lord's Supper was important.

Zwingli was primarily responsible for the view that the Lord's Supper is a memorial observance. Zwingli reduced the number of sacraments from seven to two: the Lord's Supper and baptism. At the Council of Verona/Florence in 1439-40, the Roman Church had adopted the seven sacraments of Peter Lombard as the official positions of the Church. He completely rejected the Roman position of transubstantiation and Luther's view of consubstantiation. He said that the Roman Mass was "a blasphemous undertaking, a very work of Antichrist. Christ our Redeemer gave us this only as a food and a memorial of his suffering and his covenant."[27]

For Zwingli, the Eucharist was not the vehicle of salvation that the papacy claimed it to be. Whereas Luther viewed the Eucharist as a gift from God to the church that generates faith, Zwingli believed that it was a memorial to the atoning work of Christ and should be celebrated as an act of allegiance to Christ on the part of the participant.

By the time of the Reformation, the Mass had evolved theologically to the point that only the clergy was permitted to celebrate the observance. and the congregation was relegated to the role of spectator, except at Easter. Since the service was for the clergy only, Latin was the language used in its observance.

Zwingli believed strongly that the people should be participants and that the celebration should be in the vernacular. Although he tried to persuade the Zurich city council to make the change in 1523, it was not until April 13, 1525, that the people were successful in celebrating the Eucharist as a congregation and in German. Once the reformed practice of Zwingli was in place, the Last Supper was celebrated four times a year.[28]

This theological shift in the meaning of the Lord's Supper moved the emphasis of spiritual vitality from outward works to inward relationships. This move was important for later revivals.

Baptism

Zwingli viewed the ordinances as supportive of faith, not producers of faith. Just as the Last Supper was the participants' testimony to membership in God's family, so baptism was the participants' confession of faith in Christ to the congregation. For

Zwingli, baptism was not an act of regeneration; rather, it had instructional purposes and was a sign of uniting with the church family and committing one's life to Christ.

Like the other reformers, Zwingli accepted the validity of infant baptism. He, too, insisted that the baptism of a child was an obligation and a pledge on the part of the parents to give Christian instruction to the child as the child grew into adulthood. This view was foundational for *Covenant Theology*, the theological position of many modern Protestant churches who practice infant baptism. Zwingli stressed "children born to Christian parents are heirs of the covenant given in the Old Testament and renewed in the New Testament, therefore baptism is not dependent upon personal faith since it is a sign of the predestination of the elect."[29]

Scriptures

The Bible was central in the Zwinglian reform. Influenced by Wyttenbach and Erasmus, Zwingli believed that the Scriptures were the source for truth, divine law, doctrine, church polity and practice, and guidance in life. In his disputation before the city council in January 1523, Zwingli appealed to Scripture as authority for judging church matters. When he faced Luther at the Marburg Colloquy in 1529, Zwingli challenged Luther to use Scripture to prove him wrong in his views on the Lord's Supper. For Zwingli, the Bible was the guide for Christian living.

In 1522 Zwingli preached a sermon to the nuns at Oetenbach entitled "On the Clarity and Certainty of the Word of God." He stated, "The foundation of our religion is the written Word, the Scriptures of God."[30] In thirteen of his sixty-seven theses, he stressed that God's Word could be understood only as interpreted to the individual by the Holy Spirit.

The power of the spoken word was evidenced in all of the reformers, especially Zwingli. When the proclamation of the gospel was once again the focal point of worship, the Holy Spirit anointed their preaching and moved with power within the hearts of the people. Through preaching, Zwingli changed the spiritual scenery of Switzerland and left a legacy for other preachers to follow.

Calvin, Reform, and Revival

How do revivals start? This question has been debated for centuries. Differences of opinion in this area have primarily focused upon the views of John Calvin and Jacob Arminius in the area of predestination. Since this doctrine centers on God's sovereignty, one's view of predestination will determine one's belief on how revivals begin. At the heart of predestination are divine sovereignty and human free will. This discussion raises many questions:

What role does God play in revivals?
What part does man play?
Are revivals simply the divine invasions of God into human affairs with little or no participation on the part of the Christian?

Are Christians merely pawns on God's divine revival chessboard?
Do revivals occur primarily because of the efforts of Christians in their search for spiritual fulfillment?
Are revivals the products of human formulas?
Are revivals primarily prayed down, worked up, or the result of the cooperation between God and Christians?

Jonathan Edwards and George Whitefield were staunch Calvinistic predestinarians who believed that revivals were within the sovereign will of God. John Wesley and Charles Finney were more Arminian with their focus on man's free will. They stressed that Christians, in the exercise of free will, played major roles in the emergence of revivals. Since the Reformation, leaders of both persuasions have served as revival catalysts.

Institutes of the Christian Religion

The views of John Calvin (1509-64) on predestination are found in his book *Institutes of the Christian Religion.* The event that influenced the writing of this book occurred on October 17, 1534. In protest to the Mass, some of the reformers in Paris posted placards across the city. King Francis, who was indebted to Pope Clement VII for gaining his release from Charles V's prison in Spain, supported the papacy in the suppression of reform. He responded to the placards with a vengeance. By January 1535, some two hundred reformers were imprisoned, and twenty were killed. One of the victims was Calvin's close friend, Estienne de la Forge.

In defense of his persecuted friends, Calvin finished a work that he had started while a student in Paris. It was published in March 1536 under the title *Institutes of the Christian Religion*. He prefaced the work with a letter to Francis, which is considered one of the strongest apologies for the Reformation written by any reformer. The *Institutes* were revised and expanded seven times, with the last edition published in 1559.

Predestination

Timothy George summarizes Calvin's doctrine on predestination in three words: absolute, particular, and double. By *absolute,* Calvin meant that salvation is not conditioned by man, but rests solely within the unchanging will of God. By *particular,* he meant that salvation is for individuals and not for groups of people. By *double,* he meant that some people are ordained by God to receive eternal life while others are ordained to be condemned.[31] He believed that God preordained the destinies of human beings prior to the foundations of Creation. Calvin wrote: "By predestination we mean the eternal decree of God, by which he determined with himself whatever he wished to happen with regard to every man. All are not created on equal terms, but some are preordained to eternal life, others to eternal damnation; and, accordingly, as each has been created for one or the other of these ends, we say that he has been predestined to life or to death."[32]

For those who judged from this statement on predestination that Calvin believed God to be the author of sin, he wrote, "They are ignorant and malicious who say that God is the author of sin, since all things are done by his will or ordination; for they do not distinguish between the manifest wickedness of men and the secret judgments of God."[33]

The Arminian Challenge

When Calvin died at sunset on May 27, 1564, the scepter of leadership in Geneva passed to his son-in-law and former student, Theodore Besa (1519-1605), who was also rector at the university. Within a few years, Besa had a student by the name of Jacob Arminius (1560-1609), father of Arminian theology.

The flames of controversy over predestination reached new intensity when Arminius succeeded Franciscus Junius (1545-1602) as professor of theology at the University of Leyden in 1603. He was immediately opposed on predestination by a faculty colleague, Franciscus Gomarus (1563-1641), an adamant supralapsarian Calvinist (see below). For Arminius, the views of Calvin made God the author of sin, regardless of what Calvin said.

The Arminian position was greatly strengthened when Jan van Oldenbarneveldt (1547-1619), a dominant political figure in Holland, and Hugo Grotius (1583-1645), who is considered the Father of International Law, became strong vocal supporters of the Arminian view. For their efforts, Oldenbarneveldt was beheaded by Maurice of Nassau on May 13, 1619. Grotius was imprisoned.

Following the death of Arminius in 1609, the leadership of the Arminian group was assumed by Johannes Uitenbogaert (1557-1644), a close friend of Arminius. In 1610, he, Simon Episcopius (a former student of Arminius at Leyden), and forty-two other ministers helped draft the five articles of Arminianism. These Five Articles of Remonstrance were adopted as the official positions of Arminianism on predestination on January 10, 1610.

1. Free will and human ability. Arminius taught that human nature was seriously affected by the Fall, but he denied total depravity. He stressed that every person has the opportunity to believe in Christ. His freedom rests in his ability to choose good over evil. A person has the power to cooperate with Christ and be saved or to reject Christ and be condemned. The salvation process is dependent upon the Holy Spirit, for without Him man cannot be saved. A person's contribution to his salvation is faith in Christ.

2. Conditional election. Election is determined by what man does in salvation. For Arminius, faith is not given to the lost person by God, but is the product of man's free will. It is left up to the person in regard to who is elected. God in His omniscience knows who will and who will not respond, but man in his free will determines the issue.

3. General atonement. Although Christ died for all mankind, all human beings will not be saved. The death of Christ is effectual only in the lives of those who exercise faith and choose to accept the gift of eternal life.

4. Resistible grace. The Holy Spirit works equally in the lives of all people, but through free will man has the power to reject the in-working grace of the Holy Spirit. The Holy Spirit draws to Christ only those who are willing to be drawn. The person must respond in cooperation with Christ in order to be saved. Thus, the grace of God can be resisted.

5. Falling from grace. Although there are differences of opinion among Arminians, the dominant view is that man can lose his salvation. By neglecting Christ, a person can lose his position in God's family.

The Council of Dort, 1618-19

In response to the Arminian views, the followers of Calvin met at the Council of Dordrecht, or Dort, from November 13, 1618, to May 9, 1619, in the town of Dordrecht, Holland. On April 23, 1619, they adopted the five points of Calvinism that are called supralapsarianism, five-point Calvinism, or high Calvinism.

1. Total depravity. Because of the Fall, man is unable to choose God over evil. His will is not free but is enslaved by sin, and he is unable to believe the gospel for his salvation. Salvation is not a matter of cooperation between the Holy Spirit and the lost person, but is totally the work of the Spirit. Faith is not man's contribution to salvation, but is given to the elected person as a gift from God as a part of regeneration.

2. Unconditional election. Salvation resides within the sovereign will of God. Election is not determined by one's response to God in faith; rather, God gives faith to those whom He selects for salvation. Thus, election is not determined by anything that man does, but is the result of God's selection. Salvation is God's choice of man, and not man's choice of God.

3. Limited atonement. Christ did not die for all mankind; rather, he died for the elect only. Through His death, Christ achieved the totality of salvation, including the element of faith. Thus, the death of Christ was for those whom God foreordained for salvation.

4. Irresistible grace. There are two calls of God for salvation: an outward call and an inward call. All receive the outward call, but only the elect receive the inward call. Since the inward call is necessary for salvation, only the elect are saved. It is impossible for those who receive the inward call to resist the grace of God. Thus, God's grace is irresistible.

5. Perseverance of the Saints. All who are chosen by God, are redeemed in Christ, and receive saving faith are eternally secure in their salvation. Since salvation is the work of God, He is the one who is responsible for the perseverance of salvation.[34]

Regardless of one's persuasion regarding God's sovereignty, revival is God's divine invasion into the lives of His people for the purpose of awakening them from their spiritual slumber and turning their hearts toward the eternal issues in life. Revival focuses upon the eternal springs of heavenly joy and creates an insatiable desire in the human heart for heaven's greatest treasure. This divine activity is evident in the lives of those in the sixteenth century who dared to establish heaven's standard as earth's norm.

> Revival focuses upon the eternal springs of heavenly joy and creates an insatiable desire in the human heart for heaven's greatest treasure.

The Anabaptists, Reform, and Revival

Out of the Zwinglian reform in Zurich, the Anabaptists, also called the Radical Reformers, emerged. The term *radical* was applied to the members of this group because of their adamancy toward doctrinal positions, especially in regard to religious liberty, new birth, believer's baptism, and the Lord's Supper.[35] The name *Anabaptist* was a derisive term given to them because of their rejection of infant baptism and their practice of believer's baptism. Since this was a radical departure from the church norm, they immediately encountered opposition not only from the Catholics but also from reformers. Luther called them "swarms of raving fanatics — 'too many bees chasing too many bonnets.'"[36] Other reformers called them "spiritualists" and "fanatics."

There were significant differences between the reformers and the Anabaptists. The reformers focused on altering doctrines and church practices; the Anabaptists, although stressing these issues, majored upon spiritual conversions. The reformers enjoyed political protection; the Anabaptists served without civil protection and were persecuted not only by Catholics but also by Protestants. The reformers usually served in localized regions; the Anabaptists were usually on the move. Followers of the reformers simply switched allegiance from the Roman Church to the respective reformer's position, regardless of spiritual change; followers of the Anabaptists joined the movement as results of spiritual conversions.

Some of the Anabaptist preachers served in the midst of personal revivals, as evidenced in many of their own martyrdoms and the phenomenal evangelistic results that accompanied their preaching. In some ways, they were similar to the first-century church, especially in their emphases upon conversion and the fact that they were consistently on the run as they fled persecution.

Anabaptists in Zurich, 1523-29

When Zwingli agreed with the Zurich council on the policy of caution in the debate in October 1523, some of his more avid followers, especially Conrad Grebel, Felix Manz, and Simon Stumpf, became discontented with his leadership. This disenchantment was because of Zwingli's failure to press the council to abolish the Mass and because of what these followers considered compromise on Zwingli's part in regards to other issues. On December 23, 1523, Stumpf was exiled from Zurich because of his vocal opposition to the council's decision.[37] Out of the schism that followed, the Anabaptist group was formed.

The ultimate split with Zwingli occurred following a public debate on January 17, 1525, between the two sides before the Zurich council. After the council judged that Zwingli won the debate, the Anabaptists felt that they had no recourse than to sever relationships with Zwingli. The Anabaptists, known as the Swiss Brethren in Zurich, were officially launched on January 21, 1525, when Grebel baptized George Blaurock from Chur by pouring in the home of Felix Manz.[38] Following his baptism, Blaurock baptized the other members of the group. This event was in a very real sense the birthday of the evangelical Free Church Movement. By the end of January, some eighty people were baptized. When the city leaders heard what the Anabaptists had done, they passed legislation on February 8, 1525, that levied a fine or banishment upon all who were rebaptized.

Rebaptism carried with it the death penalty. During the reigns of Emperors Theodosius (reigned 379-395) and Justinian (reigned 527-565), rebaptism was ruled to be a crime punishable by death. The edict issued by Theodosius was in response to the Donatists in North Africa.

The Donatists concluded that any priest who denied the Christian faith during the Diocletian persecution that erupted on February 23, 303, was not eligible to baptize any person. Those who were baptized by a lapsed priest received an invalid baptism. Because of these views, they rebaptized those who had been baptized by lapsed priests. This practice was creating a crisis within the Empire, and Theodosius wanted no part of a religious schism. When the emperor ruled against the practice, the Roman Church followed this edict. Justinian affirmed this edict.

Believer's baptism was an affront to the doctrinal positions of Rome and the reform leaders. The theological superstructure of the Catholics centered on the saving efficacy of baptism. The reformers accepted infant baptism as a valid expression of faith. Thus, when the Anabaptists advocated believer's baptism, they were challenging the views of both the Roman and the reformed churches. Luther wrote, "Faith does not exist for the sake of baptism, but baptism for the sake of faith. . . . Baptism is valid even though faith is lacking. . . . Baptism does not become invalid even if it is wrongly received or used."[39] In addition to the Zurich council's action in 1525, Charles V issued an edict at the Diet of Speyers in 1529 that provided the death penalty for anyone who rebaptized. On April 23, 1529, King Ferdinand of Austria ordered the death penalty for rebaptism.

For centuries, the Roman Church practiced salvific baptism for infants. The reformers retained infant baptism with their own interpretations. However, the Anabaptists understood baptism as an outward testimony of an inward change; thus, believer's baptism. From their belief about "believer's baptism," they received their name: "Anabaptists."

At first, the method of baptism was not an issue. However, in February 1525, Conrad Grebel baptized Wolfgang Ulimann by immersion in the Rhine River in the vicinity of Schaffhausen. This was the first recorded observance of baptism by immersion within the Reformation.

Conrad Grebel. Among the initial leaders of the Anabaptists was Conrad Grebel (c.1498-1526), the son of a prominent member of the Great Council of Zurich.

In November 1521, Grebel joined the followers of Zwingli. However, Grebel was far more zealous than Zwingli in his reform attempts. Through his leadership, the split between Zwingli and the Anabaptists occurred. Following the baptismal event that formed the Anabaptists in Zurich, the men began a house-to-house witnessing campaign and both baptized and observed the Lord's Supper.[40]

As they emphasized a personal relationship with Jesus Christ, the response was phenomenal. A spiritual awakening ignited in the lives of individuals and within certain communities. Persecution forced the small band of Anabaptist leaders to leave Zurich. Some journeyed to the nearby towns of St. Gall and Zollikon, preaching and witnessing as they went. A revival followed.

When the refreshing news of the message of salvation by faith in Christ was heard for the first time by the people in those small villages, a new hope sprang up in their hearts. The responses were overwhelming. On April 9, 1525, Grebel and other Anabaptist leaders baptized some five hundred people in the Sitter River at St. Gall.[41]

As the movement spread, the persecution increased. Justo Gonzalez notes that, because of believer's baptism, there were probably more martyrs among the Anabaptists than in the combined first three centuries of the Christian church.[42] Many of the Anabaptists had to go into hiding, including Grebel. On October 8, 1525, Grebel was arrested in Grunigen, east of Zurich. At the trial, the testimonies of Protestants, including Zwingli's accusation of sedition, were brought against Grebel and Blaurock. Although the evidence was extremely weak, the Anabaptist leaders were sentenced to imprisonment for an indefinite term on November 18, 1525.

While in prison, Grebel, a recognized scholar among the Anabaptists, wrote his views on believer's baptism. This document has been lost, but some of the contents are contained in Zwingli's rebuttal entitled *Refutation of the Tricks of the Baptists of 1527*.[43] At his retrial on March 5-6, 1526, Grebel was sentenced to life imprisonment. Within a few days, he escaped with the help of sympathizers and traveled through the villages of Switzerland, preaching and witnessing. During August 1526, he died at Meinfield in the Oberland.

Felix Manz. Following the youthful death of Grebel, the mantle of leadership was passed to Felix Manz (1498-1527). He was a leader in the revival at St. Gall, though his leadership was short-lived. On October 12, 1526, he was arrested in St. Gall, released for a few days, and arrested again in November. In December 1526, he and Blaurock were transferred to Zurich for trial. Since Blaurock was not a citizen of Zurich, he was whipped with rods at the Niederdorf Gate and exiled from the city.[44] However, on January 5, 1527, at three o'clock in the afternoon, Manz was drowned, symbolic of baptism by immersion, in the Limmat River in Zurich. His martyrdom exemplifies the commitment of a servant who labors in the midst of revival. As he was taken to the place of execution, he witnessed to the crowds along the way. The voice of his mother could be heard above the subdued noise of the people as she exhorted her son to remain true to Jesus Christ. As he was lowered into the icy waters of the Limmat River, his last words were, "Father, into thy hands, I commend my spirit."

Manz became the first recorded Anabaptist martyr at the hands of Protestants.[45] The courage of Manz and other martyrs was a demonstration of conviction and faith in Jesus Christ. As martyrdom became a hallmark of the Anabaptists, their opponents saw resolve that no coercion could stop. Although Manz did not live long enough to leave a legacy of writings, he did compose a hymn that is still sung among the Mennonites, "I Sing with Exultation."

George Blaurock. The first official Anabaptist was Georg Cajacob, better known as George Blaurock. After his arrival in Zurich, the name Blaurock, which means "bluecoat," was given to him because he often wore a blue coat. He was born in about 1491 in Bonaduz, Switzerland, attended Leipzig for a time, entered the priesthood, and served at Chur. He became disenchanted with the Roman Church, resigned from the priesthood, and journeyed to Zurich to join Zwingli's reform movement. When he arrived in Zurich, he was introduced to a small group, including Grebel and Manz, who were more akin in spirit with his views for reform.

Blaurock's zeal was unparalleled among the Anabaptists. Constantly on the run and often in jail, Blaurock had incredible success wherever he preached. In spite of persecution, Blaurock preached to large crowds, and the evangelistic results were phenomenal. Revival often broke out as he preached. In one service at Zollikon, 150 people made decisions for Christ.[46] Blaurock was another example of one Christian, aflame with spiritual fire, who was used of God to reach multitudes for Christ.

Music played an important role in Blaurock's ministry. He wrote two hymns that were often sung among the Mennonites. On August 14, 1529, he was arrested in Innsbruck, tried, convicted, and sentenced to death. On September 6, 1529, Blaurock was burned at the stake in Klausen, Italy.[47] With his death, the original leaders of the Zurich Anabaptists were dead.

Spread of the Anabaptists

As the Anabaptists fled to other parts of Europe, such as Moravia and Holland, they preached as they went. The Anabaptists grew rapidly. They found immediate allies in the Utraquists, the followers of John Huss. Under the leadership of Hans Hut and Leonhard Schiemer, a spiritual movement occurred in Moravia, and the Anabaptist membership grew quickly to twelve thousand. In Germany, the movement grew to more than eighteen thousand.

Their greatest success, however, was achieved in Holland under the leadership of Menno Simons and his successor, Leenaert Bouwens. By the time of his death in 1582, Bouwens listed the names of 10,378 people that he had personally baptized.[48] John Smyth and his English Separatists sought to join this group in the seventeenth century. In certain parts of Holland, one-fourth of the population embraced the views of the Anabaptists. Still, the success carried a heavy price. Paulus Scharpff noted that fifteen hundred Anabaptists were martyred in Holland by 1574.[49]

Balthasar Hubmaier in Southern Germany. Often, revivals need scholars to chronicle the events, systemize theological views, and offer defenses for the movements. The Anabaptist revival movement had that scholarship, especially in Balthasar Hubmaier (1480-1528) and Pilgram Marpeck (c. 1490-1556). Hubmaier was born in Friedberg, outside of Augsburg, and received his Doctor of Theology degree in

1512 from Ingolstadt University. He taught theology and served as the chaplain of the university church at Ingolstadt. In 1521 he moved to Waldshut on the Rhine. During 1522, Hubmaier went to Switzerland and was introduced to the Swiss reform. Upon his return to Waldshut, he searched the Scriptures in order to validate what he had heard from the Swiss reformers. On December 22, 1522, as he preached from the Gospel of Luke, the message resounded with an evangelical note and the reformer emerged. Although it is uncertain as to the exact time of his conversion, it was probably during the time of his scriptural search at Waldshut. In a letter he wrote to the city council at Regensberg in 1524, he noted that he had been a Christian for two years: "Therefore I openly confess before God and all men, that I then became a doctor and preached some years among you and elsewhere, and yet had not known the way unto eternal life. Within two years has Christ for the first time come into my heart to thrive. I have never dared to preach him so boldly as now, by the grace of God. I lament before God that I so long lay ill of this sickness, I pray him truly for pardon; I did this unwittingly"[50]

By March 1523, Hubmaier was back in Waldshut and was now a reformer. Encountering opposition from both government and church authorities, he left Waldshut on August 29, 1524, and took refuge in Schaffhausen. While in exile at Schaffhausen, he wrote a thirty-six-article document called *Concerning Heretics and Those Who Burn Them,* the most definitive work against persecution written during the Reformation. By October 1524, he was back in Waldshut, and the reform accelerated. On April 15, 1525, Hubmaier and the Waldshut church officially joined the Anabaptist movement when they were baptized by Wilhelm Reublin, the first Anabaptist to preach against infant baptism.

Through the pen of Hubmaier, the positions of the Anabaptists were crystallized and recorded. His views first appeared in 1523 in his "Eighteen Articles." At the heart of his theology was believer's baptism. In 1525, he wrote several works on the biblical meaning of baptism. His definition of baptism was a radical departure from the prevailing views of the Roman Church and the reformers:

> Baptism in the name of the Father and of the Son and of the Holy Ghost is when a man first confesses his sins, and pleads guilty; then believes in the forgiveness of his sins through Jesus Christ and therefore proceeds to live according to the rule of Christ by the grace and strength given him by God the Father, Son, and the Holy Ghost. Then he professes this publicly, in the eyes of men, by the outward baptism of water.[51]

Like the Anabaptist leaders before him, he was arrested. While in the Vienna prison, he was subjected to inhuman torture. On March 10, 1528, he was marched out to his place of execution and burned at the stake. Stephanus Sprugel, dean at the University of Vienna, provided an eyewitness account. Hubmaier was escorted by armed guards and followed by a large crowd to the place of execution. As he looked upon the pyre of brush and fagots, he rendered the testimony that marked his life during his leadership as an Anabaptist: "O gracious God, in this my great torment, forgive my sins. O Father, I give you thanks that you will today take me out of this vale of tears. I desire to die with rejoicing and come to you. O Lamb, O Lamb, take away the sins of the world. O God, into your hands I commit my spirit." Looking at the crowd, he said, "O dear brothers and sisters, if I have injured anyone, in word or deed, may they forgive me for the sake of my merciful God. I forgive all of those who have harmed me." He then spoke in Latin, "O Lord, into your hands I commit my spirit." As the executioner rubbed sulphur and gunpowder into his beard, he said, "O salt me well, salt me well."

As the flames consumed his body, he prayed, "O my heavenly Father, O my gracious God."[52] When the fire began to burn his beard and hair, he cried his last words with a loud voice, "O Jesus, Jesus."[53] Three days later, his beloved wife, Elsbeth, was thrown into the Danube River with a huge stone tied around her neck.[54] With the death of Hubmaier, not only a revival leader but also the voice and pen of the first theologian of the Anabaptists was silenced.

Michael Sattler in Southern Germany and Strasbourg. The list of martyrs among the Anabaptists is long, since very few of the early leaders died of natural causes. Their heroism paralleled the martyrs of the early church. In the martyrdom of Michael Sattler on Tuesday, May 21, 1527, an example of the cruelty inflicted upon them by others who abused power to subdue opposing views is discerned.

The indictment read: "Michael Sattler shall be committed to the executioner. The latter shall take him to the square and there first cut out his tongue, and then forge him fast to a wagon and there with glowing tongs twice tear pieces from his body, and then on the way to the site of execution five times more as above and then burn his body to powder as an arch-heretic."[55]

The torment began in the marketplace. Although a large part of his tongue was cut out, he could still speak. As he prayed for his executioners, he also exhorted them to repent. The processional to his place of execution was a mile long. Along the way, the descriptions of torture in the indictment were fulfilled. When he arrived at the appointed place, he again appealed to the crowd to repent and be converted. He lifted his head toward heaven and prayed, "Almighty, eternal God, you are the way and the truth; since no one has been able to prove this as error, I shall with your help this day testify to the truth and seal it with my blood."[56]

As the fire was consuming his life, he lifted his voice in praise to God. Moore describes the last moments of Sattler's martyrdom: "When the ropes on his hands had burned through, he raised the forefingers of both hands, thereby giving the signal he had agreed on before with his fellow believers to indicate that such a dying was bearable and that he remained in the faith. Then he cried out, 'Father into Thy hands I commend my spirit.'"[57]

While their opponents thought that persecution would end the Anabaptist movement, it only made the group spread. Like the New Testament Christians, persecution merely deepened their faith. Roland Bainton cited an Anabaptist chronicler of the Reformation period who listed the names of 2,173 martyrs and described their heroism:

> No human being was able to take away out of their hearts what they had experienced. . . . The fire of God burned within them. They would die ten deaths rather than forsake the divine truth. They had drunk of the water which is flowing from God's sanctuary, yea of the water of life. Their tent they had pitched not here on earth, but in eternity. Their faith blossomed like a lily, their loyalty as a rose, their piety and candor as the flower of the garden of God. The angel of the Lord battled for them that they could not be deprived of the helmet of salvation. Therefore they have borne all torture and agony without fear. The things of this world they counted only as shadows. They were thus drawn unto God that they knew nothing, sought nothing, desired nothing, loved nothing but God alone. Therefore they had more patience in their suffering than their enemies in tormenting them.[58]

Menno Simons in Holland and Northern Germany. Whereas the reform movements had few major leaders, the Anabaptists had many.[59] It seemed that when one was martyred, two or three would take his place. One of the most important was Menno Simons (1496-1561). It is difficult to pinpoint specific revivals in his ministry. To classify his work as revival, one must consider his life and far-reaching influence. There can be no argument that Menno Simons served with spiritual zeal that was akin to spiritual awakening, and the results were in proportion to those experienced when awakening occurs.

In 1536, Simons of Holland became officially an Anabaptist. With this decision, the Anabaptists gained their greatest leader. Under his leadership, Holland and northern Germany resounded with spiritual vitality. In April 1535 he was converted. In 1536, he made the decision to become an Anabaptist.

Simons labored initially in Holland, briefly in Freisland, and the last eighteen years of his life in northern Germany. When the edict to banish all Anabaptists from Gronigen was issued on January 21, 1539, he went to a more tolerant climate in Freisland. Constantly on the run, he preached and witnessed as he traveled. Emperor Charles V placed a price of one hundred gold guilders on his head. Amnesty was offered to prisoners for information leading to the arrest of Simons. Other rewards were offered to anyone who would help the authorities capture him. Every effort failed.

In 1543, he moved to northern Germany. The movement experienced outstanding success even though persecution awaited anyone who embraced Anabaptist views. Multitudes were converted. Churches were started and their numbers grew. Menno Simons was so successful that by the time of his death on January 31, 1561, the Anabaptists in northern Germany and elsewhere had assumed the name of Mennonites.

Simons wrote profusely and experienced astounding success in reaching converts. Among his most important works were *Christian Baptism* (1539), *Foundations for Christian Doctrine* (1540), and *True Christian Faith* (1541).[60] The themes of his ministry included Scripture as the ultimate authority, believer's baptism, and personal conversion by faith in Christ. Estep called him the "Theologian of the New Birth."[61]

Like other revival leaders throughout history, Anabaptist leaders put Christ first in life. In addition, they sealed their testimonies with their lives. Tertullian's statement, "The blood of the martyrs is the seed of the church" once again rang true among the Anabaptists.

Revival Emphases Among the Anabaptists

The contributions of the Anabaptists to subsequent revivals focused upon spiritual piety, religious liberty, Scripture, and new birth in Christ. The Anabaptists could be called the forerunners to the Pietists of the seventeenth and eighteenth centuries. Indeed, long before Spener, Francke, and Zinzendorf, the Anabaptists sounded the clarion call for piety, the hallmark of every revival.

Spiritual Piety. The Anabaptists preached and practiced piety. The people of Europe took notice of their commitment to Christ. Their opponents may have rejected some of the Anabaptist doctrines, but they could not find fault with their irreproachable lives.

In 1527 Capito, the leading reformer in Strasbourg, wrote, "I frankly confess that in most Anabaptists there is in evidence piety and consecration and indeed a zeal which is beyond any suspicion of sincerity. For what earthly advantage could they hope to win by enduring exile, torture, and unspeakable punishment upon the flesh. I testify before God that I cannot say that on account of the lack of wisdom they are somewhat indifferent toward earthly things, but rather from divine motives."[62]

Estep cites Sebastian Frank, a contemporary of the sixteenth-century Anabaptists: "The Anabaptists soon gained a large following drawing many sincere souls who had a zeal for God, for they taught nothing but love, faith, and the cross. They showed themselves humble, patient under much suffering; they break bread with one another as evidence of unity and love . . . They died as martyrs, patiently and humbly enduring all persecution."[63]

Again, Franz Agricola, a Roman Catholic theologian in the same era, testified: "As concerns their outward public life they are irreproachable. No lying, deception, swearing, strife, harsh language, no intemperate eating and drinking, no outward personal display, is found among them, but humility, patience, uprightness, neatness, honesty, temperance, straight-forwardness, in such measure that one would suppose that they had the Holy Spirit of God."[64]

The legacy of this faithful group is immeasurable in human equations. Their lives exemplified the highest Christian standards. They lived Christian lives that were patterned after the New Testament norm. Indeed, many of those early Anabaptist leaders served in the midst of revival. Roland Bainton wrote: "The worth of the Anabaptists' endeavor is not to be judged in the light of their contribution to history. They took their stand in the light of eternity regardless of what might or might not happen in history "[65]

Religious Liberty. The concept of religious liberty was a vital part of the revival movement of the Anabaptists in the sixteenth century. Almost two hundred years before John Locke of England emphasized religious liberty, the Anabaptists adopted this theme as a hallmark of their ministry. Persecuted by Catholics, Protestants, and civil governments, this group migrated to several places in Europe, seeking places to exercise faith according to the dictates of their consciences.

The Anabaptists, like the first-century Christians, were a people without a country. Because of this courageous group, religious liberty became one of the major contributions to the subsequent history of Christianity. This conviction carried with it a great price.

The Scriptures. The Bible became the foundation for the Anabaptist's faith and practice. They uncompromisingly believed that the Bible was the sole authority for the church and Christian living. Three major topics from Scripture became their cornerstones: salvation through faith, baptism, and the Lord's Supper.

While the battle cry of Luther was "justification by faith," the Anabaptists gave the expression new meaning. Luther struggled to reconcile his views on faith and infant baptism, but the Anabaptists stressed that faith is a response to God by people who have the ability to make intelligent decisions. They were immovable in their conviction that the new birth comes through faith in Jesus Christ. As a testimony to this saving faith, a person was baptized as a believer. In addition, the Anabaptists were grounded in their views on the symbolism of the Lord's Supper and baptism as for believers only. These convictions cost them their lives.

At the beginning of the sixteenth century, every nation in Europe was Catholic. By the time of the death of Scottish reformer John Knox at eleven o'clock on the evening of November 24, 1572, the religious map of Europe had been permanently redrawn.[66] The reform brought out the worst in men as intolerance led to martyrdom. It also brought out the best in men as the courage of the leaders of reform and revival and the heroism of the martyrs demonstrated that death cannot stop the march of the Church of Jesus Christ. The fires that burned within the lives of these Christians ignited hosts of Europeans to the point that history was permanently redirected. The debts that the modern Protestant churches owe to those faithful few cannot be repaid, but those debts must never be forgotten.

Questions for Discussion

1. Luther and others in this chapter show us that theology and revival go together. What theological convictions do you hold to without wavering? Do you sometimes confuse your personal preferences for unchanging truth?

2. We see various movements in this time period with varying views between the leaders. What does this teach us about how God can send revival to a variety of Christian traditions at the same time?

Introduction to Part Two
Spiritual Awakening Movements in the Modern Era

In her fascinating study of evangelical youth, author and researcher Lauren Sandler offers several observations about Christian young people today. Although not a believer herself, Sandler is a believer in movements. She makes a general observation about spiritual movements:

> Awakenings grow out of a historical moment in which social behavior has begun to deviate from traditional norms; widespread cultural disorientation and anxiety result from a time of opposing messages. A religious revival takes root, growing underground throughout the nation, eventually transforming the way we live.[1]

Sandler echoes what historians have noted. "Again and again when Christianity seemed moribund," Latourette observed, "Revivals broke out within it."[2]

More recently, Mark Shaw argued that revival movements in the twentieth century provided the force to spread Christianity globally in unprecedented ways.[3] In the pages that follow, I hope to build on what my co-author Malcolm wrote to show the reader how this has occurred in modern history. Sandler goes on, adding the specific role of the younger generation in such spiritual renewal:

> [Young people] want to reverse the flow of a river, not change its course. To reach a nation, a population needs to be redirected away from old institutions toward a radical new culture. An awakening entails young people reinventing traditional rituals, making the faith of their forefathers their own. This isn't just an observation on the MTV age—it's been the final stage of every awakening before a national transformation is complete. To hit critical mass, it takes a youth movement.[4]

People in their very nature reflect a spiritual inquisitiveness. Everyone worships something or someone. Our culture recognizes this fact. Philosopher James K.A. Smith in *Desiring the Kingdom* offers a fascinating look at shopping malls and their appeal to our worshipping tendency as they draw us in with our love of beauty. Watch zealous fans at a ball game or youth at a concert, and you will see unfettered devotion. Augustine said it well in his famous prayer: "Thou hast made us for Thyself, and our hearts are restless until they find rest in Thee."

History has been shaped more by movements than by dictators, more by revolutions than by armies. Evil movements like Nazism or benevolent movements like the abolition of slavery have shaped the story of men. Similarly, Christianity tells the story of the ebb and flow of movements. Whether reading the historical narrative of Scripture or studying the annals of church history, one can easily see the tendency of God's people to move from zealous devotion to institutionalization to spiritual deadness to the seasons of refreshing we call revival or spiritual awakenings.

Christian movements depict a variety of emphases. The story of Judges recognizes the tendency of God's people to forsake Him and then to return. The book of Acts could be described as a movement of evangelism and church planting. We read in history of missionary movements, church planting movements, people movements, and so on. Movements of revival often spawned other movements of evangelism, church planting, missions, and mercy ministries.

What Are the Marks of a Modern Movement of Revival or Awakening?

In the first chapter, Malcolm overviewed the definitions and descriptions of revival. Before we study the modern movements of God, I want to mention a few marks worth watching for as you read the history that follows, some of which are often overlooked.

First, as you have seen throughout this book, revivals are ***movements*** of God — times when God obviously works in and through His people to bring about change. Christianity in her essence is more an advancing movement than a monument to be maintained. The stories you have read and will read are the stories of movements — the advancing church in the Acts, the missionary movements of Patrick and Columba, the Reformation of Luther, the missionary expansion in the 19th century, and the remarkable spread of the gospel in China over the past two generations in our time. Movements change the world, and revival is a movement of God.

Second, ***the gospel*** marks such movements as the central idea. Ideas spur movements. Osama Bin Laden helped to spawn a terrible movement of global terrorism at the turn of the 21st century by taking an extreme idea and convincing others to give their lives for it. Martin Luther did not seek to start a movement when he nailed the 95 theses to the wall, but a movement was born nevertheless because of the ideas he presented. The major movements in history, whether good or evil, grew and spread because of ideas, and typically, these ideas that challenged the status quo of the times.

Christians believe in the Bible as the Word of God and in the gospel — the good news through the life, substitutionary death, and resurrection of Jesus — as the point of all of life. We believe the Bible is not merely a book about morality; but is primarily about reality. There is one great Story in all of Scripture, one metanarrative that makes sense of the entire Bible and all of life. In Genesis we read first of the Creation: God created an amazing world, and He created man in His image to worship Him. Because of the Fall and the reality of sin, creation has been broken, and we now need redemption. Jesus Christ came to provide our Rescue, and by faith in Him we can have life God intended. We can worship God and serve Him as a part of His Restoration, which will ultimately be enjoyed in a new heaven and a new earth.

The Bible's metanarrative follows a plotline: Creation, Fall, Rescue, and Restoration. Revival movements push forward the work of believers like a flood of spiritual renewal.

To see the Bible in terms of its overall metanarrative go to www.viewthestory.com.

Read the stories of great revivals and you will find that the preachers in these movements did not preach "how to have revival" sermons. They preached the gospel. Read the literature of those times, and you will see much about the gospel. In a real sense, a movement of revival is a movement of gospel recovery. In Josiah's day, central to the movement of God was the discovery of the Law of God that had been lost — yes; they lost the Bible in church! When churches lose a heart for the gospel and a conviction about the mission of God, they need revival. The heart of the message of revival is the gospel and those convictions that bring us back to the gospel.

Today, a growing movement of gospel recovery is spreading across the landscape of the church. This is particularly obvious in young adults. Weary of a factory-like church where attendees are basically expected to confess Jesus, show up every week at church services, and live morally, increasing numbers of young adults want to believe in something that changes everything. They hunger for a gospel recovery not unlike those we witnessed in earlier movements of God.

Tim Keller comments on why we need a focus on revival, and how the gospel is critical for such a movement:

> In other words, revivals and renewals are necessary because the default mode of the human heart is works-righteousness — we do not ordinarily live as if the gospel is true. Christians often believe in their heads that "Jesus accepts me; therefore I will live a good life," but their hearts and actions are functioning practically on the principle "I live a good life; therefore Jesus accepts me." The results of this inversion are smug self-satisfaction (if we feel we are living up to standards) or insecurity, anxiety, and self-hatred (if we feel we are failing to live up). In either case, the results are defensiveness, a critical spirit, racial or cultural ethnocentricity to bolster a sense of righteousness, an allergy to change, and other forms of spiritual deadness, both individual and corporate. In sharp contrast, the gospel of sheer grace offered to hopeless sinners will humble and comfort all at once. The results are joy, a willingness to admit faults, graciousness with all, and a lack of self-absorption.[5]

I believe that the wind of the Spirit is blowing in this gospel recovery, and I want to set my sails to that wind. So many people talk about revival as a form of behavior modification or as a means of putting a stamp on our current ministry practices instead of understanding it as a radical return to the gospel that leads to the remarkable surrender of lives for the purpose of living and sharing the mission of God.

Third, ***young people*** play a prominent role in such revival movements. Recently a former student came to see me. She currently serves in a ministry to college students on a state university campus, and sees the spiritual need there. She asked me a question, knowing my interest in young people and in awakenings: "Do you think we could see a spiritual awakening in our time?" I told her I am actually hopeful. The growing focus on the gospel mentioned above, a rising recognition that morality and institutional religion is stifling the church's mission, and a massive number of young people today actually encourages me.

The role of youth was abundantly clear in the First Great Awakening. Concerning the revival's effect on the youth, Edwards commented,

> God made it, I suppose, the greatest occasion of awakening to others, of anything that ever came to pass in the town . . . news of it seemed to be almost like a flash of lightning, upon the hearts of young people, all over town, and upon many others.[6]

He went on to argue that the Great Awakening was essentially a youth movement. If only churches would tap into the zeal of youth! I would encourage you to challenge students in the gospel and call them not to simply live a little better for Jesus daily, but to see his absolute Lordship over all of life. I could be wrong, but I believe if we in fact see a movement of God in our time, young people will be at the heart of it.

Fourth, ***small groups*** mark these movements. From the *collegia pietatus* in the early days of Pietism to the Societies of John Wesley to the coffeehouses in the Jesus Movement, small groups can be found wherever the Spirit moves. The first followers of a movement quickly identify one another and band together. You will read about the Holy Club before you learn about the Evangelical Awakening, and you are not surprised to read how a small group of ministers-in-training in the Log College of William Tennent produced key leaders in the First Great Awakening. Before Billy Graham or Bill Bright launched ministries of profound impact, they became part of a small group of people who encouraged one another to spend their lives doing something that mattered.

Fifth, a return to ***spiritual disciplines*** comes with revival movements. Believers hunger for Bible study, prayer, fasting, and other signs of healthy spiritual formation.

A sixth mark would be ***innovative*** evangelistic methods birthed in the midst of a movement led by the Spirit. John Wesley and George Whitefield did not want to leave church buildings to preach in the fields, but they had to do so, and in so doing, they reached a whole generation neglected by the church. Mass meetings by Moody after the rise of industrialization and urbanization, and coffeehouses in the Jesus Movement are other examples.

A final mark to watch for offers hope today, for it is a mark depicted in the lives of so many Millennials today: new ministries of ***social justice***. Caring for orphans has often marked revival movements as much as church planting. George Whitefield built the orphanage Bethesda, "house of mercy," because his view of the gospel did not separate his compassion for people from his proclamation of the Word. It was in fact the largest building project in the colony of Georgia at its time, and it still operates today. Francke the Pietist began an orphanage at Halle and led other social reforms while preaching Christ. Spurgeon established an orphanage, as well. John Wesley had a great impact on Wilberforce and the abolition of slavery movement. If we see revival, it will not be contained in a church building.

As you read these modern accounts of awakening, see them not only as stories that inspire, although they do. See them as a template: they can help us know how to set the sails well when the wind of the Spirit blows.

Part Two

Spiritual Awakening Movements in the Modern Era

Alvin L. Reid

Chapter 8
The Dawn of Modern Revival — Puritanism and Pietism

I preach as a dying man to dying men.
Richard Baxter[1]

One of my most memorable misadventures as a father occurred outside our Houston home in 1994. My wife, Michelle, was on an errand, so I took our daughter Hannah, not quite a year old, and our five-year-old son Josh outside. While I gathered tools to build a new flower garden, I placed Hannah in her walker to keep her close to me. I somehow forgot that walkers are indoor vehicles; they were designed to go much faster on a fast surface (like concrete) than an infant could handle.

As I became preoccupied with finding a certain tool, I suddenly realized Hannah was nowhere to be seen. My tiny tot had seized the opportunity to turn our driveway into a drag strip. She was speeding toward the street, oblivious to the steep drop-off from our driveway to the road. As I turned to give chase, I realized two things: (1) she was going to flip when she hit the drop-off and, smashing her cute, perfect face; and (2) I had no chance of catching her. Suddenly a blur came from my right. Seeing the scenario unfold, Josh rushed over to the driveway, grabbed sis by the walker, and yanked her to safety. Josh was a hero, Daddy was relieved, and Hannah was ready to do it again! She did not realize that she was heading for disaster, and or that she needed outside intervention to save her.

This parental faux pas illustrates the forces in the modern era following the Reformation and Renaissance. The modern era introduced incredible new discoveries and advances that allowed humanity to race forward facing unparalleled thrills and challenges. At the same time, the need for divine intervention in human affairs had never been greater. New technologies gave us a world of better things, but not necessarily a better world.

Increasingly in recent centuries, the place of man has been elevated as an intellectual tower of Babel has risen to displace the respect deserved only by God. The foremost effect of this trend, particularly from the Enlightenment onward, has sometimes been to throw the church headlong into heresy or spiritual deformity.

Spirituality has declined, not so much because of wholesale abandonment of the faith, but because of the indefatigable drip of our culture, pushing the conviction of a transcendent God further to the periphery. The result is a loss of the wonder of God. We overlook His awesomeness and majesty. We focus on our accomplishments and on ourselves. Even so, God continues to lavish us with vigorous showers of His presence.

During revival, we recapture the wonder of God. As the modern age has advanced, God has on occasion intervened to pour out His Spirit in mighty awakening. These times of revival remind God's people of His wonder. Wave after wave of renewal has swept the West and even the globe in recent centuries. The physical fire of Elijah's day has become the spiritual fire of awakening in our time.

The Impact of the Enlightenment

About a hundred years after the Protestant Reformation, many leading thinkers and writers in Western Europe began to debunk organized religion and exalt reason as the solution to all human problems. This rationalistic movement increased throughout the eighteenth century and came to be known as the Enlightenment.

Science

In the field of science, such men as Johannes Kepler (1571-1630), Francis Bacon (1561-1626), Galileo (1564-1641), and Isaac Newton (1642-1727) built upon the presupposition of Nicolas Copernicus (1473-1543) that the earth was not the center of the universe. The former views of man in the areas of science and creation were challenged and altered. In his *Principia* in 1687, Newton astounded the world when he proposed that creation operated as the result of gravity. As advances in science occurred, serious questions were raised about God and a person's responsibility to Him.

Rationalism

While science increasingly shaped the views of man in regard to creation, philosophical rationalism emerged. The father of modern rationalism, Rene Descartes (1596-1650), posited that the "beginning of all knowledge is doubt, and no real progress can be made until a basis, or point of departure, can be found which cannot be doubted."[2] His axiom, "*Cogito ergo sum*" ("I think, therefore I am"), and his ontological arguments for the existence of God influenced philosophical systems from his day to ours.

Building upon some of Descartes' ideas, Baruch Spinoza (1632-1677) developed a system of rational pantheism in which "God is the indwelling and not the transcendent sense of all things."[3] The doubts of rationalism were also applied to a person's relationship to God. No longer were religious ideas accepted as absolute based merely upon human assertions.

For many people, rationalism gradually replaced faith, human authority replaced God's authority, and secular society replaced the church as the focal point of life. The inversion of authority robbed man of his spiritual vitality and placed him in opposition to God. The Enlightenment replaced God with man as the center of the universe.

Deism

Within the environment of new freedoms, Deism began to spread through the influence of men like Edward Herbert of Cherbury (1583-1648) and John Toland (1670-1722). Toland's *Christianity Not Mysterious*, published in 1696, was the first "major deist manifesto."[4] Deism developed two key features: (1) it exalted reason over revelation, downgrading the authority of Scripture; (2) it moved away from any "interventionist" understanding of God; that is, it rejected the idea of divine intervention in day-to-day events.

Toland argued, "True religion must be universal, not only in the sense of calling for the allegiance of all, but also in the sense of being a religion that is natural to all mankind. Such religion is not based on particular revelations, or on historical events. But rather on the natural instinct of every human being."[5]

These ideas led to the more radical anti-Christian Deism that spread in the eighteenth century under the skeptic Voltaire (1694-1778) in Europe and Thomas Paine (1737-1809) in America. These men railed against the idea of a transcendent God actively involved in history. Interestingly, today a new form of deism threatens spiritual life, especially among youth. The National Institute of Youth and Religion contends that much of the Bible teaching youth receive in churches today can be described as "moralistic therapeutic deism," an approach focusing on morality more than gospel vitality. This approaches seeks to make youth feel better about themselves more than teaching them to worship a transcendent God, and it relegates God to church life, separated from the rest of life. This functional deism causes young people to pursue spirituality elsewhere, even though God is here, and He is not silent.

To read more on the issue of moralistic therapeutic deism and a more gospel-centered approach to relating to students see: Alvin L. Reid, *As You Go: Creating a Missional Culture of Gospel-Centered Students* (NavPress, 2013).

Empiricism

In England, John Locke (1632-1704) published his work *An Essay Concerning Human Understanding* in 1690. His view, known as empiricism, argued that all knowledge is the result of experience. In his *Treatises on Government*, he proposed revolutionary ideas on how a government operates. Locke's ideas weaved their ways into some of the governments of Europe and ultimately to America.

When people felt that they no longer served the government but that the government served them, a political ideology was unleashed that rearranged governments. This democratic philosophy was also incorporated into many denominations. Locke's views influenced a young Jonathan Edwards, who would become a leader in the First Great Awakening.

Views like this infiltrated not only the secular and academic communities but also the churches. Churches diminished in their service as spiritual beacons for man to follow as they too often adapted their standards to the world's demands and ultimately lost their spiritual identities and Kingdom purposes on earth. During this spiritual identity crisis, God began to initiate revival movements among some groups who would stand for Him in the face of the winds of change.

The Rise of English Puritanism

The Reformation spread theological truths across Europe even as the Renaissance brought many ideas to the land. In England, several dissenting groups emerged to challenge the religious status quo. One of these groups was the Puritans. When Mary Tudor ascended to the English throne in 1553 and implemented Catholic policies, many of the Protestants fled to Europe, especially to Geneva. While in Geneva, they embraced the views of John Calvin. After Elizabeth I became queen of England, many of those exiles returned to their native land, not as Anglicans, but as Calvinists. They felt strongly that English reform within the Anglican Church fell short of New Testament teachings, and they insisted upon more radical changes as they sought to purify the established church. Because of their convictions, they were called "Puritans."

Leaders of the Puritan movement included Laurence Humphrey (1527-1590), president of Magdalen College, Oxford; Thomas Cartwright (1535-1603), professor of theology at Cambridge, who proposed a revolutionary idea that churches should call their own pastors in place of appointments; Thomas Wilcox (1549-1608), a London pastor; William Travers (1548-1635), a Cambridge professor; Pilgrim's Progress author John Bunyan (1628-1688); and William Perkins (1558-1603) of Warwickshire, England. These Puritan leaders were marked by a keen desire for personal holiness. Perkins influenced many men who in turn led others to give priority to holy living. Spiritual disciplines, including prayer and fasting, were central for these leaders.[6] However, they encountered strong opposition.

In 1589 Queen Elizabeth unsuccessfully attempted to pass legislation requiring Puritans to attend the Anglican Church. At the Hampton court conference in 1604, King James I became irritated with the Puritans and declared that he "would harry them out of the kingdom if they would not conform.[7] As the Puritan movement grew, it led to several movements of revival.

Revival in London

One of the most significant revivals of the seventeenth century occurred in London in 1665. Shortly before the renewal ignited, a plague ravaged the city. In one week, ten thousand people died. "Many who were in church one day, were thrown into the grave the next," wrote Gillies, a Scottish preacher and historian who wrote a fascinating account of revivals.[8]

As people inquired desperately about their personal spiritual conditions, the English government was primarily concerned with maintaining the structure of the Anglican Church. Laws such as the Conformity Act of 1662, the Conventicler Act of 1664, and the Five Mile Act of 1665 were enacted and enforced. Yet the masses continued to listen to the nonconformist preachers. The preachers could not be silenced, and the people were not kept deaf. Churches overflowed as people crowded one another just to hear the message of eternal life.

With death so near and disease ravaging the land, people grasped for the Word of God as a drowning man seeks to catch a rope. As the plague overwhelmed the city, increasing numbers saw it as the judgment of God. "Ministers were sent to knock, cry aloud, and lift up their voice like a trumpet," said Gillies, "Then the people began to open the ear and the heart, which were fast shut and barred before; how they did hearken, as for their lives, as if every sermon were their last."[9]

Facing the possibility of death, thousands responded to the message of Christ. People desperately sought for answers, came under conviction, and were converted. Many found salvation, and spiritual fires burned in the hearts of believers.

Revival at Kidderminster

When Puritan Richard Baxter (1615-1691) assumed the pastorate in 1641 at Kidderminster, a town of three thousand people in northern England, he found the church in a dismal spiritual condition. Shortly after his arrival, he began to conduct conferences and catechisms for fourteen families a week in his church field. Through Bible classes for the people and Baxter's preaching, which possessed a spiritual power that was not known before in the church, the Holy Spirit began to move within the church membership.

Richard Baxter's Comments to Pastors, from *The Reformed Pastor*

--[Your people] will likely feel when you have been much with God: that which is most on your hearts, is like to be most in their ears.

--We must study as hard how to live well, as how to preach well. Brethren, if the saving of souls be your end, you will certainly intend it out of the pulpit as well as in it! . . . Oh that this were your daily study, how to use your wealth, your friends, and all you have for God, as well as your tongues!

--You are not likely to see general reformation [by reformation Baxter means revival], till you procure family reformation.

--The ministerial work must be carried on purely for God and the salvation of souls, not for any private ends of our own.

--Prayer must carry on our work as well as preaching: he preacheth not heartily to his people that prayeth not earnestly for them.

--Oh, speak not one cold or careless word around so great a business as heaven or hell.

--O Brethren, what a blow we may give to the kingdom of darkness, by the faithful and skillful managing of His work! If the saving souls, of your neighbour's souls, many souls, from everlasting misery, be worth your labour, up and be doing!

--I would throw aside all the libraries in the world, rather than be guilty of the perdition of one soul.

As the crowds grew, five additions to the sanctuary had to be built. The crowds still overflowed the auditorium. Previously, spiritual matters were seldom mentioned in the marketplace. After the renewal began to ignite, it was common to hear people singing the songs of the faith as they walked along the streets. As the people rejoiced in fellowship with God, multitudes were converted, including some of the most immoral people of the town.

In 1647 Baxter became critically ill and was bedridden for five months. While convalescing, he recorded his reflections on his "journey to the gates of Eternity." In 1649/1650, he published *The Saint's Everlasting Rest.* On December 4, 1655, he was scheduled to preach the inaugural message for the association of pastors in the county where Kidderminster is located. Due to illness, he was unable to fulfill the commitment. However, he expanded the message for that occasion into a book that was published in 1656 under the title *The Reformed Pastor.* This work is still considered one of the greatest works of practical advice for pastors. By "reformed," Baxter meant that the preacher must serve with a spiritual vitality. In 1657, he published *The Call to the Unconverted.* In all, Baxter wrote 168 books in his more than forty years of writing ministry.

On May 19, 1662, Parliament passed the Conformity Act forbidding nonconformist preaching. On May 22, 1662, while preaching at St. Brides Church at Blackfriars, Baxter decided he would not conform. He was deeply grieved and distraught over the intolerance the government and Anglican Church demonstrated toward those who embraced different Christian views. He labored incessantly until the act was repealed in 1672. Until his death in 1691, churches continued to experience unusual revival. Through his writings, Baxter greatly influenced the leaders of Pietism on the European continent and the leaders of the Evangelical Awakening in Britain

Selected Revivals Following the Reformation to 1700

In addition to the Puritans, other groups were also experiencing revival. Puritans advocated association with the Anglican Church, but others felt strongly that the established church in England was not going far enough in reform. Believing they should separate from the Anglican Church, these became known as the "Separatists."

Robert Browne (1550-1633) founded a Separatist congregation at Norwich in 1851. When Browne returned to the Church of England in 1585, the Separatists lost their early leader. The group struggled until John Smyth (1570-1612) joined the Separatists in 1606 and started a congregation at Gainesborough.

In addition, William Brewster (1560-1644) gathered a small group for worship in his home at Scrooby. Two prominent members of the Scrooby congregation were William Bradford (1590-1657) and Jon Robinson (1575-1625). Because of the aggressive persecution and oppression of King James I, Smyth and his congregation moved to Amsterdam in about 1608. The Scrooby congregation moved to Leyden Holland, at the same time.

Advantages Baxter noted that helped with the Revival at Kidderminster:
1. The town had not seen awakening, so a spiritual hunger existed.
2. They accepted and respected Baxter as a person.
3. There were many believers who assisted him through their godly living, people who "thirsted after the salvation of their neighbours."
4. The character of believers offered a good testimony to the community.
5. Baxter held well-attended private meetings to teach the Word.
6. In his early years, he had good health and preached in a manner that connected with the people, "for drowsy formality and customariness do but stupify the hearers, and rock them asleep. It must be serious preaching, which must make men serious in hearing and obeying it."
7. He provided Bibles to those who had none and wrote many books to help them to grow in godliness.
8. Since most of the people worked at looms in the garment industry in Kidderminister, they could read the Scripture and other books while they worked.
9. God saved many in their teens, which in turn brought conviction to their parents. This included some notoriously wicked people.
10. God used sickness to bring conviction to many.
11. He worked diligently, visiting all day on Mondays and Tuesdays in personal conferences with families, catechizing and instructing them.
12. He exercised church discipline, which helped reduce divisions among the people.
13. He had an extended ministry of many years in the same place.

Adapted from Gillies, Accounts of Revivals Online at http://quintapress.macmate.me/PDF_Books/Historical_Collections_v1.pdf

Living in Amsterdam during the pinnacle of the Arminian Controversy, Smyth adopted more Arminian views on predestination and the Anabaptist position on believer's baptism. He baptized himself by pouring, and in turn baptized the members of his congregation in 1609. When Smyth died in 1612, Thomas Helwys and John Murton assumed leadership of the group. They returned to England about 1612 to begin a new movement there; the people of this movement became known as the General Baptists.

Another group of dissenters that arose from the Puritans was the Particular Baptists under the leadership of Henry Jacob in 1616.[10] This Calvinistic group came to practice believer's baptism by immersion.

Meanwhile, the Leyden congregation flourished under the leadership of Brewster and Robinson. A small group of people from this congregation, under William Bradford, boarded the ship called the *Mayflower*, crossed the Atlantic, and landed at Plymouth Rock, Massachusetts, on December 21, 1620. They settled in the New World as they searched for religious toleration, and these Pilgrim Fathers laid the foundations for the eighteenth-century awakenings in America.

Other awakening movements broke out on the European continent. On Tuesday, March 30, 1596, some four hundred ministers and some lay people gathered behind closed doors in Edinburgh, Scotland, for a "concert of prayer" for the church and the nation of Scotland. Intermingled with their prayers were confessions of sin, humility, and wrestling with God. Within an hour, the Holy Spirit began to move among them. The church in which they met resounded with sobs and moans of contrite hearts as they wept their way to God. John Davidson, who presided over the meeting, opened the Bible to Luke 12:22 and shared from Gods Word. Following the message, the participants agreed to enter into a covenant with God and with one another. For four hours, the congregation participated in a service that was marked by unusual spiritual power, and many were converted to Christ.

Shortly thereafter, on May 12, 1596, at Dunfermline, James Melville presided over the preachers who composed the Synod of Fife. After he read from Joshua, he shared a message that was used of the Holy Spirit to cause deep conviction within the lives of those present. With groans and tears, the preachers made public confessions of ingratitude, negligence, coldness of spirit, instability, un-Christian language, and worldly lifestyles. With fear and trembling, they poured out their souls to their God, asking Him to provide mercy, grace, and spiritual strength.[11] Revival set aflame their lives.

On Monday, June 21, 1630, John Livingstone stood before a large crowd in the yard of the church in Shotts. Opening the Bible to Ezekiel 36, he read his selected text and proceeded to preach. Like a tidal wave, the Holy Spirit moved across the congregation. Many came under such conviction that they called out to God for mercy. Some five hundred people were converted in that one service. Not only did the church experience evangelistic results, but many of the Christians also enjoyed a renewed and joyful fellowship with Christ while experiencing the resurgence of spiritual power in their lives.

These and other accounts signaled the growing work of the Spirit in the British Isles. On the continent, philosophical rationalism and divergent theological views created a spiritual vacuum within Christianity that contributed significantly to spiritual declension. At the same time, strong spiritual influences in Protestant churches were used of God to create a spiritual hunger within the lives of many that served as catalysts for revival.

Pietism

Puritan William Perkins (1558-1602) influenced William Amesius and Willem Tellinck, who led the movement of Reformed Pietism in the Netherlands. Lutheran Johann Arndt (1555-1621) was another progenitor of Pietism. His work *True Christianity* (1605) was esteemed by Pietist leader Philip Spener and others. Orthodox Lutherans criticized Arndt for his emphasis on experiential religion, believing it to be rooted in medieval mysticism.

Pietism exploded with the publication in 1675 of Philip Spener's *Pia Desideria*, or "Pious Desires."[12] This classic in Christian spirituality served as a manual of reform for Lutheran churches. Under the influence of leaders including Spener, Jean DeLabadie, August H. Francke, and Moravian leader Count Nicolaus Von Zinzendorf, Pietism had a notable impact upon Lutheran, Reformed, and other churches. Pietism emphasized individual devotion to God, a conversion experience, serious Bible study, and hymn singing.

Mark Shaw observes the larger pattern and influence of revival movements:

> Christian historians such as Kenneth Scott Latourette and Andrew Walls document how a broad tidal pattern of spiritual decline and revitalization has continued down through the centuries following the close of the first century. Revivals are smaller instances of this larger pattern of decline and renewal, streams that feed this larger river. Thus times of perceived decline create the longing for change. Revivals restore the spiritual dynamics of Christianity and lead to new movements or renewed institutions. The wider consequences of revival produce the fruits of change (in small or large ways) in one's world.[13]

Pietism serves as an example of the streams noted by Shaw. Lewis Drummond call *Pia Desideria* the "manifesto of the movement" and lists eight characteristics of this "new Lutheran bolt of lightning": the new birth, religious enthusiasm, felicity or a joyous feeling of communion with Christ, sanctification, Biblicism, theological education, missionary evangelism, and social concern.[14]

Pietism can be summarized in four primary streams of influence: Lutheran, Reformed, Radical Pietism, and the Moravians.[15]

The Lutheran Stream

Lutheran Pietism focused on completing the Reformation. Its primary leaders included Spener and Francke. Philip Spener (1635-1705) was reared a Lutheran and considered himself an orthodox one, citing Luther extensively in *Pia Desideria*. He and other Lutheran Pietists insisted that they were no innovators, but were bringing the people back to the goals of Luther. He read Arndt's work and was greatly influenced by it.

Spener studied at Strasbourg University. While there, he was influenced by professor John Schmid and by the works of Martin Luther, Johann Arndt, Richard Baxter, and Theophilus Groszgebauer, the author of *A Watchman's Cry from Devastated Zion*. In 1660 Spener journeyed to Basel and then to Geneva, where he came under the influence of Jean de Labadie.

Six measures for reform in *Pia Desideria:*

1. A greater commitment to spread the Word of God. This includes pastors preaching from the entire Bible and a focus on small group Bible study.
2. A renewed emphasis on the Lutheran view of the priesthood of all believers.
3. A greater focus on the development of individual spiritual lives.
4. Truth should not be established through disputes but through repentance and a holy life.
5. Candidates for the ministry should be genuine Christians who have had spiritual training. Spener suggested Tauler's *Theological Germanica,* which Luther greatly esteemed: Arndt's *True Christianity*; and Thomas a Kempis' *Imitation of Christ* as a foundational study.
6. Sermons should not demonstrate the preacher's erudition, but rather attempt to edify.

Upon his return to Germany in 1661, Spener began a growing ministry of the Word of God. Pastorates in Frankfurt, Dresden, and Berlin helped him to become the most renowned minister of his day. He was concerned with the growing worldliness in the Lutheran church and its overemphasis on the sacraments. In 1666 Spener began the Collegia Pietatis, or "exercises of piety," a gathering of believers to study Scripture and the practice of Christianity. These meetings touched a hunger in the spiritual lives of area believers. Soon these small groups multiplied across the city.

Spener was called "a burning and shining light in his generation," and an "instrument of blessing to nations, and a father to many thousands."[16] In *Pia Desideria,* Spener offered specific guidelines for renewing the Lutheran church.

In 1683 Spener published 108 catechetical tables. His fame grew to the point that he became chief court preacher in Saxony in 1686. He also faced opposition at every turn from many clergymen. In 1690 he moved to Berlin. For fifteen years, Spener promoted Pietism in Berlin and surrounding areas. Through his preaching, the citizens of Berlin were constantly confronted with Gods spiritual demands. By the time of his death in 1705, Pietism was entrenched as the catalyst for the great Pietistic revivals of the eighteenth century. Spener's growing influence availed him the opportunity to secure the appointment of young A. H. Francke as a professor at the University of Halle.

August Hermann Francke (1663-1727), Spener's "dutiful son in the faith," was an aggressive leader who turned Pietism into a force for renewal and evangelism. At age nine, he asked his mother for a room that he could use for prayer and meditation. His desire was that God would direct his life "from first to last, to His glory, and to His glory alone."[17] At the age of sixteen, he enrolled at Erfurt and the next year transferred to Kiel University. In 1684 he entered the Leipzig University.

While he was a student, he and other students formed a Bible study group. The more time he spent studying God's Word, the more he came under conviction. The growing work of the Spirit in his life came to fruition in 1687 as he prepared a lesson on faith. He recounted the experience that changed his life: "At one time I was crying, at another pacing the floor in great unrest, then falling upon my knees, imploring Him whom I knew not. God heard and answered my prayers suddenly."[18] His dramatic conversion affected his whole life, as did the conversions of Paul, Luther, and Wesley on theirs. He believed the answer to society's ills came through leading people to a genuine conversion experience. Out of this own experience with Christ, he received an unquenchable desire to share the experience with others.

Francke and some other students formed the Collegium Philobilicum, a group that met once a week for Bible study. The rapid growth of the group and its emphasis upon piety aroused opposition from the Leipzig University administration. In 1690 the officers at Leipzig prohibited the group's meetings.

As the result of the strong opposition at Leipzig, Francke moved to Erfurt and served as an assistant in his church under Breithaupt, who was also professor of theology at Erfurt. Small groups marked the movement as Francke immediately began daily Bible studies for the students at the university and discipled people within the confines of their homes. As the waves of a spiritual awakening began to rise, Francke encountered strong opposition from local clergy among others. Within fifteen months, he was given forty-eight hours to get out of Erfurt.

On the day of his eviction, he received an invitation to teach Greek at Halle University, although the school was not yet constituted. From 1691 to 1698 he taught Greek at Halle. Because of Spener's influence, Francke was appointed as professor of theology in 1698. With this appointment, Halle became the center for the Pietistic movement.

Francke established a model community centered on a zealous study of Scripture and small group discipleship. As a part of the academic program, Francke devised numerous practical outlets for ministry. Students penetrated the slum area of Glace with the gospel. Many people were converted. Francke started a school for the children. He organized orphanages as well as schools for nobility. He initiated many benevolent ministries including a hospital, the Orphan Book Publishers, an extensive Bible distribution program, and foreign mission enterprises. He also proved to be a capable professor who attracted students from several nations.

He modeled the life of faith required to continue in revival. At one point, his funds were depleted for the various ministries. As he gave out the last of the monies, he prayed, "Lord, look upon my necessity."[19] He soon encountered a person who had traveled two hundred miles to offer him a gift.

In 1712, awakening came among exiled Swedish troops in Siberia. Officers began corresponding with Francke, and Halle responded by sending booklets and medicine. Francke also corresponded with Cotton Mather of Boston concerning missionary efforts in America.[20]

Francke possessed an aggressive evangelist's passion. A man can be at once a scholar and theologian, and a leader of awakening. His leadership helped Pietism to become an activist movement strongly committed to world evangelization. Francke launched a seven-month evangelistic tour in a time when itinerant evangelism was unknown. Under his influence, Halle became a center of awakening whose influence spread to England, Russia, and the Baltic. If Spener was the preacher of Pietism, Francke was its teacher.

The Reformed Stream

Pietism renewed the Reformed church as well. Thus, it soon spread to the Netherlands. Jean de Labadie was a key leader of Pietism in Geneva. Labadie (1610-74) preached with fire. He began as a Jesuit priest but joined the Reformed church at Montauban in 1650. He moved to Geneva and soon exerted influence through his preaching and Bible studies. Spener and Theodore Untereyck attended these Bible studies. Labadie urged clergymen to lead evangelistic efforts by preaching sermons on repentance. He made such an impression on Spener that Spener later translated some of Labadie's works into German. Spener often heard Labadie preach and attended his conventicles.

> As you read the history of revival be sure to note the impact of various leaders on one another.

On one occasion Labadie preached a series of fifty sermons on the text "Repent Ye!" In 1666, he moved from Geneva to the Wallon Church in Middleburg, Holland, and served there for three years. While at Middleburg, he wrote a monumental work entitled *Reformation of the Church through the Clergy*, which influenced the writing of Spener's *Pia Desideria* in 1675 and Francke's *Studies in Theology* in 1708.

Labadie promoted protracted meetings, multiple preachers on the same program, and simultaneous meetings in specified areas. Under his leadership, several pastors agreed to conduct simultaneous meetings in Holland. At Slius under the preaching of Pastor Koelman, "an outpouring of God's Spirit came upon the church, a great number were visibly converted; among them were those who had been deeply enmeshed in the service of the flesh and the devil."[21] Out of these revivals, a new emphasis upon personal conversion emerged.

The Dutch Pietists became known for their zealous preachers of repentance. The English Puritans influenced them greatly. Jodocus von Lodenstein (1620-77) was a key preacher.

While a student at Utrecht, Lodenstein influenced Theodor Untereyck (1635-93). In 1660, Untereyck became the pastor of the church in Mulheim in the Ruhr region of Germany. Following the examples of Lodenstein and Labadie, Untereyck also began weekly Bible studies. As a result of the weekly Bible studies in his home, revival spread from Mulheim to the lower Rhine.[21] Untereyck also helped to spread the emerging spirit of Pietism to Western Germany.

One young man who attended the small groups, Theodore Frelinghuysen, became a key personality in the First Great Awakening in the American colonies among the Dutch Reformed (see Chapter 10). Frelinghuysen's earnest preaching of repentance made a great impression on Gilbert Tennent, giving Tennent's preaching a new vitality, adding fuel to the fires of awakening in America. Frelinghuysen also encountered a young George Whitefield in America.

The Radical Stream

Radical Pietism sought to replace church forms with Christian experience. Ernst Von Hochenau (1660-1721) and Gerhard Tersteegen (1697-1769) were among the leaders of this stream. Von Hochenau experienced conversion under the ministry of Francke. Later called the "Whitefield of Germany,"[22] this great preacher proved a significant tool of God. In his *History of Evangelism* Paulus Scharpf said that von Hochenau's "revivals were so mighty, they are beyond description."[23] Hochenau spent years in prison because of his faith.

Tersteegen was both an effective evangelist and an accomplished hymn writer. A German Protestant mystic, he was converted to the Pietist movement at the age of twenty. He served as a minister and arranged devotional meetings. He translated works of French Quietists into German and wrote biographies of Catholic mystics. He wrote *The Compendium of True Godliness*, *The Hidden Life with Christ in God*, and *The Spiritual Flower Garden*.

The Moravian Stream

Nicolaus Ludwig von Zinzendorf (1700-60) was born into a wealthy family. Like George Whitefield's father, Zinzendorf's father died while he was an infant. His grandmother reared him. She was "intimately involved with the Pietist clans pushing the new university and institutions at Halle."[24] He came under Francke's influence while attending school at Halle. While there, he founded the "Order of the Mustard Seed." This organization sought to live fully consecrated to God, to avoid worldly influences such as gambling or dancing, and to participate in missionary work.

He inherited an estate at Berthelsdorf. In 1722, Zinzendorf became aware of the persecution of the Bohemian Brethren (spiritual heirs of John Huss), and he began offering asylum at the estate to these and other persecuted believers. The community that developed there became known as Hernnhut, "the Lord's watch." The diverse groups who sought asylum at Hernnhut had strained relations at times but ultimately forged a community that was united in heart, if not always in theology.

This community experienced a powerful spiritual awakening beginning in 1727. At this time, early signs of revival were emerging on the American side of the Atlantic through the ministry of Theodore Frelinghuysen. On May 11, 1727, at a singing meeting, Zinzendorf spoke on Christian unity. This began a movement of confession, prayer, and joy at the estate.

Zinzendorf himself had begun focused prayer for some of the young people at Hernnhut. His burden spread to others. Picture the scene: a wealthy nobleman on his knees, agonizing in prayer for the conversion of young girls at his estate. On August 5, 1727, Zinzendorf spent the whole night in prayer with about a dozen others. Powerful revival came on August 13 in conjunction with the celebration of the Lord's Supper. On that day, the Moravian Church was born. From August through the winter, the community "appeared like a visible tabernacle of God with men."[25] Forty-eight adults committed to cover the twenty-four hours of each day in prayer, while the children held their own meetings for prayer and praise. This practice continued for a century; thus, some will reference the One-Hundred-Year Prayer Movement of the Moravians.

Zinzendorf emphasized unity despite differences on theological points, as illustrated in the rules of the community: "Hernnhut shall stand in unceasing love with all children of God in all Churches, criticize none, take part in no quarrel against those of differing opinion, except to preserve for itself the evangelical purity, simplicity and grace."[26]

Moravians became zealously committed to missions. The first Moravians came to America in 1735 under the leadership of August Spangenberg and settled in Georgia. While headed to America, some Moravians were introduced to a young John Wesley. Wesley visited Hernnhut soon after his conversion in 1738; before that, Moravian Peter Boehler, among others, influenced him. Zinzendorf conducted three missionary forays to the Delaware and to the Iroquois Indians in the colonies, as well. While in America, Zinzendorf met with Gilbert Tennent, leader among Presbyterians in the First Great Awakening.

Contributions of Pietism

Pietism encouraged revival. This enriched many churches and groups on the European continent and influenced such subsequent revival leaders as John Wesley and Theodore Frelinghuysen.

Pietism enriched Christian hymnody. Awakenings always change the corporate worship of the church, which includes new songs (Psalm 40:3). The first organ brought to the New World came through the work of a Pietist named Kelpius. The hymns of Pietism emphasized experiential faith.

Pietism stood for social justice. The orphan asylums at Halle were a model of the benevolent way children were treated, and each child was taught a trade.

Pietism pioneered world missions. The Pietists' commitment to missions was unparalleled. One group of Pietists from Halle and the Netherlands sailed to India as missionaries in the early 1700s, preceding Carey by almost a century. Zinzendorf even taught the Moravian missionaries not to impose their culture on those they reached, which has been a subject of concern throughout the modern history of missions. Missions extended to the Virgin Islands in 1732, to Greenland in 1733, to North America in 1734, to Lapland and South Africa in 1736, and to Labrador in 1771. The influence of Pietism extended to the missionary work of David Brainerd (1718-47) among the American Indians. Whereas the ratio of Protestant laity to missionaries as a whole was 5000:1, the Moravian ratio was 60:1. By Zinzendorf's death in 1760 some 226 missionaries had been sent by the Moravians.

Pietists emphasized the authority of Scripture. This led to Bible translation in their missionary travels and made them leaders in Scripture distribution. According to one report, Halle Pietists distributed 100,000 New Testaments and 80,000 Bibles.[27] Their emphasis on scriptural authority was not without problems. Zinzendorf de-emphasized doctrine because he thought much of the preaching in his day was too stridently doctrinal. He developed personal relationships with John Wesley and George Whitefield, but Whitefield recognized Zinzendorf's weakened view of Scripture. Whitefield wrote Zinzendorf in an attempt to right some of the Moravian wrongs.[28] History is replete with examples of a genuine movement of God being sidetracked because of overemphasis in one area or another.[29] Pietism's long-term impact emphasized experience to the neglect of biblical authority.

Pietism sparked the flame of awakening in Britain and the New World. Bumstead noted:

> The [First Great Awakening] cannot be properly understood without some notion of the forces, both religious and secular, which underlay the seeming sudden explosion of spiritual concern in America beginning in 1740.
> The general movement of "experimental" (that is, experienced) religion and evangelical piety, of which the Awakening was a part, did not originate in the New World, but was rather a product of Europe in the seventeenth century.[30]

Questions for Small Group Discussion

1. We can clearly see the effects of Pietism before our time. In light of those past effects, how can you see the emphases of Pietism still affecting the world in which we live today?

2. This chapter talks about different movements. Discuss a movement that is taking place in today's culture.

3. Small groups played a major part in the Pietist movement. How does your church value and utilize small groups? How might they be a catalyst for revival?

4. If you could start a movement today, what kind of movement would it be and what might its positive results be? Use this question to help you take the "spiritual temperature" of the culture in which you live.

Chapter 9
The Evangelical Awakening in Britain, 1735-91

A very few years ago Great Britain and Ireland were covered from vice from sea to sea. . . . Out of this darkness God commanded light to shine. In a short space He called thousands of sinners to repentance.

They were not only reformed from their outward vices, but likewise changed in the dispositions and tempers, filled with. . . love to God and all mankind and with an holy faith, producing good word of every kind, word of both piety and mercy.[1]

John Wesley

"It was the best of times, it was the worst of times . . ." The words of Charles Dickens reflected the season surrounding the French Revolution at the end of the eighteenth century. They also accurately reflected the entire century concerning Christianity in the West. On the downside, higher criticism and theological liberalism emerged from the Enlightenment. The rise of liberalism in the Christian academy had sapped the life from many in the modern church. Yet the century was also "the best of times," for some of the most powerful tides of revival since Pentecost washed across much of Europe and the American colonies during the 1700s.

The mighty awakening in the eighteenth century unfolded along three geographical fronts: Europe, the British Isles, and the New World colonies. As noted in the previous chapter, the European continent witnessed the experiential emphasis of Pietism. In the British Isles, John and Charles Wesley and George Whitefield led the way in the Evangelical Awakening. The First Great Awakening set the New World colonies ablaze, powerfully affecting the settlers. Whereas chapter 8 considered Pietism, this chapter will consider the Awakening as it touched Britain. Chapter 10 features the First Great Awakening in the American colonies.

The Evangelical Awakening is sometimes called the Wesleyan Revival due to the influence of John and Charles Wesley. The earliest glimmers of revival in the British Isles came in Wales in 1735 through men like Howell Harris. The Wesley's, in particular John, certainly played a major role in the revival. Because of John Wesley's enduring leadership in Britain, the revival is dated through his death in 1791.

Eighteenth-Century England

"It would be easy to multiply testimonies showing how exhausted of living religion," says a typical description of eighteenth-century England, "how black with every kind of wickedness, was the England of that day."[2] The clergy were mostly barren in their faith, more concerned with political unity than spiritual fervency.

The Church of England obsessed over secular politics and culture. An emphasis placed upon the union of church and state by Queen Anne (1702-14) resulted in an increase in the persecution of dissenters.[3] Barely a handful of the members of the House of Commons attended church.

Although the British Isles thrived financially as a result of its international mercantilism, social conditions overall failed to see improvement. Schools were reserved for the elite. The common people in England at that time were generally ignorant and brutal. Prisons were overcrowded and squalid, complete with open sewers running through the prison cells. All too often, prisoners died due to the deplorable conditions in the jails. The theater and popular novels contributed to the moral decay.

England was entering the Industrial Revolution. People flocked to the cities, and mob violence followed. Wesley often had problems with these mobs when he preached. Infant mortality rates were appallingly high: in the early eighteenth century, the mortality rate for infants under five was 74.5 percent. Liquor consumption also had increased dramatically: from 1684 to 1735 the consumption of distilled spirits grew tenfold. Sport often consisted of unthinkable acts of cruelty to animals. Cockfighting represented one of the most popular sporting events.

One of the sources of conflict in that day concerned the desire of the leaders of both church and state in England to keep the people divided into classes. This was due primarily to a desire to prevent another "Puritan Rebellion" in the national church. The popularity of the anonymous work *The Whole Duty of Man* gave momentum to class divisions. While containing many good precepts, it nevertheless carried the theme that class divisions were divinely ordained, "and that all good subjects must faithfully perform their duties in those particular stations of life wherein it has pleased God to place them."[4] After his conversion, John Wesley rejected these views.

Prior to the Awakening, sparks flashed that served to help ignite a subsequent greater blaze. Isaac Watts (1674-1748), the father of English hymnody, preached with great effect in London. Matthew Henry (1662-1714) influenced his and following generations through his preaching and his commentary.

Still, while several prominent leaders could be seen as forerunners to revival, there is no doubt that the primary human agents in the Evangelical Awakening were John and Charles Wesley and George Whitefield.

John Wesley

John Wesley (1703-91) stands in the annals of history as one of the giants of Christianity. His contributions to Protestant Christianity are legion, and his work far transcends the limitations of his temporal life in the eighteenth century. Historians acknowledge that Wesley's Methodism ranks with the French Revolution and the Industrial Revolution as "one of the great historical phenomena of the century."[5]

Wesley's work can be examined in great detail thanks largely to his own pen. In his eight-volume *Journal*, Wesley recorded his ministry in great detail. Often, in the daily log there would be a reference to a work read by Wesley during the day while traveling, or to the location of his preaching site, or to his sermon topic.

John was the fifteenth of nineteen children born to Samuel and Susannah Wesley. John's father served as an Anglican minister. One of the most dramatic events in Wesley's life occurred in 1709. A fire destroyed the Wesley home in Epworth. Young John remained alone in the burning building. He was rescued at the last moment by a group of men. As the house burned, he appeared at an upstairs window. A neighbor stood on the shoulders of another and reached John just as the roof collapsed. John considered himself "a burning stick snatched from the fire" (Zech. 3:2, NIV). The brush with death remained near to Wesley's memory throughout his life.

Few women in the history of the church stand taller than Susannah Wesley. She taught each of her children personally. Although thirteen of her children died at a young age, illustrating the high infant mortality rate mentioned earlier, two of those who reached adulthood (Charles and John) became great champions for God. Susannah's Puritan background formed her approach to rearing her children and is worthy of study today. Family life included a disciplined schedule, with morning and evening devotions and regular times for meditation and self-examination before God. Her own spiritual journal likely influenced young John. She devoted time to discuss spiritual matters with each child.

John went to Christ Church, Oxford in 1720 and later became a fellow of Lincoln College. He earned a master's degree in 1727. He was faithful in public and private prayer and committed to his academic pursuits. Books that influenced him included *The Imitation of Christ* by Thomas a Kempis, *Holy Living and Dying* by Jeremy Taylor, and two books by William Law: *Christian Perfection* and *A Serious Call to a Devout and Holy Life*.

Charles Wesley (1707-88) came later to Christ Church. While John became by far the more prominent brother in the revival, Charles was also a key person. More emotional and sensitive than John, Charles also preached with power, often speaking to great crowds. Still, his legacy is as a writer of hymns. John also wrote hymns, but not to the level of impact or number as Charles.

The brothers became associated with William Morgan and Robert Kirkham while at Oxford. These young men practiced strict discipline in their spiritual endeavors, including visiting prisoners, aiding the poor, and observing specific study topics. The accountability group focused on daily self-examination, partook of weekly communion, and fasted Wednesdays and Fridays. Like other movements in church history (such as the Protestants and Baptists), in derision they were called the "Methodists" for their practices. The small group was soon dubbed, also in ridicule, the "Holy Club." John Wesley's work with the Holy Club began in 1729, though his conversion was not until 1738. The group remained committed to the Anglican Church. Young George Whitefield also joined the group at the invitation of Charles Wesley.

The group devoted themselves to learning about literature, divinity, and proclaiming the gospel. They also pledged themselves to ministering to the poor as they had means. Under Wesley's leadership, the group became extremely disciplined. They met every night to review and plan. The sick were visited, children were taught, and prison inmates were visited. They valued both evangelistic and social work.

After William Morgan met with a man in prison, he entreated the other men to join him in ministering to inmates. As leader of the group, John went to the bishop of Oxford's chaplain, a Mr. Gerard. He oversaw the care for the condemned prisoners.

Gerard gained approval for Wesley and the others to preach at the prison, thus facilitating an evangelistic ministry for the group.

Members of this group went to Georgia in 1735 with General Oglethorpe to serve as missionaries. On the voyage aboard the *Simmonds,* John and Charles encountered twenty-six Moravians from Germany. Charles returned to England after about a year, while John remained longer.

On February 7, 1736, the day after arriving in Georgia, John met August Gottlieb Spangenberg (1704-92), a Moravian leader. Spangenberg impressed upon Wesley to an even greater degree the importance of evangelism. Wesley's purpose in the New World was to be a missionary to the Indians. However, he encountered difficulties with the settlers in Georgia. He fell in love with Sophia Hopkey in Georgia, but his inability to decide about marriage caused her to marry another. In retaliation, John refused her admission to communion. Sophia's husband sued for defamation of her character, so John fled back to England. He returned to his homeland with a feeling of miserable failure.

On the ship and in Georgia, John Wesley had met and been deeply impressed by the Moravians. During this time of spiritual anguish, he met Peter Boehler of the Moravians. Wesley asked Boehler if he should stop preaching because of his lack of faith. Boehler replied, "Preach faith till you have it; and then because you have it, you will preach faith."[7]

Like Luther, Wesley sought salvation for a lengthy time before securing it. Before his conversion, Wesley was committed to holy living. In 1734 he stated, "My one aim in life is to secure personal holiness, for without being holy myself I cannot promote real holiness in others."[8]

Wesley's conversion came on May 24, 1738. He attended a small group meeting on Aldersgate Street. When someone read Luther's prologue to Romans, Wesley recounted, "About a quarter to nine, while he was describing the change which God works in the heart through faith in Christ, I felt my heart strangely warmed. I felt that I did trust Christ, Christ alone, for salvation."[9]

The similarity between Luther's conversion and that of John Wesley was more than coincidental. Wesley's strong sense of calling began well before his conversion. His belief in an absolute unconditional appointment by God only deepened after Aldersgate. His own words concerning his objective were: "to reform the nation, particularly the Church, and to spread scriptural holiness over the land."[10] He went forth preaching justification by faith.

If one word could describe Wesley's mission, that word would be evangelist. Immediately following his conversion, Wesley followed Paul's example and went to his "Arabia." In John's case this meant a trip to Germany to spend time with Zinzendorf and the Moravians.

In many respects, John Wesley's life mirrored the apostle Paul's, as well. Paul was characterized by unusual zeal prior to his conversion. This is likely a reason God chose him to lead the early church. Wesley's life would be characterized by strict discipline, tremendous commitment, and a passion for God.

George Whitefield

Born in Gloucester, George Whitefield (1714-70) became the most famous evangelist in Great Britain and the New World in the eighteenth centuries. His father, the proprietor of the Bell Inn, died when George was two years old. As a young lad, Whitefield's interest in acting helped to develop what would become his unusual oratorical skills. He was passionate for his schoolmaster's plays.

Whitefield entered Pembroke College at Oxford University on November 7, 1732. His seriousness and his refusal to join in the levity of the majority of students caused him to desire to be acquainted with the Holy Club. Charles Wesley invited young George to join their group.

By then these "Bible Bigots" or "Bible Moths," as the club was also called, were a subject of great derision by the student body at large. They were encouraged by the example of the apostle Paul and by A. H. Francke's *Against the Fear of Man*. These students were committed both to personal piety and to serious scholarship.

Whitefield read Henry Scougal's *The Life of God in the Soul of Man*. The book showed him that good works alone could not convert him. Whitefield wrote about its effect: "God showed me that I must be born again, or be damned! I learned that a man may go to church, say prayers, receive the sacrament, and yet not be a Christian. God soon showed me, for in reading a few lines further, that 'true Christianity is a union of the soul with God, and Christ formed within us,' and from that moment, and not till then, did 1 know I must become a new creature."[11]

For a year Whitefield earnestly travailed for salvation. But in the spring of 1735 he settled the matter and was never the same. He was twenty years old. He began immediately to tell everyone he could about the joy of salvation. Soon, a group of people he led to Christ formed a society.

> Quotes from Whitefield:
>
> *On a burden for lost people*: You blame me for weeping, but how can I help it when you will not weep for yourselves, though your immortal souls are on the verge of destruction!
>
> *On preaching*: I did not come to tickle your ears; no, but I came to touch your hearts.
>
> *On personal witnessing*: God forbid that I should travel with anybody a quarter of an hour without speaking of Christ to them.
>
> *On scholarship*: The only way to be a true scholar is to be striving to be a true saint.
>
> *On facing difficulty*: O may God put me into one furnace after another, that my soul may be transparent; that I may see God as He is.
>
> *On a disciplined life*: There is not a thing on the face of the earth that I abhor so much as idleness or idle people.[12]

Early Ministry

Whitefield was ordained into the Anglican ministry on June 20, 1736. The Wesley's had sailed to Georgia, so the young Whitefield became the leader of the Holy Club. John wrote to Whitefield from Georgia, asking him to help the work in the New World. Unable to depart immediately, Whitefield preached for almost a year to burgeoning crowds in England. His sermons were characterized not by pomp or sensationalism, but by biblical content, doctrinal emphasis, and simplicity accompanied by an enthusiastic delivery, which often included tears. His oratorical skills proved a valuable asset. David Garrick, the most renowned English actor of the period, said Whitefield could move people to tears by the way he pronounced "Mesopotamia."

Finally, on December 30, 1737, he boarded the *Whitaker*. As they were in the harbor about to embark, John Wesley returned on the *Samuel* from America. Three ships journeyed together in Whitefield's trek across the ocean, and Whitefield soon gained the confidence of those on board to the point that he would stand and preach to all three boats at once, displaying his unique vocal ability. While on board, Whitefield recorded this prayer: "God, give me a deep humility, a well-guided zeal, a burning love and a single eye, and then let men or devils do their worst!"[13]

This first of his seven visits to America lasted only five months. The trip burdened Whitefield to raise money for an orphanage built in Savannah for the many children whose parents had died due to the severity of the new land. He dubbed the orphanage "Bethesda," or "House of Mercy," and it became a model of benevolent enterprise. On the return trip, Whitefield's ship was ravaged by a storm. As another boat came by, the captain learned of Whitefield's presence. He invited the famous evangelist aboard. Whitefield's integrity is seen in his response, for he refused to leave his ship, believing a Christian should not leave danger.

While Whitefield labored in the colonies, both Charles and John Wesley were converted. Charles met Christ on Sunday, May 21, 1738, three days before John. Filled with joy over his conversion, Charles penned "And Can It Be," perhaps his greatest of over six thousand hymns:

> And can it be that I should gain,
>   An interest in the Saviour's blood
> Died He for me, who caused His pain
>   For me, who Him to death pursued
> Amazing love, how can it be
>   That Thou, my God, should die for me?

As Whitefield rejoined these brothers and others of the Holy Club, the spiritual intensity was obvious. On several occasions they spent entire nights in prayer. Though a decade younger than John Wesley, Whitefield preceded him in gathering massive crowds to his preaching.

Field Preaching

Howell Harris, a revival leader in the Calvinistic Methodist Church in Wales in the 1730s, had begun the practice of preaching in the open air. A layman, Harris followed his powerful conversion with preaching, at first to people in homes. Soon he began preaching at any public event he attended. The blessing of God marked his preaching. He called it "exhorting" because he was unordained, but gospel preaching it was! Whitefield met Harris and was influenced by him.

In 1737, while still in his early twenties, Whitefield preached to packed churches in England, often turning away hundreds and even thousands. The people's growing spiritual hunger could not be satisfied by services in church buildings alone.

Whitefield preached not only to the masses but also to the aristocracy. His growing popularity necessitated up to four sermons on Sundays. Such a pace doubtless contributed to the health woes that plagued the evangelist throughout his ministry. Constables had to be placed at the doors of some churches to maintain order due to the crowds. People often had to be turned away.

At first, many churches invited Wesley and Whitefield to preach. However, their message of justification by faith received less than enthusiastic responses from many clergymen, and invitations soon declined. When Wesley saw that the Anglican Church would not be his chief sphere of witness, he adapted by going to the various religious societies of the day. Whitefield shifted his attention to field preaching, a practice John Wesley soon adopted after serious reticence.

Whitefield first preached out-of-doors near Bristol. Jealousy among other ministers led to closed doors in the churches in that city, so he went to a notorious area of the city called Kingswood and preached in the open air. Kingswood referred to a rough, four-thousand-acre district at the edge of Bristol where coal miners lived. The miners did not mix with the other laboring classes. People shuddered at their presence, referring to the miners as "heathens" and "savages." "Why go to America to preach to the Indians?" some queried Whitefield. "Go to Kingswood, to the Colliers."[14]

For six weeks Whitefield preached at Kingswood, with thousands gripped by the Holy Spirit. Although he did not create the method of field preaching, Whitefield certainly took it to its zenith. His influence on the Wesley's led them to follow him in the practice and served to legitimize the approach. His proper Oxford training caused Whitefield to struggle at first with the concept, but on February 17, 1739, he noted in his journal:

> My bowels have long since yearned toward the poor colliers, who are very numerous, and as sheep having no shepherd. After dinner, therefore, I went upon a mount, and spake to as many people as came unto me. They were upwards of two hundred. Blessed be God that I have now broken the ice! I believe I was never more acceptable to my Master than when I was standing to preach to those hearers in the open fields. Some may censure me; but if I thus pleased men, I should not be the servant of Christ.[15]

Often Whitefield preached outside so early in the morning his hearers had to bring lanterns. His critics referred to such preaching as "that mad Trick."[16]

Whitefield invited John Wesley to preach for him in March. After some hesitancy, Wesley preached his first field sermon on March 31, 1739. In a biography focusing on Wesley's evangelism, Wood stated that only God's grace could convince Wesley to do such a task, adding, "For every age God has a program of evangelism. This was His way of reaching the masses in the eighteenth century."[17] Through field preaching, these men reached many people that could be reached in no other way. While many criticized such a strange method, Wesley said its fruits should judge it.

"I believe I was never more acceptable to my Master than when I was standing to preach to those hearers in the open fields. Some may censure me; but if I thus pleased men, 1 should not be the servant of Christ." Whitefield on his new method

Soon John Wesley focused his ministry on those not touched by the established church: the colliers, the tinners, and the left-outs of society. He became persecuted by the owners of taverns on one side, due to the loss of business his ministry caused, and by the Anglican clergy on the other because of his message.

The Methodist Pentecost and the General Awakening

On New Year's Eve, 1738, Whitefield, the Wesley's, and about sixty others gathered for a service together. In the face of rising opposition, these earnest believers encountered the presence of God. Wesley recorded the event:

> About three in the morning, as we were continuing instant in prayer, the power of God came mightily upon us, insomuch that many cried out for exceeding joy, and many fell to the ground. As soon as we recovered a little from the awe and amazement at the presence of His majesty, we broke out with one voice, "We praise Thee, O God; we acknowledge Thee to be the Lord!"[18]

This event has been called the Methodist Pentecost. Five nights later, eight of the participants prayed and discussed matters till the early morning hours. They became convinced that a great work was about to commence. Mendell Taylor argued that this meeting "might justly be marked the beginning of the revival of religion in England in the eighteenth century."[19] All-night prayers continued to characterize the ministry of these early Methodists.

At first, John Wesley's ministry centered in London and Bristol. When he would stop at an inn or in a home, individuals were converted within an hour or two. In late 1739, Wesley acquired an old cannon foundry in London. The Foundry became headquarters for the growing Methodist revival.

Whitefield's Calvinism and Wesley's Arminian tendencies caused a schism between the two friends. Wesley opposed the doctrine of predestination and supported the idea of perfectionism (i.e. that a person could attain a state of sinlessness in this life). This view would show itself in the Holiness Movement and the Oberlin Perfectionism of Charles Finney in later years. By 1741, Whitefield, returning again from the New World, felt he had to confront his old friend. Wesley had published a sermon entitled "Free Grace" arguing his position. Whitefield responded with a letter. The tone of the letter, while refuting Wesley, was marked by grace and honor.[20]

The doctrinal differences between the two caused many of Whitefield's early supporters to refuse to listen to him, choosing instead to follow John Wesley. Whitefield and Wesley were reconciled by 1743. Distinctive elements of the revival had emerged by this time, specifically Calvinistic Methodism (Whitefield), Arminian Methodism (Wesley), and Moravianism, which had been closely linked since the beginning of the movement.[21]

Different people led revival in the various parts of the British Isles. God used the Wesley brothers in London, Howell Harris in Wales, and Benjamin Ingham in Yorkshire. Whitefield affected both America and England.

Whitefield in England

Whitefield burned with a passion for God. In late 1741 he came to Bristol from the New World and preached across England, speaking to thousands with God's power upon him. He developed a routine when in Britain: he centered much of his ministry in Moorfield in London where he preached during the winter and traversed other parts of England in the warmer months. The thousands who flocked to hear him preach were for the most part favorable in their attitude toward him. Whitefield was not without his enemies, however.

On one occasion, while preaching in Moorfield in 1742, Whitefield made this telling statement: "I was honoured with having a few stones, dirt, rotten eggs, and pieces of dead cats thrown at me."[22] Still, Whitefield preached for three hours, and more than 350 people were awakened to the truth of the gospel. Few American preachers can say they have had a similar response to their preaching! The unadulterated preaching of the Word of God in any age will bring forth both those who believe and those who resist the Lord and His messenger.

A powerful incident of revival accompanied Whitefield in Cambusland, a suburb of Glasgow, Scotland. Two years prior to Whitefield's visit, a godly minister named William McCulloch began reading to his congregation testimonies of Whitefield's ministry and of the Awakening in America. McCulloch began preaching a series of sermons on the new birth. Suddenly, people were convicted of their sins. In less than three months, three hundred people were converted. Awakening spread to four nearby parishes and eventually to Kilsyth, a town twelve miles from Glasgow.

Whitefield preached twice daily to thousands in Edinburgh in June 1742, regularly visiting hospitals as well. On July 8, Whitefield arrived at Cambusland, where he preached to large crowds through the afternoon and late into the evening. Mighty revival erupted. "Such a commotion was surely never heard of, especially about eleven o'clock at night," said Whitefield. "For about an hour and a half there was such weeping, so many falling into deep distress, and manifesting it in various ways, that description is impossible."[23] The local minister followed Whitefield, preaching past 1:00 A.M. All through that night, people continued to pray and to praise God.

Benefactors such as Selina, the Countess of Huntingdon, supported Whitefield. Selina became the patroness of Whitefield. She built several chapels and proclaimed Whitefield her domestic chaplain. Whitefield had an unusual devotion to charitable causes. He preached the gospel and raised support for such causes as his orphanage in Georgia called Bethesda, those who suffered in the Boston fire of 1760, and his assistance of Ezra Wheelock in establishing his school (now Dartmouth) serve as notable examples.

In Wales, Howell Harris founded the Calvinistic Methodist movement. Whitefield presided at the group's first conference on January 5, 1743. He served as first moderator of this new denomination and traveled across Wales. The Calvinistic Methodists continued to wield significant influence in Wales for ensuing generations. Whitefield relinquished the moderatorship of the Welsh Calvinistic Methodist Church in 1749.

The Leadership of John Wesley

Biographers have been repeatedly frustrated when they have attempted to chart a step-by-step account of Wesley's travels. There is simply too much to include. Wesley was driven by the conviction that, as long as he had breath this side of eternity, he would spend his life sharing the gospel. He covered nearly 250,000 miles, mostly on horseback. He preached over 40,000 sermons and wrote approximately 250 books and tracts. He used his saddle as a library chair, reading books as he rode upon horseback. He spent so much time in the saddle that he has been dubbed "The Evangelical Centaur."

In his field preaching, Wesley sought the most opportune place to preach in each town he visited. He used town squares, marketplaces, castles, hillsides, and any place that would help the message to be heard. He generally stood on a chair or a table. In later years, Wesley was able to preach indoors more often as well. He preached in town halls, workhouses, hospitals, prisons, asylums, and in whatever church invited him — Anglican, Presbyterian, Independent, Baptist, and Quaker.

For decades Wesley preached with great popularity among the common people. Many clergymen opposed his emphasis on justification by faith and his methods, such as field preaching. On one occasion, an ox was chased into his congregation as he proclaimed the Word. Another time, a bull was used in an attempt to disrupt the meeting. He was hit with stones, forced to preach over the noise of clanging church bells, and verbally ridiculed. Wesley planned his travels to allow as many stops as possible. He made use of the printing press; notices were sent ahead. People from surrounding villages flocked to his sermons.

Wesley's organizational acumen is obvious when one notes the rise of societies in his ministry. Societies dotted the British landscape of his day for a variety of purposes. Wesley formed small groups that copied the societies in the nation. Wesley encouraged his converts to remain loyal members of the Church of England.

He had no desire or intent to form a denomination outside of it. Early in the Awakening, Wesley began forming a staff of lay preachers. He nurtured them like a father, and insisted on strict discipline. He maintained a standard of personal discipline that gave him credibility with the leaders.

Wesley began early in his ministry to organize people into small groups for study and spiritual growth. One reason he did so was that George Whitefield had asked John to aid him in the task of organizing new converts. Whitefield's great preaching brought multitudes to salvation, but he knew that it would take a man like Wesley to organize the masses. Another major factor in Wesley's use of small groups is found in the fact that he also had great success as a preacher. Although not the orator Whitefield was, Wesley nonetheless drew crowds at all times of the day.

The Holy Club had been a model of small group success. In Georgia, Wesley recommended that his hearers form themselves into a society to meet once or twice weekly. His visit to the Moravians in Europe gave him another look at the concept. The Moravians had embraced the idea of small groups as part of the larger movement of Pietism described earlier.

As Wesley presented his message, many came seeking further spiritual advice. While it is true that some mocked Wesley, many were drawn to him. As more and more people continued to entreat Wesley to spend time with them, he began to meet with them on Thursdays. Thus Wesley began to use societies.

As the societies developed, Wesley was opposed by many of the Anglican clergymen. Charges arose that Wesley was beginning a new church. Wesley denied this and said he did not even administer the sacraments in a society. It could be that Wesley desired Methodism to create a kind of "central hall of piety" within the Church of England. At one point Wesley, in a letter, replied to a man making charges of beginning a new church by saying, "No. This society does not separate from the Communion of the rest of the Church of England."[24]

The societies began by the end of 1739. The broader movement of Methodism, which eventually did break with the Church of England, had several streams of origin. Some of the early societies in London included those at Baldwin Street, Nicholas Street, Weavers Hall, Castle Street, and Gloucester Lane. The definition of a united society was "a company of men having the form and seeking the power of Godliness, united to prayer together, to receive the word of exhortation, and to watch over one another in love, that they may help each other to work out their salvation."[25]

The growth of the societies brought about the need for leadership. A notable feature of Wesley's system of leaders was the development of lay leadership it achieved. The structure of the societies was as follows: the converts were gathered after a six-month probationary period into bands of approximately ten members, each with a leader. Membership cards were given and attendance was checked. Wesley ruled the whole system with great personal authority.

Wesley disciplined himself quite severely. This self-discipline played a major role in the societies. He would have a personal inquisition of himself weekly on Saturday evenings. While a strict disciplinarian who expected the same of others, he was also a realist. For example, when a certain lady joined a society; Wesley wrote to her, telling her that she should know that all society members would not act as they should. He counseled her, "When you see anything amiss, remember our Lord's word: 'what is that to thee? Follow thou me.'"[26]

The continued growth of the movement caused Wesley to divide the societies into smaller groups. These groups were in a constant state of growth and development.

Five groups developed throughout Wesley's ministry. The *United Societies* became the largest. These simply consisted of "awakened persons." Part of this group, who had experienced the "remission of sins," was more closely united into *Bands*. Drakeford notes that the Bands were in many respects the forerunners of modern group therapy. Those even more faithful, who "walk in the light of God," composed the *Select Societies*. The fourth group was made up of those who had shipwrecked their faith. They were called the *Penitents*. The Select Society and Penitents were on opposite sides of the spectrum. The *Class Meeting* began originally as a means of raising money. The distinctive of this organization was in its training program that developed to train the lay leadership to serve in varying capacities.

Wesley formed rules for the United Societies to aid in the disciplinary process. He drew much of his information for these rules from Jeremy Taylor, especially his books *Holy Living* and *Twelve Rules of a Helper*. Wesley had one standing prerequisite for those who desired to join a society: "A desire to flee from the wrath to come, and to be saved from their sins."[27]

There were general rules to be followed in order for one to give evidence of their desire of salvation. First, they were to avoid evil, such as taking God's name in vain, drinking liquor, fighting, buying on credit, wearing jewelry, laying up treasures on earth, etc. Second, they were to do good deeds, such as helping the poor. Third, they were to observe the ordinances of the Lord. The leaders were responsible to give account of anyone in their classes who habitually broke these rules.

Wesley also gave many strict orders concerning the skill of preaching, ranging from how to pronounce certain words, to always kneeling down in public prayer, to abstaining from singing "hymns of your own composing."[28]

The basic biblical text for the meetings of the societies was James 5:16: "Confess your faults one to another, and pray for one another, that ye may be healed." The meetings were to begin precisely on time, follow a set format, and include the investigation of one another. Five questions were always asked of each member, and others could be added. These five questions show the high accountability involved.

The Five Questions Asked at Society Meetings; [29]
1 What known sins have you committed since our last meeting?
2. What temptations have you met with? How were you delivered?
4. What have you thought, said, or done, of which you doubt whether it be sin or not?
5. Have you nothing you desire to keep secret?

Wesley's rigidity in matters of discipline can be seen clearly in his "Directions Given to the Band Societies" on December 25, 1744:

> I. Carefully to abstain from doing evil; in particular-
> Neither to buy nor sell anything at all on the Lord's Day.
> To taste no spirituous liquor, no dram of any kind, unless prescribed by a Physician.
> To be at a word both in buying and selling.
> To pawn nothing, no, not to save life.
> Not to mention the fault of any behind his back, and to stop those short that do.
> To wear no needless ornaments, such as rings, earrings, necklaces, lace, ruffles.
> To use no needless self-indulgence, such as taking snuff or tobacco, unless prescribed by a Physician.[30]

Such accountability groups have historically proved a significant factor in the spiritual growth of Christians. Wesley later divided England into five circuits. His base for ministry was the Foundry building in London that he had purchased in 1739. He set up a national organization in the colonies in 1784. The eventual break with the Anglican Church did not officially come until after Wesley's death.

Wesley's success is astounding. Although only five feet three inches tall and 128 pounds, he stood as a spiritual giant. At his death in 1791, there were 79,000 Methodists in England and 119,000 around the world. Within 110 years there were nearly 90,000 churches with members, teachers, scholars, and adherents numbering more than 40 million! Wesley's circuits led to the circuit-riding preachers famous in the Second Great Awakening. Wesley's preachers lived extremely sacrificial lives. They often lived in poverty. Sometimes there was no provision for their wives and children.

Whitefield, known for his saying that he would rather "burn out" than "rust out," followed a similarly grueling schedule on two continents. These men truly preached in season and out of season. Wood made an apt comparison between men like these and staid, slothful ministers: "We cannot but be struck by the contrast between Wesley's incessant ministry and the vegetable existence of a Parson Woodforde, who found one sermon each Sunday more than enough."[31]

While neglecting one's family or ravaging one's health do not portray virtue in themselves, these examples also indict those in our day who think more of salary packages and comfort than of a wholesale abandonment to God.

Revival in Wales

Revival came to the nation of Wales as well. In fact, the awakening in Wales preceded that in England. Griffith Jones (1683-1761), called the "Morning Star of the Methodist Revival," preached with power twenty years prior to John Wesley's conversion. He founded schools that taught tens of thousands in Wales to read the Bible in their language. According to Simon, the schools prepared the people "for the appeals that were subsequently made to them by the evangelist who passed from village to village like flames of fire."[32]

While Jones witnessed revival in his own ministry, one of the more significant aspects of his ministry was his impact on the young clergyman Daniel Rowland (1713-90). Rowland, a fine athlete and intellectually gifted man, came to Christ under the preaching of Jones. Rowland preached with power. "They fall almost as dead by the power of the Word, and continue weeping for joy, having found the Messiah; some mourning under a sense of their vileness, and some in the pangs of the new birth!" So observed Harris in March 1743. "The power at the conclusion of his sermons was such that multitudes continued weeping and crying out for the Saviour and could not possibly forbear."[33]

Harris (1714-73) was converted May 25, 1735. He experienced a powerful personal revival a few weeks later on June 18, 1735:

> I felt suddenly my heart melting within me like wax before the fire with love to God my Saviour; and also felt not only love, peace, etc. but longing to be dissolved, and to be with Christ; then was a Christ soul which I was totally unacquainted with before, Abba Father! Abba Father! I could not help calling God my Father; I knew that I was his child, and that he loved me, and heard me. My soul being filled and satiated, crying, "Tis enough, I am satisfied. Give me strength, and I will follow thee through fire and water."[34]

That fall Harris began visiting people house to house. The growing spiritual interest of the people led to large gatherings in the homes. Family worship became a priority while church attendance swelled. However, local clergymen all attacked this unordained preacher. Harris' own mother and brother viciously ridiculed him. Soon his effectiveness led to preaching out-of-doors. His influence on Whitefield has been noted. Harris read Jonathan Edwards' *Narrative of Surprising Conversions* in early 1738 with great interest. By the end of that year, news had come of an outpouring of the Spirit in London through Whitefield. Though opponents attacked Harris verbally and physically, he served the Lord with indefatigable zeal. He founded many societies.

Two other men completed the quartet of significant leaders in Wales. William Williams (1717-91) is remembered as a hymn writer. The final Welsh preacher of note was Howell Davies, who had been a pupil in Griffith Jones's schools. He and the other were mightily used of God in the eighteenth-century awakening.

Impact of the Evangelical Awakening

Evangelistic Results. Untold multitudes were converted in the Evangelical Awakening. In times of awakening, new or renewed evangelistic methods emerge. These included *field preaching*, which opened the gospel to the masses. Although opposed by many, this became a critical tool for Whitefield, the Wesley's, and others. *Printed literature* served as excellent kindling for the revival flames. Sermons, tracts, and revival reports aided the spread of the Awakening. John Wesley has been called the

"Father of the Religious Paperback" due to the thousands of letters, sermons, and tracts he published. His journals are a personal compendium without peer. He published *A Christian Library* consisting of spiritual readings from the church fathers through the Puritans and Pietists. *Lay preachers* also spread the Word of God. Many of the converts became lay preachers who carried on the work.

Music. Hymnbooks existed before the Evangelical Awakening, but Charles Wesley made the hymnbook a tool of evangelism. Charles penned over six thousand hymns, while John wrote many as well, and Whitefield penned a number. Sallee noted the influence of the Moravians on the brothers: "The Wesley's' association with the Moravians during the trip and then in Georgia had an important influence on what was to become Wesleyan hymnody. Its immediate effect was to introduce to congregations an enthusiastic type of hymn singing quite foreign to the sober singing of the metrical psalms. It also revealed the spiritual possibilities of the hymn."[35]

The impact of their songs is hard to overestimate. To a largely illiterate population, the hymns taught doctrine and, due to their application oriented messages, Christian experience. They sang the gospel to those in their day. I am convinced we need to learn to sing the gospel well to our culture today. For the leaders of this awakening, the music became a means to further the Awakening. Their hymns "combined the revivalist's fervor with the cooling elements of disciplined poetry and biblical theology."[36] Recent artists like Lecrae have found ways to use the medium of hip-hop to communicate the gospel and theology to youth.

At this same time, Isaac Watts began composing hymns. His hymns, including "When I Survey the Wondrous Cross" and "We're Marching to Zion," set a new standard for English church songs, thus his title: the "Father of English Hymnody." By the turn of the new century more than 130 hymn collections had been printed. Ellsworth summed up the impact of hymns and gospel songs: "Music played a vital role in this period of revival. Early in the Awakening the wide use of singing, particularly the singing of groups of young people along the cities and roads of the countryside, had a profound impact. Thousands of nominal Christians were caught up in evangelistic fervor that shattered old forms and traditions and opened new channels of spiritual growth for entire congregations."[37]

Missionary Expansion. Leaders of the Evangelical Awakening were committed to evangelizing the world. Whitefield's seven excursions to the New World will be noted in chapter 10, as will the Methodist efforts in America.

Impact in Issues of Social Justice. One of the overlooked marks of awakenings has to do with their impact on social ministry and on calling for justice for the oppressed. Wesley and his Methodist followers openly opposed the slave trade. Wesley corresponded with William Wilberforce, the man responsible more than any other for the abolition of slave trading by the British in 1807. Converted slave trader John Newton had led Wilberforce to Christ.

The Wesley's and Whitefield had visited the prisons regularly while in the Holy Club at Oxford. Prison reformer John Howard was encouraged by John Wesley in his efforts to bring about a change in the dreadful prisons in England and around Europe. Wesley also set up schools to educate children, focusing on evangelism. One of the effects of this awakening was its impact on Robert Raikes and the Sunday school movement. "Without doubt," said Taylor, "this was one of the major streams of evangelical power to flow from the great revival."[38] John Richard Green wrote:

> [The revival sought] to remedy the guilt, the ignorance, the physical suffering, and the social degradation of the profligate and the poor. It was not till the Wesleyan impulse had done its work that this philanthropic impulse began. The Sunday Schools established by Mr. Raikes of Gloucester at the close of the century were the beginnings of popular education. Human sympathy with the wronged and afflicted raised hospitals, endowed charities, built churches, sent missionaries to the heathen, and Wilberforce in their crusade against the iniquity of the slave-trade.[39]

Britain experienced the Evangelical Awakening, but no revival of such magnitude swept France. Instead, the French Revolution brought a bloodbath. How did Britain avoid a similar experience? More than a few historians have argued that the Evangelical Awakening helped prevent a similar result in Britain.

Questions for Small Group Discussion

1. What were three major results stemming from the Evangelical Awakening?
2. Give an example of the impact John Wesley and George Whitefield had in the Evangelical Awakening. Discuss whether or not that impact is still in effect today or whether it is needed.
3. If an awakening occurred today and had similar types of results in the different areas mentioned above, which result would be the most vital and why?
4. What can John Wesley's use of societies teach us about the importance of organization, even in spiritual movements?

Chapter 10
The First Great Awakening in America, 1726-70

In the years 1734 and 1735, there appeared a very great and general awakening, in the county of Hampshire, in the province of Massachusetts Bay, in New England also in many parts of Connecticut. Since this, there has been a far more extensive awakening of many thousands in England, Wales, and Scotland and almost all the British provinces in North America. . . . About two years ago, a very great awakening and reformation of many of the Indians, in the jerseys, and Pennsylvania~ even among such as never embraced Christianity before and within these two years, a great awakening in Virginia and Maryland.
Jonathan Edwards[1]

The testimony above illustrates the remarkable effects wrought by the First Great Awakening. A sense of awe swept the colonies as they were overwhelmed by torrents of this movement of God. For most historians, the paradigm for spiritual awakenings in the modern era is this revival that swept the American colonies in the eighteenth century.

Like the incoming tide, which connects individual puddles of water as it swells toward the shore, the Awakening quickly swept across the colonies with the force of a spiritual tidal wave. The colonies were touched from north to south and east to west. Multitudes professed changed lives. Churches were planted and strengthened, missions enterprises birthed, and theological convictions hammered out on the anvil of the Reformation were renewed and given fresh vigor. The Awakening affirmed both the importance of Christian experience and doctrinal fidelity. Institutions ranging from orphanages to colleges dotted the landscape.

The earliest signs of awakening came in 1726, although its greatest impact came in the 1740s. As revival rains waned in the North by 1750; they intensified in the southern colonies in the years following. By 1770, the year of George Whitefield's death, the Awakening's fire dampened as the growing conflict of the Revolutionary War loomed.

Conditions before the Awakening

By the turn of the eighteenth century, Europeans enjoyed life in thirteen colonies. The population had grown dramatically: from 75,000 in 1660 to almost 1.6 million in 1760. In addition, a rich ethnic diversity and a concomitant denominational variety characterized the colonists. Germans, Swiss, and Dutch joined those settling the New World from the British Isles. Anglicans, Congregationalists, Baptists, Quakers, Lutherans, the Dutch Reformed, Presbyterians, and some Roman Catholics made up the majority of religious groups. Due to the rapidly expanding slave trade, the African population swelled, particularly in the southern colonies.

Along with a new world and a new way of life, the colonists discovered hardships. Wars and skirmishes were frequent, including various intercolonial wars and battles with different Indian tribes. Particularly in New England, the colonists faced a continual fear of confrontations with Indians.

Church life had become established in the colonies by the early eighteenth century. Congregationalists dominated New England, Presbyterians were predominant in Pennsylvania and New Jersey, and Anglicans (Episcopalians) settled mainly in Virginia. However, like the children of Israel who had a tendency to forget the LORD after settling in the Promised Land, the ensconcing of church life led to a rote religiosity among parishioners and a professional formalism among the clergy across traditions.

Heimert and Miller summarized the concern in the colonies: "What concerned American Protestants, after the first planting of Massachusetts Bay, was the sterility, not of colonial soil but of its spiritual life."[2] The spiritual lethargy resulted in a twin problem which brought the need of awakening to the forefront: deviant orthodoxy (a departure from historic Christian belief) and dead orthodoxy (correct belief devoid of corresponding Christian behavior).[3] Consistently in Scripture and history, one sees this two-headed beast confront God's people. Either problem — laxity in devotion or compromising the Word of God — comes to the same end: a heart turned away from God.

An example of the tendency toward dead orthodoxy was the annual fast day in Puritan New England. Days of fasting began in New England as early as the 1620s with remarkable effects. In 1622, the year following the famous thanksgiving of the Pilgrims, a serious drought threatened the crops. The authorities appointed a day of prayer and humiliation. Providentially, the rains fell, commencing a second ceremony of thanksgiving.

In 1631 Governor Winthrop realized the colonists did not have enough provisions to make it through the approaching winter. The authorities "called for a day of humiliation — upon which the *Lyon* came into view. The ship bringing supplies returned in harmony with the prayers of the people."[4]

Because of the early success, authorities ultimately proclaimed annual fast days. The Massachusetts General Court voted to hold a day of fasting on January 19, 1637. The fast days developed into opportunities for community gatherings rather than outcries to God. Like the children of Israel, the colonists lost their intimacy with God in the externals of ceremony.

There was an irony that developed: the gathered community, while losing their focus on God, still gave their attention to the fast day sermon. Faithful ministers eventually saw the fast day sermon as a means to exhort the people to return to their God. Increase Mather, Thomas Thatcher, Joseph Rowlandson, John Cotton, and others recognized the spiritual declension among the people. Their fast day sermons in the latter half of the seventeenth century developed into the sermonic form known as the Jeremiad. The preacher first stated a problem in the community. Following this, the minister described the judgment of God for the problem, proposed a way by which the community could be reformed, and warned the people lest they ignore his counsel.[5]

Following the example of the Old Testament prophets, pastors called people to renew their covenant with God, believing such a return would lead to a general revival.

By the turn of the eighteenth century, however, most ministers believed only united, earnest prayer could bring a divine outpouring, which would then lead the people to return to God. Whereas "reformation of manners" was the heart cry of New England Puritanism in the 1690s, "revival of religion" became the phrase used in the 1720s to describe the only antidote for the spiritual declension. In other words, rather than calling the people to change so that God would pour out His Spirit, ministers began calling people to seek God's face in prayer in order that He would lead the people into revival, which in turn would initiate a moral reformation.

The most obvious example of deviant orthodoxy was the Halfway Covenant in New England. Confirmed in 1662 by the Massachusetts Synod, the covenant gradually gained acceptance in virtually every Congregationalist church in New England. The text of the covenant in part said:

> The children of the church-members as well as their parents, and do not cease to be members by becoming adult, but do still continue in the Church, until in some way of God they be cast out; and . . . they are subject to Church-discipline, even as other members, and may have their children baptized before themselves be received to the Lord's Supper; and yet that in this way there is no tendency to the corrupting of the Church by unworthy members, or of the Ordinances by unworthy partakers.[6]

As a result, members became content with their halfway status, leading to churches filled with unregenerate members.

The ultimate end of this compromise of evangelical conviction was seen in the ministry of Solomon Stoddard (1643-1729), the powerful minister of the Congregationalist church in Northampton, Massachusetts. Stoddard had in fact seen several instances of robust revival in his pastorate. His ministry in many ways was admirable, but his view, known as "Stoddardeanism," taught that the Lord's Supper was a converting ordinance; further, he argued that one must assume a person already a saint if he accepted the creed and faithfully attended worship and communion. This example, with others noted above, demonstrated the need among the colonists for God to "rend the heavens and come down" (Isaiah 64:1).

Rather than calling the people to change so that God would pour out His Spirit, ministers began calling people to seek God's face in prayer, in order that He would lead the people into revival, which in turn would initiate a moral reformation.

The Awakening in the Middle Colonies

The awakening moved along three primary fronts. The middle colonies, particularly Pennsylvania and New Jersey, saw the earliest manifestations of the Spirit. New England soon followed, notably through the ministry of Jonathan Edwards. Later the southern colonies experienced similar phenomena. George Whitefield's itinerant ministry helped unite individual revivals into a Great Awakening.

Dutch Reformed pastor Theodore Jackobus Frelinghuysen (1691-1747) in New Jersey experienced the first sparks of the Awakening's fire in the year 1726. In 1739, George Whitefield called Frelinghuysen "a worthy old soldier of Jesus Christ, . . . and the beginner of the great work which I trust the Lord is carrying on in these parts."[7]

A German-born son of a Dutch Reformed pastor, Frelinghuysen came to the colonies in 1720 to serve as pastor of four Dutch Reformed churches in the Raritan Valley of New Jersey. He was influenced by Dutch Calvinism and by Pietism. He came to the New World with a burning passion for revival in the Dutch Reformed Church. He commented on the spiritual laxity in the churches he served: "While horse-racing, gambling, dissipation, and rudeness of various kinds were common, the [church] was attended at convenience, and religion consisted of the mere formal pursuit of the routine of duty."[8]

Frelinghuysen determined to bring a fresh vigor to the faith through evangelistic preaching, church discipline (especially related to observing the Lord's Supper), and zealous visitation. He preached that an obvious conversion experience was necessary. His preaching on the necessity of conversion, particularly when aimed at church members, brought a spirit of revival, many new believers, and controversy among some members and other Dutch Reformed ministers. Many members welcomed his leadership, though some fought unsuccessfully for his removal. Ultimately, the revival birthed in New Jersey led Frelinghuysen to itinerate from Neshaminy, Pennsylvania (site of the Log College of the Tennents – see below), to Long Island, New York. Many church members were converted under his ministry, a mark of deep revival.

In 1725, a group of Dutch Reformed ministers led by Domine Boel published the Complaints, seventeen accusations charging Frelinghuysen with doctrinal error and improper practice. They particularly criticized his itinerant ministry. Frelinghuysen responded with three messages that were received with great effect. Following this, Frelinghuysen confronted Boel with these words: "Is this not the doctrine of the Reformed Church? I care not what ignorant, carnal men say behind my back. They are greatly deceived if they imagine they will thus put me to shame, for I would rather die a thousand deaths than not preach the truth."[9]

Despite opposition, revival flourished. It reached its climax in 1726 and was especially effective among the youth of the four churches served by Frelinghuysen. The spirit of revival spread to many Presbyterians. The Dutch Reformed Church eventually split into prorevival and antirevival groups. The revival in New Jersey is a fitting reminder that revival is like a fire: some draw near to it for its warmth while others fear the pain it can bring.

Frelinghuysen shared a common theological feature with the Reformation and other awakenings: an emphasis on the necessity of conversion that came through justification by faith alone. Frelinghuysen promoted two significant innovations, as well.

First, he developed the practice of small group devotional meetings not unlike those of the Pietists of Germany. Second, he transformed the voorlessers ("helpers") into lay preachers. When he was away to minister to others Frelinghuysen appointed one or two men to preside over the devotional meetings. The success of this approach is seen in that by 1736 the United Consistory of the Dutch Reformed Church elected one or more helpers for each church.

The key impetus to the revival among Presbyterians came through the Tennent family. The Scotch-Irish family came to America in 1716, eventually settling in Pennsylvania. William Sr. (1673-1746) was concerned about the dead orthodoxy in the churches. He built a log cabin as a theological training center for his sons. He trained Gilbert (1703-64), the oldest, and eventually his three remaining sons along with about fifteen others. His curriculum was critical in the future development of leaders in the Awakening. Subjects included languages, logic, and theology. Most importantly, however, he instilled in each student a passion for evangelism, for a devotional life, and for the Word of God. William Sr. had an ability to draw the most promising young men to his "Log College," as his detractors deemed it. Many of these students became revival leaders themselves.

The influence of William Sr. has for too long been underestimated in the history of revivals. Through the students in his Log College and the many other log schools arising from his originality, his impact spread far beyond his personal ministry. The contemporary movement toward mentoring in ministry training could learn from William Tennent's work. George Whitefield commented on the school on one of his visits:

> The place wherein the young men study now is, in contempt, called The College. It is a log house, about twenty feet long, and near as many broad; and, to me, it seemed to resemble the school of the old prophets. That their habitations were mean, and that they sought not great things for themselves, is plain. From this despised place, seven or eight worthy ministers of Jesus have lately been sent forth; more are almost ready to be sent; and the foundation is now laying for the instruction of many others.[10]

The Log College eventually developed into the College of New Jersey and subsequently Princeton University. It has been deemed the forerunner of modern seminaries. Many of the college graduates started log colleges of their own. The impact of the Log College led to a continual founding of schools as Presbyterians moved westward. In fact, at least sixty-three educational institutions were spawned by its example, and the cumulative years of pastoral ministry from Log College graduates alone were 426.[11]

Gilbert Tennent emerged as the most capable revival leader. He was appointed to plant a Presbyterian church at Brunswick, New Jersey, in 1726. At this time, he experienced a serious affliction, which affected his commitment to God. Gilbert pledged to serve the Lord faithfully, particularly in the cause of evangelism. Like his father, Gilbert was concerned that many church members and several ministers had never been converted. Immediately following the illness, an effusion of the Spirit's power marked his ministry.

Around this time, Gilbert Tennent met Frelinghuysen and recorded the following impressions: "I had the Pleasure of seeing much of the Fruits of his Ministry. This together with a Kind Letter which he sent me respecting the Necessity of dividing the Word aright excited me to great Earnestness in ministerial Labours."[12]

Whitefield called Gilbert and his peers the brightest lights in the colony of Pennsylvania. Like other preachers of the Awakening, Gilbert preached the necessity of conversion. He preached "terrors" to unawakened sinners and applied the balm of the gospel to those under conviction. As many were awakened, he emphasized the preaching of doctrine. His style of preaching differed from that of the staid Edwards or the oratorically gifted Whitefield. His preaching style was more an extension of his personality than a technique to gain results. His preaching's impact on Whitefield was clear. "He convinced me," said the young evangelist, "that we can preach the Gospel of Christ no further than we have experienced the power of it in our hearts."[13]

Gilbert Tennent was mightily used of God in the cause of revival. He preached his most famous sermon, "The Danger of an Unconverted Ministry," in Nottingham, Pennsylvania, on March 8, 1740. He railed against ministers in the synod, declaring that many were unregenerate and therefore unfit to preach the new birth. He concluded with an invitation to the people to seek churches that provided profitable teaching. Unlike our time, when switching churches happens constantly, calling believers to move from one church to another for sound preaching was virtually unheard of. The sermon indicted the entire Presbyterian ministry, especially those opposing revival. It was published and distributed widely.

The result was a division among Presbyterians in 1741 between the "Old Sides" and the "New Sides," anti-revival and pro-revival groups, respectively. Gilbert and others argued for conversion experience validated by a changed life as necessary for church membership. In addition, the New Sides believed ministers should not only be educated, but should also give evidence of an inward, divine call.[14] The Old Sides opposed the enthusiasm of the Great Awakening.

Among the New Side churches revival flourished. Old Side ministers declined from twenty-five to twenty-two for the period 1745-58, while New Side ministers increased from twenty-two to seventy-two. Through the leadership of Gilbert Tennent, an agreement was reached between the parties in 1758. The united Presbyterians continued to grow rapidly through the time of the Revolutionary War.

The revival spread through the ministry of the Tennent sons and others. John Tennent witnessed a strong movement of God in Freehold, New Jersey. His brother William Jr. (1705-77) followed him to the church, and the revival spread. John Rowland, who through the influence of the Tennent's and others was the first minister licensed in the Presbyterian denomination that was not first approved by the synod, saw a powerful revival at his church in Maidenhead and later at Hopewell and Amwell.

Jonathan Dickinson (1688-1747) became a member of the Philadelphia Presbytery in 1717. He affirmed and defended the ministry of Whitefield and was close friends with the young David Brainerd. He wrote a popular tract supporting the revival while opposing fanaticism. Dickinson later became moderator of the Synod of New York. This Synod granted a charter for what became the College of New Jersey. Dickinson was named the first president.

Jonathan Edwards and the Awakening in New England

The Great Awakening in New England centered on the ministry of Congregationalist pastor Jonathan Edwards (1703-58) and subsequent itinerant visits by George Whitefield from England. Edwards' place in early American Christianity stands without peer. He is remembered for his preaching, philosophical contributions, theological formulations, and his personal piety. Oliver Wendell Holmes echoed the opinion of many when he called Edwards and Benjamin Franklin the two most significant thinkers in early America.

Rev. and Mrs. Timothy Edwards welcomed baby Jonathan into their home on October 5, 1703, the only son among eleven children.[15] Timothy and Esther Stoddard Edwards lived in the same modest flat the entirety of their sixty-three years of marriage. Young Jonathan quickly distinguished himself as a prodigy. He read Latin by age six, and by thirteen read the writings of Locke with great pleasure. He wrote remarkable treatises, including *Of Insects* at age eleven, writing *Of the Rainbow* at about the same time, and finishing *A Facetious Rebuttal to the Notion of a Material Soul* before his thirteenth birthday. He graduated as valedictorian from Yale at age sixteen.

Following his graduation, Edwards briefly served as pastor of a Presbyterian church. Soon thereafter, he earned his M.A. at Yale and was employed as a tutor for the school for two years. During this time, he wrote his *Diary* and *Resolutions*. *Diary* consists of brief statements about his daily relationship with God. A total of seventy resolutions make up the latter work.

Edwards's conversion came following a bout with pleurisy, which caused him to fear for his life. He lived a disciplined life in the mode of his Puritan forefathers. His voluminous appetite for reading was satisfied with a variety of tastes. His writings reflect a broad knowledge of the Bible. He also searched out books with which he disagreed, which explains in part his aptitude toward apologetic and polemical writing. Fasting and prayer characterized his life; he spent days in prayer and fasting often during the course of a year. His *Memoirs* record how, as a boy of only seven or eight, he prayed five times daily in secret prayer. He also, with the help of schoolmates, built a booth in a swamp designed to be a place of prayer.

Edwards married Sarah Pierrepont, who has been recognized along with Susannah Wesley as one of the models of a godly woman in Christian history. In 1726 he became associate pastor to the famous pastor Solomon Stoddard at the distinguished Congregational church in Northampton, Massachusetts. Stoddard, Edwards' maternal grandfather, was so famous he was called the "Pope" by some and the "White God" by some Indian tribes. After Stoddard's death in 1729, Edwards became pastor of the church. Edwards' Northampton pastorate became a lightning rod for the growing thunderclouds of awakening.

In the Puritan style, Edwards preached on Sundays and gave a Thursday lecture. He averaged thirteen hours daily in his study. His penchant for writing demonstrates the breadth of his intellect and his piety.[16] His writings include works on philosophy and theology; however, Edwards' writings related to revival require attention for the present study. No individual in history, with the arguable exception of Charles Finney, has produced more significant writings on the subject of revival than Jonathan Edwards. His writings provide a thorough history and defense of the awakening in his day.

Before the widespread awakening of the early 1740s, several localized revivals occurred in New England. Edwards' first record of revival, the *Narrative*, chronicled the Valley Revival of 1734-35. Edwards was only thirty-one when revival came. He began by noting five church revivals under Solomon Stoddard's ministry in Northampton during 1679, 1683, 1696, 1712, and 1718. The Valley Revival was so named because it spread from Northampton up and down the Connecticut River valley.

Several factors contributed to the revival's origin. Concerned about the dullness of the people toward the faith, Edwards called his people to honor the day of the Lord. This caused some to grow concerned over their laxity. This concern increased following the conversion of several families in the nearby town of Pascommuck.

Edwards also encouraged youth to form small groups for prayer and discussion, which many adults joined as well. Edwards repeatedly commented on the preeminent role young people had in this and subsequent revivals. The death of two young people in separate incidents added to the growing seriousness of the people. One young man who was highly respected died suddenly in June of 1734. Edwards preached a message on the untimely nature of death, which strongly affected the youth, encouraging further devotion to small group prayer.

Revival erupted when Edwards preached a series of messages on justification by faith. He himself was amazed at what he termed the "surprising works of God." He wrote that, for some time in Northampton, the only topic of discussion was of spiritual matters. Many persons came to Christ as a result of the supernatural activity of God. A frivolous young woman's dramatic conversion was the first of many. More than three hundred professed faith in Christ in only six months.

By the spring of 1735, the church filled to capacity each week. Often the entire congregation was moved to tears, due in some cases to joy and in others to sorrow for sin. In the months of March and April, nearly thirty were added to the church, while a spirit of revival moved many believers. People came from other areas to see the amazing work. Many of them were awakened and spread the revival elsewhere. Edwards recorded that no less than twenty-seven towns ultimately experienced revival. Soon Edwards' church counted more than six hundred members, encompassing virtually the entire adult population of the town.

The *Narrative* had a powerful effect on both the contemporary scene and on the century following. It was immediately published and sent to England. Miller commented on its impact there: "Without exaggeration one may say that the Narrative did for bewildered English nonconformists of 1736 what Goethe's Werther did for young German romantics. It perfected a formula for escape from an intellectual dilemma by opening an avenue into emotion and sensibility."[17]

The *Narrative* also had an impact on a young John Wesley. Wesley read the account in 1738, writing in his journal that this movement was surely from the Lord. As a result, he "was led to desire earnestly that England might not lay behind America in that path of grace."[18] In addition, Whitefield read the work while in Georgia in 1738.

Beyond recording the events of Northampton, Edwards mentioned other signs of revival he had discovered:

> The Rev. William Tennent, a minister who seemed to have such things much at heart, told me of a very considerable revival of religion under the ministry of his brother the Rev. Gilbert Tennent, and also at another place, under the ministry of a very pious young gentleman, a Dutch minister, whose name as I remember was Frelinghousa.[19]

Edwards saw the Valley Revival as not only an outpouring of God's Spirit, but also a doctrinal corrective against the rising tide of Arminianism. While demonstrating utmost respect and courtesy toward his grandfather, Edwards confronted the teachings of Solomon Stoddard with which he disagreed.

The Awakening reached its climax across New England in 1740-42, particularly through the itinerant work of George Whitefield. In October 1740, Whitefield came to Northampton on a visit to the Edwards family. A fresh awakening followed his visit there. A letter by Edwards to a Boston pastor described the work of God in 1740-42. As had occurred in 1734-35, Edwards wrote that the entire town was transformed into an unusual God-consciousness. During the summer of 1741, meetings frequently continued all through the night.

Due to his growing reputation as a preacher following the Valley Revival, Edwards occasionally traveled to other churches to speak. Other pastors in Connecticut and New Jersey followed Edwards' example of brief itinerant journeys with the permission of their congregations. He preached exegetical sermons in the Puritan tradition. He typically stood in the pulpit with his manuscript in one hand and a candle in the other. Early in his ministry, sermon manuscripts were read; after Whitefield visited Northampton, Edwards began using outlines instead. Winslow offers a telling glimpse of a Sunday in Northampton during Edwards' day:

> It was on Sunday morning at the ringing of the meetinghouse bell that Northampton had its best chance to know "Mr. Edwards," as he mounted his high pulpit and in a quiet voice, without movement or gesture, laid down his doctrine. . . . the piercing eyes went everywhere, the thin tones reached the dim corners of the gallery. Every word was distinctively spoken. . . . This delicate-looking young man had something to say, and strangely enough his fragility seemed to increase his power. [20]

On July 8, 1741, he preached his most renowned sermon, "Sinners in the Hands of an Angry God," which spurred profound brokenness and repentance in the church at Enfield, Connecticut. Not all of his sermons were in the imprecatory style of "Sinners." In fact, revival came to Northampton in 1740 in the midst of a series on the love of Christ from 1 Corinthians 13. Still, the impact of "Sinners" should not be overlooked. The sermon's impact drew from Edwards' imagery. Based on the text, "Their foot shall slide in due time" (Deut. 32:35, KJV), Edwards' thesis was: "There is nothing that keeps wicked men at anyone moment out of hell, but the mere pleasure of God." His powerful imagery was almost visceral in its effect:

> The God that holds you over the pit of hell, much as one holds a spider or some loathsome insect over the fire, abhors you and is dreadfully provoked. His wrath toward you burns like fire; he looks upon you as worthy of nothing else but to be cast into the fire. . . . it is nothing but His hand that holds you from falling into the fire every moment.[21]

He concluded the message with an appeal to flee the wrath to come and follow Christ. What happened as he delivered the message?

> The effect of the sermon was as if some supernatural apparition had frightened the people beyond control. They were convulsed in tears of agony and distress. Amid their tears and outcries the preacher pauses, bidding them to be quiet in order that he may be heard.[22]

In January of 1742, he preached for several weeks in Leicester, where again awakening erupted. While on that tour, he asked a Reverend Buell to preach in Northampton. When Edwards returned, he remarked that "almost the whole town seemed to be in a great and continual commotion, day and night, and there was indeed a very great revival of religion."[23] In May, Edwards led the people to affirm a covenant before God, followed by a day of fasting.

In 1741 Edwards published *The Distinguishing Mark of a Work of The Spirit of God*, a collection of sermons, which included five "marks" that illustrated the Spirit's true activity in revival. During the years following the apex of revival, Edwards produced many important writings. His *Some Thoughts on the Revival of Religion in New England* described the mighty revival in the early 1740s. This treatise revealed Edwards as the champion of the New Lights, or prorevival preachers. He unequivocally affirmed the work as a movement of God. The work is divided into five parts. In part 1 he argued that revival is a glorious work of God that should be judged a posteriori, not a priori. In other words,

> We are to judge the effects wrought; and if, upon examination of that, it be found to be agreeable to the word of God, we are bound to rest in it as God's work; and shall be like to be rebuked for our arrogance, if we refuse so to do till God shall explain to us how he has brought this effect to pass, or why he has made use of such and such means in doing it.[25]

Edwards added that judging a priori is "too much for the clay to do with respect to the potter." In other words, revival should be judged by its fruits. Part 2 formed a discourse on the need and obligation to promote the revival. He charged pastors not to be envious of those ministers whom God had chosen to carry on this work more than they. In part 3 of *Some Thoughts* he admitted the revival had been abused by some.

Five marks of a revival according to Jonathan Edwards:[24]

1. When the operation is such to raise their esteem of that Jesus who was born of the Virgin, and was crucified without the gates of Jerusalem; and seems more to confirm and establish their minds in the truth of what the gospel declares to us of his being the Son of God, and the Saviour of men; is a sure sign that it is from the Spirit of God.

2. When the spirit that is at work operates against the interests of Satan's kingdom, which lies in encouraging and establishing sin, and cherishing men's worldly lusts; this is a sure sign that it is a true, and not a false spirit.

3. The spirit that operates in such a manner as to cause in men a greater regard to the Holy Scriptures, and establishes them more in their truth and divinity, is certainly the Spirit of God.

4. If by observing the manner of the operation of a spirit that is at work among a people, we see that it operates as a spirit of truth, leading persons to truth, convincing them of those things that are true, we may safely determine that it is a right and true spirit.

5. If the spirit that is at work among a people operates as a spirit of love to God and man, it is a sure sign that is the Spirit of God.

In part 4, Edwards cited what should be corrected or avoided to promote the work. He warned against spiritual pride, exclusivism, and people who claimed God had spoken to them in impressions, which might or might not have anything to do with Scripture. The final section gave specific examples as to how one might promote the revival, including confessing faults, the conversion of ministers, true worship, moral duties to the community, frequent public recommitment to God, and most importantly, prayer and fasting.

In 1746 Edwards wrote *Religious Affections*, which presented his philosophy and psychology of religion. He defended outward expressions of Christian living as not only acceptable, but also as normal. However, he cautioned in part 2 that outward signs of piety did not in themselves prove genuine religious affections. In other words, one could "fake it" by demonstrating fervor, knowledge of Scripture, hard work, or other means. In the third section, the heart of the treatise, he listed twelve distinctive traits of true affections. The last is most significant: Edwards said a true Christian will act like one; Christ-like practice will not produce salvation, but it is a natural result of conversion. Other writings in the category of revival included a treatise on prayer entitled *An Humble Attempt to Promote Explicit Agreement and Visible Union of God's*

People, in Extraordinary Prayer, for the Advancement of Christ's Kingdom on Earth, which played an important role in the Second Great Awakening (see Chapter 11).

As time passed and the effects of the revival diminished, Edwards faced increasing opposition to revival in his congregation. In 1748 he refused to admit an applicant without a public profession of faith. In 1749 he published his *Humble Inquiry* to explain his views on requirements for church membership. He was unable to win most church members to his side. After two stormy years, a council was summoned with the result that Edwards was dismissed in 1750.[26]

Edwards traveled west to the frontier town of Stockbridge, where he served as a missionary to the Mohawk and Houssatunnuck Indians. Here he wrote several important works. He published *Freedom of the Will* in 1754 as a defense of Calvinist dogma and a polemic against Arminianism. In September 1757, the trustees of the College of New Jersey (Princeton) asked him to become the next president. He arrived at the school in February 1758. Unfortunately, he and died from a smallpox inoculation on March 22, 1758, at the age of fifty-four.

David Brainerd (1718-47) was influenced by Edwards, and was engaged to his daughter before his untimely death. He experienced a powerful conversion in 1739 and entered Yale soon thereafter. He was expelled from Yale after commenting that one of the faculty had no more grace than a chair. His noted his remorse for the statement and its consequences repeatedly in his *Diary*. Ebenezer Pemberton (1705-77) influenced young Brainerd to give his life to evangelizing the Indians. "My great concern," Brainerd wrote, "was for the conversion of the heathen to God."[27]

Brainerd's sacrificial commitment to reach the Indians was blessed by God. On one occasion, for example, the Susquehannah Indians demonstrated unusual brokenness from Brainerd's preaching — drunkards bowed in repentance, — young and old were broken under the force of the Spirit.

Jonathan Edwards admired Brainerd. Edwards' daughter Jerusha was engaged to the young preacher. Unfortunately, Brainerd died just before his thirtieth birthday from tuberculosis. Brainerd's *Diary* has influenced countless believers to live sacrificial lives. It played a key role in the life of Henry Martyn, the great missionary to India.

Nathaniel Leonard of Plymouth, concerned by the Sabbath-breaking and tavern-frequenting in his area, called his church to observe annual days of prayer and fasting for revival. Local authorities had attempted unsuccessfully to curb the rowdies by imposing a 9:00 closure on the taverns. However, when the fire of the Great Awakening came to the town, frequenters of the taverns forsook humanly distilled spirits for the sweet wine of the Spirit of God.

In Boston, churches agreed to fast and pray for an outpouring of the Spirit in 1722 and 1734. When the Great Awakening rocked that city, a similar season of prayer was held in 1742. The difference was that the focus of this season was thanksgiving for the abundant blessings of God in the Great Awakening.

In Gloucester, Massachusetts, John White led his church to set aside a day for prayer and fasting after reading Edwards' *Narrative*. The church soon experienced an awakening of its own. Seasons of revival also came following seasons of prayer and fasting in Halifax, Wrentham, and Middleborough, Massachusetts, and Portsmouth,

New Hampshire. Over twenty-five individual narratives of revival following the pattern of Edwards' *Narrative* were composed. [28]

The awakening was not without its problems. James Davenport (1716-57) did much to discredit the awakening in New England with his fanaticism. He set out to follow the pattern of Whitefield and Tennent, jealously desiring to become one of the great awakeners. An example of his bizarre behavior came on March 6, 1743, when he led a public burning of theological books. Davenport proceeded to throw his trousers into the fire, moving about in his underclothing. The local court pronounced him deranged, and he was ultimately deported to Long Island from Connecticut. He then published *Confessions and Retractions* in 1744, repenting of much of his behavior.

On the other extreme was Charles Chauncy, a liberal Boston pastor who lumped Davenport, Whitefield, and Tennent together as censorious enthusiasts who played to the emotions of their hearers. He attacked Whitefield and Tennent for their itineration and complained of numerous problems with Davenport, including an occasion where two women were supposedly put into a trance following his influence. Davenport was undoubtedly an extremist. Chauncy was inaccurate, however, when he considered Whitefield and Tennent in the same camp.

Chauncy tended toward focusing on the role of the mind in religious experience, whereas Edwards, though certainly one who affirmed the place of the intellect, said true religion could not be divorced from the affections or passions. In his insistence on an enlightened mind over against raised affections, Chauncy "increasingly preached a 'liberal gospel' and was therefore a precursor of the Unitarianism that would flourish in eastern Massachusetts."[29]

Edwards' *Some Thoughts* and Chauncy's *Seasonable Thoughts* clearly display the developing tension between evangelical and rational theology. John Smith portrays Edwards as a mediator between Davenport's emotionalism and Chauncy's rationalism.[30]

The Unifying Impact of George Whitefield

God used George Whitefield with great effect throughout the colonies as a traveling evangelist. He crossed the Atlantic to the colonies from his native England seven times (1738, 1739-41, 1744-48, 1751-54, 1754-55, 1763-65, 1769-70). His most powerful visit came during his second campaign. On September 14, 1740, shortly before his twenty-sixth birthday, Whitefield began a tour of New England, described by Gaustad as "the greatest single evangelistic tour in New England's history."[31] His itinerant ministry throughout the colonies fanned the flames of localized revivals into the inferno of the Great Awakening.

Benjamin Franklin, although himself a Deist, published many of Whitefield's sermons and recognized the unusual elocution of the young minister. On one occasion, Franklin estimated that Whitefield spoke to twenty-five thousand people in the open air. Considering Whitefield's ability to persuade, note this account by Franklin when Whitefield was raising money for his orphanage:

I silently resolved he should get nothing from me. I had in my pocket a handful of copper money, three or four silver dollars, and 5 pistoles in gold. As he proceeded I began to soften, and concluded to give the copper. Another stroke of his oratory made me ashamed of that, and determined me to give the silver; and he finished so admirably that I emptied my pocket wholly into the collectors dish, gold and all! [32]

Whitefield's enormous popularity and evangelical fervor led to massive crowds. For a time he was the most popular figure in America. Crowds by the thousands thronged to hear him on his journeys. While in Boston on his second campaign, over fifteen thousand came to hear him. This was greater than the population of the city! During his time there, two ministers in Boston stated that more people came to them for spiritual aid in one week than had done so in the previous twenty-four years combined. He preached virtually every day and generally several times daily.

A memorable account of Whitefield's immense popularity is seen in an account by Nathan Cole, an unlearned farmer who heard of Whitefield's visit to Middletown after the evangelist visited with Jonathan Edwards. Cole recorded how the announcement of Whitefield's coming to preach brought people of the entire countryside to hear him.[33]

The conversion of Nathan Cole:

I was in my field at work; I dropped my tool that I had in my hand and ran home to my wife, telling her to make ready quickly to go and hear Mr. Whitfield [sic] preach at Middletown, then run to my pasture for my horse with all my might. . .

As I came nearer to the road, I heard a noise something like a low rumbling thunder and presently found it was the noise of horses' feet coming down the road. . . . I turned and looked towards the [Connecticut River] and saw the ferry boats running swift backward and forward bringing over loads of people. . . . The land and banks over the river looked black with people and horses. All along the 12 miles I saw no man at work in his field, but all seemed to be gone.

When I saw Mr. Whitfield come upon the scaffold, he looked almost angelical, young, slim, slender youth before some thousands of people with a bold, undaunted countenance. . . . he looked as if he was clothed with authority from the Great God, and a sweet solemn solemnity sat upon his brow, and my hearing him preach gave me a heart wound. By God's blessing my old foundation was broken up, and I saw that my righteousness would not save me.

By 1740 Whitefield faced increasing numbers of detractors, particularly among the clergy. Challenging the status quo — even for the sake of the gospel — brings opposition. A pamphlet entitled the Querist vilified him, and a tract by professors of Harvard charged him with excessive enthusiasm. He was also attacked for his itinerancy. Whitefield listened to his critics and agreed with points he considered valid. However, he would not deviate from his conviction about evangelical tenets or from his conviction that the Awakening was indeed a work of God's Spirit.

Like Wesley, Whitefield made use of his published sermons. Whitefield's relation to other revival leaders helped to unite the various revival movements. Gilbert Tennent followed Whitefield's powerful ministry in Boston; under Tennent's leadership, revival continued for a year and a half.

Whitefield united the revival movements. This was due in part to his itineration and in part due to the fact that he sought a trans-denominational ministry. One of the criticisms he received concerned his willingness to work across denominational lines. It has been said that Whitefield was the first American hero, the first American celebrity, and the best-known person in the colonies in the mid-eighteenth century.

Whitefield served Christ as a peerless evangelist whose preaching led to the conversion of countless souls. Dargan boldly declared: "The history of preaching since the apostles does not contain a greater or worthier name than that of George Whitefield."[34]

Whitefield also emphasized social ministry. His best-known example was the orphanage he founded called Bethesda in Georgia. The orphanage provided both a source of joy, because of the children who were helped and the many similar enterprises the institution inspired, and of sorrow, because of the nagging debt associated with it.

Whitefield embarked on his seventh trip to America in 1770. After some time at Bethesda, he preached from Philadelphia through New England. In Newburyport, Massachusetts, he preached his last sermon. On September 29, he spoke to a gathering from his window until the candle in his hand burned out. Early the next morning his earthly candle ceased to burn.

Awakening in the South

The Awakening in the South in many ways followed much of what occurred in the North. The primary denominations affected were the Presbyterians, the Baptists, and the fledgling Methodist movement that leaped across the Atlantic and spread through the southern colonies.

The southern phase of the Awakening followed that of the North chronologically. It bore the stamp of the frontier because the colonies in the South were less established than those up the Atlantic seaboard. In addition, more Baptists were affected in the South than in the North. By far, the greatest Methodist gains came from Virginia southward. To the current day, the most prominent historic denominations in the South are Methodists, Baptists, and Presbyterians.[35]

The official church in the colony of Virginia was the Episcopal Church. Like the Anglican Church in England, the American counterpart did not adequately meet the spiritual needs of its parishioners. Unlike the English Awakening led by official ministers (the Wesley brothers and Whitefield), the movement in Virginia began with the laity.

Layman Samuel Morris and several friends were concerned about the teachings of their local rector. Because of concern for his own spiritual growth and that of his neighbors, in 1740 Morris began reading Whitefield's published sermons, Luther's *Commentary on Galatians*, the writings of Bunyan, and similar materials to a small group. This practice became so popular that "reading houses" were built. Soon, Morris began to be asked to read to other congregations. His itinerant, spontaneous ministry was a source of awakening to many.

The Presbyterians

As news of the reading houses spread, Presbyterian evangelist William Robinson investigated reports of the ensuing revival. Robinson was a graduate of Tennent's Log College. Upon his arrival in Hanover, Virginia, Robinson discovered reading halls packed with individuals dissenting from the Episcopal Church. These persons had experienced awakening in their own lives but subsequently had no real identity with the church. In fact, when Robinson inquired as to their creed, they called themselves Lutherans because the writings of Luther were read in their meetings. Robinson helped several of the groups to become Presbyterian churches. Another Log College graduate, Samuel Blair (1712-51), became pastor of Fagg's Manor, Pennsylvania, in November 1739. He began a school similar to the Log College, training several important leaders. A powerful revival came to his church in 1740, due in part to a visit by George Whitefield. Blair was the most scholarly of the Log College graduates.

Samuel Davies (1723-61) studied in Blair's school at Fagg's Manor from 1738-46. Davies was sent in 1748 at the age of twenty-five to follow Robinson and serve as pastor in the Hanover area. Davies organized the first Presbytery in the South, the Hanover Presbytery. An outstanding preacher and a great humanitarian, his itinerant preaching helped to continue the fires of revival in the area that began under Morris and extended throughout Virginia and North Carolina. Davies is also known for his efforts toward religious toleration. He secured legal permission for itinerant ministries. In addition, he ultimately won religious toleration for dissenters in Virginia under the Act of Toleration of 1689. From 1753-55, he traveled with Gilbert Tennent to the British Isles to raise money for the College of New Jersey. Davies became president of the school in 1759 following Edwards' death. Ironically, a pupil of one of the Log College graduates ultimately became president of the school the Log College became! Davies continues to be one of the most respected names in Presbyterianism.

The Baptists

Baptists in the South experienced a surge in growth; from 1755 to 1792, Baptist churches in the South grew from 28 to 441, more than 1,500 percent! This remarkable growth can be attributed in large part to the Great Awakening.[36]

Baptists in New England were generally suspicious of the Great Awakening. Still, Baptist churches there grew from 21 to 286, an increase of over 1,000 percent.

Some slowly warmed to revival fires due particularly to the influence of Isaac Backus (1724-1806). Converted in 1741 under Eleazor Wheelock's preaching, Backus became a New Light Congregationalist in 1745. After becoming convinced about immersion, he became a Baptist and was immersed on August 22, 1751. During the years following, he saw revival come in his own ministry. From 1756-66 he traveled fifteen thousand miles as a pastor-revivalist. Besides his well-known fight for religious toleration, Backus and other ministers in New England set up a concert of prayer, which served to bridge the gap between the First and Second Great Awakenings (see chap. 11).

Perhaps the most remarkable example of growth among Baptists in the south was the Sandy Creek Church in North Carolina. Separate Baptists from New England named Shubal Steams (1706-71) and Daniel Marshall (1706-84) had both been strongly influenced by the preaching of Whitefield. The Congregationalist Steams became a Baptist in 1751; Marshall, who married Stearns's sister Martha, turned to the Baptist denomination from Presbyterianism in 1754. With a total of eight families, they migrated to Sandy Creek, North Carolina, where they formed the first southern Separate Baptist Church in 1755. On a personal note, I had the joy of preaching in the Sandy Creek Baptist Church in August of 1996. What a thrill to stand at a monument erected at the place Stearns led in communion 240 years earlier!

Within only a few years, membership of Sandy Creek grew from 16 to 606. Historian Morgan Edwards observed:

> Sandy-creek church is the mother of all the Separate-baptists. From this Zion went forth the word, and great was the company of them who published it: it, in 17 years, has spread branches westward as far as the great river Mississippi; southward as far as Georgia; eastward to the sea and Chesopeek Bay; and northward to the waters of Potowmack; it, in 17 years, is become mother, grandmother, and great grandmother to 42 churches, from which sprang 125 ministers, many of which are ordained and support the sacred character as well as any sort of clergy in America.[37]

In 1760 Marshall organized the first Separate Baptist congregation in Virginia, and ultimately founded eleven others. One of his converts, Colonel Samuel Harris, was powerfully moved during revival services with the result that he immediately began preaching with unusual effectiveness.

People would travel from far and near to hear Harris, forming what was at least a prototype of the camp meetings of the Second Great Awakening. Such meetings were also characterized by emotionalism, which would have been negatively received in New England, but caused no severe problems in the more primeval frontier.

Baptist Isaac Chanler (1701-49) came from England to Charleston, South Carolina, at the age of thirty-two. He became pastor of a Baptist church there. Whitefield had witnessed an effusion of spiritual life there previously. At his departure, he encouraged the local ministers to continue the revival work through weekly lectures. Chanler became one of the lecturers, exhorting the people to continue in the grace of God.

The Methodists

Methodism constitutes the final stage of the First Great Awakening. Some place Methodism at the beginning of the Second Great Awakening. The first official Methodist work was established in the 1760s. By 1783 there were about fourteen thousand Methodists in the colonies. As Methodism originated in England, the first Methodist societies in the New World considered themselves a part of the established Episcopal Church rather than a separate entity.

A petition to the legislature of Williamsburg in 1776 said the Methodists were "a religious society in communion with the Church of England" who desired to "strengthen and support the said established church."[38] The fledgling Methodist movement was restricted mostly to the South. Sweet recorded a total of 3,148 Methodists in 1775, of which 2,384 were in the South.[39]

The first prominent leader of Methodists was Devereux Jarratt (1733-1801). Born to a nominally Anglican family, Jarratt came to Christ through the influence of a Presbyterian family he served as a tutor. Though he began ministry training for the Presbyterian Church, he was unconvinced of the Reformed teaching on election. He ultimately sailed to England where, in 1762, he was ordained into the Anglican Church. Whitefield and Wesley, whom he heard while in the mother country, influenced his preaching. Thus, when he returned to Virginia, his ministry style reflected Methodism more than traditional Anglicanism. He preached conversion through repentance and faith, set up small group meetings, and founded Methodist societies. Because his preaching featured spiritual vigor unlike that of other Anglicans in his area, many flocked to his services. Ultimately, he preached to crowds out-of-doors due to the large numbers. A powerful revival ensued through his leadership, although traditional ministers opposed him. The strongest effects came from 1764-72. His ministry at the parish of Bath in Virginia grew from less than ten people to almost one thousand in only a decade. Beyond his ministry in the parish he itinerated for a radius of hundreds of miles.

Robert Williams came from England to become one of the first Methodist itinerants in the colonies. It was his work as a book publisher that distinguished Williams. He published many of John Wesley's sermons and hymns, and his publications helped to spread the First Great Awakening among the Methodists. Francis Asbury, the dominant person in early American Methodism, said at Williams' funeral in 1775, "perhaps no man in America has been an instrument of awakening so many souls as God has awakened by him."[40]

Francis Asbury (1745-1816) began his work in the New World with Richard Boardman in New York. Wesley had charged Boardman with overseeing Methodist work in America. Ultimately, Asbury's superior vision, tenacity, and effort led to his becoming the general assistant in charge of America as assigned by a letter from Wesley on October 10, 1772. By the time of his death in 1816, Asbury had traveled 275,000 miles on horseback, preached 16,500 messages, and ordained some 4,000 preachers. Probably the most significant contribution of Asbury was the introduction of circuit-riding preachers. The circuit riders would play a critical role in the Second Great Awakening in the West.

The Revolutionary War caused a schism between Asbury and both John Wesley and other American Methodist ministers. Wesley remained loyal to Britain. Asbury and Jarratt were two of the few leaders who remained in America after the war began to expand. The result was the formation of the American Methodist Episcopal Church on December 24, 1784.

Contributions of the First Great Awakening

Heartfelt Religion. The First Great Awakening brought a renewed focus on experimental piety. The fresh emphasis on Christian experience went beyond what the Reformers or the New England Puritans had acknowledged. Edwards and others championed the role of both the intellect and the emotions as significant features of genuine Christianity. He wrote a treatise on religious affections arguing for their role in one's life.

Focus on Prayer. Tennent, Whitefield, Edwards, and other leaders of the First Great Awakening were men of prayer. Edwards urged fellow ministers to "be much in prayer and fasting, both in secret and with one another. It seems to me, it would become the circumstances of the present day, if ministers in a neighborhood would often meet together, and spend days in fasting and fervent prayer among themselves."[41]

Edwards believed God's sovereignty extended to the prompting of prayer among his people: "So it is God's will that the prayers of his saints shall be on great and principal means of carrying on the designs of Christ's kingdom in the world. When God has something very great to accomplish for his church, it is his will that there should precede it the extraordinary prayer of his people."[42] Edwards wrote *A Humble Attempt to Promote Explicit Agreement* to encourage others to pray.

Evangelism and Missions. The First Great Awakening brought new methods of evangelism. One of the most notable innovations was the practice of itinerancy. While not unknown before this era, it became an accepted and effective tool for spreading both the gospel message and the good news of local revivals. Many pastors took extended tours during the Great Awakening. These included Gilbert Tennent, Benjamin Pomeroy, Eleazar Wheelock, Jonathan Parsons, Andrew Croswell, Samuel Buell, and Philemon Robbins.

The evangelization of Indians became a major concern for revival leaders. John Sargeant (1710-49) was sent by the Society for the Propagation of the Gospel as a missionary to the Housatonic tribe in Stockbridge, Massachusetts. He experienced success, including baptizing 182 Indians. Jonathan Edwards, after being terminated from his church at Northampton, served as a missionary in Stockbridge during the 1750s. David Brainerd experienced an awakening among the Indians.

Theological Renewal. The First Great Awakening gave rise to two important issues in theology. First, it championed the emphasis of both the Reformation and the New Testament on justification by faith. This was the consistent message of revival preachers of various denominational stripes. Second, in many respects the revival brought a renewal of Reformed theology. Most of the leaders were Reformed theologically.

Work Toward Social Ministry and Justice Issues: *Education*. The birth of institutions of higher learning was one of the long-term effects of this movement. The Log College foreshadowed modern seminaries. In Philadelphia, a tabernacle erected for Whitefield's meetings became a charity school, which in turn led to the University of Pennsylvania. Eleazar Wheelock (1711-79) began a charity school for Indians in 1754. George Whitefield helped Wheelock and Indian preacher Samson Occam raise money for the school in England. The institution ultimately became Dartmouth College in New Hampshire. Numerous other schools emerged in the years following.

Orphanages. Bethesda in Georgia founded by Whitefield characterized the awakening. As in other great movements of God, a renewed care for the helpless resulted from the revival.

The reality nevertheless exists that, even in times of great spiritual movement, fallen men can still miss God's best. We see this in the First Great Awakening, for Whitefield and Edwards, as great as they were, had a blind spot when it came to the issue of slavery. Whitefield showed unusual care for the African slaves at Bethesda and preached the gospel to them, but he did not seek to abolish the practice. John Wesley, who influenced Wilberforce in the effort to end slavery in England, proved to be more faithful to the gospel in this instance. I sometimes wonder if the church 200 years in the future will look at the American church of our time and question why the gospel did not move us more to forsake materialism and care for the poor and disadvantaged. The fact remains that God condescends to use balls of clay for His glory, even when we miss the mark at times. We cannot excuse Whitefield or Edwards for their views toward slavery and their involvement in the slave trade. Others such as Benjamin Franklin, George Washington, and many of the founders of our nation shared in this blind spot. Even noting the reality that they were a product of their times does not excuse them. We can be reminded by their lives that God still uses imperfect men in genuine revival, which means there is hope for us. Moses, David, Peter, Luther, and many more in Scripture and history lived less than perfect lives, reminding us that God is both the One Who judges sin and the One Who extends mercy to use sinful men in His work.

Questions for Small Group Discussion

1. In what ways did laymen and young people contribute to the First Great Awakening in America?

2. Which church had the greatest impact among Baptists? In light of that, do you think your church could have a similar impact?

3. Small group devotions turned out to be a great idea in this awakening and innovative in its time. What innovative ways can you use to reach people?

4. Assuming that you are reaching people in very fruitful ways on a consistent basis, what improvement can you make in doing this? Keep in mind that even Edwards and Whitefield failed to try to abolish slavery.

Chapter 11
The Second Great Awakening in America, 1787-1843

The noise was like the roar of Niagara. The vast sea of human beings seemed to be agitated as if by a storm. I counted seven ministers, all preaching at one time, some on stumps, others in wagons . . . . Some of the people were singing others praying, some crying for mercy in the most piteous accents, while others were shouting most vociferously.
James Finley at Cane Ridge[1]

The Revolutionary War (1776-83) secured the freedom of the colonies and marked the beginning of a new nation. At the first census in 1790, there were four million Americans. The largest cities at the time were New York (population 50,000), Philadelphia (28,000), and Boston (25,000). The following states were added soon after the nation's birth: Rhode Island (1790), Vermont (1791), Kentucky (1792), Tennessee (1796), Ohio (1803), and Louisiana (1812).

Revival can be described as a renewed passion for God. By 1800 revival had swept across Britain and much of Europe.[2] Camp meetings, college revivals, and foreign missions enterprises are but a glimpse of the portrait painted by the Second Great Awakening. This mighty moving of the Spirit of God ushered in what Latourette called "the Great Century" because of the rapid spread of the faith in the 1800s. The Second Great Awakening in America affected a greater region and more people than the First, for the young nation had expanded both in geography and population.

The Second Great Awakening can be dated with its beginnings around 1787. It continued to 1843. Orr and Cairns divide the period into two distinct awakenings,[3] but I am convinced the awakening was a single movement, though containing at least three significant aspects: the college and church revivals of the eastern seaboard, the camp meetings of the West, and the subsequent ministry of Charles Finney and others.

Conditions Prior to Revival

The First Great Awakening had waned considerably by 1750. While spiritual tides continued to swell in the South, particularly through Methodists and Baptists, the more established middle and northern sections of the country witnessed a severe decline in spiritual life.

War had no small effect: the French and Indian War (1754-63) and more importantly the Revolutionary War (1776-83) sidetracked the pious for the urgent task of freedom. In fact, many ministers left their churches to join in the fight. The practical result was the neglect of corporate worship and more than a few abandoned churches. While the revolution was being won to secure fundamental freedoms, the religious convictions of many people were being lost. Promiscuity, profanity, gambling, and drunkenness increased.

Another irony of the war was that the French, who so aided the colonists militarily to secure their freedom, simultaneously introduced much of the spiritual and moral refuse of the Enlightenment to the New World. Skepticism and Deism came through the writings of Voltaire, Rousseau, and David Hume. The influence of these and others especially infected the minds of students in the young colleges of the new nation. Voltaire boasted that his *Candide* would sell at a premium within thirty years while one would be unable to give away a Bible. You should note that in 1789, immediately following the Revolutionary War, the French Revolution began. Many thousands of French people were killed in the Reign of Terror from 1793-94.

Many ideas from Europe were accepted and promoted by Americans. Thomas Paine, Ethan Allen, and others opposed biblical Christianity. These ideas gained popularity in the colleges. Paine's *The Age of Reason* was published in France and sent to the United States. Paine ridiculed the Christian belief in divine revelation.

In a Christ-honoring twist of fate, it was at the colleges where revival began to break forth in the early stages of this awakening. Revival often begins at times and in places where circumstances appear most bleak, and this awakening was no exception. Added to these conditions was the migration of many Americans westward across the Appalachians to the western frontier. This uprooted many from their cultural and spiritual heritage.

In the East: Colleges and Churches Come Alive

For the most part, the awakening in the East affected local congregations and college campuses. The role of itinerants such as Whitefield, so instrumental in the First Great Awakening, was minimal until men such as Asahel Nettleton and Charles G. Finney came on the scene well into the nineteenth century.

The spiritual temperature of the colleges measured at a tepid level. William and Mary, founded in the seventeenth century to give a pious education to Anglicans, now debated such topics as whether Christianity had been helpful or harmful to humanity. Bishop Meade of Virginia wrote of the impact of such ideas on students: "Infidelity was rife in the state, and the college of William and Mary was regarded as the hot-bed of French politics and religion. I can truly say that then and for some years after in every educated young man in Virginia whom I met I expected to find a skeptic, if not an avowed unbeliever."[4]

Only two students at Princeton professed to be Christians in 1782. Still, a dying tree can in fact bear good fruit. The waves of revival soon swept campuses into the growing tide of awakening.

Hampden-Sydney

The first college revival came to Hampden-Sydney in Virginia beginning in 1787. Four young men — William Hill, Cary Allen, James Blythe, and Clement Read – – were crucial to the revival. Allen became a Christian during a fall vacation in 1787. Hill was converted soon thereafter. Hill soon encountered Blythe, who had also been under deep conviction. These two teamed with Allen and then Read to meet for prayer, study, and worship. Once again, a small group gathering for prayer played a vital part in revival.

At first these students met in a forest away from the campus, then in a locked dorm room. They feared the wrath of the reprobate student body. When they were discovered, they were ridiculed by students who threatened the uncovered "fanatics." A near-riot ensued that had to be stopped by two of the faculty.

President John Brown Smith, himself converted in the First Great Awakening, was moved to tears. He sternly reprimanded the persecutors and invited the four believers to meet in his parlor the following Saturday. Revival soon followed, affecting no less than half the student body. It spread to surrounding counties as testimony about the revival was shared.

The campus was visited periodically by revival during the next three decades. In both 1789 and 1822, revival spread from Hampden-Sydney to Liberty Hall in Virginia (now Washington and Lee University). Daniel Baker studied at Hampden-Sydney when a fresh wave of the Spirit came in 1812. Clement Read, a student when revival first came in 1787, preached in the college church the day Baker united with the congregation. Baker came to Princeton in 1813 and was the human impetus for revival at that school over the following years. Over the following decades, Baker had an unusually blessed ministry of evangelism in the South.

Yale College

Timothy Dwight (1752-1817), the grandson of Jonathan Edwards, became president of his alma mater in 1795. At the time, Yale had 110 students. The spiritual condition of the college was deplorable. Noted preacher Lyman Beecher described the college before Dwight:

> Before he came [the] college was in a most ungodly state. The college church was almost extinct. Most of the students were skeptical, and rowdies were plenty. Wine and liquors were kept in many rooms; intemperance, profanity, gambling, and licentiousness were common. That was the day of the infidelity of the Tom Paine school.[5]

Beecher added that the "infidel" student body liked to take the names of their heroes, calling one another Voltaire, Rousseau, D'Alembert, and others.

The brilliant and erudite Dwight faced the problem squarely. He took the questions of the skeptics and answered them. He preached on the subject "Is the Bible the Word of God?" for six months in chapel. Beecher, a student at the time, said that as a result "all infidelity skulked and hid its head." By 1797, students had formed the Moral Society of Yale College to assist in improving conditions.

The change was gradual until the spring of 1802, when two seniors publicly professed their faith in Christ. Quickly, dozens were powerfully awakened. Of the 230 students enrolled at that time, about half of the seniors entered the ministry, and sixty-three students were converted. Bennett Tyler, who would later become a significant pastor in the awakening and compile an important collection of accounts of church revivals in New England,[6] was a sophomore at Yale in 1802 and was powerfully impressed by the revival. Incidentally, in the twenty-five accounts of revival gathered by Tyler, no less than twenty emphasized the role of youth in the movements. Revival came again in 1808, 1813, and 1815. Significant leaders of the Second Great Awakening, including Beecher, Tyler, and Asahel Nettleton, came from the Yale campus.

The Haystack Revival at Williams College

Samuel Mills' father served as a pastor in Torrington, Connecticut. A revival there in 1798 made a strong impact on the younger Mills. Williams College in Massachusetts experienced an awakening in 1804-6. Mills came as a student during this time. He met with a group of students twice weekly for prayer. On a warm August day in 1806, a rainstorm drove the group to seek shelter at a large haystack. Sheltered from the wind and rain at the haystack's side, the men continued in prayer. While there, Mills proposed a mission to India. Thus, historians have referred to the meeting as the "Haystack Revival."

In 1808 the group organized to study and pray for missions. After seminary graduation, Mills and others of the "Brethren" (their group's name) asked the General Association of Massachusetts to send them to India as missionaries. This Association formed the American Board of Commissioners for Foreign Missions on June 28, 1810. This was the first official foreign missions organization in the United States. The first missionaries included Adoniram Judson, Samuel Mott, Luther Rice, Gordon Hall, and Samuel Newell. Mills stayed behind in part because of his ability to promote the cause of world missions in America. Other colleges witnessed revival, including Amherst and Princeton.

Churches Come Alive through Prayer

Earlier in the eighteenth century, John Erskine of Scotland published a memorial to encourage prayer for an outpouring of God's Spirit. Jonathan Edwards' *A Humble Attempt to Promote Explicit Agreement and Visible Union of God's People in Extraordinary Prayer for the Revival of Religion and the Advancement of Christ's Kingdom* was based on Erskine's memorial. In 1784, Erskine sent Baptist leaders John Ryland and Andrew Fuller the treatise. Thus began what was soon a "concert of prayer" throughout England. Soon, reports of revival also spread across the nation.[7] In 1794, Baptists Isaac Backus and Stephen Gano, along with more than twenty other New England ministers, distributed a circular letter calling believers to pray for a general awakening. The letter below called for a "concert of prayer." Notice that the italicized words are the complete title of Jonathan Edwards' earlier treatise.

> The call to prayer by New England ministers:
>
> To the ministers and churches of every Christian denomination in the United States, to humble in their endeavors to carry into execution *the humble attempt to promote explicit agreement and visible union of God's people in extraordinary prayer for the revival of religion and the advancement of Christ's Kingdom on earth.*
>
> In execution of this plan, it is proposed that the ministers and churches of every Christian denomination should be invited to maintain public prayer and praise, accompanied with such instruction from God's Word, as might be judged proper, on every first Tuesday, of the four quarters of the year, beginning with the first Tuesday of January, 1795, at two o'clock in the afternoon, if the plan of concert should then be ripe for a beginning, and so continuing from quarter to quarter, and from year to year, until the good Providence of God prospering our endeavors, we shall obtain the blessing for which we pray.[8]

This simple, local, church-based call to prayer spread across New England. All the major denominations supported this call to prayer. Methodists observed the concert from 1796 to the close of the century At about the same time, Presbyterian pastor James McGready, who would later be important in the frontier camp meetings, wrote a prayer covenant enlisting believers to pray every Saturday evening, Sunday morning, and the entire third Saturday of each month for revival in Logan County, Kentucky, and throughout the world. Orr argued that the awakening became "great" following the movement of prayer.

By 1800 Backus rejoiced: "The revivals of religion in different parts of our land have been wonderful."[9] Revival had begun in isolated places before 1795. A powerful revival touched both the First and Second Baptist Churches of Boston during the winter of 1791-92. Edward Griffin reported revival in Yarmouth, Maine, in 1791. He witnessed revival under his own ministry beginning in 1792 in New Salem, Connecticut. By 1799 Griffin stated that fifty to sixty congregations in his region were "laid down in one field of divine wonders, and as many more in different parts of New England."[10] By 1798 reports of deep brokenness for sin and changed lives indicated a powerful awakening in West Simsbury, Torrington, New Hartford, Northington, and many other towns in Connecticut and surrounding states. In 1798, the Presbyterian General Assembly set aside a day of fasting and prayer for the spiritually destitute frontier, two years before the camp meetings.

Revival spread through Baltimore into the rest of Maryland and into Delaware. Methodist hymns echoed from fields, workshops, and logging camps. Congregational pastors launched *The Connecticut Evangelical Magazine* in 1800 to spread revival by publishing reports of it. The inaugural issue commented that the nation was witnessing an outpouring of the Holy Spirit not seen since the 1740s. Other issues included reports from across the nation.

The Western Camp Meetings

Spiritual conditions were worse in the West than in the East. The few who professed religion were mostly Deists and Unitarians. In the 1790s, the population of Kentucky tripled, but the number of Methodists there declined. On a trip to Tennessee in 1794, Francis Asbury wrote, "When I reflect that not one in a hundred came here to get religion, but rather to get plenty of good land, I think it will be well if some or many do not eventually lose their souls."[11] The dramatic change wrought by the awakening is seen in Asbury's life, for one decade later he proclaimed the year of 1804 the greatest year for religion in American history.

Part of the reason for the spiritually destitute condition in the West stemmed from a lack of ministers. In addition, the few ministers there had a difficult time adjusting to the frontier. A pastor simply could not "do church" on the frontier in the same manner as the Atlantic coast churches. Today, many pastors struggle to take a timeless gospel to a rapidly changing world in a timely manner. We could learn from the sacrificial service of leaders in the frontier, many of whom died young in their efforts to evangelize in the hard places.

> Today, the urban centers of America have become the hard places that the frontier represented two centuries ago.

Most people were preoccupied with their own survival in the wilderness. Methodist circuit riders covered vast territory with little resources. So, the task of reaching the frontier was far from simple.

James McGready

Unfortunately, many ministers and church members were transformed by the culture rather than affecting change. But not all were. As God used Edwards, Whitefield, and Dwight as catalysts for awakening east of the Appalachians, He used James McGready (1758-1817) on the frontier. McGready had studied in a log college in Pennsylvania similar to that of the Tennent's. He observed stirring revival while pursuing his studies. He experienced further revival in 1789 in Virginia, where he visited Hampden-Sydney College and its president, John Blair Smith.

McGready was an outstanding preacher with a stirring delivery. He served as a pastor in North Carolina, where his preaching resulted in an outbreak of revival in 1791, following which more than a dozen towns were touched. While there, he also encouraged many men to enter the ministry. Minister Robert Wilson commented about the unusual number of men entering the ministry at that time: "Either they will be despised and loaded with reproaches from every quarter or they will be instruments in the hand of God in producing a glorious revival."[12] Several of these went to Kentucky, as did McGready, and played pivotal roles in the great revival there. These included Barton W. Stone and William McGee.

McGready came to Logan County in southern Kentucky in 1798 to serve as pastor of three churches: Red River, Gasper River, and Muddy River. Logan County was well known for its reprobate character. Famous Methodist revival leader and circuit rider Peter Cartwright knew the area well:

> Logan County, when my father moved into it, was called "Rogues Harbor." Here many refugees from all parts of the Union fled to escape punishment or justice; for although there was law, yet it could not be executed, and it was a desperate state of society. Murderers, horse-thieves, highway robbers, and counterfeiters fled there, until they combined and actually formed a majority. Those who favored a better state of morals were called "Regulators." But they encountered fierce opposition from the "Rogues," and a battle was fought with guns, pistols, dirks, knives, and clubs, in which the "Regulators" were defeated.[13]

In 1797 and 1798, signs of revival occurred in the Gasper River church and then at the others. A communion service was held in July 1799, at the Red River church. The Lord's Supper was observed only rarely in Presbyterian churches at this time, so when it was held, services were extended over a weekend. Often visitors would come from other congregations for the services from Friday through Monday.

The next month, a similar occurrence came to a communion service at Gasper River. Momentum was growing for an even greater revival. In September, McGready said the services at Muddy River were "the greatest, the most solemn and powerful time of any that had been before."[14]

The "Great Revival" of the West began in June 1800 when several hundred members of McGready's church gathered for a joint communion service at Red River. There was a great sense of expectancy based on the years of prayer and the prior revival. Other ministers there included those who had surrendered to the ministry in North Carolina under McGready's leadership: John Rankin, William Hodge, and William McGee. McGee's brother John, a Methodist minister, came also. After three normal days on Friday, Saturday, and Sunday, the Spirit broke through — a woman began shouting at the sudden assurance of her salvation, which led to the congregation as a whole becoming broken.

Methodist John McGee, who had come to the camp meeting along with several from different denominations, said: "I turned to go back and was near falling; the power of God was strong upon me losing the sight of the fear of man, I went through the house shouting and exhorting with all possible ecstasy and energy, and the floor was soon covered with the slain."[15]

Camp Meetings

A second sacramental service was scheduled for the Gasper River church the following month. Hundreds came — many from distant points — with plans to encamp for the weekend. Most refer to this event as the first true "camp meeting." Again the Spirit of God moved. Revival began to break out among the people beginning on

Saturday evening. Ministers counseled all through the night. McGready wrote of the service on Sunday:

> After the congregation was dismissed the solemnity increased, till the greater part of the multitude seemed engaged in the most solemn manner. No person seemed to wish to go home — hunger and sleep seemed to affect nobody — eternal things were the vast concern. Here awakening and convening work was to be found in every part of the multitude; and even some things strangely and wonderfully new to me.[16]

Spontaneously, camp meetings sprouted across the land of Kentucky and Tennessee. Methodist James Finley, while noting peculiarities in the meetings, said the closest parallel was the revival at Pentecost recorded in Acts 2. Many ministers and others who attended these meetings continued to spread the news that revival was touching the frontier.

One such minister was Presbyterian pastor Barton Stone (1772-1844). Stone, who later founded the Disciples of Christ church, had known McGready from the early 1790s. In 1801 he attended a camp meeting in Logan County and was amazed. After telling his own congregations at Concord and Cane Ridge (near Lexington) about the revival, he determined to have a similar meeting in August of 1801. It was publicized for a month prior.

On Friday, August 8, 1801, the people came. Estimates indicate that as many as twenty to twenty-five thousand arrived by wagon, on horseback, and on foot. Preachers across the hillsides stood to proclaim Gods Word. Some stood on wagons, others on fallen trees. Makeshift pulpits were used in abundance. At least eighteen Presbyterian and even more Methodist and Baptist ministers were counted.

Untold lives were changed in this overwhelming event, which has symbolized the Second Great Awakening in the West. It is also the meeting known for the abnormalities associated with the camp meetings. The emotional, primitive lifestyle of the frontier created an atmosphere prone to excesses.

Historian John Boles categorized six varieties of unusual phenomena: falling down, rolling on the ground, jerking motions, barking, dancing, laughing uncontrollably, and singing uncontrollably.

Boles on the inaccurate overemphasis on these exercises:

These grossly exaggerated revival exercises, which have been cited widely to discredit revival, were probably restricted to a comparable few. Only among some of the splinter groups that developed in Kentucky did they become ultimately respectable. Except at the very start, they were never a significant factor in the camp meetings.[17]

Some unusual phenomena came during the First Great Awakening, but they were quickly quieted by leaders. The leaders in the camp meetings were perhaps so overwhelmed that they did not adequately deal with the emotional aberrations. It must also be pointed out that this was a frontier people given to more primitive forms of expression. This can be seen not only in the emotional excesses, but also in the many new denominations and sects who prospered among the religiously revived but spiritually shallow frontier Christians. To use the paradigm of Richard Owen Roberts, that revivals tend to be either "Word-centered" or "experience-centered,"[18] the revival in the West was definitely more experienced based than in the East. Also, the vast numbers caused no small problem for sound guidance. Such unusual phenomena do not in themselves disqualify the camp meetings as examples of genuine, God-sent revival.

As a result of the meeting at Cane Ridge, religious matters became the dominant topic of conversation along the frontier. As Dr. George Baxter traveled through the land, he observed that "a religious awe seemed to pervade the country."[19] Other camp meetings were held across the frontier, and the land that had been so cold to spiritual matters began to warm in the glow of the Spirit's fire.

In addition, similar meetings were reported in the South. A four-day meeting in 1802 at a small Presbyterian church in Georgia erupted in revival. Soon, five to eight thousand were in attendance. From Ohio down through Tennessee, Georgia, and the Carolinas, revival spread through camp meetings. Two new denominations, the Christian Church and the Cumberland Presbyterians, arose during this time.

The awakening affected churches dramatically. The Elkhorn Baptist Association saw its twenty-nine churches report only twenty-nine conversions in 1799. In 1801 this same association reported 3,011 additions by baptism and testimony. A total of twenty-one new churches were formed in 1801-02. In 1803 Francis Asbury said that reports of awakening came from every state in the union and almost every Methodist circuit.

The circuit-riding preachers of the Methodist Church helped to spread much of the revival's fire. Circuit riders often traversed dangerous avenues in order to bring the gospel to the frontier. One-half of these brave soldiers of the Cross died before their thirty-third birthdays. One Presbyterian observed on his travels through Kentucky that he could not "find a family whose cabin had not been entered by a Methodist preacher."[20]

One such preacher, Peter Cartwright (1785-1872), traveled across the dangerous frontier for a generation. He brought roughly ten thousand frontier people into the church, preached nearly fifteen thousand sermons, and traveled on eleven circuits during his career. A tough, daunting man who enjoyed debate, Cartwright was suited for the rigorous demands of the frontier. He was also outspoken in his opposition to slavery.[21] James Finley, involved in the work at the earliest camp meetings, later became a circuit rider. Another Methodist itinerant of note was the eccentric preacher Lorenzo Dow (1777-1834).

Beyond renewed vigor and manifest conversions, the camp meetings also provided a means for church expansion. Churches flourished — especially Methodist and Baptist churches. The Methodist Church was the most numerous religious group in America by 1844.[22] Many new groups arose. Barton Stone eventually left Presbyterianism to form the Disciples of Christ. Thomas Campbell soon joined him. More unusual groups, such as the Shakers, also arose at this time.

Revival Extends and Broadens

The War of 1812 brought a spiritual lull, but revival returned with new force after 1815. Joshua Bradley published a record of over one hundred powerful revivals from the years 1815-18. Accounts of revival touching churches, schools, and communities demonstrate the depth of the movement, as well.[23] During this time, some remarkable preachers helped to further revival. Asahel Nettleton (1783-1844) attended Yale during a time of revival. Nettleton was converted in 1801. He met Samuel Mills in 1807 while at Yale. Nettleton desired to be a foreign missionary, but his health would not allow it. Nettleton witnessed powerful revival in his ministry, leading him to become an itinerant preacher. His approach followed the pattern of earlier, Calvinistic ministers. His preaching was described as bold, warm, and plain; not graceful, but anointed.

An example of the effect of Nettleton's ministry was seen in Saratoga Springs, New York, in 1817. An observer, calling the scene "beyond description," reported that the place was so full many could not fit in the building: "Did you ever witness two hundred sinners, with one accord in one place, weeping for their sins? . . . I felt as though I was standing on the verge of the eternal world; while the floor under my feet was shaken by the trembling of anxious souls in view of a judgment to come."[24]

Nettleton's ministry began in Connecticut and Rhode Island, where he became familiar with James Davenport's earlier fanaticism. This doubtless caused Nettleton to be concerned with excesses in revival. A powerful revival attended his ministry in Stonington, Connecticut. Similar stirrings came to Waterbury, Connecticut, as well as Malta and Schenectady in New York. Nettleton was one of the earliest itinerant preachers born in America to have long-term success.

Dr. Noah Porter recorded the efforts of revival under Nettleton's ministry in Farminghouse, Connecticut. In 1821 the town was awakened to the extent that a holy hush covered the area. "There was no commotion, but a stillness, in our very streets," said Porter, "and a solemnity in almost all, which forcibly impressed us [that] God was in this place."[25] Most of Nettleton's preaching was in small towns and villages, yet he is credited with at least twenty-five thousand conversions.

Nettleton became one of the foremost critics of Charles Finney's "New Measures" and of his practice of itineration without receiving permission from area ministers. He did not attack Finney personally or attack Finney's motives; however, he did seek to point out concerns over Finney's theology and his new measures. After an attack of typhoid fever in 1822, Nettleton never regained his prominence. He was instrumental in the founding of Hartford Seminary in 1833 where he served as an adjunctive faculty member.

Lyman Beecher (1775-1863) graduated from Yale in 1797 where he was converted under the ministry of Timothy Dwight. Two of his children have also been remembered: Harriett Beecher Stowe, author of *Uncle Tom's Cabin*, and minister Henry Ward Beecher. Lyman Beecher and Nettleton were close friends. Beecher witnessed powerful revival in his ministry as pastor in Litchfield, Connecticut, and in

Boston. He later became president of Lane Seminary in Cincinnati from 1832-51. His moral crusading served to demonstrate how evangelism and social reform could be linked.

James Caughey (1810-97) was a significant Methodist preacher in North America and Britain. Reports of revival across the young nation came during the late 1820s. Numerous colleges were set aright spiritually: Centre College in Kentucky, Franklin College in Georgia, Dickinson in Pennsylvania. At about this time, Daniel Baker (1791-1857), mentioned earlier in conjunction with the revival at Hampden-Sydney, witnessed revival through his ministry Throughout the 1830s and 1840s, he served the Lord as an evangelist across the South, often spurring revival movements among believers as well as the conversion of sinners.

Great revival always leads to significant evangelism and church growth.

Baptist Jacob Knapp (1799-1874) saw awakening under his ministry beginning in the 1830s. Around this time, another man emerged as both a leader in revival and the center of controversy: Charles Grandison Finney.

Charles Finney and the Continuation of Revival

The Second Great Awakening flourished in much of the country into the 1830s and early 1840s. Many areas and leaders were involved in the work. However, no one was more prominent than a former law student who set parts of the Northeast on fire with revival. In fact, in the modern history of spiritual awakening, few are better known than Charles Grandison Finney (1792-1875). His writings on revival, especially his *Lectures on Revival of Religion*, or *Revival Lectures,* have influenced countless believers through the current day. Drummond observed: "Finney is the 'father' of many modern evangelistic philosophies and revivalistic methods."[26]

Born into an irreligious home, Finney studied law in Adams, New York. He was unimpressed with the spiritual life of the churches he attended; yet he became the music director for a Presbyterian church due to his musical ability. Finney and pastor George Gale often debated points of Scripture. Some young people began to pray for Finney's conversion; one would later become his wife.

At the age of twenty-nine, Finney determined to settle the issue of his own salvation. After a lengthy time of conviction, on October 10, 1821, he determined to resolve the issue. By that evening, he had experienced a life-changing conversion. He recorded the event: "The Holy Spirit descended upon me in a manner that seemed to go through me, body and soul. I could feel the impression, like a wave of electricity, going through and through me. Indeed it seemed to come in waves of liquid love, for I could not express it in any other way."[27]

His transformation amazed the townspeople of Adams. Even pastor Gale was dumbfounded that Finney could be genuinely called a Christian. After his conversion, Finney began to preach immediately while pursuing theological studies under Gale. Revival ensued in Adams and the surrounding area. Finney called the region the "burned over district," because in his view so many had been converted in previous revivals that no fuel remained to burn a fire of revival in his time. But as he exhorted his hearers to respond to the gospel openly and publicly, remarkable numbers responded.[28] Somewhat embarrassed by his pupil at first, in later years Gale joined with Finney in support of the revival.

Revival came to nearby Evans Mills and Antwerp under Finney's ministry. Upon arriving in Antwerp, Finney was appalled at the profanity in the town. He recorded in his *Memoirs* that the whole atmosphere of the town was poisoned by vulgarity.[29] This caused him to spend most of Saturday and the early hours on Sunday in prayer.

When Finney arrived at the church, it was packed. Preaching from John 3:16, he soon noticed some of the most profane men in the town in attendance. Finney personally addressed the men, saying with tears that the damnation they were cursing at one another would become their own fate. Virtually everyone attending was moved to brokenness and tears. He preached like a lawyer trying a case — his sermons were logical, convincing, and delivered with great unction. Like Wesley and Whitefield a century earlier, he sought to communicate to the common man.

These localized revivals were the beginning of Finney's "nine glorious years" from 1824-32, the greatest years of Finney's efforts. In 1825, a significant revival erupted in Oneida County in western New York that continued until 1827. Finney began his ministry there with a strong appeal to prevail in prayer. Finney then preached in nearby Rome. Finney preached twenty consecutive nights, while prayer meetings filled the daylight hours. The meeting moved from a church to a large hotel and then to the courthouse. In twenty days, some five hundred were converted. One convert was Reverend Gillet's wife, who was also the sister of Samuel Mills.

One example of the unusual activity of the Spirit at that time occurred at the hotel where Finney stayed while at Utica. Even stagecoach travelers were overwhelmed by the power of God:

> The stages, as they passed through, stopped at the hotel; and so powerful was the impression in the community, that I heard of several cases of persons that just stopped to dine or to spend a night, being powerfully convicted or converted before they left the town. Indeed, both in this place and in Rome, it was a common remark that nobody could be in the town, or pass through it, without being aware of the presence of God; that a divine influence seemed to pervade the place, and the whole atmosphere to be instinct [filled] with a divine presence.[30]

During this time, Finney began to develop certain innovations called "New Measures." These measures have been the source of controversy from Finney's day until ours. Finney argued that he never did many of the things his opponents charged.

Some of these methods originated before Finney; he merely popularized them. For example, Shubal Steams used protracted meetings sixty years before Finney.[31]

Finney's New Measures:

Finney used innovative evangelistic techniques, and these became known as "New Measures." Some of these techniques included:

1. Anxious meetings. For those in Finney's meetings who appeared concerned or "anxious" about their salvation, separate meetings were assembled to give counsel as to how one might be saved.

2. House-to-house visitation. Finney would go to a person's home to give instruction concerning personal salvation.

3. Anxious seats. Typically, a pew designated for persons anxious about their salvation was made available in meetings. Some came to the bench before the service, some after. The practice actually began in Methodist camp meetings. Finney began using these following the Rochester Revival of 1831.

4. Prayer innovations. Certain New Measures related to prayer. Unlike other clergy of his day, Finney spoke to God in common language, which some called "vulgar." He also advocated allowing women to pray publicly and encouraged people to pray for lost people by name in public.

5. Protracted Meetings. Meetings were held several nights consecutively.

Small towns in surrounding areas also experienced revival. Finney often spoke of a "spirit of prayer" which preceded these movements. While in Utica, Finney went to a factory in the area. Workers reportedly began to fall under conviction as Finney gazed at them. The owner stopped work so that the people could attend to their spiritual lives.

In 1826, a meeting of ministers including Asahel Nettleton was held in New Lebanon, New York, to consider Finney's New Measures. At this conference, charges were lodged against Finney. Finney said the charges were not representative of his meetings, except the accusation that women were allowed to pray aloud. The subject of the meeting was Finney's methodology, not his theology, which was coming under increasing scrutiny. "It is not entirely clear," wrote Nettleton biographer Thornbury, "why Finney's Pelagian tendencies had not come under scrutiny."[32] Lyman Beecher offered the following evaluation of the two men at New Lebanon: "[Nettleton] was old and broken. Mr. Finney was young and robust. The one was reverential, timid, secretive; the other bold, striking, demonstrative."[33]

For more than a decade following the conference, Finney preached in meetings across the Northeast, where he witnessed revival among believers and conversions among the lost. Finney's successful preaching in Presbyterian churches led to several months of revival centered in a German church-house that held three thousand. A powerful movement continued for a year and a half. From there, he preached primarily in Reading, Pennsylvania, followed by Lancaster in the late spring of 1830.

The single greatest series of meetings in the ministry of Charles Finney came in the Rochester revival of 1830-31. A spirit of revival was already swelling across the area when Finney's preaching commenced. At Finney's arrival, huge crowds thronged to hear the revivalist. Not only did revival result in multitudes following Christ, but also some forty men entered the ministry, many as foreign missionaries.

The *Rochester Observer* reported the universal impact of the revival as it affected students, mechanics, professionals, and politicians. The *New York Evangelist* echoed the sentiment: "So large a proportion of men of wealth, talent, and influence have rarely, if ever, been known to be the subjects of revival in that vicinity."[34] During the Rochester revival, the father of A. H. Strong came to faith. The younger Strong himself met Christ in a later Finney revival.

Finney preached ninety-eight sermons in Rochester from September 10, 1830, to March 6, 1831. Lyman Beecher, who had seen mighty movements of the Spirit earlier at Yale and in his own ministry, called the Rochester revival the "greatest revival of religion that has been since the world began."[35] It was at Rochester that the "anxious seat" came into practice. Finney called any persons under conviction to come forward to certain seats, "and offer themselves up to God while we made them subjects of prayer."[36] The first time he did this, far more came than he expected. Revival touched a large high school in the town, resulting in the conversion of nearly every student and the principal.

Many leaders in the city were saved. A lawyer who became district attorney for Rochester told Finney years later that the population of Rochester had increased two-thirds from the revival in 1830, but the crime rate reduced by two-thirds over the same span. Many townspeople wrote letters across the country reporting the revival, whereupon many churches in different states, after reading the letters, also experienced revival.

Finney paid a high price to be a part of such a movement of God. By 1832, after preaching with great effect in Boston (where he worked with Beecher), his health was broken. Several physicians said he had consumption, yet on he preached. He ultimately took the pastorate of the Second Free Presbyterian Church on Chatham Street in New York. However, he was soon found to be suffering from cholera, rendering him unable to preach for many months. Under his brief ministry there, no less than seven new churches were planted.

The influential Tappan brothers and other laymen determined to build a new facility on Broadway. Finney became the pastor. That the new church was Congregationalist and Finney was a lifelong Presbyterian seemed to be a nonissue. The Broadway pulpit provided Finney with another means of great influence. Before this influence could be seen, however, Finney took a lengthy voyage to the Mediterranean to assist his poor health.

On Finney's return, Joshua Leavitt, editor of the *New York Evangelist*, asked the now-famous preacher to write a series on revival to help the paper's sagging subscription. Instead, Finney volunteered to deliver a series of lectures on the subject Leavitt could copy and publish. The Friday night lectures became the classic *Lectures on Revival of Religion*, also known as the *Revival Lectures*. Finney preached one lecture a week over the winter of 1834-35.

The *Revival Lectures* demonstrated a much stronger emphasis on human agency than earlier writings, such as those of Jonathan Edwards. Finney actually never saw the lectures until they were published. He gave them extemporaneously. Often, he did not determine the subject of the next lecture until he saw the report on the last one. Leavitt copied the lectures feverishly by longhand, capturing about one-third of the content of the live lectures.

The impact of the publication of his lectures amazed Finney:

> These revival lectures, meager as was the report of them, . . . have been instrumental, as I have learned, in promoting revivals of religion in England, and Scotland, and Wales, on the Continent in various places, in Canada east and west, in Nova Scotia, in some of the islands of the sea, and in fact throughout the British colonies and dependencies.[37]

In 1835, Finney became professor of theology at Oberlin Institute (later Oberlin College). He spent half of each year at his New York pastorate and half at the school in Ohio. Oberlin became a leader in opposing slavery. The first coeducational institution of higher education in the nation, it admitted women and blacks without discrimination. While at Oberlin, Finney's view on Christian perfection developed. Many Methodists and others eventually adopted his "Oberlin Perfectionism". In 1851, Finney became Oberlin's president.

Finney saw occasional movements of revival in succeeding years. One stirring example was a powerful revival in Rochester, home of his earlier great meeting. Finney increasingly spoke out against social ills, including slavery, alcoholism, prostitution, and materialism. One example of his influence was George Williams, the British founder of the Young Men's Christian Association (YMCA) in 1844. He occasionally preached in Britain, preaching for nine months in Whitefield's tabernacle on one visit.

Charles Finney stands as a watershed figure in the history of American Christianity. The ultimate impact of Finney on the Second Great Awakening was the emergence of a new understanding of revival. This view, generally called "revivalism,"[38] placed much more emphasis on the role of man in revival's birth and effects. Thus, while in the First Great Awakening a controversy arose between those in favor of revival and those who opposed it, in the Second Great Awakening the great rift was between two groups of prorevivalists.[39] On the one hand, the Calvinistic heritage of Edwards was seen in Asahel Nettleton and others. On the other hand stood Finney and his focus on man's role in addition to the work of God.

Finney's views gave impetus to a more man-centered focus on revival. Orr succinctly explained the difference between the two groups, while also noting the important difference between evangelism and revival:

> There is controversy here and there between followers of Finney, who said that "revival is nothing more than the right use of appropriate means," and those who

> believe, like Edwards, that it is a work of God. Evangelism, most certainly, is the right use of appropriate means, as Finney said. There is also a sense in which any congregation, anywhere, which resolves to live up to the light it already possesses will experience a measure of revival. Edwards rather spoke of an outpouring of the Spirit and that is not the work of man.[40]

Finney's preaching and writings served as a catalyst to revival and to the conversion of multitudes. He emphasized the gospel's impact on the individual and on culture. He led in confronting social issues, including slavery and the lack of equality in educational opportunities. In response to a brand of Calvinism that virtually ignored the responsibility of man, Finney argued for a much greater role of human instrumentality both in salvation and in revival. As is often the case however, his efforts swung the pendulum too far, creating their own set of unintended consequences.

Finney's *Revival Lectures* offer an invaluable compendium of information to be studied and have themselves served as a catalyst for revival in the lives of many who read them. His discussions on praying for revival and hindrances to revival, for example, should be heeded today. Many of his "New Measures," as they were called, are familiar customs in churches today. Many would be surprised to know that such practices as praying for lost people by name, women praying in public, and the anxious seat — a forerunner to the modern use of the public invitation — were innovations by Finney. And, in a move considered scandalous at the time, Finney changed the practice of a Sunday service and a weekday lecture to successive nightly service — the aforementioned "protracted meeting." Winthrop Hudson called this approach "the camp meeting brought to town."[41] Finney also employed what some today call "seeker services," services designed intentionally for bringing lost people to hear the gospel.

Finally, on Finney's behalf, one should remember that he ministered in a time of great revival rarely seen in history. Untrained in theological matters and a young Christian when he began to encounter the movement of God, his life provides a good argument for a gospel-centered theological education. He failed to distinguish between the blessing of God in awakening and the activity of man to "capture" such blessing. Finney later retracted some of his overemphasis on human agency. In a small publication of letters produced later in his ministry, Finney stated:

> I have thought that, at least in a great many instances, stress enough has not been laid upon the necessity of Divine influence upon the hearts of Christians and sinners. I am confident that I have sometimes erred in this respect myself. . . . I have laid, and I doubt not that others also have laid, too much stress on the natural ability of sinners, to the neglect of showing them the nature and extent of their dependence on the grace of God and the influence of His Spirit. This has grieved the Spirit of God.[42]

Finney's legacy has unfortunately served to muddy an understanding of biblical revival.[43] Dr. Robert Baird estimated that twenty-six thousand of the thirty thousand ministers in the U.S. in 1844 "were more or less committed to what had come to be known as the revivalist 'new measures.'"[44] There has been a devaluation of the sovereignty of God in American Christianity for a long time. Far too many see the key to revival in what the church does, rather than looking to the One whom alone can "rend the heavens" (Isa 64:1). It is clear that Finney's views soon ruled the day in the practice of the local church, leading eventually to programmatic ministry and too much focus on what people can do for God over what God does in and through His people.

In a general sense, one can see Finney's influence continuing in Wesleyan, Nazarene, and many Pentecostal and Charismatic traditions that are more Arminian in heritage. The legacy of Edwards can be seen in Presbyterian and other more Reformed groups. Many leaders today who focus on revival tend toward the views of Edwards, while many apply the views of Finney o evangelism. An example of the latter is the use of the expression "revival" to refer to a four- or seven-day series of meetings (called "protracted meetings" in Finney's day). Such meetings can be helpful in evangelism in any generation. They should be described as mass evangelism rather than revivals, however.

Unfortunately for many American evangelicals, the word revival has come to refer only to an evangelistic campaign.[45] Although revival has continually occurred along the lines of the earlier understanding of those in the First Great Awakening, for many churches today the term revival has lost its value.

J. Edwin Orr, a leading evangelical awakening scholar in the last century, has best summarized Finney:

> As a gospel tactician, Finney was second to none. As a strategist, his practice was better than his theory. Finney went to the extreme of stating that revival of religion was nothing more or less than a result of the right use of appropriate means. His own expectancy of revival seemed justified by the results reported almost everywhere in his services. Unfortunately, besides encouraging many a local pastor or evangelist to expect revival, Finney's theory encouraged a brash school of evangelists who thought that they could promote genuine revival by means chosen by themselves in times chosen by themselves. The use of means was often blessed with Spirit-filled men, but with less Spirit-filled agents it gave rise to a brand of promotional evangelism, full of sensationalism and commercialism. It must be concluded that Finney's theory applied to evangelism, not outpourings of the Spirit.[46]

Enduring Impact of the Second Great Awakening

Great revival always leads to significant *evangelism and church growth.* This was certainly the case with this awakening. From 1800 to 1830 Presbyterians grew fourfold, from about 40,000 to 173,329. Baptists experienced dramatic growth, from 872 churches and 64,975 members in 1790 to 7,299 churches and 517,523 members in 1836. The Methodist Church, after rapid gains in the latter eighteenth century, actually lost some 11,000 members from 1793-95. But phenomenal growth in the Second Great Awakening resulted in 1,323,361 members by 1850. New methods emerged, including camp meetings and Finney's New Measures.

The greatest long-term impact of the awakening came in the form of *new societies and agencies*, many of which remain active today. The New York Missionary society emerged in 1796, founded by Presbyterians, Baptists, and Dutch Reformed to reach the Indians. Congregationalists formed the Missionary Society of Connecticut in 1798 to establish new churches in frontier areas. The Massachusetts Society, founded in 1799, supported 224 missionaries by 1824.

By the turn of the century, such enterprises literally exploded. The American Board of Commissioners for Foreign Missions began in 1810. Two of the first missionaries, Adoniram Judson and Luther Rice, became Baptists while en route to Burma. Rice formed the General Missionary Convention of the Baptist Denomination in the United States for Foreign Missions in 1814.

In this same period a shoe cobbler in England named William Carey uttered his famous words, "Expect great things from God, attempt great things for God." Carey challenged the church of his day to take seriously the Great Commission. In 1793, Carey, his wife Dorothy, and four young children sailed to India, taking the gospel to the nations as the young collegians in America would not many years following.

Samuel Mills itinerated three thousand miles through the western frontier on mission work. His work was influential in beginning the American Bible Society. In 1817 Mills helped form the American Colonization Society. He died at sea while returning from Africa, where he discovered a location to return freed American slaves. Magazines began that promoted missions endeavors: *Connecticut Missionary Magazine*, *Missionary Herald*, *Evangelical Intelligence*, and *The Analytical Repository*.

The American Bible Society and the American Education Society came along in 1816; the American Colonization Society in 1817; the American Tract Society in 1825; and the American Home Missions Society in 1826. In 1791 the first Sunday school union was formed in Philadelphia. The New York Sunday School Union was established in 1816. The American Sunday School Union organized in 1824 to establish a unified effort for the growing Sunday school movement.

Social effects were felt as well. One cannot underestimate the impact of the Great Awakenings on the cultural fiber of America, particularly in the nation's formative years. Lacy stated succinctly: "The Great Awakening of the eighteenth century prepared the way for Independence and the New Republic; the Great Revival of the 1800s saved the new nation from French infidelity, crass materialism, rapacious greed, godlessness, and out breaking violence on the frontiers."[47] Some of the new societies were directly aimed at social reform: the American Temperance Society in 1826; the American Peace Society in 1828; and the American Antislavery Society in 1833.

The Young Men's Christian Association (YMCA) began as an evangelistic outreach. It also became known for its positive influence on society as a whole. YMCA founder George Williams was profoundly influenced by Finney's writings shortly after his conversion. He and a group of others began the association on June 6, 1844. Finney was a foremost spokesman against the scourge of slavery. Lyman Beecher also led efforts in social and moral reform. His daughter, Harriet Beecher Stowe, wrote the famous book *Uncle Tom's Cabin*.

Education was renewed as well. By the end of the awakening, the colleges in the nation were operated, "from boards of trustees down to senior tutors, by ministers and devout laymen."[48] The beginning of the modern seminary movement is traced to Andover Theological Seminary in 1808, although earlier prototypes, like the Log College, had existed. One reason for the need of such schools was the rise of ministers out of the college revivals.

Princeton Seminary began in 1812; Yale Divinity School in 1822; and Hampden-Sydney established a theological library for ministry students. The first Baptist seminary was Newton Theological Seminary, begun in 1824. Oberlin Seminary, later led by Finney, opened in 1835. In 1780 there were nine schools of higher education in America. By 1861, there were 182. States or municipalities founded only 27 of these. The Presbyterians founded 49 schools; Methodists, 34; Baptists, 25; Episcopalians, 11; and Congregationalists, 21.

Finally, the *music* in the churches was changed. This can be seen especially in the influence of the music from the camp meetings. The style of camp meeting songs developed into the gospel hymn, marked by a verse and chorus; they were notorious musically for their sentimentalism. Lorenz stated the reason for their songs:

> A new kind of hymn was needed for this new feeling. Watts and Wesley and other eighteenth-century English hymnists had written hymns that expressed the emotions of the newly converted, and these were whole-heartedly adopted. But new hymns, and especially new tunes, had to be found that equally conveyed the sense of the exhilaration, even the ecstasy, which newborn souls needed to express.[49]

The camp meetings were not complete without song after song. *The Southern Harmony*, a collection of camp meeting songs published in 1835, sold 600,000 copies over twenty-five years.

Finney worked closely with local churches in urban centers, so a different sort of revival song was needed to reach the people in the cities. The church hymnals set too high a standard for some tastes, but the typical camp meeting songbook's standards were too low. Thus Finney used Thomas Hastings, who published an early hymnbook, as a musician in the urban setting.

Revival is a fresh passion for God. May we desire to be as passionate for God in our day as the preachers, students, and camp meeting Christians of the eighteenth century.

Questions for Small Group Discussion

1. What are a few positive things that occurred within the college revivals? Could we see a movement on a college campus like these today?

2. Today, urbanization of the world provides great evangelistic opportunity amidst the mass of people inhabiting so many cities. What did Charles Finney do to aid churches in urban centers?

3. Finney developed innovative methods that caused controversy. How should we deal with those with whom we disagree? What role does a humble attitude play in answering this question?

4. For college students: What kind of things are you doing to reach your fellow college students in light of what we see from the collegiate revivals that took place?

Chapter 12
The Layman's Prayer Revival, 1857-59

Lord, what wilt Thou have me to do?
Jeremiah Lanphier

A lone figure stood at the corner of a busy intersection in the heart of New York City. His heart weighed heavily in his chest, broken for the purposeless, despondent masses of New York, what could a single lay missionary do? He had been diligent in his efforts of personal evangelism, street preaching, and door-to-door witnessing. His burden for the throngs of people had forced him to his knees. Could he ever have imagined what would soon come about? Within a matter of months, more than fifty thousand people would gather daily for prayer!

Jeremiah Lanphier (b. 1809) was that lone man. He prayed "Lord, what wilt Thou have me to do?" out of his passion for the salvation of the residents of New York City. On September 23, 1857, he knelt in prayer, alone in a quiet room, shortly after the noon hour. Lanphier's intercession ascended from the upper lecture room of the Old North Dutch Reformed Church.

Any outpouring of the Spirit has its origin in the heart of God Himself. But, while conceived in the Father's love for His people, it is birthed in the burden of believers who experience an overwhelming sense of urgency in prayer. As the familiar saying of Matthew Henry goes: "When God desires to do a fresh work, He sets His people to praying." A faithful few given to desperate, concerted prayer can provide the spark for a mighty revival. This is seen nowhere more clearly than in the Layman's Prayer Revival of 1857-59.

While occasional glimmerings of revival sprouted in American soil in the 1840s and 1850s, a noticeable loss of spiritual fervor came across the nation during this time. "For several years, from 1843 to 1857," wrote Beardsley, "the accessions to the churches scarcely equaled the losses sustained by death, removal or discipline, while a widespread indifference to religion became prevalent."[1]

Then God again touched His church with revival. The Layman's Prayer Revival has been the subject of extensive research for only the past generation. Perhaps due to the lack of a well-known leader, its lack of controversy, and its interdenominational character, the awakening has often been overlooked.[2] J. Edwin Orr began the scholarly interest in this awakening. He personally examined this movement more than any other, calling it the greatest revival he ever studied. In his book *Light of the Nations*, a survey of the advance of Christianity in the nineteenth century, Orr gave great attention to the Prayer Revival. At first, historians were skeptical. Martin Marty of the University of Chicago reviewed the book and criticized Orr for giving too much attention to the awakening. However, church historian Edwin Gaustad commended Orr for the valuable contribution of his research. Perry Miller of Harvard called the awakening "The Event of the Century."[3]

Spiritual Declension before Revival

The effects of the Second Great Awakenings had waned by the late 1840s. Economic prosperity turned the hearts of people from God. During the 1840s, the United States acquired much of the land that comprises the southwestern United States from Texas to California. The Conestoga wagon, the railroad, and the telegraph precipitated the westward advance. The vast resources found across the Great Plains, the mineral-rich mountains, and the gold of the west coast helped to push the United States to the forefront of the Industrial Revolution. The number of Americans working in manufacturing increased fourfold from 1820 to 1860.

On March 4, 1857, president James Buchanan stated in his inaugural address that, because of the unparalleled financial success of the United States, "No nation has ever before been embarrassed from too large a surplus in its treasury."[4] He observed further that corruption was thriving as a result of the love of money over public virtue. As Candler described the scene: "Men forgot God in pursuit of gold."[5]

At the height of this economic boon, a financial panic sent shock waves across the nation. In the fall of 1857, the "excessive railroad building, over speculation and a wildcat currency system"[6] led to a major banking crash. On October 14, the United States banking system collapsed. Thousands of people in the industrial centers of the East were devastated.

Many church leaders attributed the bank panic to God's judgment upon America's sin and called believers to prayer and fasting. Some today have reduced the Prayer Revival to nothing more than a human response to economic panic that can be explained sociologically. This was the conclusion of William McLoughlin, who followed a sociological approach to the study of spiritual awakenings. Orr objected to such reasoning:

> It is fashion among the uninformed and the skeptical to dismiss the 1858 Revival as hysteria following the bank panic of October 1857. This view, which is ideological rather than historical, ignores the fact that the prayer meetings began during the month before the financial crisis prostrated business; its evangelistic phase began in Canada which was not affected by the crash; rural areas remote from the city experienced revivals three months after the panic; and the cities were not swept by the enthusiasm until six months after the crash, when the newspapers at last publicized it. It is foolish to ignore the bank failures as a factor, but even more foolish to consider them the major factor, in the light of the fact that most bank failures (including 1929) have not at all produced religious revivals.[7]

Samuel Prime, editor of the daily *New York Observer,* who in 1858 penned a narrative of the awakening in New York, demonstrated that the union prayer meetings, which were so critical to the awakening, had already begun by the time of the bank panic. He further noted, however, that the thousands of businessmen who suddenly found themselves unemployed, "in their want of something else to do, assembled in meetings for prayer."[8]

A second factor regarding the revival's genesis beyond the economic consideration was the ominous cloud of slavery. While Finney and others had been tireless in their efforts to stop this inhuman practice, the schism between the North and South continued to grow until the Civil War. During this time, the Supreme Court handed down the Dred Scott decision, and *Uncle Tom's Cabin* was published. Pulpits began to focus on this issue as well.

By the 1840s, many people thought the spiritual condition of the nation had declined noticeably. The *New York Observer* ran articles in 1844 bemoaning the paucity of revivals. By 1845, it entreated: "Dear Christian brethren, we must have revivals or we are undone."[9] Denominational gatherings decried the loss of religious commitment.

An increasing emphasis on human agency in revival, due in large part to Charles Finney's influence, also turned many eyes from gazing upon the only true Author of revival. The sentiment of human agency is seen in the following quote from the *Independent* in 1854: "Brethren, if you will, follow the above directions for two months, and do not enjoy a revival or religion of the old stamp, you may tell me that public, that I am no prophet."[10]

Religious extremism contributed to the spiritual need. William Miller, who predicted wrongly the coming of Jesus in 1843 and 1844, caused no small stir that resulted in apathy from his botched predictions. The theologically untrained Miller first said the Lord would return on April 23, 1843. Many became convinced of his views. Material possessions were abandoned, great meetings were assembled, and ascension robes were made. Both this prediction and the later one of March 22, 1844, were shown to be spurious, bringing disrepute to Christianity in the minds of many.

Revival Beginnings

The Prayer Revival began with several unrelated movements of revival that ultimately became one. There was no planning, no major call to prayer, no attempt to propagate revival. A contemporary of the revival said, "This advent was so sudden and heralded, that ministers were in many cases taken by surprise, and scarcely able to realize that awakening [was] breathing on the hearts of their congregations."[11]

Before the 1857-58 awakening, several sources recognized the need for a general awakening. American Baptist pastor Henry Clay Fish wrote *Primitive Piety Revived*, and British Methodist minister William Arthur (who visited America) wrote *The Tongue of Fire*. Both emphasized the need for a general outpouring of the Spirit. Orr noted that both books reiterated Jonathan Edwards's earlier "pleas for explicit agreement and visible union of the people of God in extraordinary prayer for the revival of religion and the advancement of Christ's kingdom on earth."[12]

Local churches experienced revival "puddles" prior to the flood of awakening. In January of 1857 the *New York Observer* cited local revivals in many states from New York to Ohio and in Canada. Revival swept the Baptist church in

Lawrence, Massachusetts; the church added 317 new members in less than a year, 210 of those by baptism. The church had only 164 members at the beginning of that year.

After a time of prayer and fasting, a similar movement touched Pittsfield. Over five hundred decisions were recorded; one out of every fifteen residents came to Christ in a short period. Baptists and Methodists in South Carolina saw similar phenomena in 1857. At the First Baptist Church of Beaufort, the church was shaken, which resulted in 428 new believers baptized in four months. A similar movement came to Methodist churches in Columbia.

Orr believed the earliest signs of revival came in Canada. In 1855 a powerful revival shook the campus at Acadia College in Wolfville, Nova Scotia. Isaiah Wallace, a student who was converted at the time, became a revival leader among Canadian Baptists. He witnessed revivals in local churches for the following several years. Fifty years after the college awakening, he said, "Whatever success may have attended my life's work in the Lord's service is traceable, in some degree at least, to that gracious renewing in 1855."[13] Presbyterian, Baptist, and Methodist churches developed a burden for revival, especially in Canada West (modern Ontario). The Presbyterian Synod called a concert of prayer early in 1857.

Walter and Phoebe Palmer conducted evangelistic meetings among the Methodists in Canada. Phoebe Palmer was one of the first prominent female preachers in America. She became an advocate of the view of complete sanctification, which could be traced through the Wesleyan and Holiness traditions. Orr specifically cited a revival movement that began in the midst of such services in Hamilton, Ontario, led by the Palmers beginning October 1857. The first day, 21 persons professed faith in Christ. Soon, about 40 people a day were being saved. On the last Sunday in October, close to 100 were converted.

A national journal in New York City proclaimed a "Revival Extraordinary" had erupted in Ontario. "The work is taking within its range persons of all classes," the article observed. "Men of low degree, and men of high estate for wealth and position; old men and maidens and even children are seen humbly kneeling together pleading for grace. The mayor of the city, with other persons of like position, are not ashamed to be seen bowed at the altar of prayer."[14]

The camp meetings of the Palmers in Ontario and Quebec drew 5,000-6,000 people. By April of 1858, a Methodist newspaper reported that revival had spread over virtually the entire country.

Later, news of the union prayer meetings in the United States led to similar revival movements in Canada. Meeting halls were filled with praying saints: 1,000 in Brandton, 5,000 in Newburgh, 8,0000 in Brockville.

The growing spirit of revival similarly touched the Presbyterians in the United States. On December 1, 1857, a three-day conference was called in Pittsburgh for the purpose of seeking revival. More than 200 ministers met to discuss the need for a general awakening. Much of the meeting was spent in prayer.

As a result, the pastors were encouraged to preach on revival the first Sunday of the New Year to be followed the next Thursday with a day of fasting and humiliation. A similar conference was held in Cincinnati following the first. By this time, many were beginning to discuss a "great revival" that had ensued. This conference became a great prayer meeting that spread out to touch the city.

The *Baptist Watchman* in Boston devoted space to promote prayer for revival beginning with the New Year issue of 1857. Sunday school played a part as well. For example, in New York City a massive Sunday school outreach campaign was launched in September of 1856. All denominations were encouraged to join the effort, which went block by block to enlist people for Sunday school. Similar plans were followed in Hanford, Buffalo, Boston, and Detroit. This effort helped to lay the groundwork for the emerging revival.

The Union Prayer Meetings

I will never forget the comments of an elderly saint at a prayer conference I led in Texas. "The only place you will ever find power coming before prayer," he said, "is in the dictionary."

As noted earlier, the power of prayer was demonstrated in the union prayer meetings inaugurated by Jeremiah Lanphier. In fact, the name given to the general awakening is taken from these meetings, which began in New York and spread nationwide. Prayer meetings rather than preaching services became the means for spreading revival fire. Certainly preaching played a vital role; but in most cases, preaching services came as a result of prayer meetings. As the revival spread to the British Isles, preaching took on a more prominent role.

Calls to prayer had begun in some denominations before the New York union meetings. Thus, the union prayer meetings that began on Fulton Street were not the only prayer meetings, but the most significant meeting began at the North Dutch Reformed Church on Fulton Street.

The residents of New York City exhibited a deep decline in godly affections. The old downtown North Dutch Reformed Church employed Jeremiah Lanphier to influence their area for the gospel. He had been converted in the year 1842 at a tabernacle constructed by Charles Finney. Lanphier was a forty-year-old single businessman filled with enthusiasm. Like most leaders of this revival, Lanphier served as a layman. It is more difficult to identify key preachers as major leaders in this movement as with previous leaders like Wesley, Whitefield, Edwards, Finney, or others.

Lanphier began his assignment on July 1, 1857. He put together a folder describing the church and commending his lay missionary work. He gave the folder to everyone he met. He passed out Bibles and tracts. While he found some success, he was overwhelmed at the enormity of the task. He prayed, "Lord, what wilt Thou have me to do?" This led him to a novel approach.

Lanphier had found prayer to be a great source of comfort. He had noticed how the businessmen were "hurrying along their way, often with care worn faces, and anxious, restless gaze."[15] He presented to the church board the idea of a prayer meeting for businessmen. Their response was less than enthusiastic, but they agreed to allow Lanphier to proceed. Determining that the noon hour was the most feasible time for a prayer meeting, he printed and distributed a handbill publicizing the meeting. He promoted the meeting with great zeal. Lanphier distributed the following handbill in New York City during 1857:[16]

The Handbill of Lanphier:

How Often Shall I Pray?

As often as the language of prayer is on my heart; as often as I see my need of help; as often as I feel the power of temptation; as often as I am made sensible of my spiritual declension or feel the aggression of a worldly spirit. In prayer we leave the business of time for that of eternity and intercourse with men for intercourse with God.

[Backside of the handbill:]

A day prayer meeting is held every Wednesday from 12 to 1 o'clock in the Consistory building in the rear of the North Dutch Church, corner of Fulton and Williams streets. This meeting is intended to give merchants, mechanics, clerks, strangers and businessmen generally an opportunity to stop and call on God amid the perplexities incident to their respective avocations. It will continue for one hour; but it is also designed for those who find it inconvenient to remain more than 5 or 10 minutes, as well as for those who can spare a whole hour. Necessary interruption will be slight, because anticipated. Those in haste often expedite their business engagements by halting to lift their voices to the throne of grace in humble, grateful prayer.

Lanphier's own description of the birth of the noonday meetings, which began on September 23, 1857, is moving:

> Going my rounds in the performance of my duty one day, as I was walking along the streets, the idea was suggested to my mind that an hour of prayer, from twelve to one o'clock, would be beneficial to businessmen, who usually in great numbers take that hour for rest and refreshment. The idea was to have singing, prayer, exhortation, relation of religious experience, as the case might be; that none should be required to stay the whole hour; that all should come and go as their engagements should allow or require, or their inclinations dictate. Arrangements were made, and at twelve o'clock noon, on the 23rd day of September, 1857, the door of the third story lecture-room was thrown open.[17]

At first, Lanphier prayed alone. Then, one joined him, and by the end of the hour there were six. Prayer meetings had been held before, but this was different. Former meetings tended toward formalism and routine. These meetings inaugurated by Lanphier were free and spontaneous.

The following Wednesday, there were 20, and on the third, 30 to 40. Those present determined to meet daily rather than weekly. On October 14, over 100 came. At this point, many in attendance were unsaved persons, many of whom were under great conviction of sin. By the end of the second month, three large rooms were filled.

Almost simultaneously, prayer meetings were begun across the city. Many churches sponsored such meetings without knowledge of other activity similar to their own. Within six months, fifty thousand were meeting daily in New York, while thousands more prayed in other cities. On March 17, 1858, Burton's Theater near the North Dutch Church opened for noon prayer. The theater was filled to capacity by 11:30 A.M. Henry Ward Beecher spoke to three thousand gathered there on the third day. Evening preaching services soon accompanied the daily prayer meetings. Lanphier and the church set up seven rules for the meetings:

1. Open with a brief hymn.
2. Opening prayer.
3. Read a passage of Scripture.
4. Take time for requests, exhortations, and prayers.
5. Prayer would follow each request or at most two requests, while individuals were limited to five minutes of prayer/comments.
6. No controversial subjects were to be mentioned.
7. At five minutes before 1:00, a hymn was sung so the meeting could end at 1:00 promptly.[18]

Such rules illustrate the fact that, while revival is a spontaneous movement marked by a departure from normal services, offering guidance need not hinder the work of the Spirit.

Both religious and secular publications reported on the phenomenon. The *New York Herald* reported meeting places, denominational affiliation, and the number of those attending. The numbers reported on March 26 included the following:[19]

Fulton Street	Dutch Reformed	300
John Street	Methodist Episcopal	600
Burton's Theater	Union Service	1200
Ninth Street	Dutch Reformed	150
Pilgrims Church	Congregational	125
Waverly Place	YMCA	200
Madison Square	Presbyterian	250

Typically the meetings featured hymn singing, Bible reading, and brief exhortations, but the bulk of time was spent in intercession. Prominent among the requests were burdens for lost friends or relatives. In fact, in stark contradiction to the typical prayer meetings of our day, requests were almost exclusively about spiritual needs. Prayers for physical needs seemed insignificant in light of the stark spiritual needs of the day.

Amazing answers to prayer were recorded across the nation. One man spoke of his burden for an unconverted son. This son, who had traveled across the world, was converted soon after the request was made at Fulton Street. One young man came to the meeting seeking salvation. He was converted after hearing a request by a mother for her son. "It struck me that that was from my mother," the youth reported. "After meeting I got sight of that request. And sure enough, it was from my mother, in her own handwriting."[20]

The overall spirit of the meetings was one of deep love for Christ. Many unchurched residents were amazed at the love among believers, the prayer, and the answers to prayer. People came from as far as St. Louis to be a part of the movement of prayer. The meetings were multi-denominational and cut across economic lines. In fact, the first meeting of six men represented no less than four denominations. Thus they were called "union" prayer meetings because of unity despite the differing backgrounds of the participants.

The strong emphasis of the meetings was the conversion of the lost. Lanphier's personal journal noted times when evangelistic tracts were distributed at the meetings. Churches experienced revival, and evangelistic harvests grew out of the prayer meetings: 75 were converted in a Brooklyn church revival meeting, 115 professions of faith occurred in a few days at a church in the Catskills, and 3,000 were converted in two months in Newark.

Other churches began morning prayer meetings at about the same time. Churches in New York and Brooklyn commenced praying without knowing what others were doing. Churches in Philadelphia had begun praying in September of 1857 for revival. Several churches from various denominations exchanged pulpits in the Thanksgiving season to encourage prayer for revival. News of the prayer meetings in New York led to a gathering in Jaynes Hall that recorded 6,000 men coming together at noon for prayer. Requests for prayer came by the thousands. At one of these meetings, George Duffield wrote the song "Stand up for Jesus."

Ultimately, a tent was erected for evangelistic services, which recorded more than 150,000 in attendance over a four-month period. Some 10,000 came to Christ during this time. Baptist churches alone, which had averaged only a 2.5 percent growth for the years 1853-57, posted a remarkable 19 percent growth in 1858. Other denominations posted similar records. Two meetings in Pittsburgh recorded about 1,000 conversions each. Reports of revival in towns and churches have been found for no less than sixty-five Pennsylvania towns.

The spirit of prayer led to unusual effectiveness in preaching. While a movement of prayer, the revival yet featured significant sermonic content. By the fall of 1858, large halls in New York City were filled to capacity: The Cooper Institute, where 2,500 gathered and thousands were turned away, while the Academy of Music filled throughout the winter every Sunday night for gospel preaching.

Prime noted, however, that the secret of the Prayer Revival was the largely unnoticed churches where God moved mightily: "I have reason to know, and with intense pleasure stated here, that some of the most remarkably favored churches have been those that are out of the great centers of attraction, in the retired or waste places of the city."[21] In addition to preaching, tracts were used both in the promotion of revival and in the cause of evangelism.

This revival was unusually free of the emotional excess that characterized many of the camp meetings in the Second Great Awakening. Perhaps due to the focus on the prayer meetings, the Prayer Revival was characterized by a calm, deep solemnity.

A person living at the time wrote:

> The most crowded meetings were solemn by their deep and strange stillness; the most thorough conviction and terrible anxiety showed themselves in concentrated meditation and half-suppressed and deep drawn sighs; while the joy and hope and forgiveness told of its presence by tears which made the eyes they moistened more radiant than ever.[22]

The Awakening became so popular that leading secular papers such as the *New York Herald* published "Revival Extras" to report revival accounts from across the nation.

> The unchurched residents of New York City were amazed at the love among the believers, the prayer, and the answers to prayer.

Revival Spreads

Simultaneously, revival came to areas across the nation. In Boston, a daily prayer meeting had been going on for years before 1858. As news of the growing prayer movement in New York came to Boston, a businessman's meeting for prayer was set in the South Church downtown. The first day, the place was so filled some could not enter. Charles Finney, in the latter stages of his ministry, was preaching at the Park Street Church in Boston. He described the revival that soon swept Boston as "too general to keep any account at all of the number of converts, or to allow any estimate being made that would approximate the truth."[23] Across Massachusetts some 150 churches reported revival.

Nearby Connecticut was also hit with a wave of unusual prayer meetings. Rhode Island experienced unprecedented movements of the Spirit in 1858. Again, prayer and evangelism coupled to bring amazing results. In Pawtucket, more than 100 people came to Christ in a short time. More than one hundred professions of faith were recorded at a small Baptist church in Warren. Some three-dozen towns reported revival.

In Maine, the church bells tolled daily, calling thousands to prayer. Revival came to towns including Saco, Dear Isle, Beddeford, and Bargon. Similar accounts can be traced to Vermont and New Hampshire. Possibly one hundred towns in these small states experienced some form of revival spirit.

A study of documents during this time reveals that revival touched every major city in the Midwest: Cincinnati, Cleveland, Louisville, Indianapolis, Detroit, Chicago, and St. Louis. In only two months in the state of Ohio, 200 towns recorded twelve thousand conversions. Prayer meetings sprang up everywhere. In Indiana, 150 towns experienced renewal.

One of the most moving accounts out of the Prayer Revival came from the town of Kalamazoo, Michigan. At a prayer meeting there, a man in attendance related the following account:

> At our very first meeting someone put in such a request as this: "A praying wife requests the prayers of this meeting for her unconverted husband, that he may be converted and made a humble disciple of the Lord Jesus." All at once a stout burly man arose and said, "I am that man, I have a pious praying wife, and this request must be for me. I want you to pray for me." As soon as he sat down, in the midst of sobs and tears, another man arose and said, "I am that man, I have a praying wife. She prays for me. And now she asked you to pray for me. I am sure I am that man, and I want you to pray for me."[24]

Five other men made similar statements. The power of God fell upon that meeting and that town. In a brief period, almost five hundred conversions came to the town.

Wisconsin and the area of Minnesota also reported revival. Baptist churches in Illinois received more than a thousand converts a month. Chicago saw many prayer meetings and a spirit of revival in 1858, as well.

Many reports of revival came from ships entering U.S. ports. Hoffman said it seemed there was "a definite zone of heavenly influence" across the eastern seaboard.[25] The battleship North Carolina was anchored in New York City's harbor with more than a thousand-man crew. Four sailors began a prayer meeting on the ship. The Spirit filled them to the point that they began to sing. Some of the ungodly crewmen heard the singing and began to mock the young believers. They were almost immediately gripped with conviction for their attitude, whereupon they began to cry for mercy.

Night after night, meetings were held, and nightly, hardened sailors were broken in repentance and faith. Ministers were eventually sought out from the shore to assist in ministering to the sailors. At this time, the *North Carolina*, a veritable revival center, served as a receiving ship for the navy. This ship served as the one through which crewmen changed assignments. Thus, the tides of revival literally spread across the seas.

Over the past two centuries, spiritual awakenings have moved with particular impact on college campuses. The *Oberlin Evangelist* proclaimed that the greatest benefit of the Second Great Awakening came on college campuses. Colleges experiencing revival included Oberlin, Amherst, Dartmouth, Middlebury, and Williams. Yale recorded the most powerful movement of awakening since 1821. Almost half of the 447 students professed conversion. Out of an enrollment of 272 at Princeton, 102 students were converted, and 50 entered the ministry. The University of Virginia experienced a revival that featured extensive prayer meetings. A practical result was the formation of the first college organization of the YMCA. Baylor University and other schools in the South responded similarly.

There is some debate concerning the extent of the Prayer Revival in the southern half of the United States. Certainly the abomination of slavery kept many in the South from the hand of God. But revival did occur in some circles. Finney wrote that revival completely missed the South because of slavery. Beardsley said basically the same thing some sixty years after the fact. However, these men underestimated the grace of God in touching the hearts of those who would return to Him.

Orr and Candler argued convincingly that many churches in the South experienced revival. In particular, churches that included black slaves in worship seemed to be blessed by the touch of God. In one year, 1858, the Methodist Episcopal Church in the South added 43,388 members and "probationers;" 10,117 were black. The Anson Street Presbyterian Church in Charleston, South Carolina, was awakened in 1858. The majority of the members were black. Black pastor John Girardeau preached regularly to crowds of fifteen hundred to two thousand. The revival in Charleston began with a prayer service that grew until the church was full. Then, the fire fell. The attendees began to sob softly, like the falling of rain; then, with deeper emotion, to weep bitterly, or to rejoice loudly, according to their circumstances. It was midnight before Girardeau could dismiss his congregation. The meeting went on night and day for weeks. Large numbers of both blacks and whites were converted and joined churches of the city.

During this period, revivals occurred over practically the whole country, and large numbers of young men were brought into the church. Dr. Girardeau frequently referred to this as the "Lord's mercy in gathering His elect for the great war that was soon to sweep so many of them into eternity."[26]

In the Southwest, news of the Fulton Street prayer meeting led a missionary among the Choctaw Indians to observe the hour of prayer as well. Many Indians participated, with many coming to Christ as a result.

Revival during the Civil War

One of the reasons the Prayer Revival received less attention by historians is its short-lived nature. After cresting in 1858, there was an abating of the Spirit's fire. This was due mainly to the growing tensions that erupted in the Civil War. John Brown's raid and the election of Abraham Lincoln exacerbated the schism between the North and South.

However, this does not mean all signs of revival had vanished. By the end of 1859, there were still many large gatherings for prayer. Prayer conventions continued to be called in 1859 and 1860. The specter of war and the corresponding national furor over slavery brought the attention of the nation to a more sinister, although unfortunately necessary, subject: the Civil War.

Orr considered the question of the awakening's relationship to the Civil War: "It served and fortified the churches for the great trauma. While the younger generation sallied forth for battle, home churches, as the war progressed, showed no diminishing of zeal."[27] Similarly Hoffman wrote: "As a result of the revival the nation entered the dark days of the Civil War with a deeper faith in God and a firmer belief in the efficacy of prayer."[28]

An evangelistic and social agency called the Christian Commission served the armies of the North. This organization was born out of the Prayer Revival. The Commission continued the prayer movement by leading evening prayer meetings in every Union post it served.

Other factors played a part in revival, particularly in the southern armies. Prayer and fasting were frequent and fervent. Tracts produced by the various societies proved instrumental in the conversion of many. Thousands of Bibles provided to the soldiers were received gladly. In addition, many of the leaders, particularly Robert E. Lee, were committed Christians in spite of the failed cause for which they fought.

The war went badly for the North in the early stages. President Lincoln once commented that he was concerned that the rebel soldiers were praying more fervently than those of the North. The U.S. Senate passed a resolution asking the president to observe a national day of fasting and prayer. He set apart April 30, 1863, as a national day of humiliation, prayer, and the confession of national sins. The tide of war turned soon thereafter, including the defeat of Confederate troops led by Lee at Gettysburg on July 3.

Throughout the war, reports of localized revivals among the Union soldiers were given: on the Potomac, at Windmill Point, and through the ministry of D. L. Moody in occupied Nashville.

During the horrors of the Civil War, when over 600,000 Americans were killed at the hands of their countrymen, revival touched many in the Confederate army. Books written by eyewitnesses carry accounts of the Spirit of God moving in wartime.[29] Thousands of soldiers came to Christ during the fury of the conflict.

Both the North and the South had chaplains among their ranks. In addition to Moody, many lesser-known chaplains assisted in ministering to northern troops; the famous prayer warrior E. M. Bounds served as a chaplain, as well. The newly formed Southern Baptist Convention employed as many as 75 missionaries to the Confederate armies. Episcopalians furnished a hundred chaplains and missionaries; Methodists supplied nearly two hundred. The work of these men, along with Christian generals such as Lee and "Stonewall" Jackson, impacted the soldiers. The very rigors of war doubtless impressed the soldiers, as well. Like Jonah, who was used of God despite his attitude toward the Assyrians, the South was touched by revival despite their own prejudice.

The Prayer Revival laid the foundation that would give spiritual resources that would help the nation survive this conflict. Roy Fish notes that one of the "major functions of the great awakening of 1858 had to do with its preparation of the country for its fratricidal war which clouded the horizon."[30]

A powerful revival was reported in Fredericksburg, Virginia, in 1863 under the general leadership of Methodist chaplain W B. Owen. Services outgrew the local churches; some five hundred professions of faith were recorded. Chaplain William Jones arrived on the thirty-first day of revival. Another minister there, a Dr. Stiles, said the work was "widening and deepening, and ere it closes, it may permeate the whole army of Northern Virginia."[31]

Similar movements came at Dalton, Georgia, in 1863-64, and along the Rapidan River in Virginia. A key leader at the Rapidan River Revival, which came after the bloody conflict at Gettysburg, was John A. Broadus of Southern Baptist Theological Seminary renown.

The Awakening and the Subsequent Ministry of D. L. Moody

The Prayer Revival made perhaps its most notable impact on an individual in Chicago. As early as January 1857, revival fires burned in parts of the Windy City. The YMCA held prayer meetings like those in New York. A young man named Dwight Lyman Moody attended the meetings. Born at Northfield, Massachusetts, on February 5, 1837, Moody lost his father as a four-year-old and grew up in abject poverty. While only a teenager, young Moody became a successful shoe salesman. His Sunday school teacher at the Mount Vernon Congregational Church, Edward Kimball, won Moody to Christ.

In 1856 Moody moved westward to Chicago. He sought greater avenues for success in business. He united with the Plymouth Congregational Church, filling four pews each Sunday with young men he had invited. He eventually began a mission Sunday school, reaching the most destitute youths in Chicago. Soon, six hundred attended.

During the Prayer Revival, Moody's heart was stirred. Biographer John Pollock said: "The revival of early 1857 tossed Moody out of his complacent view of religion as primarily an aid to fortune." He wrote to his mother about his attendance at the prayer meetings: "I go every night to meeting — Oh, how I do enjoy it! It seems as if God were here Himself."[32]

Orr once recounted a conversation with a church historian about the revival of 1857-59. As he described his research into the "revival of '58," the historian asked, "What started that? Moody?" Orr replied, "No, Moody did not start the '58 revival, the '58 revival started Moody."[33] Moody also prayed in 1899, the year of his death, that the church would be quickened again as it had been in 1857.

Although never ordained to the ministry, D. L. Moody became one of the most effective and famous servants of Christ since apostolic days. His citywide campaigns came at a pivotal time in American history. Cities were rising to unparalleled prominence. His urban campaigns had unprecedented impact.

For example, a three-month campaign in Chicago during late 1876 recorded this impact: cumulative attendance of 900,000 in a city of 400,000; 6,000 converts; large numbers of new members added to area churches for months. Additionally, thousands of ministers attended a convention during the period. Streetcars were set up to provide transportation to the Tabernacle. Chicago's leading newspapers featured front-page coverage of his services almost every day. Moody's sermons were often printed verbatim the day following each service.

In 1871 Moody met Ira Sankey (1840-1910) in Indianapolis, thus, the first itinerant music-preaching team was born. Another musician who affiliated with the Moody-Sankey team on occasion was Philip P. Bliss. Beginning in 1875, Sankey and Moody used Bliss's collection *Gospel Hymns and Sacred Songs*. Other collections by Bliss and Sankey included some of the great hymns of that day, such as Sankey's "The Ninety and Nine" and "A Shelter in the Time of Storm;" Bliss's "Wonderful Words of Life" and "Almost Persuaded;" and Fanny Crosby's "Rescue the Perishing."

The Impact of the Moody-Sankey Crusades:

The religious fervor that Moody and Sankey generated in Chicago in 1876 was part of a broader phenomenon extending to other major urban centers in America. From 1875 to 1877, Moody and Sankey conducted revival campaigns in New York, Philadelphia, Brooklyn, and Boston. Thousands crowded the meeting places wherever they went. Collections of Moody's sermons and Sankey's gospel hymns were printed and became overnight best sellers. Moody and Sankey became household names among both the churched and the unchurched. A Moody and Sankey revival was a religious and social event of large significance for many urban dwellers in nineteenth-century America. Denominational distinctions were set aside, and thousands of evangelical Christians came together to work as one for the revivalists. Religious experience and theological questions were, at least temporarily, established as topics of central importance to large numbers of the public. Lethargic churches were enlivened, and membership in many increased dramatically.

Darrell M. Robertson, *The Chicago Revival of 1876 Society and Revivalism in a Nineteenth-Century City* (London. Scarecrow Press, 1989), 1-2.

Moody's final campaign came at the brink of the new century in November 1899. The impact of many of the efforts of Moody and music evangelist Sankey was particularly effective in the evangelization of sinners; more often than not, however, genuine revival erupted in the process of his meetings as well.

Other Continued Signs of Revival

Beyond Moody, pastors and itinerants reported renewal and evangelism through their ministries during the Prayer Revival. Henry Ward Beecher, son of Lyman, was a pastor who attended to unusual signs of the work of God. He addressed a prayer service in Burton's Theater on March 20, 1858, in which 3000 attended. Many more were turned away. He continued to be involved in the work of revival.

Theodore Cuyler's role in the history of youth ministry:

September 1860 an incident of historical importance in the development of youth societies occurred: a young people's prayer meeting was formed in Brooklyn's Lafayette Avenue Presbyterian Church. Its format, according to its pastor, Theodore Cuyler, was the highly successful prayer-meeting approach of the YMCA — the example and model Cuyler needed for his congregation. When 40 youth and young adults signed the constitution he had developed, they agreed that the purpose of their society should be the conversion of souls, the development of Christian character, and the training of new converts in religious work. Significantly, this statement of purpose later found its way into the constitutions of youth societies organized by most of the principal denominations.

Karen E. Jones and David Rahn, *Youth Ministry That Transforms* (Grand Rapids: Zondervan, 2001), 28.

Theodore Cuyler, pastor of the Market Street Church in New York City, said in 1858: "The glorious work of that revival kept many of us busy for six months, night and day."[34] Cuyler later went to pastor a church in Brooklyn that became the largest Presbyterian Church in America. He played a role in the history of youth ministry as well, organizing a prayer meeting of spiritually hungry youth during this season of revival. While organized student ministry common in churches today is a more modern phenomenon, we see early seeds for such ministry in the work of Cuyler.

Many itinerant evangelists experienced powerful results during the height of the Prayer Revival. Even in the years following, men including Jacob Knapp (1799-1874), A. B. Earle (1812-1895), Payson Hammond (1831-1910), Emerson Andrews (1806-1884), James Caughey (1810-1891), Herman Humphrey (1779-1861), and Sam Jones (1847-1906) experienced unusually blessed results. Revival was reported in the ministries of such men again and again. Major denominations encouraged evangelists in their work as a rule, making possible the citywide campaign ministries of Moody, R. A. Torrey, and J. Wilbur Chapman in successive years. To quote Orr on the awakening's impact on mass evangelism:

> Modern mass evangelism, the citywide campaigns supported by a major number of churches of all the denominations, arose from the 1857-58 awakening. During all the previous 120 years — from Whitefield to Finney — nothing like a citywide cooperative campaign had ever been held. Unity and fraternity in the 1858 Revivals made possible Moody's great campaigns of the nineteenth century's fourth quarter.[35]

A. B. Earle, a Baptist evangelist used mightily of God during the revival's height, continued to see powerful outpourings. In Canada during 1858, revival spread so profoundly that on one occasion Earle was one of five ministers baptizing new believers simultaneously because of the massive numbers. "I went out at midnight near my boarding-house," Earle wrote concerning another Canadian village, "and could distinctly hear the voice of prayer in the houses, in the barns, in the fields, in the streets."[36] In New York during the year 1858, he preached in churches that could not contain those desiring to attend. At one church, a group of ladies began a prayer gathering on Saturday nights during Earle's ministry that continued at least ten years later.

Revival came to other locales as well: three months of continuous preaching in Boston in 1862; a general awakening in Fall River in 1863; in 1864 thousands came to services in Springfield (hundreds had to be turned away) and 600 were added to the churches of that town. The awakening in Springfield spread to neighboring towns in the region. Similar occurrences came to Vermont and New York in 1866, and later to the western U.S. An estimated 150,000 were converted under Earle's ministry.

Edward Payson Hammond was a New England Congregationalist who played a part in the Scottish Revival of 1859-60. In the United States, he experienced an unusually effective ministry. He preached ten weeks consecutively in Philadelphia and witnessed quite an outpouring in Maine. A report came from Detroit in 1864 of a general awakening led by Hammond. He is best known as an effective evangelist among children.

Jacob Knapp, a Baptist evangelist whose ministry began in the 1830s had his ministry renewed in 1858. He had earlier been charged and then cleared of wearing old clothes to collect better offerings. He was powerful as a preacher of the gospel and in the anti-slavery movement. James Caughey was a Methodist who also labored in America and Britain.

Awakening Overseas

The Prayer Revival offers further evidence of the role of testimony in the spread of an awakening. The news of the union prayer meetings in New York gave impetus to revival in the British Isles. Commenting on the remarkable growth in the number of prayer meetings in England, John Lorimer stated: "Had it not been for the revival in the United States, we might safely say no such meetings would have been called into existence."[37] Some groups had commenced praying before the news from America came. The testimony of revival in the United States turned the spiritual heat considerably warmer in the mother country.

In 1856 a Mrs. Colville came to Ireland from England to testify of the grace of God from house to house. One man her witness impressed was James McQuilkin. A small group began meeting for prayer in September 1857 in Ireland. McQuilkin, John Wallace, Robert Carlisle, and Jeremiah Meneely thereafter founded the Believer's Fellowship Meeting. This small group grew to about fifty and sparked a flame of revival that spread across the country over the next two years. The awakening became known as the Ulster Revival of 1859. In the town of Conor, six of the nine saloons were closed. John H. Moore, a Methodist minister in Conor who had influenced McQuilkin, led revival movements through open-air meetings. Such hymns as "Just As I Am" and "All Hail the Power" were frequently sung. Often, ministers had to counsel with convicted persons into the early morning hours.

Wales experienced a similar powerful awakening in 1859. "The work of a century is crowded into a year," wrote Thomas Phillips of the awakening.[38] Phillips witnessed the impact that one year of deep revival can have on a nation. Wesleyan Humphrey Jones (1832-95) and Calvinistic Methodist David Morgan (1814-88) were instrumental in the revival. Jones focused his preaching to the church, exhorting them that "an awakened church is to be the principal instrument in converting the world."[39] Many churches in the principality began to hold joint prayer meetings. Awakening touched their meetings as it did the campus of the College of Trevecca. All denominations were warmed by the revival's glow. Phillips surveyed forty locales in Wales to investigate the awakening's impact. He estimated that of the thousands of converts won to Christ, only one in twenty failed to live consistently for Christ.

Reports from the Prayer Revival in America only helped revival in Ireland. In August 1858 a group from the Presbyterian Synod in Ireland visited the Fulton Street meetings. After the group's return, a letter was sent from the assembly to encourage revival prayer. Cairns estimated that revival in the British Isles brought one million people to Christ. He traced such movements as the Salvation Army and the Keswick conventions to the revival.[40] In 1859 revival came to Broughshane in Ireland. Presbyterian minister Archibald Robinson and his people had been praying for revival, but they were surprised when it came in such an extraordinary manner.

A national movement of prayer came also to Scotland. More than forty thousand were praying continually for revival when the Spirit was poured out in 1858. News of the "Great Revival" in America, as it was called, fanned further the revival's flames. Some converts became outstanding Christian leaders. These included Professor James Off and Professor Simpson, James Chalmer of New Guinea, James Gilmour of Mongolia, Mary Slessor of Calabar, and John McNeil. In Ulster, more than one hundred prayer meetings sprouted in one district alone during 1859.

Moody witnessed robust revival on his journeys to England. In 1872 he met Henry Varley. During the visit, he heard Varley say, "The world has yet to see what God can do with one man fully consecrated to Him." Moody determined to be such a man to the glory of God, and Varley's phrase has since been associated with Moody.

On this junket, Moody preached at the Arundel Square Church. He was so surprised at those who responded to his invitation that he repeated it. Within ten days, four hundred united with the church. It was later disclosed to him that a woman named Marianne Adlard, an invalid, had been praying for revival in the church. The tide of awakening that lapped British soil more than a decade earlier arose again in the 1870s. Powerful revival often accompanied Moody and Sankey on British tours, including tours in 1873-75,1881-84, and 1891-92. In Glasgow, more than 30,000 people thronged into the largest hall to hear the evangelist. Thousands were converted. Social enterprises, including an orphanage, emerged.

During the latter half of the nineteenth century in England, Charles Spurgeon led in a period of continuous revival. Spurgeon (1834-92), the "prince of preachers," witnessed perpetual revival for many years while pastor of the Metropolitan Tabernacle in London. He serves as a model for pastors of one who walked in revival in his personal life, and whose influence therefore far transcended his own impressive abilities.

Revival in Spurgeon's congregation can be traced to the prayers of his people. The invitation of the congregation to the young Spurgeon when he became pastor stated in part, "We pray that the result of his services may be owned of God, with an outpouring of the Holy Spirit, and a revival of religion in their midst."[41] While only a small group constituted his congregation early in his ministry, there was a deep earnestness in their prayers. "Sometimes they seemed to plead as though they could really see the Angel of the Covenant present with them, and as if they must have a blessing from him," Spurgeon remembered. "More than once we were all so awe-struck with the solemnity of the meeting that we sat silent for some moments while the Lord's Power appeared to overshadow us."[42]

The phenomenal growth and spirit of revival that came to the New Park Street Chapel (which became the Metropolitan Tabernacle) is an example of a church ministering in the midst of awakening. Spurgeon attributed much of his success to his "Furnace," a group of hundreds of laymen who prayed in the basement as he preached.

Another minister used of God in this era was William Booth. Both William and his wife Catherine were both born in 1829. William became a pastor in 1851. In 1858 he was ordained and sent to minister with the Methodist church at Gaterhead. For two years, revival advanced. The place where the church met became known as the "converting shop." During the 1860s, the Booths went to the East End section of London, where poverty was indescribable. The conversion of sinners there became the birth of the Salvation Army. The army continued to spread news of the gospel and Holiness doctrine for generations.

Revival reports came from Northern Ireland, England, Scotland, Wales, South Africa, Scandinavia, Switzerland, and Germany. In South Africa, Andrew Murray (1828-1917) served as a catalyst for revival after about 1860. His writings, including *Absolute Surrender* and *With Christ in the School of Prayer*, have burned a desire for revival into many who have read them. I was introduced to them in 1981, and their influence on my life has been great.

Impact of the Layman's Prayer Revival

The awakening provided a testimony to the Word of God in revival. Of the national awakenings in America, this was the only awakening without a well-known leader. It came unexpectedly, which may explain the great unity among believers. Differences between denominations were minimized in the prayer meetings. Churches in the same region, though of differing traditions, united for the cause of revival.

The evangelistic impact was impressive. Almost every denomination recorded significant increases in the late 1850s. The proportion of church members to the total population jumped by 50 percent from 1850 to 1860. Roy Fish found that Baptists saw 650 new churches birthed during this period.[43] Estimates of conversions ranged from 300,000 to 1 million. Beardsley believed half a million were converted, while Orr and Candler said the number had to be nearly one million. Specific approaches of ministry were emphasized, including prayer and evangelism; lay preachers, such as Lanphier; house-to-house visitation; evangelistic literature; open-air preaching; youth and children's evangelism; and music in evangelism.

Urban evangelism developed as people flocked to cities due to the Industrial Revolution. Moody made effective use of massive citywide crusades, which fit the times well. His work in cities has been emulated for a century, and it demonstrates an effective example of applying the unchanging gospel to a given era.

Sankey served as a model for emerging music evangelists. "The Ninety and Nine," "Jesus of Nazareth Passes By," and other songs he penned made a great impact on believers and unbelievers alike. Lord Shaftersbury did not exaggerate when he said, "If Moody and Sankey had done nothing else but teach us 'Hold the Fort' their visit would have been worthwhile."[44] Sankey and Philip P. Bliss published *Gospel Hymns and Sacred Songs* in 1875, which included hymns of Sankey, Bliss, and Fanny Crosby (1823-1915). Between fifty thousand and eighty thousand copies were sold by 1900.

An aspect of awakenings is the evangelistic advance seen in missions efforts. The next great wave of missions involvement following the Second Great Awakening emerged in the form of the Student Volunteer Movement, the seeds of which can be traced at least in part to the Prayer Revival. British athlete C. T. Studd had surrendered his life to God and to missions at a D. L. Moody crusade. Six others joined Studd to form the "Cambridge Seven." The result of the Student Volunteer Movement was some 20,500 students involved in foreign missions over the next fifty years. Tucker said that half of the Protestant foreign missions force in the early twentieth century came from student volunteers.[45]

D. L. Moody's influence in the calling of the 1886 Northfield Conference held at Mount Hermon, Massachusetts. This led ultimately to thousands committing their lives to missions over the ensuing decades. At the first conference, 100 students of the 250 in attendance volunteered for overseas service. This "Mount Hermon Hundred" was John R. Mott. Two years later the Student Volunteer Movement was formally organized with Mott as its first chairman. The theme of the movement became "the evangelization of the world in this generation."

At Moody's meetings in Belfast, ninety men gave their lives to missions. In Britain, the International Missionary Council, dated by Latourette to the Liverpool Conference in 1860, was made up of friends of the Prayer Revival. Baptist missionary to the Congo George Grenfell was first spiritually impressed during the Prayer Revival. Converts of the revival included missionaries Mary Slessor of Calabar, West Africa; Christina Forsyth of South Africa; James Chalmers of Indonesia; Timothy Richard of China; and James Gilmour of Mongolia. Powerful revival came through the ministry of Andrew Murray in South Africa beginning in 1860. Among Southern Baptists, Lottie Moon came to Christ under the preaching of John Broadus. Moon set the standard for thousands of Southern Baptist missionaries to encircle the globe in ensuing generations.

Lay involvement during this time was obvious. Many men were reported to have taken time off work simply to witness to others. Lay organizations such as the Young Men's Christian Association were strengthened. Later, the Young Women's Christian Association and the Young People's Society of Christian Endeavor were formed. The Sunday school and city missionary groups received impetus from the burgeoning movement of laymen. There were certainly important ministers, including Henry Ward Beecher, Jacob Knapp, Norris Kirk, and Charles Finney in his latter years. However, the primary catalyst for the movement was the laity.

The social effects of revival were profound. Beardsley wrote:

> As the Great Awakening enabled the feeble colonies to pass through the baptismal fires of the American Revolution and preserved the religious institutions of the country from complete impairment in that struggle, so the Great Revival of 1857-1858 served to prepare the people and sustain them in the fearful cataclysm which swept over our country in the early sixties and threatened to blast forever our free institutions. . . . The revival nerved and fortified the church for this fearful struggle.[46]

Beardsley argued further that the revival that occurred in the southern armies prepared them for their defeat. The United States Christian Commission was born from the YMCA and the Prayer Revival. It provided ministry to soldiers in the Civil War.

The impact of the revival on William Booth and the Salvation Army has already been noted. Thomas J. Barnardo was a product of the revival in 1859 in Ireland. He began taking in orphans, and by his death he had cared for some sixty thousand children in the homes he founded.

Moody, himself never ordained, saw the need for schools to train "gap men," laity who were equipped with the Scriptures. Thus the Moody Bible Institute was born in 1883. A. B. Simpson of the Student Volunteer Movement began Missionary Training College (today Nyack College).

Studies indicate that more than 90 percent of Americans pray. However, if that many Americans really prayed; we would live in a different society than we do today. I thank God for Christians like Lanphier, who did not say they believed in prayer, but who prayed believing in God! May God raise up a generation of such men and women, so that five, ten, and twenty years from now we will be amazed at how God has used people such as we.

Questions for Small Group Study

1. In times of calamity in his day and age, Lanphier's response was to pray. Think of some major nationwide and/or worldwide calamities that have happened recently. What has been the cultural response at the time?

2. In speaking of revivals and the agents that propel them into success, who is the bigger agent, God or man?

3. What happened at Burton's Theater? What might a contemporary parallel look like?

4. Briefly recall the impact of the Moody-Sankey ministry. Why was this effective then? What might be effective today?

Chapter 13
The Global Awakening, 1901-10

I believe the world is upon the threshold of a great religious revival, and I pray that I may be allowed to help bring this about. I beseech all those who confess Christ to ask Him today, upon their knees, if He has not some work for them to do now. He will lead them all as He has led us. He will make them pillars of smoke by day and pillars of fire by night to guide all men to Him.

Evan Roberts[1]

Around the year 1700, God visited continental Europe in the Pietistic Revival. Around the year 1800, He brought the Second Great Awakening to America. Around the year 1900, a global revival occurred that touched not only the West, but also many other points around the globe. The Global Awakening did not penetrate as deeply as earlier great revivals, nor did it continue as long in influence as did the First and Second Great Awakenings. In this awakening, however, God visited not only America and Europe but also many regions around the world.

A revival movement can be compared to a war in its impact. World War I and II had unparalleled global impact geopolitically. More recently, Operation Desert Storm in 1990-91 involved dramatically less soldiers, campaigns, and overall impact than World War II. But for a soldier in a live battle, war is equally real. Similarly, the First Great Awakening had a more profound impact in the specific region of the American colonies than the Jesus Movement of the 1960s and 1970s or the Welsh Revival of 1904. But for those involved, whether on a college campus or in a local church, the movement of God changed the trajectory of those touched.

Mark Shaw argues there are actually no less than eight global revival movements across the span of the twentieth century. His work *Global Awakening* would be a good place to start for those who desire to study a wider ethnic, geographical, and global perspective of more recent revival movements. Other writers demonstrate the global impact of Christianity over the past century or more. In *The Next Christendom*, author Philip Jenkins maintains that by 2050, the geographic center of Christianity will be in the global South — Africa, Asia, and Latin America — instead of in Western Europe and North America. The following summarizes some of the more noteworthy movements at the turn of the new century. With so many regions affected, it is difficult to determine a clear time frame. The first decade denotes the most significant period.[2]

The Welsh Revival of 1904-05

As a college student, I journeyed to Wales on two trips as part of a choir tour with my university. I discovered why Wales is known as the "Land of Song." I have long loved this land, as one of the first revival movements I heard of was the Welsh

Revival of 1904-05. This movement of God spread from Wales to other countries, including the United States. The British principality of Wales had been blessed repeatedly in earlier revivals. It has duly been called the "Land of Revival" as well as the "Land of Song." Griffith Jones, Howell Harris, Daniel Rowlands, William Williams, and Christmas Evans led earlier awakenings. The 1859 awakening in Wales was reported around the world. The land was set ablaze by the Moody-Sankey meetings in the late nineteenth century.

In 1904 God again visited the Welsh nation. Before the revival, there were several calls to prayer. Dean David Howell, in an article published one month before his death in 1902, decried the situation in the churches:

> The preaching, it is said, is able, scholarly, interesting, and instructive; it is however accompanied with but little unction and anointing. The terminology of former ages, such as conviction, conversion, repentance, adoption, mortification of sin, self-loathing, and such like, has become to a great extent foreign and meaningless. But what of the remedy? The principal need of my country and dear nation at present is still spiritual revival through a special outpouring of the Holy Spirit.[3]

When Howell's message was published in a magazine in January, 1903, it "caused a deep impression throughout the Principality."[4]

The earliest signs of renewal are actually traced to the United States, where W S. Jones, pastor of the First Welsh Baptist Church in Scranton, Pennsylvania, became broken before God in his personal life. His personal revival led him to resign his church and return to Wales in 1897. Before his personal revival, Jones' preaching had been eloquent and erudite but aimed solely at impressing his hearers.

Jones influenced many young ministers. These preachers began meeting together for prayer in 1903. They invited the esteemed F. B. Meyer to speak to them. He instead invited them to attend the Keswick meetings at Llandrindod in August. God touched many.

There had been other precursors to revival, such as the Forward Movement of the Calvinistic Methodist Church, the work of the Salvation Army, and particularly the Keswick Conventions. In July 1902 a Keswick Convention featured the formation of a circle of prayer for revival around the world. The prayer focused on God's promise, "I will pour out my spirit on all flesh" (Joel 2:28). Reports increased about individuals and groups being burdened with a spirit of prayer. Revival leaders included David Thomas, Rhys Thomas, Read Harris, Mrs. Jessie Penn-Lewis, and R. B. Jones.

Joseph Jenkins

Another of the earliest signs of a growing awakening came in the ministry of pastor Joseph Jenkins at New Quay, Cardiganshire. Jenkins' great-grandfather was one of the first in the preaching bands organized by Howell Harris during the Evangelical Awakening. Andrew Murray's book, *With Christ in the School of Prayer*, had stirred

Jenkins deeply. In November 1903 he began a Young People's Meeting to battle their growing worldliness. A shy young girl following an evening service in January 1904 visited Jenkins. The next week, the first Sunday in February, Jenkins asked for testimonies during the Young People's Meeting following the morning service. Then he asked for responses to the question, "What does Jesus mean to you?" That same young, poor Welsh girl, Florrie Evans, spoke in a trembling voice: "If no one else will, then I must say that I do love the Lord Jesus Christ with all my heart." Her sincere, earnest confession had the effect of a lightning strike of the Spirit in the congregation. Person after person arose and made full surrender to Christ. Jessie Penn-Lewis, who experienced the revival personally, observed: "It was the beginning of the visible manifestation of the Spirit breaking out in life-streams which afterwards would touch thousands of souls."[5] The news of the service spread throughout the area as young people testified in other churches. Once again we see the vital role of youth in God-movements.

Within six months, a growing sense of revival spread throughout New Quay and surrounding areas. In August 1904, the second Keswick Convention at Llandrindod included personal testimonies of the activity of God. The conference experienced an outpouring of the Spirit like none prior. In September 1904 Seth Joshua (1858-1925), a respected evangelist in the Methodist Forward Movement, came to Jenkins' church to lead special services. Joshua related how "he had never seen the power of the Holy Spirit so powerfully manifested among the people as this place just now." Commenting further, he said on September 20, "I cannot leave the building until 12 and even 1 o'clock in the morning. I closed the service several times and yet it would break out again quite beyond the control of human power."[6]

The Ministry of Evan Roberts

Joshua then went to Newcastle Emlyn, where a coal miner in his twenties named Evan Roberts (1878-1951) heard him at the last service. Roberts came from a humble, religious family. The devout lad took a Bible everywhere as a child. Early in his life, he dreamed of revival. At age 14, the young coal miner had a page of his Bible scorched at 2 Chronicles 6, where Solomon prayed for revival. Perhaps Evan saw this as prophetic, for when he became world-famous, the Bible was displayed in photographs around the world. Roberts followed Joshua to Blaennannerch. The Thursday morning service closed with Joshua praying, "Lord. . . Bend us." Roberts went to the front, knelt, and with great anguish cried, "Lord, bend me." Reflecting on that prayer, Roberts later said the impact of his commitment had this effect: "I felt ablaze with a desire to go through the length and breadth of Wales to tell of my Savior; and had that been possible, I was willing to pay God for doing so."[7]

Immediately, Roberts began to go to various towns to speak of his changed life. The presence of the Spirit was obvious, but this demonstrated only a foretaste of a deeper work to come. "Oh, Syd," Roberts said to his best friend Sydney Evans in late 1904, "We are going to see the mightiest revival that Wales has ever known — the Holy Spirit is coming just now." In great anticipation, he added, "We must get ready.

We must get a little band and go all over the country preaching." Suddenly Roberts stopped, looked at Sydney, and said, "Do you believe that God can give us 100,000 souls now?"[8] Within six months, 100,000 were converted in Wales.

Roberts felt impressed to speak to his home congregation. On October 31 he took a train home to Loughor. He was allowed to speak only following the regular Monday night prayer service. Seventeen people remained to hear Roberts. The next day he spoke at a nearby town. On November 2 in nearby Moriah, Roberts began to speak about four requirements for revival:

1. You must put away any unconfessed sin.
2. You must put away any doubtful habit.
3. You must obey the Holy Spirit promptly.
4. You must confess Christ publicly.

These became known as the "Four Points." Within one week, much of Loughor had been changed. Meetings lasted until four in the morning. Prayer sparks revival's fire, while testimony fuels the flame. For the next several months, Roberts and others traveled across Wales giving testimony to the power of God. Thousands came to hear him. Chapels were filled across the land. Services would break forth in singing, in prayer, and in testimony. In fact, some called the awakening a singing revival because of the prominence of song in the services. The burden of Roberts' message was to obey the Holy Spirit, while his rallying cry was "Bend the Church, save the world."

As God answered this burden, even the newspapers published the results. In two months, 70,000 were converted, 85,000 in five months, and more than 100,000 in six months. Judges were presented with white gloves signifying no cases to be tried. Alcoholism was halved. At times, hundreds would stand to declare their surrender to Christ as Lord. Restitution was made. Gamblers and others normally untouched by the ministry of the church came to Christ.

The esteemed G. Campbell Morgan recalled a conversation with a mine manager about profanity. The manager told him, "The haulers are some of the very lowest. They have driven their horses by obscenity and kicks. Now they can hardly persuade their horses to start working, because there is no obscenity and no kicks."[9]

Morgan attended some of the meetings during the revival. He was amazed at the antinomy of disorderliness and yet a sense of order. It was God-organized chaos. Confession of sin marked the meetings, as well. "I have never seen anything like it in my life," Morgan said, "While a man praying is disturbed by the breaking out of song, there is no sense of disorder, and the prayer merges into song, and back into testimony, and back again into song."[10]

I fear we may be so afraid of wild fire that we could miss the real fire of God. When we pray, "God, take control," do we really mean, "God, don't let things get out of control?"

Morgan rightly observed that the Welsh Revival began neither with Roberts nor with anyone else, nor did Roberts claim to be its progenitor. He did play a prominent role in it. The Welsh Revival demonstrated that, although the idea of revival had been understood more in terms of citywide crusades, the God of heaven will still move to send an outpouring of the Spirit.

The Welsh newspaper *Western Mail* published the following report on November 10, 1904:

A remarkable religious revival is now taking place in Loughor. For some days a young man named Evan Roberts, a native of Loughor has been causing great surprise at Moriah Chapel. The place has been besieged by dense crowds of people unable to obtain admission. Such excitement has prevailed that the road on which the chapel is situated has been lined with people from end to end. . . .

Many who have disbelieved Christianity for years are returning to the fold of their younger days. One night, so great was the enthusiasm invoked by the young evangelist that, after his sermon which lasted two hours. The vast congregation remained praying and singing until two-thirty in the morning. Shopkeepers are closing early in order to get a place in the chapel.

Roberts had his detractors. His emotionalism opened the way for particularly virulent attacks. Roberts' arduous schedule and the criticism ultimately took its toll. After a week of rest in February 1905, Roberts continued for about a year. He then went into seclusion for a long period at the home of Mr. and Mrs. Jessie Penn-Lewis. From that time onward, he gave himself to prayer more than preaching.

Other Revival Movements

Local revivals occurred independent of Roberts' ministry: in December 1904 at North Wales led by Hugh Hughes and through the ministry of Joseph Jenkins, Seth Joshua, Evan Lloyd-Jones, Keri Evans, and many others in 1905. In fact, in November of 1904 when Roberts spoke at Loughor, several regions experienced revival simultaneously.

Perhaps you are a pastor reading this in the middle of serving a difficult church. Be encouraged by this account: A minister in Morriston had resigned from his church, so distraught from battling with deacons that he determined to leave the ministry for secular work. He then read a book on the Spirit-filled life and heard about the growing revival. After attending one of the meetings, he surrendered fully to God while alone in a back street. The following Sunday, he gave a report to his church. The Spirit of God descended with power. His resignation was rejected, and the deacons were changed. In the last five weeks of 1904, 185 converts were won to Christ in that church.

Report after report came from Church of England and Free Churches of revival. Unholy church members repented or were converted. In one church, the pastor confronted a deacon about his worldliness. After conversion, the deacon began testifying of the mercy of the Lord. On a Sunday morning soon after this, the church had its "Pentecost" — a service of open confession and conversion, with people falling prostrate before God. In the following weeks, scores of the unchurched poured into the church. Many of the converts had been described as beyond hope before the revival.

At Rhos in northern Wales, revival erupted in November 1904. R. B. Jones led ten meetings there. On the last day, the service continued unabated for twelve hours. A Liverpool correspondent recorded his impressions of revival there:

> If I had been asked a month ago whether a revival was probable in Wales I should have answered No. It seemed to me that the Higher Criticism had wrecked the ordinary machinery of a revival. Oddly enough the Revivalist is one who, according to his own story, was at one time deeply interested in the Higher Criticism, and preached the "new theology." He felt, however, emptiness and coldness in his sermons. Attendance at a convention held in Llandrindod led to a crisis in his life. He felt himself to be a new man, and since then the writings of the higher critics have lost their attraction for him.[11]

The services in Rhos started the same day Roberts spoke in Loughor. Two children were overheard in Rhos giving their understanding of revival:

> "Do you know what happened at Rhos?" the first asked.
> "No, I don't, except that Sunday comes every day now."
> "Don't you know?" said the first again.
> "No, I don't."
> "Why, Jesus Christ has come to live in Rhos now."[12]

At Llanerchymedd, three days of special meetings were held. On the first night, 67 people came to Christ. The second night, the preacher spoke on the holiness of God. A college student arose and took a pipe out of his pocket. He handed it to the speaker. Another student on his knees cried out to God in repentance for his use of tobacco. Others did the same until the desk was covered with tobacco and pipes. Until 12:45 A.M. people came into the church house to be saved. At least 111 were converted at this meeting.

At another place, following the work of the Spirit, 260 converts were added to one church in a short time. At a church in Dowlais, some 170 were added in six months. On and on the reports went. The revival cut across denominational lines. In Rhos, the Vicar was fully devoted to the revival; in one service, a Baptist minister began the service and a Welsh Calvinistic Methodist minister closed it. The revival featured a strong emphasis on witnessing and a special emphasis on the work of the Holy Spirit. Numerous reports of unusual occurrences came as well: some were delivered immediately from strong drink, while others received physical healing.

In August of 1904, R. A. Torrey held a crusade in Cardiff that saw the conversion of many and a deepening hunger for God. Others reported similar results.

A Revival Participant Reports "Boiling" for Christ

How very cold and formal the prayers of the Church have been for many a year! But for the last four months there has been everywhere a marked change — the prayers have been boiling and whole multitudes have been thrown into a state of extraordinary fervor. It rejoices me to see the rising generation boiling with a great enthusiasm in the service of Christ — the mark of the "boiling" will be on them as long as they live. None are the same after boiling as before. Hundreds of our young men and women had been brought up religiously in the home and the church; but their religion was cold, formal, following routine. . . .

Behold the difference! Now our young people flock to the services. Prayers flowed spontaneously from their lips like water from the spring, praise ascends to heaven like the carol of bids in spring. . . . All the chapels are crowded, the valleys and mountains ring with praise . . . gamblers refuse money won by bets made before conversion, . . . prize-fighters are now soul-winners, . . . enemies are made friends. Scores of pages can be filled with as striking conversions as any in the annals of the Christian Church.[13]

The Welsh Revival is dated 1904-05, because during those years, it was at a fever pitch. The revival continued to touch the nation for many years following. Orr determined that the total number of conversions was one-tenth of the population.[14] Perhaps the reason it was so powerful for such a brief period was due to the emotion expressed. Another factor could be that singing rather than preaching characterized the revival. As important as singing is, no doubt the preaching of the Word would have served to deepen the revival's impact. In fact, if revival begins with prayer, and if testimony fuels revival, then the preaching of the Word gives focus to revival.

Visitors came from around the globe to partake of the spiritual fruit. James Stewart of Edinburgh offered these characteristics of the revival. It was a revival (1) for young people; (2) of singing; (3) of prayer; (4) of soul-winning; and (5) of personal experience.[15]

The Awakening in America

The latter decades of the nineteenth century in America featured the painful period of Reconstruction, as well as continuous westward advance and increasing industrialization. By the end of the nineteenth century, the automobile and the motion picture were born. The telephone, typewriter, electric light, phonograph, and electric motor spawned numerous commercial enterprises.

Urbanization grew as swiftly as technology. This set the stage for the citywide evangelistic efforts that exploded at this time. Industries offered jobs for Americans and for the unprecedented numbers of immigrants — nine million from 1900-1910. Many of the immigrants were Roman Catholics from Europe, changing to some degree the religious landscape of the nation.

The United States emerged as a world power by 1900. The nation annexed Hawaii and received the Philippines, Guam, and Puerto Rico from Spain following the

Spanish-American War. In 1901 President McKinley was assassinated, thrusting Vice President Theodore Roosevelt into the highest office.

Spiritual life ebbed, although there were some bright spots. American Protestantism continued to grow through the last decades of the nineteenth century. D. L. Moody's campaign ministry was effective, as was that of Sam Jones in the South. Moody led the vanguard of evangelists who promoted evangelism through the businesslike practices of organization and planning. Still, even Moody's impact in the cause of revival and evangelism diminished toward the end of the century: "The religious excitement that followed Moody and Sankey in the mid-1870s was not equaled in the remainder of the nineteenth century."[16] The evangelist's influence went far beyond his campaigns, however. In 1889 he founded the Moody Bible Institute in Chicago. R. A. Torrey, the evangelist/revivalist, also served for a time at the Moody Church.

In the South, blacks thronged to the churches. The chief black institution following Reconstruction was the local church. In the South at this time, virtually every African-American was a church member. In 1886 the National Baptist Convention had been established and became the largest African-American denomination. The African Methodist Episcopal (AME) Church became the second largest tradition, and it also grew out of the post-Civil War South.

But on the horizon, trends were emerging that would strangle the spiritual life of the nation. One factor was the rise of liberal thought in the form of higher criticism. Theological schools were gradually drawn into a perspective that diminished the role of the spiritual life. Walter Rauschenbusch led the way in focusing on the social implications of the gospel. While the Social Gospel Movement emerged to combat societal ills, it also served to blunt the focus on the evangelistic imperative.

The incipient decay of conviction wrought by theological liberalism infected countless churches. Darwin's *The Origin of Species* influenced both the scientific and religious communities. While liberalism seeped into the halls of academia and infected many churches, there were new evangelical movements as well. Dispensationalism, the Holiness movement, and Pentecostalism spread through many churches and traditions.

At the same time new religious sects emerged. Mary Baker Eddy founded the Church of Christian Science in 1879. Charles Taze Russell organized what became the Jehovah's Witnesses in 1884.

A Movement of Prayer

In places across the United States and around the world, believers began a groundswell movement of prayer. In the United States, the Methodist Episcopal Church ushered a call to prayer. Following a decline of almost twenty-two thousand members in 1899, leaders of the denomination asked churches to set apart the days from March 25 to April 1 as a season of fasting or abstinence and prayer:

> We ask you to assemble yourselves in your accustomed places of worship at least once each day, humble yourselves before God, worship Him, personally lay aside

every weight and the easily besetting sin, and make earnest supplication to Him. We ask, also, that in your private and family prayers you will daily implore God's mercy for the revival of His work of grace in each heart throughout all our borders.[17]

Others issued similar calls to prayer and to a greater commitment to evangelism: the Presbyterian General Assembly in Philadelphia in 1901, the triennial meeting of the National Council of the Congregationalist Churches in 1904, and others. Penn-Lewis recorded a gathering of several hundred at "an Institute in America" (likely Moody in Chicago) who prayed each Saturday night beginning in 1898 for "world-wide revival."[18] News of the Welsh Revival contributed to the spirit of revival in the United States. By 1905, national reports frequently spoke of awakening.

February 12, 1905, was declared a Universal Day of Prayer for students by the World Student Christian Federation. Scores of colleges joined in the call to pray. In 1905 Yale University professor Henry Wright observed more spiritual interest than he had ever seen. Colleges and seminaries reporting revival during the period included: Bowdoin in Maine; Cornell; Rutgers; Princeton Seminary; Randolph-Macon and Emory and Henry College in Virginia; Trinity College in North Carolina; Emory and Mercer in Georgia; and Ouachita in Arkansas.

Schools birthed in some way out of the awakening included Biola in California and Southwestern Baptist Theological Seminary in Fort Worth. Southwestern's birth in the first decade of the twentieth century came in no small measure because of the "widespread evangelism, great revivals, mass movements to win to Christ lost men everywhere" and the "necessity for more and better preachers."[19] The seminary began on Baylor's campus in 1905 under the leadership of B. H. Carroll. Asbury College in Wilmore, Kentucky, witnessed a great moving of the Spirit, which ignited missionary E. Stanley Jones, a student at Asbury at that time.

Reports of Revivals in America:

Moody Bible Institute: "The revival has come."

Newark, N.J.: "Pentecost was literally repeated during the height of revival."

New England Baptists: "The churches were obviously in the midst of a revival of greater power and extent than New England had known since 1858."

The Northfield Conference (founded by D. L. Moody): "Open confessions" came that "almost defy description."

Orr's observation: "'The cause of revival was greatly helped in the Southern Baptist Convention by the warm interest of its leading scholar in Louisville, Kentucky, E Y. Mullins."

Louisville, Kentucky: "The whole city is breathing a spiritual atmosphere. Salvation is the one topic of conversation."

Florida: Revival there was called "part of the mighty movement the world over."

Houston: "A tidal wave of spirituality has rolled through the city."

Methodists in Michigan: "A most gracious religious awakening."

Kansas City: "Greater Kansas City has been passing through a season of spiritual awakening, and the Revival of 1905 will go down in history as anew spiritual epoch."

Methodist editorial: "A great revival is sweeping the U.S. Its power is felt in every nook and corner of our land."

The Baptist Home Mission Monthly: "The tidings of revival come from every side."[20]

Baylor University was awakened under the leadership of W. W. Hamilton. Throughout the nights, students prayed and sought spiritual counsel: "Songs in the night were not unusual while some lost one arose from his knees to grasp the hand of his teacher and his fellows and tell of his surrender to Christ."[21] Similar awakenings touched Decatur Baptist College, Howard Payne, and other schools.

The Role of the Urban Evangelist

Accompanying the movement of prayer was an attempt by denominations to reach the rapidly growing cities. We cannot separate effective evangelistic methods from the cultural milieu at a given time. The rise of cities and the Industrial Revolution led to mass production in factories. One would not be surprised to find that — in an era of mass production — the mass evangelism meeting would also be effective. Following the model of Moody, revival of believers and the evangelization of sinners overlapped in the ministries of a train of itinerants. Whereas the central figure in the 1857-59 awakening was the layman, the crucial person in America in the years after 1900 was the itinerant preacher. An example of this is seen in such organizations as the new evangelism division of the Southern Baptist Convention's Board of Domestic Missions (now called the North American Mission Board), which began as a team of itinerant preachers to help the churches. Perhaps no time in history witnessed the consistent impact made by evangelists in the cities and towns of the nation as occurred in the early twentieth century.

Moody influenced Reuben Archer Torrey (1856-1928), who then became the first evangelist to go literally around the world with the gospel. While in seminary, Torrey was exposed to higher criticism, which served to erode his convictions. He ultimately abandoned liberal influences; however, this experience no doubt motivated him to emphasize the authority of Scripture.

Torrey became superintendent of Moody's Bible Training Institute (later Moody Bible Institute) in 1890. Torrey later served as pastor of the Chicago Avenue Church, averaging over 2000 members at the time. A biographer recorded that, from Torrey's first Sunday, "the power of God fell, and from that day till he left America there was never a single Sabbath without conversions."[22]

From 1899 to 1901 Torrey led a prayer gathering of three to four hundred in Chicago each Saturday night, specifically entreating God for revival. He and a few others often continued to pray in his home until three in the morning. On one such occasion, he prayed specifically for the opportunity to preach around the world. From 1902-06, Torrey indeed traveled around the world with meetings in Japan, China, and Australia. Musician Charles Alexander joined him in Australia, and the two enjoyed unusual success with more than twenty thousand conversions in five months. After reading Finney's autobiography, Alexander resolved to become a personal soul-winner. He went to study at the new Moody Institute in Chicago, where he met Sankey and other music evangelists. In 1906 Torrey's Toronto meetings included the conversion of Oswald J. Smith, who later became a famed preacher.

Torrey's preaching appealed to reason more than to the emotions. He preached and wrote for the twin causes of revival and evangelism. He also made a marked impact on doctrinal trends in America. He was instrumental in meetings that ultimately led to the publication of the *Fundamentals*, published to battle the growing tide of liberalism. He was unabashedly committed to the inerrancy of Scripture.

Torrey had a deep burden for revival in his life. After reading George Muller's *Life of Trust*, Torrey determined to forgo receiving a salary and to live by faith in God's provision. At the turn of the century, he became convinced revival was near. He observed ministers and believers discussing, expecting, and beseeching God for revival. Torrey emphasized the critical role of prayer in revival. He then observed the contemporary trend toward revival praying:

> Here and there God is laying upon individuals, ministers, and churches a burden of prayer that they have never known before. Ministers are crying to God day and night for power. Churches and portions of churches are meeting together in the early morning hours and the late night hours crying to God for the latter rain. There is every indication of the coming of a mighty and widespread revival. The only thing needed to bring this fire is prayer.[23]

J. Wilbur Chapman (1859-1918) was born during the Laymen's Prayer Revival. The Presbyterian Chapman struggled with his assurance of salvation until an encounter with D. L. Moody in 1878. Following a service, Moody counseled Chapman in the inquiry room. Using John 5:24, Moody stayed with Chapman until he achieved assurance of salvation. Following seminary, Chapman served as pastor in Indiana, Ohio, and New York. Chapman then served as pastor of the Bethany Presbyterian Church in Philadelphia for two terms, divided by three years of itinerant evangelism from 1892-95. His final pastorate was at the Fourth Presbyterian Church in New York City. The church grew dramatically during his four years there from 1899-1903. Also, for fourteen years, beginning in 1885, Chapman spoke each summer at the Winona Bible Conference in Indiana. Chapman also served as the leader in evangelism for the Presbyterian denomination beginning in 1901.

In 1904 Chapman began conducting citywide mass meetings with elaborate organization. He understood the difference between evangelism and true revival, saying, "The effective cause in all true revivals is the life-giving, light-imparting, quickening, regenerating and sanctifying energy of the Holy Spirit, converting the hardened sinner and reclaiming the backslidden and dormant believer."[24]

Chapman placed a great emphasis on prayer for the success of his campaigns. He used many preachers in simultaneous campaigns across a city. Those of a certain denomination would utilize an evangelist from their tradition, thus increasing the cooperation between groups. In much of his ministry, he teamed with Charles Alexander, who had also worked with R. A. Torrey.

In the year 1900, Mordecai Ham began preaching the gospel full-time. Ham was energetic and bold. His boldness can be seen in the following incident in which he encountered a notable infidel:

> I asked someone to hitch up a horse and take me to call on some of the worst sinners in the community. We trailed one into a corn field — he was reputed to be the biggest infidel in the county and was leading his children to follow after his infidelity. I went to the spot of the field where I had seen him, but failed to find him. I heard a noise from a corn shock where he had hidden. I grabbed his leg and pulled him out. He hollered,
>
> "Oh, you've got me!"
>
> "Yes, I have," I returned.
>
> "What are you going to do with me?"
>
> "Ask God to kill you"
>
> "Oh, don't do that!" he shouted.
>
> I asked, "Why not? You say you don't believe there is a God, so prayer shouldn't trouble you, but if there is, then you are not fit to live because you are leading more than forty of your children and grandchildren into damnable infidelity." He then began to tremble and to beg me not to pray for God to kill me. I said, "All right, I shall pray for God to save you." I led him to Christ right there in the field and then said, "Now you can take me to see all your children and grandchildren." At the close of the meeting I not only baptized him but every member of his family that was old enough to be baptized.[25]

While this is neither a typical illustration of Ham's ministry nor a model of ministry one would necessarily follow, it is offered to demonstrate the boldness of Ham and others like him who were used of God in revival.

Billy Sunday (1862-1935) rose to prominence as an urban evangelist after the turn of the century. This fiery emotional former baseball player preached for the gospel and America and against alcohol. His ministry was marked by the erection of tabernacles with floors covered in sawdust. "Hitting the sawdust trail" became a moniker for Sunday's calling people to follow Christ. Musician Homer Rhodeheaver joined Sunday in 1910. Methodist Sam Jones continued his ministry from the nineteenth century. Jones preached primarily in the South. Baptists George Cates and W. W. Hamilton had strong ministries, especially in the South and among Baptist churches. Cates preached for one hundred consecutive days on the atonement.

Rodney "Gypsey" Smith (1860-1947), an evangelist from England, conducted his first tour of the United States in 1889. A powerful revival came to Boston during his campaign there in 1906. A similar result came in Brooklyn in 1907. He continued to travel around the world for years to come.

Revival across the Nation

Individual towns and cities reported localized awakenings in the first decade of the new century. Newcastle and Wilkes-Barre, Pennsylvania, experienced such in 1903-04. Likewise, a campaign led by Wilbur Chapman in Pittsburgh brought true revival to believers as well as evangelistic results. Over six thousand people joined the city's churches as a result of the effort. Similar results came to Philadelphia under the leadership of Chapman and singer Charles Alexander, working with numerous other evangelists and musicians in the year 1908.[26]

A cooperative effort between churches in Schenectady, New York, witnessed such results that secular papers featured headlines entitled "The Power of Prayer" and "Fires of Pentecost." A Christian publication reported: "the revival became the absorbing theme. Saloons and theaters were almost emptied. Those who frequented them are largely found in churches."[27]

A week of prayer in a Presbyterian church in Troy stretched into an awakening that affected no less than twenty-six churches. "Syracuse aroused" provided the byline for the report on the Chapman meetings where 45 churches participated in that city in 1906. Revival reports also came from Boston, Connecticut, and Rhode Island.

Perhaps the greatest ministry of Chapman came in 1908 in Philadelphia. He teamed with 21 other evangelists with an average of 35,000 people attending nightly services for six weeks. A total of 10,000 people professed faith in Christ. A convicted embezzler received Christ in jail during the effort. He was later seen at an altar while on bond. He was praying with the man who had convicted him. Similar results came the following year in Boston.

Revival touched college campuses, such as Denison University in Ohio in 1906. R. A. Torrey held a citywide effort with unusual results continuing for thirty days in Cleveland during 1907. Methodists in Michigan considered the early 1900s as a time of awakening unheard of for many years for decades. In Burlington, Iowa, stores and factories closed between 10:00 A.M. and 11:00 A.M. to allow employees to attend services.

In Colorado, a day of prayer was scheduled on January 20 at the time Chapman was beginning a campaign. The day drew thousands of people into churches and public buildings for prayer. The mayor requested that stores be closed, and most were. Local schools were closed. The *Watchman* reported "the Colorado legislature postponed business in order to attend the prayer meetings. Schools were closed and the entire city engaged in prayer and evangelism."[28] Chapman preached with mighty results along the western U.S. in 1905.

A united prayer emphasis led to a spirit of revival in Paris, Texas. Similar events led to reports proclaiming revival had come across the state. The Southern Baptist paper *Baptist Standard* reported instances of revival. In Houston, revival was so strong "the gambling dens have been closed and the gambling gentry ordered out of the city."[29] Powerful movements came to Fort Worth, Marshall, and other cities in Texas.

Evangelist Mordecai Ham, renowned for being the preacher under whose ministry Billy Graham was converted, preached a seven-week meeting in New Orleans in 1906 with noticeable effect. Similar meetings came through the ministry of George Cates in Mississippi. In 1907 the governor of the state came to Christ under Cates' ministry. Chapman preached in a Mobile, Alabama campaign that affected the churches and the lost. Atlanta newspapers reported that almost a thousand men were praying for revival in that city during 1904. Chapman preached there for three weeks in January to packed auditoriums. The former governor was so impressed that he financed the publication of five thousand copies of a sermon by Chapman, which were distributed across the city. Similar reports came from across the South, particularly through the ministry of powerful itinerants: Ham and then Cates in Paducah, Kentucky, and Ham in Louisville.

The Pentecostal Revival

The Global Awakening included the birth of the Pentecostal Movement, which has spread around the world over the twentieth century faster than any other tradition. The roots of Pentecostalism go back to Methodist Perfectionism that arose in the nineteenth century. Early examples of such thought included a booklet entitled *The Christian's Manual* and *A Treatise on Christian Perfection, with Directions for Obtaining that State*, published by the Methodist Episcopal Church in 1825. Phoebe Palmer became the leader of the Holiness Revival beginning in 1835.[30] Another stream came through the Oberlin Perfectionism espoused by Charles Finney.

The Holiness Movement developed as a reaction to religious deadness in the nineteenth century. It particularly opposed the growing secularism, modernism, and institutionalism of the church. Those involved had no plans to start new denominations. The Holiness Movement was conservative in theology and grew out of meetings for prayer and Bible or prophetic studies. The movement united in the Wesleyan dogma of entire sanctification, often referred to as a "second blessing."[31] The Revival of 1857-58 helped spread the Holiness Movement. It was the doctrine of a second crisis experience marked by glossolalia that would become the most widely known feature of Pentecostalism. Orr observed that the "rise of the Pentecostal denominations was as much an aftermath of the awakenings of the earlier twentieth century as the rise of the Baptist and Methodist denominations was to the precedent awakenings of the seventeenth and eighteenth."[32]

The Pentecostal Movement can be traced to Charles Parham (1873-1929), who was ordained at age nineteen in the Methodist Episcopal Church. From 1894-99 he served as a nondenominational evangelist. In October 1900, Parham opened a Bible school named Bethel College in Topeka, Kansas. At a watch-night (December 31, 1900) service, Agnes N. Ozman asked that hands be laid on her to receive the Holy Spirit to go to the foreign field. Parham reported: "A glory fell upon her, a halo seemed to surround her head and face, and she began speaking in the Chinese language."[33]

On January 3, 1901, several students began speaking in tongues as well, including Parham. Not all students agreed with the events that transpired. A few left, while one in particular, S. J. Riggins, said everything was a farce.[34]

From Topeka, the center of the movement soon shifted to Houston. Parham founded a Bible school there like the one in Topeka. One of Parham's students in Houston was a black man named William J. Seymour (d. 1923). A visitor from Los Angeles during this time, Neeley Terry, was impressed by Seymour and recommended him to be pastor at her church. Seymour accepted the call to California. In his first sermon, Seymour preached on Acts 2:4, explaining the new Pentecostal experience that occurred in Houston. This was new to Holiness groups in Los Angeles. The people in the church were offended and felt Seymour was speaking heresy. When he returned for the evening service, Seymour was locked out of thc building. He was then invited to a church member's home to conduct prayer meetings and soon was asked to conduct services at the home of a Baptist at 214 North Bonnie Brae Street. On April 9, 1906, unusual events transpired:

> They shouted three days and three nights. It was the Easter season. The people came from everywhere. By the next morning there was no way of getting near the house. As the people came in they would fall under God's power, and the whole city was stirred. They shouted until the foundation of the house gave way, but no one was hurt. During these days, there were many people who received their baptism who had just come to see what it was. The sick were healed and sinners were saved just as they came in.[35]

The group rented a larger building at 312 Azusa Street. It was from the Azusa Street Mission that Pentecostalism spread around the world. The revival that began there lasted three years without a break.

The revival in Los Angeles was not totally unexpected. F B. Meyer had preached in the city, arousing a spiritual interest. Another precursor of the movement was an evangelist named Frank Bartleman, who held a meeting in January 1905 at a Methodist church in Pasadena. More than two hundred came to Christ in three weeks. In April he heard of the revival in Wales and began leading groups to pray for a similar occurrence.[36] Another person who prepared the way was a Baptist minister named Joseph Smale. Upon returning from a trip to Wales, Smale began leading people to pray for revival.

As news of the revival at Azusa Street spread, many came to observe what was transpiring. W H. Durham from Chicago and G. B. Cashwell from North Carolina were two of the many ministers who came to Azusa Street. Both returned as advocates of the Pentecostal experience, and both experienced similar movements to those in California. The Pentecostal Holiness Church was born out of Cashwell's influence. At one of Cashwell's meetings A. J. Tomlinson had a Pentecostal experience. Tomlinson became a main leader in the Church of God (Cleveland, Tennessee).

Aimee Semple McPherson (1890-1944) was converted in Los Angeles. She organized the International Church of the Four-Square Gospel (incorporated 1927). A black man named Charles H. Mason left Los Angeles to begin a ministry in Memphis,

Tennessee. Out of this ministry came one of the largest Pentecostal bodies in the world — the Church of God in Christ. In 1914, many Pentecostal ministers met in Hot Springs, Arkansas. They saw a need to organize, especially for the sake of missions. Using the Bible as the infallible rule of faith and conduct, the Assemblies of God were born.

Pentecostalism spread internationally at an incredible pace. The movement shared some traits with the larger awakening and with past revivals: it was interdenominational, touched the masses, and emphasized evangelism and missions. Like some other movements, it tended at times toward emotional extremes. The Pentecostal Revival emphasized tongues and healing.

Throughout the twentieth century, Pentecostalism has helped the evangelical church to reexamine the role of the Holy Spirit. It has further demonstrated a model of missionary zeal through its rapid spread worldwide. It further offers an example of a movement that went too far in its emphasis. The phenomena of tongues and emphasis on healing have been a source of controversy and division in twentieth-century Christianity. Pentecostalism has too often emphasized experience to the neglect of gospel-driven theology.

Pentecostal revivalism illustrates the dynamic quality of spiritual awakenings. Throughout history, genuine revival has always been accompanied by some degree of phenomena. As Edwards argued in his treatise *Distinguishing Marks*, phenomena alone do not demonstrate whether a movement is from God or not. At the same time, the fear of unusual phenomena could prevent believers from trusting God to work in their midst. We must keep the tension between standing on truth and trusting a mysterious God Who works through frail servants.

One way to explain this danger is to illustrate it on a continuum.

Two Extremes in Understanding Revival

Propositional————————————————Experiential

On one side of the continuum are those devout believers who focus exclusively on the propositional side of the faith. For them, commandments are primary, standards obligatory, and rigidity is too often their testimony. The danger for this group is to define revival so narrowly that the very Spirit of God has no freedom to move as He wishes: revival is welcome if it conforms to certain standards of worship, polity, and doctrinal schemes. These sincere believers are so afraid of wildfire they might miss the real fire of revival.

On the other side rests the overemphasis on experience. How easily human nature leads us to this side! Pietism and the camp meetings of the Second Great Awakening stand as illustrations. These were without a doubt movements of God, but at times their experientialism overshadowed God's Word. The Pentecostal Revival stands as another example of this danger. The vast multitude of people touched by the Pentecostal Revival and later the Charismatic movements have been sincere. That being said, these movements have too often emphasized phenomena over biblical revelation, emphasizing experience over doctrine. Unusual phenomena should not be ignored. They should, however, be seen as occasional rather than normal. The normative record of God's Word should measure any occasional phenomena.

Let me apply this personally. There have been times in my life when the Lord has spoken to me clearly, if not audibly. I have also on occasion seen the Lord do things that can only be described as the extraordinary work of a sovereign God. Still, while I rejoice in these occasions, I know I can daily, regularly, consistently go to the unchanging Word of God to hear Him speak. While God occasionally speaks in a variety of ways, He consistently and unambiguously speaks through Scripture, and He will never contradict His Word.

The Pentecostal Revival offers another example of a movement of God colored by experientialism. Hummel provides a helpful analogy: "Like other powerful movements in the churches history, the charismatic renewal (and Pentecostalism in general) has its peculiar dangers. The rushing stream not only waters the countryside but also throws debris on the riverbank."[37]

The Awakening around the Globe

After a century of aggressive missions expansion worldwide, Christianity was positioned to spread revival far beyond the West. The Global Awakening witnessed unprecedented revival blessings geographically. As Jesus said in Acts 1:8, as His followers obeyed His call to be witnesses to the uttermost, Christianity has become a truly global faith.

As news of the Welsh Revival traveled to other lands, a spirit of revival accompanied the testimonies. Japan, South America, Australia, and New Zealand all reported revival. Thus, by the turn of the twentieth century, significant revivals erupted at points around the globe. This is the major reason for referring to this revival as a global awakening. Europe, Norway, Denmark, England, Sweden, Germany, and even France reported revival.[38]

In London, John R. Mott, leader in the World Student Christian Federation, experienced unusual results at campaigns at Oxford and Cambridge in 1905. Similar events came during Mott's return to the schools in 1908. Over the next fifteen years, more than a thousand students went forth as missionaries from the Student Volunteer Union of Great Britain and Scotland, a third of them to India.

A mass harvest of the lost came in Indonesia. Called by some "The Great Repentance," the seven-year movement of revival reportedly saw mass conversions, leading the Christian population to escalate from 100,000 to 300,000.[39]

A revival of significant proportions touched parts of India. In Assam, spurred both by a movement of prayer and by reports from the Welsh revival, revival erupted and spread. Similar reports came from Khasi.[40] In 1897, leaders of the Student Volunteer Movement called for a day of prayer for an awakening in India. It became an annual event. Pandita Ramabai (1858-1922), a woman converted from Hinduism, saw awakening through her leadership south of Bombay. Reports of the Torrey-Alexander campaign and of the Welsh Revival encouraged the revival in her area. A particularly powerful work of the Spirit came on June 30, 1905. Groups went forth to minister, often witnessing revival.

Revival in India came through the ministry of Presbyterian missionary John "Praying" Hyde (1865-1912). When he graduated from McCormick Theological Seminary in 1892, twenty-six of his forty-six classmates were pledged to foreign missions. The Student Volunteer Movement had influenced Hyde. Beginning in 1904, a powerful revival came to Hyde's ministry. Open confession, days of prayer, and multitudes of conversions marked those days. In 1904 Hyde and others in the Presbyterian mission developed the Punjab Prayer Union.

Southern India witnessed awakening through the mission work of the Brethren, the London Missionary Society, and others. It was here that Amy Carmichael served. She and others prayed for revival to come as it had in Wales. In one decade, Christians in India grew in number sixteen times faster than the Hindu population. Revival came on October 22, 1906. Carmichael described the scene: "Soon the whole upper half of the church was on its face on the floor crying to God. . . . The sound was like the sound of waves or strong wind in the trees."[43] Baptist missionaries were among those involved in revival in northern India.

Praying Hyde's Five Questions

Praying Hyde and the Punjab Prayer Union kept these five questions at the center of their ministry:

1. Are you praying for quickening in your own life. . . . your fellow-workers, and in the church?
2. Are you longing for greater power of the Holy Spirit . . . Are you convinced that you cannot go on without this power?
3. Will you pray that you will not be ashamed of Jesus?
4. Do you believe that prayer is the great means for securing this spiritual awakening?
5. Will you set apart one-half hour each day . . . to pray for this awakening . . . ?[42]

The "Korean Pentecost" began on January 6-7, 1907. Following weeks of prayer by missionaries through the winter of 1906 and encouraged by the revival in Wales, a series of meetings at the New Year's beginning erupted in revival. Missionaries wisely gave limited guidance to the confession and restitution that ensued. A missionary gave testimony to the work of revival in India following the Welsh revival. During the winter of 1906-07, missionaries met each night to pray for awakening. When revival began in January, relationships were restored, restitution was made, and great examples of sacrifice were reported.[44]

Jonathan Goforth (1859-1936) was another missionary who witnessed a spiritual awakening in his ministry to China. Following his escape from the horrors of the Boxer Rebellion in 1900 and the death of scores of missionaries, Goforth returned to China. The writings of Finney made a profound impact on the Presbyterian missionary. Further, he witnessed the Korean revival while on a trip there in 1907. Upon his return, he gave testimony to the power of God in Korea. The testimonies created a hunger among the missionaries and Chinese believers for revival. Beginning in 1908, revival came to Manchuria. Following a season of repentance that included Christians who had to deal with their enmity toward those who massacred so many Christians less than a decade earlier, a great evangelistic harvest ensued.[45]

In Australia, news of the Welsh Revival along with a Torrey-Alexander crusade furthered the awakening there. Reports of revival also came from New Zealand, the Philippines, and Indonesia.

South Africa reported revival during the decade, as well. Rees Howells took the fire of God from his native Wales to the mission field. In South Africa, he founded the Bible College of South Wales in Swansea. Revival sprcad to the school. One student from Latvia, upon graduation, carried this same fire to Russia. He personally built two hundred churches in Eastern Europe. Other points in Africa, including Zambia, Cameroon, and Malawi, saw awakening. A hundred prayer meetings in Malawi led to unprecedented confession of sin and brokenness. By 1910, a series of services included one Saturday when 2500 Africans began simultaneously confessing their sins following the costly confession of a leader. The sound was described as that of a rushing mighty wind like at Pentecost. The 1910 Edinburgh Missionary Conference reported, "by far the greatest progress of Christianity in Africa has been achieved in the past decade."[46]

In Latin America, awakening caused phenomenal growth. Evangelical churches grew from 132,388 communicants in 1903 to 369,077 in 1910.

Impact of the Global Awakening

In a general sense, the most significant impact of the Global Awakening was its reminder that *the Sovereign God of the universe yet initiates revival.* In spite of technological advances, the greatest need of humanity is to encounter God personally.

The awakening *emphasized the importance of the Scriptures* as foundational for the Christian life. Faced with the deadness of theological liberalism on the left and experiential overzealousness to the right, the church can confidently stand on the Word of God as the arbiter of truth and the guide for times of revival.

Evangelistic results paralleled earlier awakenings, except that this time the impact was seen worldwide. Methodists in the North grew by 35,000 annually during 1901-04. In 1905 the number was 78,090, and it grew to 119,000 in 1906. The Southern Baptist Convention recognized "there has come about an awakened interest in the subject of evangelistic work."[47]

'The effective cause in all true revivals is the life-giving, light-imparting, quickening, regenerating and sanctifying energy of the Holy Spirit, converting the hardened sinner and reclaiming the backslidden and dormant believer." J. Wilbur Chapman

Social effects included organizations that affected change. The interdenominational Layman's Missionary Movement began in 1906. The Men and Religion Forward Movement began in 1910. Various denominations and groups, including the Young Men's Christian Association, the International Sunday School Association, and the Gideon's met to organize revival fruit.

Missions also advanced. E. Stanley Jones, one of the most effective and inspirational missionaries in the twentieth century, committed himself to missions following the revival at Asbury College, where he was a student. Missionaries including Goforth, Hyde, and Carmichael were often catalytic in revival movements in foreign lands.

The story of revival coming at the dawn of a new century offers hope for our generation. Surely we can follow the example of those before us to set aside special times of prayer and fasting to seek the Lord.

Questions for Small Group Study

1. What are Evan Roberts' four marks of revival? Do they still hold the same importance today?

2. If you were in the place of Florrie Evans and had the opportunity to be the first to speak, would you be willing?

3. Give your understanding of the Pentecostal movement today as it relates to its uprising during these awakenings.

4. The Welsh revival went to from a national movement to a global one. Can you think of any spiritual movements today that have become truly global in nature? Why is this the case, or why is it not the case?

Chapter 14
Recent Regional and Specialized Awakenings

If that train comes by I'm going to be on it, I'm not going to get left.
C. B. Hogue[1]

My generation has never seen a mighty outpouring of the Spirit in America like the great awakenings of old. We can only read about past great awakenings. Still, even our day is not without a witness that a living God moves in our time. The good news of the past two generations relates more to the global spread of Christianity in places like China, sub-Sahara Africa, and Latin America.

It seems that, from a global perspective, the West has been passed by the developing world as the place where God's Spirit is at work today. But history yet offers hope to our generation. Despite the absence of a great revival in our lifetime, regional and specialized awakenings have occurred in the twentieth century. These movements can give us hope that even in materialistic, secularized America, God could yet move again to revive His church.

In this chapter I will attempt to overview some, though certainly not all, of the revival movements in the twentieth century beyond the Global Awakening of 1901-10.

Two specific eras of mild or specialized revivals form the content of this chapter: the Mid-Century Revival and the Jesus Movement of the early 1970s. Neither of these movements rival earlier, greater awakenings. However, their chronological proximity to the contemporary setting makes their study significant.

Mark Noll has noted the remarkable spread of the faith in modern times:

—This past Sunday it is possible that more Christian believers attended church in China than in all of so-called "Christian Europe." Yet in 1970 there were no legally functioning churches in all of China.

—This past Sunday more Presbyterians were at church in Ghana than in Scotland, and more were in congregations of the United Presbyterian Church of Southern Africa than in the United States.

—This past week in Great Britain, at least fifteen thousand Christian foreign missionaries were hard at work evangelizing the locals. Most of these missionaries are from Africa and Asia.

—In a word, the Christian church has experienced a larger geographical redistribution in the last fifty years than in any comparable period in its history, with the exception of the very earliest years of church history. Some of this change comes from the general growth of world population, but much also arises from remarkable rates of evangelization in parts of Asia, Africa, Latin America and the islands of the South Pacific — but also from a nearly unprecedented relative decline of Christian adherence in Europe.

Taken from Mark A. Noll. *The New Shape of World Christianity: How American Experience Reflects Global Faith* (Kindle Locations 153-170). Kindle Edition.

As noted earlier, awakenings can be understood with the analogy of wars. The First Great Awakening's impact is not unlike that of the First World War in its widespread and long-term affect. The Jesus Movement would be more like its contemporary war in Vietnam. The latter conflict does not compare to the First World War, but to those involved, it was just as real. "Lesser" revival movements may have less impact globally or over time than great awakenings, but for those touched by God in those movements, the encounter is just as real. The Shantung (or Shandong) Revival swept parts of China in the early 1930s. In this movement, missionaries including Lutheran Marie Monsen and Southern Baptists C.L. Culpepper, Mary Crawford, and Bertha Smith played key roles. This revival offers a helpful study in the importance of leaders making their relationships with one another right as a part of God's reviving work. Readers unfamiliar with this movement can read about this remarkable work of God online.[2] The East African Revival touched that great continent, as well. The ministry of John Sung and others in China bear further study, as does the Indonesian Revival in 1970. Space will simply not allow for the description of other lesser (though important nonetheless) awakenings.

The Mid-Century Resurgence

The years 1949-60 demonstrated a time of effective evangelism in American churches. The era has also been described as a period of general revival, although this is more open to debate. J. Edwin Orr, historian Clifford Olmstead, Fred Hoffman, and professor Arthur Johnston all agreed that genuine revival characterized the period.[3] Johnston even called the era the "Fourth Great Awakening." I agree with Orr, who referred to the decade as the "Mid-Century Resurgence." Orr said the revival was a true awakening, but one which "by no means reached the effectiveness of either of its predecessors in the eighteenth century or the nineteenth."[4]

Edward Elson echoed the sentiment of many when he stated that in the United States "the days since World War II have been days of expanding religious activity."[5] In 1959 Gerald Ira Gingrich believed he was "in the midst of a revival of Christianity" in his days. He compared the 1950s with twelve earlier revival movements: the Wesleyan Revival; the Great Awakening; the Revival of 1800; Finney's revivals; the Revival of 1857; and those of Moody, Chapman, Torrey, Gypsy Smith, and Billy Sunday, along with the Welsh Revival and the Korean Revival. Gingrich cited characteristics to buttress his view that revival was occurring: key leaders, deep prayer, a high place given to Scripture, open confession of sin, and multitudes of conversions. He considered Billy Graham to be the unparalleled leader in the contemporary revival. Graham himself said the following in 1954:

> A religious revival unparalleled in modem history is sweeping like a prairie fire across the English-speaking world. It is a spiritual awakening in which millions are turning to God. . . . I have talked with hundreds of thousands of men, women, and children in America, England, continental Europe, and Asia. Everywhere I have seen living evidence of this groping for spiritual foundations.[7]

Certainly there was a need for spiritual renewal in mid-twentieth-century America. The post-World War II era was a time of moral decline: one divorce for every four marriages, alarmingly high for that day; six million alcoholics; etc. Like the time prior to the 1857-59 awakening, a growing prosperity captured in the "pursuit of the American dream" taxed the spiritual fortitude of the land. Liberalism had become securely entrenched in schools of higher learning, including most seminaries.

The Mid-Century Resurgence featured a rejection of theological liberalism and the Social Gospel Movement. Two obvious streams of renewal occurred in the decade. The first was a resurgence of conservative, evangelical Christianity as seen in such examples as the ministry of Billy Graham and *Christianity Today* magazine. The second was the Charismatic Revival featured by the ministries of Oral Roberts and others. An offshoot of the era was the "peace of mind" movement of Norman Vincent Peale, a theologically anemic approach to Christianity.

The 1857-59 Prayer Revival was assisted in its spread by the rise of the telegraph. Similarly, the 1950s revival was the first to profit from radio and television. Prayer played a vital role. On one occasion, 30,000 people, the largest crowd ever assembled in Iowa for prayer, met at the steps of the state capitol in Des Moines.

Religious activity and revival are not synonymous. Still, statistics for the decade bear studying. Church attendance was at an all-time high in the year 1955. Approximately 49 percent of Americans attended church on an average Sunday that year, compared with 37 percent in 1949 and 39 percent in 1950. In 1954 Congress added the words "under God" to the pledge of allegiance to the flag. They also instituted a prayer room in the capitol. Religious books outsold all other categories in 1953.[8]

The Southern Baptist Convention witnessed its greatest years of advance in its history to that point in the 1950s. The denomination grew from seven million members to nine and one-half million from 1949 to 1960. In 1951 the Convention passed a resolution allowing the Home Mission Board and other agencies to work outside the South.

Revival among Youth

Evangelical schools experienced powerful revival movements around the year 1950. Theological compromise had crept into denominations by means of their schools. Ironically, theological renewal has often begun there as well, for campuses provide a fertile field for revival. In one instance, four men became deeply burdened for revival: William Dunlap, Jack Franck, Edwin Orr, and Billy Graham. Both Graham and Orr were particularly used of God in awakenings at schools. Orr presented a series of lectures at Bethel College and Seminary in Minneapolis in 1949. A powerful revival ensued. Bethel president Henry C. Wingblade later reported:

> I think none of us will forget that week, especially the climactic day, which was Thursday. The student body as a whole were on their faces before God in prayer,

asking for His heart-searching, confessing before Him every known sin, and being willing to make any restitution that might be necessary. There have been many great meetings in the history of our school, but this was certainly one of the greatest experiences we have ever had. It is all by Gods grace — we have nothing to boast about.[9]

Other campuses touched by the testimony of revival at Bethel included St. Paul Bible College; Northwestern College and Seminary, where Graham was president; and several other schools. A student awakening came at Northern Baptist Theological Seminary in Chicago in 1949-50. Scores of colleges eventually experienced some degree of divine visitation. Asbury College, scene of a great stirring in 1905 and later in 1970, was shaken in 1950. A Thursday chapel led to brokenness and confession that continued with few lulls for 118 hours. Students from the college took the spirit of revival through their testimonies to many states.

Baylor University in Texas experienced revival in the early 1950s. Billy Graham's visit provided a time of open expression of the revival that was already touching a number of students. Many students who later became effective leaders in the Southern Baptist Convention were affected by revival: Jess Moody, Bo and Dick Baker, and Howard Butt, to name a few. Also, a student at the nearby Methodist College came to be a part of the Baylor revival. At this time, the young man gave his life to Christ. Thus Robert E. Coleman, author of *The Master Plan of Evangelism*, came to know the Master.

Many students noticed a rise in spiritual interest during the fall of 1949 at Wheaton College. Youth for Christ founder Torrey Johnson spoke at a series of meetings at the Wheaton Academy in January 1950. The week was marked by unusual answers to prayer and times of confession of sin. The Academy began praying fervently for similar services scheduled at the college. The first services on Sunday night and Monday seemed fairly normal. A day of prayer was announced for Tuesday.

During an afternoon session, a humble and respected professor named Clarence Hale confessed his sin of speaking unkindly to students about a faculty member. Several students followed his example. Following his Wednesday evening message, guest speaker Dr. Edwin Johnson asked for a few testimonies. Senior Bill Kornfield had asked Johnson earlier in the day for permission to speak that night. He was the first to share. Testimonies continued all through the night. Mary Dorsett reported on the revival:

As with other revivals, the testimonies and confessions followed a Spirit-ordained order. Most were very brief, lasting only a few minutes, and although specific in the naming of sins such as cheating, pledge-breaking, pride, bitterness, resentment, etc., they avoided the sensational. . . . At first fifty to one hundred students stood for hours, waiting their turn at the microphone. Finally someone suggested that they sit in the faculty or choir seats behind the podium while waiting to testify In addition to the main meeting, faculty and staff also counseled and prayed with students in a smaller room in Pierce Chapel.[10]

For thirty-nine consecutive hours — Wednesday night until Friday morning – – students met in chapel. A University of Chicago student heard what had happened and came to see. He was ultimately converted there, as was a high school student who said he was drawn inside as he drove past the campus at eleven o'clock. A Friday evening praise service lasted many hours.

The Rise of Parachurch Ministries

The decade would also witness the birth of the most influential evangelical organization among college students: Campus Crusade for Christ, International (now known simply as Cru). Bill Bright founded Cru, the world's largest evangelical parachurch organization, in 1951. He had experienced personal revival in 1947 while at a meeting at Forest Home Christian Conference Center in California. Henrietta Mears, then director of education at First Presbyterian Church, Hollywood, spoke with Bright and the son of the senior pastor. Bright said, "As we continued to talk, suddenly the Holy Spirit enveloped us."[11] During that encounter with the Lord, Richard Halverson entered the room. He was defeated, thinking of leaving the ministry. The Spirit touched his life, as well. Bright noted how all three men have since had significant ministries: Louis Evans Jr., the pastor's son, became a significant Presbyterian minister, including spending time as pastor of the National Presbyterian Church. Halverson became chaplain of the United States Senate. Bright subsequently founded Cru. He called that moment in 1951 "a sovereign act of God when He gave me the vision for Campus Crusade for Christ."[12]

Bright continued to hold forth the light for the twin necessities of any generation — evangelism and revival — until his death in 2003. He organized an advisory board that included Henrietta Mears, Billy Graham, Navigators founder Dawson Trotman, and Edwin Orr. The Bright family frequently lived in the Orr's home in the decade while he was away on his travels.

Orr and some recently converted movie stars gathered with Henrietta and Margaret Mears to form the Hollywood Christian Group. Those involved included Roy Rogers, Dale Evans, Tim Spencer, and Stuart Hamblin. Hamblin had been converted at Graham's Los Angeles Crusade. Ronald Reagan, president of the Screen Actors Guild, once directed part of the program.

Dawson Trotman had founded the Navigators organization in the 1930s, but it experienced phenomenal growth in the 1950s. Youth for Christ started in the 1940s. It too exploded as a ministry in the next decade. Many of the dominant parachurch ministries still active today were born within a 10-15 year period in the middle of the twentieth century:

—Young Life: 1942
—Youth for Christ: 1944
—The first Urbana gathering of InterVarsity: 1948
—The Billy Graham Evangelistic Association: 1950

—World Vision: 1950
—Campus Crusade (or Cru, as it is now called): 1951
—Compassion International: 1952
—Fellowship of Christian Athletes: 1954
—Operation Mobilization: 1957
—Youth With a Mission (YWAM): 1960

Billy Graham

While a distinction must be made between an evangelistic crusade and an outpouring of the Spirit, the two can overlap. Many of Moody's crusades in America and England brought powerful revival as well as a harvest of souls. The same is true of Billy Graham's ministry, particularly in his early years. The amazing success of Graham's 1949 Los Angeles Crusade immediately thrust him into the leadership of the growing spirit of renewal. His crusades, his leadership, and his personal character serve as a model for those who would be leaders in a time of awakening.

Graham was converted under the ministry of evangelist Mordecai Ham in a crusade in Graham's hometown of Charlotte, North Carolina. Before his conversion, Billy's father and a group of godly businessmen prayed "out of Charlotte the Lord would raise up someone to preach the Gospel to the ends of the earth."[13] This group invited Ham to Charlotte, and young Billy met the Savior.

Graham served as an evangelist for the fledgling Youth for Christ organization in 1945. He passed through a serious time of spiritual testing shortly before his Los Angeles crusade. His friend Charles Templeton had rejected the authority of Scripture and ridiculed Graham's convictions. After a time of struggle, Graham experienced personal revival and a deep time of consecration to the Word of God. Following a talk with Orr at Forest Home, Graham placed his Bible on a stump, declaring, "I accept this book by faith as the Word of God."[14] From that point onward, Graham was ready for God to use him in an uncommon manner.

The Los Angeles Crusade of 1949 actually began eighteen months earlier in the prayers of the saints. Armin Gesswein directed a prayer effort across denominational lines. At one pastor's prayer conference sponsored by Gesswin in 1949, the principal focus was awakening. A spirit of revival fell on the meeting, raising the anticipation of those attending for a general outpouring of the Spirit. Orr spent one month leading the prayer movement for the crusade.

On several occasions, the crusade was almost cancelled. A six-thousand-seat tent served as the facility for the crusade as it commenced on September 25, 1949. For weeks, Graham preached with success, but no revival came. Though scheduled to conclude on October 16, the committee met and determined to continue. The following evening, entertainer Stuart Hamblin's conversion caused no small stir. The crusade made the front page, and crowds expanded to fifteen thousand. Graham continued to see unusual services in other cities: Boston; Columbia, South Carolina; Atlanta; and others. Harold Ockenga reported on Graham's time in New England: "For two hundred years there has been no such movement in New England," Ockenga said. "George Whitefield was the last man who stirred New England in such a way."[15]

From the 1950s until the new millennium Billy Graham has continued to serve the Lord as the man who has preached the gospel to more people than anyone in history. He has been a personal confidant to many presidents, organized evangelistic meetings all over the globe, and continues to make an impact through family members including his son Franklin, Franklin's son Will, and his daughter Ann Graham Lotz. In 2013, at the time of his 95th birthday, Graham's Billy Graham Evangelistic Association led the My Hope campaign, which wed an evangelistic message from Graham shown in homes, combining the local community with mass evangelism.

The Charismatic Revival

In the late 1940s and 1950s, a renewal movement known as the Charismatic Revival/Movement was born. Although it began in small Pentecostal churches following World War II, its rise was most notable through certain charismatic evangelists who quickly developed unusual authority in the Pentecostal world. Richard Riss, writing from the Pentecostal Charismatic tradition, referred to the "healing and latter rain movements" as "two parallel movements within Pentecostalism"[16] during the Mid-Century Revival. Prominent in the Healing Revivals were Oral Roberts, William Branham, and Kathryn Kuhlman. The Latter Rain Movement focused on the immediate return of Christ.

In 1960 Dennis Bennett, rector of Saint Mark's Episcopal Church in Van Nuys, California, told his congregation he had a Pentecostal experience that included speaking in tongues. This event received widespread media coverage and was followed by similar reports from other denominations and within Catholicism. This rising Charismatic Movement was not synonymous with revival, but it demonstrates the growing spiritual currents during the decade.

David Harrell conducted extensive research into this movement focused on healing and other miracles. While these Pentecostal leaders in many ways resembled earlier revivalists like D. L. Moody and Billy Sunday and admired the ministry of Billy Graham, "they were not part of the same revivalistic stream."[17] While salvation was preached, this renewal placed its emphasis where the New Testament does not: on the miraculous healing of the body. Whereas earlier leaders in revival at times witnessed miraculous healing, divine intervention, and remarkable answers to prayer, they placed a priority on the preaching of the gospel over such manifestations,

The revival in the 1950s, while genuine, was not without its weaknesses. Orr rightly noted that it was "accompanied, and, in a national sense, overwhelmed by a sense of 'mushiness' about the faith."[18] The revival did not deeply affect the fabric of American society, as seen in its failure to abate the movement of culture into the turbulent sixties. Nevertheless, one should not dismiss the multitudes of changed lives wrought by the season of awakening.

Reports from around the Globe

One of the most recognized regional revivals in the twentieth century came to the Hebrides Islands in the midst of the British Isles. Duncan Campbell was mightily used of God in this revival. Campbell had been rescued after being severely wounded in World War I. At that time, he experienced a convincing personal revival he called a "baptism in the Holy Spirit," an empowering to work for God. He led seven other wounded soldiers to Christ before his rescue.

During the Hebrides Revival, Campbell's two-week evangelistic mission on the Island of Lewis extended for two years! The power of God was manifested in a deeply convicting manner.

Like most movements in history, prayer preceded the revival. The new minister at Barvis determined to spend Tuesday and Friday evenings in prayer in a barn. He and a small group continued to intercede for three months. When Campbell came for his two-week mission, no one came to Christ until the final service. The latter was reserved particularly for those genuinely seeking salvation. At the last service, seven youths met the Master. When the benediction concluded, people headed toward the door. To their surprise, the congregation noticed a great mass of people had gathered outside "as if drawn by an unseen hand."[19]

The crowd thronged into the church building. Many cried out for mercy; more were converted. Whole families were transformed. Singing was almost angelic, and the people of the island were filled with awe. Remarkable testimonies emerged. On one occasion, a preacher went to a dance hall. After he spoke there, many came to Christ, including the master of ceremonies. In one village, a prayer meeting began. A minister in the town who opposed the revival led many to join his opposition. Thirty believers gathered to take the matter before the Lord. At about midnight, Campbell asked the local blacksmith to intercede. The simple worker begged God to move, stating the Lord's honor was at stake. The place shook like an earthquake, as the early church experienced in a time of prayer as recorded in Acts 4:31. When Campbell pronounced the benediction at 2:00 A.M., the village was ablaze with God! People were leaving their homes and coming to the church in brokenness before a holy God.

On another occasion, Campbell went to preach at a convention in Bangor. Seated on the platform before he was to speak, Campbell was gripped with the conviction that he must leave that place and go to the island of Bemeray. He had never been there and knew no one on the island. But, like Abraham in Genesis, he arose the next day and went. When he arrived, having told no one on the island he was coming, he was soon informed, "Hector McKennon was expecting you to arrive today he has initiated a meeting at the church at 9:00 tonight and he expects you to address it."[20] While Campbell was still at Bangor, a man on Berneray had spent an entire day in prayer for revival on the island. He became convinced God had heard his prayer and would soon answer.

When Campbell spoke that evening, the service was very normal. The man who had prayed so diligently said to Campbell, "God is hovering over us, and He will break through at any moment!" As they left the service, Campbell recorded what he saw: "Suddenly, the elder stands, takes off his hat: 'Stand, Mr. Campbell. God has come! See what is happening.' And I looked toward the congregation and I saw them falling on their knees in the heather. I heard the cries of the penitent. And that meeting that began at 11:00 that night continued on the hillside until 4:00 in the morning."[21] Campbell said every home on the island was touched by revival.

A revival was reported in East Africa that began in Kenya and spread outward. Times of prayer, fasting, and confession marked the revival. Its effect served to build the "fellowship of brethren in Christ recognizing no barriers but sin."[22]

Hansen and Woodbridge summarized the effect of the movement that spanned several decades in the middle of the 20th century:

> The so-called East African Revival nursed the health of a growing church that would survive severe persecution and genocide during the latter half of the bloody twentieth century. Observers of the awakening insist the world has never seen anything like it. Decades later, nearly all of East Africa's Protestant church leaders had been shaped by the revival.[23]

A significant feature of this movement was the growth of the church in the face of tremendous persecution at the hands of men like Idi Amin in Uganda. Hansen and Woodbridge quoted Anglican Bishop Festo Kivengere who commented on the cost of revival:

> "Revival doesn't come to respectable Christians," Kivengere wrote before the persecution chased him from Uganda. "If you think that because you're a good church member, or because you belong to such and such an organization, you're going to be revived, you had better forget it. The basis of revival is men and women shattered by their failures — aware that all is not well, helpless to do anything about it."[24]

Reports came from the Pacific realm, as well. Billy Graham witnessed unprecedented crowds in Australia and New Zealand. On the Atlantic side, Orr personally witnessed a remarkable movement of the Spirit in Brazil in the early 1950s. The growth rate of Christians in Brazil during the 1950s was twelve times that of the general population.

The unprecedented growth of Christianity in South Korea in the twentieth century can be traced to revival movements that touched the peninsular nation in the early 1950s. William Allen gave an eyewitness report from the beginning of the decade. He observed more than four thousand believers meeting at 5:00 A.M. to pray, twenty-five thousand receiving Christ in six weeks, and hundreds of Christians praying all night for several days in succession.[25]

The Jesus Movement

Older readers of this book can remember some of the features that burst onto the Christian scene around 1970: the "one way" sign, index finger pointed skyward;

youth musicals like *Good News* and *Tell It Like It Is*; youth choir tours; guitars and drums introduced into Sunday services, to the consternation of many; "Jesus Freaks;" Christian coffeehouses; and Christian bumper stickers. These are only a sampling, some serious and some superficial, of the impacts of the youth awakening known as the Jesus Revolution, the Jesus Generation, or the Jesus Movement. The year 1970 marked a cultural watershed in this century for the church as significant shifts came, like Evangelism Explosion witness training and the rise of the megachurch. The year 1970 certainly was vital for me, for that year, as my little Baptist caught the heat of the Jesus Movement; I met the same Jesus so many young people were proclaiming with such passion.

The Jesus Movement can be classified as a specialized revival, as it primarily affected the younger generation. Features of earlier movements reappeared, including brokenness over sin, a passion for the lost, a spirit of prayer, and sacrificial obedience. Because it mainly touched the youth culture, it tended to be idealistic and superficial. In some way, it paralleled the secular youth protests of the 1960s and 1970s. The war in Vietnam, the Civil Rights movement, environmental concerns, campus dissent, and other phenomena formed the milieu out of which this youth movement arose.

Some have reduced the Jesus Movement to the "Jesus Freaks," a term generally employed to refer to the new and obviously non-establishment Christians, also known as "Jesus People" or "Street Christians." These were the members of the youth population who had dropped out of mainstream society and met Christ. *Time*, *Look*, *Life*, and *Newsweek* magazines reported on this countercultural group. However, the movement went far beyond this segment.

Richard Lovelace referred to the Jesus Movement as "a general spiritual awakening in America during the 1970s."[26] Three streams flowing in this youth awakening included: (1) the Jesus People; (2) youth in traditional churches and parachurch youth organizations such as Campus Crusade for Christ; and (3) elements of the charismatic renewal. *Time* magazine distinguished three groups: (1) Jesus People, (2) traditional youth ministries, and (3) the Catholic Pentecostals.[27]

The charismatic renewal marked a significant feature of the movement, continuing the twentieth-century trend of parallel revival movements in both Pentecostal and non-Pentecostal streams of conservative, evangelical Christianity. In the early 1970s, massive Charismatic megachurches dotted the horizons of cities across the land. The Charismatic Movement in the 1970s was more middle-class than the Pentecostalism of the early 1900s, representing what some called "the Second Wave of the Pentecostal movement" following its birth as described in the previous chapter. Also, those involved in this newer movement tended to stay within existing denominations, whereas the Pentecostal revival spawned a number of new traditions.

The Jesus People

Duane Pederson coined the terms "Jesus People" and "Jesus Movement" after he began the underground *Hollywood Free Paper*. Secular press recognized the more counter-cultural aspect of the movement:

> Jesus Freaks. Evangelical hippies. Or, as many prefer to be called, street Christians. Under different names . . . they are the latest incarnation of that oldest of Christian phenomena; footloose, passionate bearers of the Word, They evoke images of St. Francis of Assisi and his ragged band of followers, or of the early Salvation Army, breaking away from the staid life of congregations to find their fellow man in the streets.[28]

In San Francisco's Haight-Asbury district, a movement began that saw "flower children" turn from drugs to Jesus. In Southern California, a similar movement began at the same time. Ted Wise converted from a lifestyle of drug addiction in 1966. Wise and his wife began witnessing in Haight, the mecca of the counter-culture. In 1967, Wise began a coffeehouse ministry called "The Living Room." Small group coffeehouses would mark the movement and correspond to the practice in past movements. For two years, this ministry continued, and some thirty to fifty thousand young people made contact with the coffeehouse. At the same time, Wise began a Christian commune called "The House of Acts."

Calvary Chapel in Costa Mesa — the church I would call the Mother Church of the Jesus Movement — became literally deluged in the earliest storms of the Jesus Movement. In 1970 two thousand youth were baptized in the Pacific Ocean by pastor Chuck Smith. Smith said the movement there was preceded by his preaching on the subject of agape love for two and one-half years. Calvary Chapel began holding three weekly youth nights with as many as two thousand in attendance. The services lasted three to four hours and included gospel rock music, prayer, and a quiet, peaceful Bible study. Lonnie Frisbee later moved from Haight to Costa Mesa, where he and his wife, Connie, opened the House of Miracles under Calvary Chapel's sponsorship. Soon, other ministries like the House of Miracles spread around the West.

The First Presbyterian Church in Hollywood sponsored The Salt Company beginning in 1967, a coffeehouse ministry pastor Don Williams described as "a cross between Disneyland's Main Street and Knott's Berry Farm."[29] Larry Norman, a leader in Jesus Movement music, often performed at the coffeehouse. Duane Pederson received help in printing and distributing his *Hollywood Free Paper* from the Salt Company and First Presbyterian. A young artist named Lance Bowen helped with the layout and cartoons for the *Free Paper*. Bowen originated the key Christian symbol of the Jesus movement: an upheld fist with index finger pointing to heaven with a small cross above it, and stenciled beneath: the slogan "One Way."

In 1969 the Christian World Liberation Front (CWLF) was founded on the radical campus of the University of California at Berkeley. Jack Sparks, a Ph.D. and former professor of statistics at Penn State, started the organization. Modeled after the radical left but based on a Christian witness, the CWLF soon began an underground paper, *Right On*, which was similar in jargon to the other papers in the counterculture. Sparks began his organization with a commune in his home; by 1971, some thirty-two communes with six hundred Jesus People had spread around the Bay area. This organization eventually became the Spiritual Counterfeits Project, a cult-watching organization.

Linda Meissner came to Seattle from New York in 1968 to set up the Teen Center. She also opened The Ark and The Eleventh Hour coffeehouse. She later moved the coffeehouse to a larger building and renamed it the Catacombs. By 1971, it was one of the largest coffeehouses in the movement. They also used the underground paper *Agape* and the evangelistic Jesus People's Army.

As is often the case in movements, particularly those with a bit more heat than light, some aberrant movements developed at the same time. The Children of God and The Way, International, represent two cults that arose from the Jesus Movement. Meissner's group merged with the Children of God in 1974, although she later left. As the book of Acts records not only the expansion of the early church but also the rise of ill-advised groups and individuals like Simon (Acts 8) and the Judaizers (Acts 15), so modern movements have their dark side.

Southern Baptist Arthur Blessitt became known for his ministry through the Christian nightclub His Place on Sunset Strip in Southern California. Later, he was best known for trekking across the country carrying a large wooden cross. Blessitt's ministry caused many to turn to Christ and spurred many believers to a more radical commitment to Christ. However, he was also prone to hyperbole, and ultimately saw his ministry fade. Still, he made a significant impact on many during the years of the Jesus Movement.[30]

Sammy Tippit led a street-witnessing ministry in Chicago known as "God's Love in Action." Tippit's ministry continues to flourish, particularly in Eastern Europe. Denny Flanders in Washington, D.C., began Maranatha, aimed at Washington's underground. The Jesus People, USA, began in Chicago. This group continues to minister in that city through social ministries and beyond Chicago through its *Cornerstone* magazine and the Rez (Resurrection) Band.

Unique ministries developed as the numbers of Jesus People swelled. Coffeehouses were a common phenomenon, becoming evangelistic centers where refreshments were served, music was played, and youth off the street could take refuge. Most evenings featured a Bible study, group discussion, and spiritual help. The coffeehouses became fertile ground for the rise of Christian rock music. Hundreds spread across the country: The Vine coffeehouse near Los Angeles; The Fisherman's Net in Detroit; Agape in Columbus, Ohio; Powerhouse in Las Vegas; and the Apple in Fort Wayne, Indiana, where the Christian group Petra began.

Festivals, marches, and rallies also began to emerge. The Faith Festival in Evansville, Indiana, held from March 27-28, 1970, was the first major Christian festival. In 1971 a Faithfest had fifteen thousand in attendance. On March 9, 1971, the first of a series of rallies in Chicago drew nine thousand. At a rally for Jesus in Belmont Plateau, Philadelphia, more than five thousand listened to the testimonies of converted drug addicts and others.

Evangelical leaders and Megachurches influenced by the Jesus Movement:
—Harvest Christian Fellowship in Riverside, California: Over twelve thousand members. Pastor and founder Greg Laurie was converted at Calvary Chapel. The church began as a Bible study in 1972.
—Elmbrook Church in Milwaukee: The church grew from 350 to 2,000 in 1970-72 as a result of the Jesus Movement. The large influx of young people led to several relocations and a reorganization of the church. Pastor Stuart Briscoe initiated small group ministries to assimilate new members.
—Willow Creek Community Church near Chicago, Illinois: Perhaps the most studied church in America, and perhaps the largest in attendance at over fifteen thousand, Willow Creek began in 1972 with Bill Hybels and a few friends who formed the Son Company, a band who played "high voltage Christian rock music." Hybels and others recognized that the time was right for radical changes in ministry, observing, "It was the time of the Jesus People and One Way bumper stickers."
—Tom Elliff, head of the International Mission Board and 1996-97 SBC President: Elliff was a student at Southwestern Seminary in 1970 when revival came there. The result: "It ushered into my life an awareness that God's work moves on the basis of prayer. . . . From that moment on, I saw that God would do his greatest work as a result of prayer. I've never been able to shake that conviction since."
—Henry Blackaby, author of Experiencing God: Henry was in Canada during a mighty revival in 1970: "When I accepted the call to go to Saskatoon as a pastor, God used the prospect of a spiritual awakening there to affirm my call-a spiritual awakening that started there spread all across Canada in the early 1970s." [Taken from *Experiencing God*][31]

The movement overall featured a deep conviction about evangelism. The twin slogans "One Way Through Jesus" and "Jesus Is Coming Soon" brought a sense of urgency to young believers. Those involved in the movement desired to share their joy for Jesus with others. Witnessing was both spontaneous and organized.[32] Creative methods were employed, including tracts, stickers, and T-shirts.

By early 1971, revival fires spread from the West Coast to Canada to Florida. Vancouver, British Columbia, reported by this time over a dozen communes and three coffeehouses, along with prayer groups meeting in the high schools and universities. A festival sponsored by the Jesus People of Milwaukee, Wisconsin, held in Duluth, Minnesota, turned into genuine revival that continued for over forty days.

Traditional Churches and Ministries

Many Evangelical churches and ministries openly supported and joined in the Jesus Movement. There were many established churches and ministries that missed the movement, often wary of the longhaired youth, the new music, and its non-traditional bent. Billy Graham, who wrote a book in favor of the movement, credited Campus Crusade for Christ with playing "a major role in sparking the new Jesus Revolution."[33] Jack Sparks was a Crusade staffer when he began the Christian World Liberation Front.

Hal Lindsay, who flamed the apocalyptic fervor so prevalent in the movement with his book *The Late Great Planet Earth*, left Campus Crusade and administered a commune in Southern California called the J. C. Light & Power Company. Campus Crusade (known now as Cru) spawned many Jesus Movement ministries, and their materials received wide usage.

Campus Crusade held a major event at Expo '72 in Dallas, Texas. At that time, it was the most massive gathering of students and Christian laymen to descend on one city. Some 80,000 delegates came to the weeklong training conference in June 1972 in Dallas, Texas. A crowd estimated at 150,000 attended a Saturday Jesus music festival that lasted eight hours. People came from all fifty states and from sixty-eight nations, with the focus of the meeting being world evangelization. *Life* magazine, perhaps the most popular of the time, featured a cover story and multiple-page spread on the Expo.

In 1970 Asbury College experienced a powerful revival that spread to many other campuses. Although some students had been gathering to pray for spiritual awakening, revival came suddenly out of a chapel service on Tuesday, February 3, 1970. The dean of the college was scheduled to speak. Instead, he shared his testimony briefly, and then opened the floor for others. Near the end of the normal chapel hour, students were invited to come to the altar for prayer. A mass of students responded, while others continued to testify. The revival spread to Asbury Seminary the next day. For 185 continuous hours, students met in the college chapel to pray, sing, and testify. Henry C. James noted the tremendous response to the revival from across the country:

> Before long, appeals began coming from other campuses for Asbury students to come and tell the story. This intensified the burden of prayer even as it heightened anticipation of what God was going to do. . . . With the dispatch of these witnesses, the local revival began to take on the dimensions of a national movement. By the summer of 1970 at least 130 colleges, seminaries and Bible schools had been touched by the revival outreach.[34]

Asbury students spoke at the South Meridian Church of God in Anderson, Indiana. Revival erupted which included nightly services from February 12 to April 12 without a break. Similar experiences came to churches across the country as students traveled to tell the story. Robert Coleman, author of *The Master Plan of Evangelism,* taught at Asbury at the time and edited a book about the movement. The book, called *One Divine Moment,* featured testimonies from other places as well, including Southwestern Baptist Theological Seminary. One of my colleagues read the book while a college student and experienced personal revival. Saskatoon, Saskatchewan, also reported revival. Beginning at Ebenezer Baptist Church, a weeklong campaign spread into months. The meeting moved into larger facilities with attendance in the thousands.[35]

The Southern Baptist Convention offers an interesting study in the impact of the Jesus Movement. The years 1971-75 remain the most productive period in number of baptisms in the convention's history. More than 400,000 baptisms were recorded for each of those years, a high mark never attained before or since. It is interesting to note that, while these years saw the greatest evangelistic results ever, the percentage of youth baptisms was even higher than the number of total baptisms. In other words, the primary numerical growth in the early 1970s was due to youth baptisms. The highest percentage of youth baptisms to total baptisms came in 1972 (30.8 percent of 445,725 baptisms), followed by 1971 (30.7 percent of 409,659), then 1973 (28.9 percent of 413,990). Later years, when more than 400,000 baptisms were recorded (including 1980, 1981, 1982), the percentage of youth baptisms was never more than 25.2 percent. Also, the ratio of youth baptisms to total youth population has never equaled the percentages of 1971 or 1972 in the years since. It is interesting to note that the greatest years of youth evangelism came at the same time as the Jesus Movement. To offer a comparison, note that in 1972, the SBC reported 137,000 youth baptisms, the all-time high to date. In 2011, with more Millennial teens than the Baby Boomers of the 1970s, and with far more Southern Baptists, the denomination baptized just under 80,000.

It is also interesting that, in the 1970s, the six SBC seminaries experienced significant across-the-board enrollment increases, perhaps reflecting the numbers of young people entering the ministry out of this youth revival. Some would note the possibility to young people entering seminary to avoid the draft, but the numbers continued to surge after the Vietnam conflict ended.

Many denominational leaders spoke of revival, especially among the youth.[36] Russell Richardson of Illinois said, "A spirit of revival seems to be in many churches and associations." In 1972, Harold P. McGlamery, evangelism director for Colorado, said, "Spiritual tides of revival seem to be running high in Colorado. . . . Some churches are experiencing almost continual revival, and the trend seems to be spreading rapidly."

F. M. Dowell in Tennessee reported in 1972, "a great spiritual movement has been reported all across our state." The evangelism report in the Kentucky Baptist Convention annual contained a paragraph about the Jesus Movement. In addition, the 1971 report of the Home Mission Board Evangelism Section reported "continued signs of spiritual awakening in our Convention, *especially among the youth*."[37]

In 1971, editors of the thirty-two Baptist state papers voted the Jesus Movement the third most important story of the year among Southern Baptists. Several editorials were written about the movement. Scores of Southern Baptist churches were positively influenced by some aspect of the movement, including Castle Hills, San Antonio; Rehoboth, Atlanta; Roswell Street, Marietta, Georgia; First Baptist, West Palm Beach, Florida; and First Baptist, Houston.[38] I interviewed dozens of leaders who were in some way influenced by the Jesus Movement. Many are currently in positions that have given them a forum to encourage many to pray for yet another great awakening.

Perhaps no church experienced a greater blessing from the Jesus Movement in the SBC than First Baptist, Houston. When John Bisagno came as pastor in 1970, the church was in decline, with only a handful of youth or young adults. Bisagno cast a vision for reaching the youth, saying he would rather see teens yelling for Jesus in church than sitting in a park smoking pot. Bisagno brought youth evangelist Richard

Hogue to conduct a SPIRENO (Spiritual Revolution Now) campaign to Houston. For four months, Hogue "blitzed the high schools and junior highs with rock-rhythm Jesus music and Hogue's electrifying announcements that 'the Jesus Movement is here.'"[39] When the meetings began, they were so packed they had to be moved to the Houston coliseum. The entire process saw an incredible 4,011 recorded professions of faith, 95 percent of them youth. First Baptist baptized about one thousand, while an intensive follow-up effort led planners to conclude that 70 percent of the converts were baptized in some church.

First Baptist Church baptized 1,669 that year; the first year an SBC church broke the one thousand barrier, and an increase of 1,274 over the previous year's leader in the convention. The church had to hire a full-time minister of follow-up! First Baptist set the pace for the many contemporary Southern Baptist megachurches across the nation. "The SPIRENO revival led by Richard Hogue," Bisagno surmised, "was probably the most important factor that God used in reviving the work here."[40]

Much of the heat of the Jesus Movement was lost before it greatly affected denominations. Many traditional churches were unwilling to accept the zeal and uniqueness of the Jesus Movement. We must be wary of expecting revival to fit our stereotypes. Part of the reason for the hesitancy of conventional churches to embrace the movement was the anti-institutionalism of many of its adherents, which led some in the Jesus Movement to ignore the biblical significance of the local church. The overemphasis on experience and theological superficiality kept the renewal from being more deeply entrenched as well.

Tom Elliff, SBC president in 1996 and a student at Southwestern Seminary in 1970 when it was touched by revival out of the Asbury college revival, said: "All that energy, enthusiasm, and excitement was like water on hot pavement, because it didn't have a theological container."[41]

Still, across the nation, each time I talk about the Jesus Movement, I meet someone whose life was radically and permanently changed in that time of revival.

The Impact of the Jesus Movement

The impact of the Jesus Movement can still be seen. First, it caused a *revolution in church music and in worship styles,* either to the delight or the dismay of many believers. The scores of contemporary Christian Music (CCM) stations across the nation and the abundance of praise choruses in churches were unheard of prior to 1970. Two streams of influence merged to form the new music of the Jesus Movement. One was the rise of folk music that led to youth choir musicals such as *Good News, Celebrate Life, Tell It Like It Is*, and many others. Youth choir tours were at their peak during the early 1970s, spreading the gospel through song across North America. One summer, my youth group went on such a tour, seeing people come to Christ at every stop along the way.

The other stream — and the more controversial — was the rise of indigenous Christian rock music. As is often the case in times of social unrest in a given cultural context, the late 1960s created a growing interest in spirituality among young people.

Contemporary Christian music (CCM) began in the coffeehouses and youth fellowships of the period and mushroomed into a $500 million industry annually by 1990. John Styll, president of the Gospel Music Association in 1993 and publisher of *Contemporary Christian Music* magazine, summarized the advent of the genre: "Contemporary Christian Music was born out of the counterculture movement of the 60's. Disillusioned hippies who found the answer in Christ used their most natural means of expression — music — to proclaim the joy of their salvation and to share Christ with others. It wasn't organ music either. It was the music they understood."[42]

Dozens of "Jesus rock groups" had begun playing in Southern California. Pat Boone was openly involved in the new music of the Jesus Movement. Larry Norman, called the "Poet Laureate" of the Jesus Movement by some, was one of the best-known leaders of Jesus Movement music. His simple ballad about the second coming of Christ, "I Wish We'd All Been Ready," became a signature song of the movement. Some referred to Chuck Girard and his group Love Song as "the Beatles of the Christian music world". At The Adam's Apple coffeehouse in Fort Wayne, Indiana, the Christian rock group Petra got its start. In Nashville, the Koinonia coffeehouse was seminal in the rise of Contemporary Christian Music (CCM). Artists such as Amy Grant, Brown Bannister, and the group Dogwood spent a great deal of time at Koinonia. Likewise, the Jesus festivals provided a forum for musicians to share their songs. Unfortunately, as CCM has become institutionalized, it has become more of an industry than a ministry for many.[43] While the new musical styles among the youth gradually gained favor in churches through the youth musical and the rising popularity of contemporary Christian music, many sounds were not necessarily as desirable to the ears of the traditional church.

The music of the Jesus movement changed the worship styles of countless churches and paved the way for more recent worship movements. Without a Jesus Movement, youth today might not be enjoying the worship at such mega-conferences as the Passion movement today.

Interestingly, a second feature related to the Jesus Movement was *the rise of the modern megachurch*. The Jesus Movement did not cause the rise of modern megachurches, so common in cities across America today. But many individual megachurches were hatched from the incubator of the youth renewal. Calvary Chapel offers the most notable example. The church has become a quasi-denomination, with hundreds of Calvary Chapels springing up across America and in other nations. Many of the churches affected by the Jesus Movement were independent charismatic congregations. From 1970 to today, large churches have grown exponentially, adopting much of the newer music and reaching many of the younger people along the way. First Baptist Houston, mentioned earlier, would be an example of a Southern Baptist megachurch touched by the Jesus Movement.

A third way the Jesus Movement has continued to make its mark is seen in the *rise in focus on prayer and spiritual awakening* in the years following its end. Peter Wagner argued that the church in the latter 20th century was in the midst of the "greatest prayer movement of all time."[44] He dated the growing emphasis on prayer to the year 1970. The ministry of prayer and spiritual awakening at the North American

Mission Board, led for years by Henry Blackaby and now led by Gary Frost, had its beginnings during the Jesus Movement. C. B. Hogue had seen his church in Ada, Oklahoma, touched by revival through the visit of students from Asbury College. When he came to serve as vice president for evangelism at the Board in the early 1970s, Hogue brought a deep burden not only for evangelism but for spiritual awakening as well: "I came to the conclusion that we did need to have something that would spark interest, create desire, develop a prayer process that would help to bring awakening. That is when I instituted the Office of Spiritual Awakening. . . . I saw what could happen in a local church. And consequently I wanted to see that same thing happen over all the country."[45]

Hogue invited Glenn Sheppard to direct the Personal Evangelism Department. Sheppard had been radically affected by features of the Jesus Movement while a student at Southern Seminary. Hogue added to Sheppard's job description an emphasis on spiritual awakenings. In 1980 Sheppard was named Special Assistant in Spiritual Awakening, and devoted his efforts fully to the task of assisting Southern Baptists to pray for genuine revival in our land. Henry Blackaby held the office later. He had been personally involved in the Canadian revival in 1970. A retrospective on the Jesus Movement in 1982 stated: "One thing is certain, more Southern Baptists are talking about spiritual awakening today than at any time in the past 50 years. More than 2,000 Southern Baptist churches have groups praying for spiritual awakening."[46] In recent years a growing interest in prayer for revival has come from pastors and leaders in various traditions.

Nancy Honeytree, one of the early Jesus Movement musical artists, offered an interesting comment about the enduring impact of the Jesus Movement today: "The Jesus Movement was a very specific 'workers' revival. Many of those who got saved are now in ministry and in place for the next revival, which I believe will cross every barrier: age, denomination, and race."[47]

I must agree with Orr that, when compared to awakenings in 1858 and 1905, for example, the "1970 awakening made up a minor visitation, not a major one."[48] That being said, I close this section with the question Orr asked following the quote above: "If so much good arose from a minor movement, what could a major one do?"

Impact of These Twentieth Century Movements

These various movements remind us of *the role of youth in awakenings*. While we have seen no great awakening in the West for a long time, God stirred multitudes of young people in the Jesus Movement and on many college campuses. I still meet people today whose trajectory was changed for the rest of their lives by a brief visitation from God in revival on their college campuses.

That such movements are, from our perspective, spontaneous and arise often outside the dominant church culture should remind us to be aware of God's work beyond our normal patterns of church life. Who would have thought a bunch of converted hippies and new ministries like coffeehouses would have the affect they do today? With the phenomenon of the third place as seen in such venues as Starbucks today, could we envision a movement of God happening not first in a church building among church goers, but at a Starbucks among friends?

Questions for Small Group Study

1. What parachurch ministries are you or your church a part? Or, more specifically, in what type of parachurch ministry might you serve?

2. These revivals spread by use of the technology of their day. TV aided the Asbury revival and the Jesus Movement, for instance. Do you think social media (Twitter, Facebook, etc.) could play a similar role in revival today?

3. Here you begin to see the rise of Billy Graham's ministry. What preachers and biblical teachers do you listen to, given that this millennium is the age of the podcast?

4. By way of more of a discussion than questioning talk about the role of youth not only in this specific chapter, but also thus far in this reading as a whole. What are the possibilities for the youth you know?

Chapter 15
Revival in Our Time

When the fire is falling, get as near as you can to the flame.
Roy Fish[1]

Our generation stands at a unique time in history. We live not only at the beginning of a new century, but in recent years we were the second generation since our Lord walked upon the earth to usher in a new millennium. Could we see a divine visitation like the revivals in the past in our time?

I hope the preceding survey of historic revival movements has pointed out the irony that great revival often comes in times when the possibility of revival seems so remote. Some of the greatest movements of God came in dark spiritual times. Our day is filled with much darkness. Our culture has been described as post-Christian, or even anti-Christian. Tolerance is promoted as a virtue while conviction is disdained as a vice. Increasingly, leaders in evangelical Christianity decry our lack of theological depth and historical awareness. A focus on popular culture leaves the serious believer perplexed about the future.

But we can have hope, and this is where history becomes our friend. Out of the spiritual darkness of the Middle Ages, God brought a Reformation. When the Enlightenment began spreading rationalism and secularism across the West, God sent a succession of mighty awakenings. In our day, when the skies seem dark, we can see light on the horizon.

Many have concluded that the only hope for America is revival. Pause for a moment and ponder: what if the current events propel us to pray and to seek the mercy drops before the shower, the sparks to a yet greater flame! Could it be that examples such as those above are an indication of the beginning of a mighty movement of God for which so many have prayed?

Is a great revival at hand? At the time of this writing, our nation as a whole is not in revival. But our God is alive and at work.

Revival in Brownwood, Texas

On January 22, 1995, an unusual service at Coggin Avenue Baptist Church in Brownwood, Texas, became the beginning of a movement of spiritual awakening in that town.[3] Commencing with a testimony given by college student Chris Robeson, people began responding in the service with tears and brokenness. The early service extended through the Sunday school hour, past the 11:00 service, and into the early afternoon. The spirit of revival there quickly spilled over to the nearby campus of Howard Payne University. Students from Howard Payne and Coggin Avenue pastor John Avant have crisscrossed the nation sharing revival testimonies. The revival spread as students from other schools have likewise gone forth to give testimony to the activity of God. Campus after campus and church after church have experienced varying levels of deep brokenness, often including hours of open confession of sin.[4] Characterized by brokenness, confession, and repentance, the revival has set ablaze scores of colleges, seminaries, and churches from Texas northward through the heartland, and from Boston to California.

The movement was reported by religious and secular news media, from *Christianity Today* to the Phil Donahue Show. Wire services and the Internet scattered seeds of renewal as well, while fax machines (this was still a few years before the social media explosion of the current day) spread the tidings of revival news at a record pace. The *Houston Chronicle*, *Fort Worth Star-Telegram*, *Dallas Morning News*, and other major newspapers carried features of the revival. But the primary means by which the movement has spread is through the testimony of students and others.

After the momentous day on January 22, Avant prayed the following: "Lord, we call out to You for genuine awakening on Howard Payne's campus, that could send out literally hundreds and hundreds of students to every corner of this nation and world with afire of revival in their hearts." These words proved to be prophetic. In the coming weeks, students from Howard Payne University did go out, if not in hundreds, at least in twos, fours, and fives, to spread the news of a true movement of God on their campus.

Like any other movement of God's Spirit, what occurred in January 1995 did not come out of a vacuum. John Avant's passion for revival was ignited through the teaching of Roy Fish, professor of evangelism at Southwestern Baptist Theological Seminary. Fish's course on the great awakenings led Avant to do doctoral work with him. While a student in Fish's History of Spiritual Awakenings seminar, Avant joined with four other students in an accountability group — Steve Gaines, Doug Munton, Preston Nix, and me. In the pattern of earlier, more extensive revivals, a small group of like-minded individuals played a role in preparation. The group, along with our wives, has continued to seek God's face and pray for revival.

Avant soon learned what Arthur Wallis said: "Let us face it on our knees before God, revival is costly."[5] After serious discussions with a megachurch went awry, Avant confessed, "I was angry with God." Suddenly, in 1992, in the midst of preaching in Indianapolis, Avant became ill. The undiagnosed illness racked his body to the point that he could hardly continue his ministry. The only thing the doctors could tell him was that he had some type of viral condition, and they could not find a cure. The condition caused Avant to yield himself to God whether he ever got well again or not. This purging process ultimately led Avant to Coggin Avenue Baptist Church in Brownwood, Texas. The illness did not begin to go away until he was actually on the church field in Brownwood.

Brownwood is a small town in west central Texas and the home of Howard Payne University, a Texas Baptist college with about fourteen hundred students. There had been terrible immorality at Coggin Avenue, serious sexual sin in the leadership. There were some wonderful people, but some serious problems as well. The longer Avant remained, the more it appeared that everything he tried to do to lead the church met with opposition.

Slowly, things began to turn; a hunger and expectancy developed. People began to sign up for classes to study materials entitled *Experiencing God*. Eventually, three hundred people had been through the seminar. The people began to thirst for God a little more. The normal evening services were cancelled so the entire congregation could study *Fresh Encounter*, a study of the principles of revival. The people began to hunger yet more; however, there was still no genuine revival.[6]

Then God began to do some unusual things: remarkable conversions, answered prayer, families restored. One man in the church with a torrid reputation in the community experienced personal revival after almost committing suicide. God took hold of the man's life and radically changed him, to the point that everyone who knew him could not miss what had happened. He began to share his life and the desperate situation out of which God had taken him. God began to change people's lives through him. One day, he stood up and shared his testimony before a packed church, filled with people who knew what he had done. He said, "Men, some of you are right where I was," and they were.

A man named Fernando Hernandez became an unlikely tool in the hand of God. A former cocaine addict, he was convinced God had a plan and purpose for him to move to Brownwood. He began an effective ministry to the gangs in Brownwood. Avant met him and led Coggin Avenue Church to support his ministry among the gangs. There was only one problem: the charismatic church in town was already giving him some financial support. Soon, Coggin Avenue unanimously voted to have a joint mission effort between a Baptist church and the charismatic church.

While recognizing doctrinal differences, the two groups began to fellowship together. The charismatics were saying, "You mean you don't hate us?" And the members at Coggin said, "No; you don't hate us?" They said, "No." Avant started baptizing kids from the gangs. As of the beginning of spring 1995, he had baptized 30 gang members.

Pastors began to witness the mighty power of God when the charismatic church and the Baptist church worked together. Pastors began to pray from many denominations: Nazarene, Church of Christ, Methodist, Baptist, Pentecostal, and Assembly of God. The pastors started to pray, "God, we don't care about our differences; we just want to see Jesus come into this community." God began to unify the churches, and *Experiencing God* began to sweep across different denominations.

The charismatic church had a group studying *Experiencing God* that was led by a Presbyterian, full of charismatics, meeting in a charismatic church, with a Church of Christ pastor attending, using Baptist materials. The charismatic pastor said, "It has got to be revival!"

A hunger for revival also developed at Howard Payne University as students began to develop a desire to see the Lord in a new way. People prayed, believed, and hoped that God might bring revival. There was a growing, building sense of expectancy. Many thought revival would come in February of 1995, because that was the time when Henry Blackaby, author of *Experiencing God* and *Fresh Encounter*, was scheduled to come to town for the annual revival services at Howard Payne University That seemed to be the perfect time, but God had other plans.

Revival did come, but in an unlikely manner. Avant started a sermon series that Sunday morning, January 22, on the Ten Commandments entitled "What Must Go That God Will Come." The early service on January 22 began as normal at about 8:30 A.M., with the auditorium about half full. But there was something different. Usually few if any students attended the early service, but this Sunday, there were about 30 university students present. When the invitation came, Chris Robeson, a student leader on campus, came forward and asked if he could speak. Ordinarily, Avant would have told Chris to talk to him after the service, but God led the pastor to allow him to speak.

Chris stood at the pulpit and read Joel 2:12: "Return to me with all your heart, with fasting, with weeping, and with mourning." He began to weep and cry out to the Lord. He shared his desperate burden that the time had come for revival. People began to stream down the aisles. A woman in the church challenged the people that they were not a praying church and that they must begin to pray and seek God diligently. She asked, "If we don't turn back to Him in prayer, what is God going to do with us?" People started coming to the microphone spontaneously, sharing scripture and sharing their hearts.

It came time for Sunday school, but it was obvious that the Lord was dealing with the people in a deep way. Avant told the people that they could stay, go to their classes and tell others to come to the services, or go to their classes for the Sunday school hour. Most of the people stayed. The service continued with praise, prayer, sharing, and singing all through the Sunday school hour. People were coming to the altar broken for sin.

People began to come in for the 11:00 service. They didn't know what was going on, but they joined in seeking God. Many of them came spontaneously to kneel at the altar. The venue services are broadcast live on the radio at 11:00, but this day the entire structure for the service had changed. As the service was going on the air, it was in the midst of an invitation. People were streaming down the aisles. It was obvious they were ready to respond. Twenty-two people were saved or called to the ministry during that invitation.

Meanwhile, in Pioneer, Texas, a rancher who was a strong believer had to go take care of a cow that was giving birth to a calf that morning, and thus he could not go to church services. He had with him a fifty-year-old ranch hand. Due to the cold, they sat in the truck and listened to Coggin Avenue Church's service on the radio. The ranch hand was so moved that he asked how to receive Jesus. The rancher told him, and he received Jesus that day. He asked what to do next, and he was told to be baptized. They couldn't find a church in that little area with a baptistry, so they found a pastor who later baptized him outside on that cold day.

The same day, Rocky Creek Baptist Church experienced revival. First Baptist, Santa Anna, a small community close to Brownwood, had twenty-seven commitments to Christ that day and forty-eight decisions in all. It was the greatest harvest of people coming to know Jesus they had ever seen. Trinity Chapel, another church in the area, also broke out in revival on January 22.

That night, Coggin had a joint service scheduled with their Hispanic mission. The group had already begun to experience something of a revival themselves, with a new pastor and new growth. The auditorium was packed with whites, blacks, and Hispanics. God fell on that service. Although the Brownwood community struggled with racial problems, the altar filled with people from various races crying out to God. Avant baptized sixteen young people that night.

In the ensuing weeks, individuals continued to testify to revival in their own lives. Senior adults shared their testimonies in both the early and late morning worship services about what God was doing in their hearts in revival. A man told how he had prayed for forty years that God would send revival. People were overwhelmed. People were baptized weekly. In the following weeks, the messages on foundation convictions from the Ten Commandments fueled the revival with biblical kindling.

Home prayer meeting groups sprang up in the church. Similar groups began meeting on the Howard Payne University campus. The Howard Payne newspaper, *Yellow Jacket*, reported "Revival an Everyday Occurrence for Students." A strong revival movement came to campus, not among all the students, but among a large number who were daily walking with God in revival.

Henry Blackaby came to preach at Coggin on February 11. That day, the largest attendance in the history of the church, maybe twelve to thirteen hundred people, packed into the services. The power of God came. People responded with brokenness and repentance as Henry preached.

Sunday night, twenty to thirty churches, some from out-of-town, canceled their services and came for the service, which lasted more than three hours. At one point, all the pastors and staff members came to the altar. On Monday, God began to work in a powerful way on campus. As Henry shared in chapel, there were deep movements and responses among the students.

Tuesday night, public expression was given to what was already happening in many students. That night, six or seven hundred students filled the auditorium. At the end, Henry called on two students to testify. The first said, "You think that I have been such a good Christian, but I've been wearing a mask. Tonight I am taking off the mask." He laid down on his face before the Lord on the platform. The other student shared about his own sin. The male students came and gathered around them. Then a young woman came and shared how she and other women had not been helping the men. She said they were ashamed of the way they had been dressing. A hundred or more women came to the stage, weeping.

Dozens of people began coming to the microphone. Three to four hundred students came to the altar. Confession of sin went on for three hours. By eleven o'clock, the students finished. As they finally finished, they gathered around the piano and sang praises to the Lord. Some stayed up all night, seeking God in prayer in their dorms. Avant and Blackaby left to speak at the North American Convocation on Revival in Little Rock.

On February 26, Avant spoke at the Greater Faith Community Church, a predominantly African-American church. The charismatic church in the town joined in the services. Avant preached on the subject of how revival can end racism. The service lasted three and one-half hours and was filled with brokenness.

That same evening, students from Howard Payne testified at Jersey Village Baptist Church in Houston where I had been speaking for four consecutive Sunday nights. I witnessed a stirring of the Spirit each week. I had talked to John Avant about God's work in Brownwood. He sent two students to testify on February 26. Two of the students, a young man named Kelly Parrish and a young lady named Brandi Maguire (who are now married and church planters), spoke boldly about all night prayer meetings and changed lives at Howard Payne. Instead of preaching, after the testimonies I admonished the congregation with the Four Points of Evan Roberts: 1) Confess every known sin, 2) Lay aside every doubtful habit, 3) Obey the Holy Spirit promptly, and 4) Proclaim Jesus publicly. People began to respond with prayer requests, testimonies, and much brokenness. As one would share, others would gather around that one to pray. A woman told of her distress that her unbelieving husband opposed her church attendance. Several woman with lost husbands banded with her and they sought the Lord on the spot. Families were restored, ministry happened, and songs were sung spontaneously.

Then something happened I will never forget. A young lady stood before the church and said, "I'm pregnant, I'm scared, and I need help." Ladies young and old gathered around her to love on her and to pray for her. This prompted a mom in the church to share how she had almost had an abortion years ago because of a pregnancy outside marriage, but she had kept the baby, and her now thirteen-year-old daughter wept beside her. Others encouraged the youth who had just discovered and confessed her sin. I never really talked to her that night, because there were so many people. But I did hear that she determined not to have an abortion but to give the child up for Christian adoption.

I helped write a book after this movement that is now out of print. I mentioned the young lady in that book. Eight years later, in 2003, I received an email one morning that said the following:

> Dr. Reid:
>
> I am not sure if you remember me, but I was the fifteen-year-old pregnant girl. I wanted to let you know that I recently sought out a copy of the book and began to read it for the first time in many years, and the passage about me brought me to tears. I wanted to thank you for putting my story in there. . . . I was glad to read something done entirely by a stranger and get an outside perspective of that situation after [finding] healing. I would love it if in some, even small, way helped another person, . . . I also wanted to give you an update on me. I recently graduated [from College] and am married to the most wonderful man I have ever known. I am planning on going to medical school and becoming a pediatrician.
>
> I placed my two-day-old son for adoption. . . . He is a wonderful, almost eight-year-old, stubborn boy. His parents are wonderful and I am truly blessed to be allowed the chance to know him as he grows. He and his younger brother were ring bearers at my wedding. I could not have imagined what my life would have been like without him.

Revival changes our lives, and the lives of others. What a testimony to the gospel and the forgiveness found in Christ!

On March 1, Avant spoke to a packed chapel audience at Southwestern Seminary. Avant shared the story of what God had done. Howard Payne students had shared in some of the seminary classes the day before. Some seminary students were so moved they had stayed up all night praying and fasting for revival. President Ken Hemphill wisely allowed the students to stay beyond normal chapel time. They began public confession that continued for hours. They confessed all forms of sin, adultery, lust, pornography, greed, and racism. Every time students confessed, other students gathered around them, loved them, and prayed for them. When the confessions finally ended, students continued to pray. As students went to their churches that evening, tremendous revival movements followed in area churches.

Many churches experienced similar movements. In March at the First Baptist Church, Corinth, Texas, pastored by Doug Munton, one lady was so broken for her attitude that she and her husband washed the pastor's feet in an evening service to demonstrate her repentance.

One of the deepest movements came to Wheaton College near Chicago. Howard Payne students Brandi Maguire and James Hahn were invited to speak at World Christian Fellowship (WCF), a student-initiated, student-led gathering with a focus on world missions. More than double the normal attendance of 450 students gathered on the evening of March 19 to hear testimonies about the movement of God in Brownwood. There was an undeniable sense of anticipation in Pierce Chapel. As Brandi shared, a "holy hush" began to permeate Pierce Chapel. She concluded by saying with deep emotion, "My heart is broken for you, that you will break your hearts before the Father, because He desires that." Then she sat down.

James Hahn followed Brandi, describing how he had become rather cynical about the prospects of revival at Howard Payne during his three and a half years there. James talked about how God had done a deep work in his own life and how he had been humbled to the point where he publicly confessed his sin in front of fellow students. He said, "I went up [to confess] more scared of God's judgment than that of my peers."

Students began to come to the microphones following the testimonies. As each moment passed, lines at the microphones grew until they wound halfway back the outside aisles of Pierce Chapel. Students, one after another, openly confessed sin in their lives: bitterness, lust, anger, jealousy, pride, cheating, racial prejudice, hatred, addictions of all kinds, theft, cynicism, materialism, competitiveness, and broken relationships.

What took place as students continued to share was a beautiful picture of the body of Christ in action. After each confession, a group of five to twenty-five people would gather around the person who had confessed and would minister love, acceptance, and encouragement. There was a continual flow of people into and out of the auditorium all evening as people left to call friends or to go and bring them back to Pierce.

At 6:00 A.M., there were more people in Pierce than had begun the previous evening. It was determined that another meeting should be held Monday night at 9:30 P.M. Matt Yarrington, head of WCF, encouraged the group to focus on three things in the days ahead: prayer, the Scriptures, and mutual accountability. He challenged people only to confess publicly if they were truly repentant — not only sorry for their sin, but ready to turn from it. He referred to things people may have in their dorm rooms as "hidden provisions for defeat," things that would trip them up in the days ahead. A student then read from Mark 9:42-47 and talked about getting rid of the things that caused students to stumble. Students began bringing to the stage books, magazines, videos, alcohol, drugs, CDs, a credit card (symbolizing a bondage to materialism), a rose (symbolizing a destructive relationship). These and many other items were placed there by students hungry to get right with God. It was wonderful to see how deeply God was at work; it was depressing to see what people had been hiding away in their rooms. It took five garbage bags to gather up everything. Tim Beougher, a professor of evangelism at Wheaton at the time, observed first hand the power of God at work, and edited a book entitled *Accounts of a Campus Revival* about the movement.

For the next three nights, through Thursday, March 23, students flocked to impromptu services that met for four to five hours each evening. The services moved to College Church on Wednesday. By Thursday night, the days of confession were followed by an expression of praise to the gracious God who had touched so many in a beautiful way. Having seen the ugliness of their sin, the contrast of the beauty of Christ and His work came clearly into focus.

On that night, an invitation was offered for those sensing God's call into full-time ministry. Between two and three hundred gathered at the front and up the center aisle of the church. The service concluded with a time of praise and worship.

Howard Payne, Southwestern Seminary, and Wheaton are only three examples of the scores of other schools touched, as well. Dozens of schools across the nation were affected at some level. Some had only brief visitations, but others continued for weeks and months. Wesley Duewel has well noted that, even when revival sweeps powerfully for only a day or two, as happens at times on a college campus, "more spiritual transformation has resulted than from months and years of ordinary Christian life and witness."[7]

During the biennial meeting of the staff of Campus Crusade for Christ (now Cru) in Fort Collins, Colorado, in July 1995, revival ignited among the participants. More than four thousand United States staff members plus many international workers heard Nancy Leigh DeMoss of Life Action Ministries speak on Monday morning of the conference. Spontaneously, the Holy Spirit worked the process of conviction in the lives of the people. The service on that Monday lasted until after midnight. For two days and more than eighteen hours, the people confessed, shared, and received cleansing. Staff members had come to the meeting with expectation of God's movement, and they were not disappointed as God worked powerfully in the conference.

Experiencing God

In the sixteenth century, pastor Richard Baxter wrote of the role of writings in furthering the season of awakening among his people. Malcolm and I pray that this book might encourage some to seek God afresh. One of the catalysts for spiritual renewal in the lives of believers and churches in recent years are the works of Henry Blackaby and Claude King called *Experiencing God* and *Fresh Encounter.* Blackaby has had a passion for revival and awakening since he was a lad in his native Canada. Hear his story:

> My heritage goes back to England where several of my family were graduates of Spurgeon's College at a time when Spurgeon was trying to win England to Christ. I grew up in a town in Canada where there was no evangelical witness to Christ. My father served as a lay pastor to help start a mission in that town. Way back in my teen years I began to sense a deep burden for communities all across Canada that did not have an evangelical church. In 1958 when 1 was in seminary, God assured me that He loved my nation enough to want to bring a great movement of His Spirit across our land. When 1 accepted the call to go to Saskatoon as a pastor, God used the prospect of a spiritual awakening there to affirm my call — a spiritual awakening that started there spread all across Canada in the early 1970s.[8]

These materials swept the nation, spreading across many Christian traditions, leading countless individuals to personal renewal and churches to encounter God in real and fresh ways. *Experiencing God* was founded on the following principles:

1. God is always at work around you.
2. God pursues a continuing love relationship with you that is real and personal.
3. God invites you to become involved with Him in His work.
4. God speaks by the Holy Spirit through the Bible, prayer, circumstances, and the church to reveal Himself, His purposes, and His ways.
5. God's invitation for you to work with Him always leads you to a crisis of belief that requires faith and action.
6. You must make major adjustments in your life to join God in what He is doing.
7. You come to know God by experience as you obey Him and He accomplishes His work through you.

Promise Keepers

In 1996 more than one million men from different races and denominations gathered in stadiums to glorify God. I was in Charlotte with 60,000 men on June 21-22. On that Saturday, a satellite linkup enabled over 110,000 men in Charlotte and Denver to worship together for a period of time. With the intensity of a Super Bowl crowd, men were proclaiming their love for God and their families. Promise Keepers has gripped the hearts of millions. In addition to the arena meetings involving primarily laymen, in February 1996 the largest gathering of evangelical pastors in human history met in Atlanta, Georgia, in the Promise Keepers Clergy Conference.

Football coach Bill McCartney (b. 1940) founded Promise Keepers. McCartney met Christ as Savior through an organization under the umbrella of Campus Crusade for Christ in 1974. McCartney came to the University of Colorado to lead their football program from disarray to the national championship.

In March of 1990, after the Colorado Buffaloes had just won their national title, McCartney and his friend, Dave Wardell, conceived the Promise Keepers idea. Wardell taught in the physical education department at the university. McCartney recalled his passion: "More than anything, God has put in my heart to witness a tremendous outpouring of His Spirit among men. I envision men coming together in huge numbers in the name of Jesus, worshiping and celebrating their faith together. I long to see men openly proclaiming their love for Christ and their commitment to their families."[9]

Seventy-two men gathered with the same vision. They underscored the need for integrity if the movement was to honor Christ. They came to realize that integrity meant keeping one's word. So, Promise Keepers was born. The vision at first was to build a ministry to touch Colorado. At one point, Gary Smalley asked the men to pray about the possibility that this would become a national, even international ministry.

The next year, 4,200 gathered in Boulder, and the vision grew. It was about this time that the issue of racial reconciliation became a critical component in the movement. In 1992 some 22,000 met, followed by more than 50,000 in the summer of 1993. By 1994, more than 275,000 from every state gathered in seven arenas. In 1995 the number reached 720,000, an increase of 10,000 percent in five years! The figure topped 1.2 million in 1996. The movement encouraged men to hold one another accountable to deeper commitments to Christ, His church, and their families.

The Promise Keepers movement has waned in recent years. It was not synonymous with revival; however, many thousands of men have experienced personal revival, and more than a few churches have been touched afresh by God through the movement. In fact, one might argue that the movement was a specialized revival that touched the lives of countless men. McCartney himself had a vision for Promise Keepers to be a catalyst for awakening. "We have been called to be a spark in God's hand for a spiritual awakening in this country and around the world," McCartney claimed. "We want to sound the trumpet for genuine spiritual, biblical revival."[10] The materials produced and the vast meetings continually sounded the call for revival.

Promise Keepers was founded on "Seven Promises:"

> 1. A Promise Keeper is committed to honor Jesus Christ through worship, prayer, and obedience to God's Word through the power of the Holy Spirit.
>
> 2. A Promise Keeper is committed to pursue vital relationships with a few other men, understanding that he needs brothers to help him keep his promises.

3. A Promise Keeper is committed to practice spiritual, moral, ethical, and sexual purity

4. A Promise Keeper is committed to build strong marriages and families through love, protection, and biblical values.

5. A Promise Keeper is committed to support the mission of his church by honoring and praying for his pastor and by actively giving his time and resources.

6. A Promise Keeper is committed to reach beyond any racial and denominational boundaries to demonstrate the power of biblical unity.

7. A Promise Keeper is committed to influence his world, being obedient to the Great Commandment (Mark 12:30-31) and the Great Commission (Matt 28:19-20).

Other Significant Developments

At the end of the twentieth century, a variety of convocations, summits, and gatherings illustrate the continuing interest in spiritual awakenings. On February 14-17, 1995, the same week of the campus revival at Howard Payne University, the North American Convocation on Revival convened in Little Rock, Arkansas. Brothers Bill and Jim Elliff organized the meeting to focus on biblical, theological, and practical tenets of revival. Leaders from numerous denominations gathered to hear speakers including Richard Owen Roberts, Timothy George, Paul Cedar, David Bryant, and Dennis Kinlaw. Henry Blackaby spoke to the gathering, as well. He arrived directly from the Brownwood revival, bringing John Avant with him. On February 16, Avant described the Brownwood revival to the convocation. It was as if the Lord were saying, "This is how revival looks." The convocation met again in 1996.

Bill Bright of Campus Crusade for Christ observed a forty-day fast in late 1994 to call attention to spiritual awakening. In December he led in a three-day meeting focused on fasting and prayer. More than six hundred came to Orlando for the gathering. Another meeting was held in November 1995 and again in 1996. Of particular importance is the interest in fasting. In times of true revival, self-denial becomes a priority. Fasting, almost an unknown subject to many evangelicals only a decade ago, has suddenly become a subject of great interest.

In the annual sermon at the 1996 Southern Baptist Convention in New Orleans, Ronnie Floyd, pastor of the First Baptist Church of Springdale, Arkansas (now Cross Church), called the denomination to set aside October 30, 1996, as a day of fasting for revival. Thousands of church leaders responded to his appeal. Floyd observed a forty-day fast himself in 1995 and another in 1996. In an unprecedented move, 1996 SBC president Tom Elliff called for a day of prayer for awakening on the six SBC seminary campuses. More recently, Floyd has led pastor-focused prayer meetings calling for revival in our time. In January 2014, 374 pastors and other leaders met for two days of prayer for revival in Atlanta.

For the past several years, a movement called Passion has brought together thousands of young people to worship Jesus. Could this be a sign of the work of God afresh in our midst? A gospel recovery sweeps many churches with a renewed focus on exalting Christ throughout the Scripture and on the gospel's power in all areas of life. A missional movement and church planting movements illustrate the point that God continues to work among His people. At the same time, the fastest growing religious group in the United States is the "nones,"[11] and a rising tide of social unrest toward historic biblical views on issues like the sanctity of life and homosexuality test the conviction and compassion of followers of Christ.

As we stand in the early days of the third millennium, what should be the focus of prayer for contemporary churches concerning revival?

Is the greatest need family values, and thus the central request should concern the home?

Is moral rot our great enemy, so that our cry to God emphasizes a need for moral reformation?

Are the great social issues in our time worthy of our greatest affection, so that we lead churches to emphasize the fighting of injustice above all else?

Ethical restructuring as a primary focus leads to short-lived changes. History's shores are awash with shipwrecked ethical theories and utopian dreams. Other issues are good and important, but too often the good has taken the place of the best. Such changes are best accomplished when a greater focus captures our affections, the kind of affections only the Spirit of the Living God can inspire. Ethical solutions create moral changes that glorify activists; divine solutions create holy results that glorify God.

If we are to see an awakening in our day, let the revival for which we pray be a revival of holiness — a revival marked by an awesome respect for a sovereign God, gospel centrality, brokenness over sin, and a passion for the glory of God. Our survey of revivals throughout history has hopefully provided a foundation for an understanding of what happens when an outpouring of the Holy Spirit comes. While different details can be gleaned from various movements, one thing is constant: the holiness of a sovereign God.

May the God who flooded the temple in Isaiah's day fill our hearts today. Let us say with one voice: "Will you not revive us again, that your people may rejoice in you?" (Psalm 85:6, NIV).

Questions for Small Group Study

1. What is the one thing that keeps you from surrendering everything for Jesus?

2. What can you do as an individual, in your family, in your small group, and in your church to be in a position to set the sails where the Spirit moves?

3. Can you say that you genuinely hunger for a movement of God?

A Concluding Challenge
Ronnie Floyd

God is up to something special in America. As I left a recent prayer gathering with pastors and leaders, I am convinced more than ever that the Lord is stirring up men of God all across this nation. In another time God spoke through a pastor to stir revival in America. Puritan theologian and pastor Jonathan Edwards' treatise A *Humble Attempt to Promote Explicit Agreement and Visible Union in Extraordinary Prayer for the Revival of Religion and the Advancement of God's Kingdom* stirred believers in his day and in the generations following to seek God in revival.

From Edwards' writings three ideas speak to us today: the need for explicit agreement, visible union, and extraordinary prayer. We who know Jesus and love His gospel must come together, setting aside secondary matters to agree that He is our only hope to bring revival to the church and awakening to our nation. We must embrace visible union, showing the world we believe in a God who still moves in great power today. We must come together in extraordinary prayer, desperately seeking His face. And God is calling many to this in our time!

Seeing several hundred pastors and ministers crying out to God for revival and awakening at a recent gathering in Atlanta, with men lying on their faces in humility, pouring out their prayers not just for others, but for their own spiritual condition, and praying for one another, brought great joy and hope to us all.

Something happens when believers — and in particular the shepherds of God's flocks — come together to intercede for the churches of America. Many report personally developing a growing burden for the world to be reached for Jesus Christ. The answer in the church and in our nation for the issues we face is a major move of God. He is placing a strong burden and growing a sense of holy desperation in our midst. We are anticipating the next great move of God! This is occurring because of extraordinary prayer.

It was said of Jesus: "And he did not do many mighty works there, because of their unbelief." (Matthew 13:58 ESV) God is raising up a generation who do believe, who hunger for biblically-based, theologically-balanced, spiritually-empowered revival and awakening, so that we can see the Great Commission escalated as our priority and accelerated to its completion in our generation.

Pastors, gather your people to pray. Leader, call together those you lead to seek the Lord. We are now seeing churches set aside an entire Sunday morning worship service in order to pray in an extraordinary way. God is moving. We must reach this world for Jesus Christ. The hour is critical. The time is short. This is why we need to join together in extraordinary prayer. We are encouraged by reports of God's work in many churches in America and even more by testimonies across the globe; still, we are all aware of the great need for spiritual revival in the church. We need a fresh, mighty moving of God that awakens the church from spiritual slumber and moves us into an aggressive mobilization to see America and the world come to faith in Jesus Christ and Him alone for their eternal salvation.

Spiritual awakening can occur in America. This awakening is so needed. When God comes upon the church, the church is mobilized, resulting in great numbers of people coming to Jesus Christ. When this occurs, regions are impacted, families begin to live differently, cultures can be changed, and cities can be shaken for Christ.

"Oh, that you would burst from the heavens and come down!" (Isaiah 64:1 NLT)

For More Information

For speaking on the subject of revival, awakening, prayer, and evangelism, contact:

Malcolm McDow — Malcolmmcdow@yahoo.com

Alvin L. Reid — areid@sebts.edu
Website www.alvinreid.com
Twitter @alvinreid

Let It
Begin In Me
TURN // PRAY // UNITE
in humble repentance from every sin God reveals to us
with urgency for spiritual recovery and awakening
with other believers in spreading the hope of revival
ONECRY
A Nationwide Call for Spiritual Awakening
To learn more about OneCry and to join the movement, visit
www.OneCry.com
OneCry is a partnership led by Life Action Ministries
©2011 OneCry: A Nationwide Call for Spiritual Awakening. All rights reserved.

END NOTES

Chapter 1

1. Jonathan Edwards, *Puritan Sage: The Collected Writings of Jonathan Edwards,* ed. Vergilius Fern (New York: Library Publishers, 1953).
2. J.Edwin Orr, "Revival That Rocked the World," *Moody Monthly*, June 1986, 68-71; *The Outpouring of the Spirit in Revival and Awakening and Its Issue in Church Growth* (Pasadena, Calif.: by the author, 1984), 3-6; *The Fervent Prayer: The Worldwide Impact of the Great Revival of 1858* (Chicago: Moody Press, 1974); "Revival and Evangelism," *World Evangelization,* March 1985, 6-7. For a detailed discussion of Orr's view, see Douglas Munton, "The Contributions of Edwin On to an Understanding of Spiritual Awakenings," (Ph.D.diss., Southwestern Baptist Theological Seminary, 1991).
3. Frank Grenville Beardsley, *Religious Progress through Religious Revivals* (New York: American Tract Society, 1973), 170. Also see Beardsley, *A History of American Revivals*, 1st ed. (New York: American Tract Society,1912), passim.
4. Henry T. Blackaby and Claude V. King, *Fresh Encounter* (Nashville: Broadman & Holman, 1996), passim.
5. There are no attempts to go into the meanings of the Hebrew and Greek words outside the parameters of spiritual awakening. For example, *chodesh* refers to the sacred months in relation to religious festivals. These annual events were looked upon as times of refreshing and starting anew. However, one New Testament word that deserves mention is *eknepho*. It means "to be sober" and "to come to one's senses." This word conveys the idea that revival is the restoration to spiritual sanity. In Luke 15: 17, Jesus indicated that salvation is also a restoration to spiritual sanity.
6. For further discussion of these words, see Robert Young, *Analytical Concordance to the Bible*, 22nd. ed.(Grand Rapids, Mich.: Wm. B. Eerdmans Publishing Company, n.d.). Also see William Gesenius, *A Hebrew and English Lexicon of the Old Testament*, trans. Edward Robinson, 2 vols. (Oxford: The Clarendon Press, reprinted, 1952). See Gerhard Kittel, ed., *Theological Dictionary of the New Testament*, 10 vols. (Grand Rapids: William B. Eerdmans Publishing Company, reprinted, 1978).
7. When *Chalaph* is used as an intransitive, *hiphil*, it means "renewed." This usage is found in Job 14:7 and Isa.40:31, among others.
8. In Ps.85:6 the writer says, "Wilt thou not revive us again?" In Isa. 38:16 the word is used to express the idea "make me strong again."
9. This word and its derivatives occur five times in the New Testament: Heb.6:6; 2 Cor.4:16; Eph.4:23; Titus 3:5; and Rom. 12:2.
10. Earle Cairns, *An Endless Line of Splendor: Revivals and Their Leaders from the Great Awakening to the Present* (Wheaton, Ill.: Tyndale House, 1986), 22.
11. C. E. Autrey, *Revivals of the Old Testament* (Grand Rapids: Zondervan Publishing House,1960), 13.
12. Richard Owen Roberts, *Revival!* (Wheaton: Ill: Tyndale House, 1982),16-17.
13. Stephen Olford, *Heart Cry for Revival* (Westwood, N.J.: Fleming H. Revell, 1962), 17. For a study in the criticisms of revival, see William G. McLoughlin, Jr., *Modern Revivalism: Charles Grandison Finney to Billy Graham* (New York: Ronald Press, 1959), 339.
14. Orr, *Fervent Prayer*, vii.
15. Spiritual awakening is synonymous with living the Spirit-filled life. In Ephesians 5:19, one evidence of being filled with the Spirit (Eph. 5:18) is having a song, or joy, in the heart.

The Christian has three relationships: with God, others, and self. In revival, the Christian is in right relationship in all three areas.

16. See Albert Barnes, "Vindication of Revivals and Their Influence upon This Country," *The American National Preacher*, W.H. Bidwell, ed. (New York: Brick Church Chapel, 1841), 21. Second Great Awakening (1787-1843). These dates vary according to historians.

17. See J. Edwin Orr, *The Flaming Tongue* (Chicago: Moody Press,1973).

18. See Wesley L. Duewell, *Revival Fire* (Grand Rapids, Mich.: Zondervan Publishing House, 1995), passim.

19. Because of the lack of leadership and resistant from many churches, the Jesus Movement arguably did not enjoy the results that it could have had. The revival leader in Scripture who did not meet these standards was Jonah.

20. E. M. Bounds; *Power through Prayer* Grand Rapids, Mich. Zondervan Publishing House, 1970), 12.

21. Charles Finney, *Lectures on Revival of Religion* (n.p.: Fleming H. Revell Co., n.d.), 1. In the Old Testament, some of the Judean revivals occurred in the midst of reform. Even in reform, the spiritual declension was evident.

22. James Burns, *Revivals*: *Their Laws and Leaders*, (London: Hodder and Stoughton, 1909),32.

23. Ibid.

24. Jonathan Edwards, "Thoughts on the Revival of Religion in New England," in *The Complete Works of Jonathan Edwards*, ed. Sereno E. Dwight (Edinburgh:The Banner of Truth Trust,1834), passim.

25. Finney, *Lectures on Revival*, 5.

26. Burns, *Revivals*, 36.

27. Confessions of this nature are evidenced, among others, in the Jesus Movement. For an account of the confessions in the Asbury revival of 1970, see Robert Coleman, ed., *One Divine Moment* (Old Tappan, N.J.: Fleming H. Revell Company,1970).

28. The year 1770 is given in correlation with the death of George Whitefield. The work of Isaac Backus, Devereaux Jarrett, Daniel Marshall, and Shubal Stearns in the southern colonies was part of this awakening.

29. The date of 1787 is selected because of the spiritual movement at Hampden-Sydney.

30. This designation is given to this spiritual movement because it impacted every continent and many nations around the world. Some have called this the Revival of 1904-1908. However, the date of 1901-1910 is given in order to include the Pentecostal revival in America and other spiritual movements already in existence in 1904.

31. The Shantung Revival ignited with Marie Monsen as early as 1925. In 1927, C. L. Culpepper experienced revival. Great spiritual movements occurred from 1930 to 1935. The Second World War curtailed this revival. See C.L. Culpepper, *The Shantung Revival* (Dallas, Tex.: Crescendo Publications, Inc., 1971).

32. This designation is given to this revival because of the time frame. Its origin is set with the Billy Graham Los Angles Crusade in 1949. Many colleges and churches experienced renewal. It also includes, among others, the Hebrides Revival that ignited in 1949. Duncan Campbell became the revival leader of this movement. For a discussion of Campbell's leadership, see Andrew Woolsey, *Duncan Campbell* (London: Hodder and Stoughton, 1974). It also includes the Asbury Revival in 1958.

33. Burns, *Revivals*, 56.

34. W. B. Sprague, *Lectures on Revival in Religion* (Carlisle, Penn.: The Banner of Truth Trust, 1978),13.

35. Burns, *Revivals*, 23.

36. Brian Edwards, *Revival!* (Durham, England: Evangelical Press, 1994), 44.

Chapter 2

1. The tablets of Tel-el-Armana disclose the extensive education given to Egyptian royalty. In Acts 7:22, Stephen acknowledges Moses' education.
2. In 1Kings 12:38, Jeroboam, when he became king of the Northern Kingdom, erected the golden calf in Bethel and Dan as the method by which the Israelites would worship God.
3. D. Martyn Lloyd-Jones, *Revival* (Westchester, ILL: Crossway Books, 1987), 153, 157.
4. Jeroboam, Nadab, Baasha, Elah, Tibni, Zimri, Omri, and Ahab.
5. The Omride dynasty had three kings; Omri, Ahab, and Jehoram.
6. C.F. Keil and F. Delitzch, *Commentary of the Old Testament*, vol. 3 (Grand Rapids. Mich.: Wm. B. Eerdmans Publishers, reprint, 1976), 22.8
7. Simon DeVries, *Word Biblical Commentary* (Waco, Tex.: Word Book Publishers, 1985), 204.
8. Other names for Asherah were Astarte and Ashteroth.
9. Merrill Unger, *Unger's Bible Dictionary* (Chicago: Moody Press, 1974), 30.
10. Keil and Delitzch, *Commentary of the Old Testament*, Vol. 3, 244.
11. Ibid., 243.
12. Walter C. Kaiser, Jr., *The Quest for Renewal* (Chicago: Moody Press, 1986), 72.
13. Pfeiffer, *Old Testament History* (Grand Rapids: Baker, 1993), 331-343
14. John Calvin, *Jonah* in *Commentaries on the Twelve Minor Prophets trans.* John Owen (Grand Rapids, Mich.: Baker Book House, reprint 1979), 22.
15. David Noel Freedman, ed. *The Anchor Bible Dictionary* vol. 4, (New York: Doubleday, 1992), 1118.
16. Arthur Buttrick, ed., *The Interpreter's Bible Dictionary* vol. 2, (New York: Abingdon Press, 1962), 966. Also, see C.E. Autrey, *Renewals in the Old Testament* (Nashville: Broadman Press, 1968(, 71.
17. Keil and Delitzch, *Commentary of the Old Testament*, vol. 3, 390.
18. Calvin, *Jonah*, 22.
19. Cited in Keil and Delitzeh, *Commentary of the Old Testament*, vol.10, 380.
20. F. W. Farrar, *The Minor Prophets* (New York: Fleming H. Revell Company, n.d.), 236-37.
21. The entire biblical account of Jonah and Nineveh has become a battleground for critics. Instead of a historical account, the book of Jonah is looked upon by some as either legend, myth, poetry, drama, or some other type of literary production. In these views, the book contains moral lessons to be considered but not history to be accepted.
22. Josephus, *Antiquities*, IX, 10, 2. Adam Clark adopted this view. See Clark, 699
23. Calvin, *Jonah*, 29.
24. Freedman, *Anchor Bible Dictionary*, vol. 3, 938.
25. Farrar, *Minor Prophets*, 238.
26. Keil and Delitzch, *Commentary of the Old Testament*, vol. 10, 393.
27. The Hebrew word for "prepare" means "to count," "appoint," "designate," "ordain," or "set apart." This word can include the use of available natural means, or it can convey the idea of creation. It is the same word used in reference to the gourd or palchrist tree in chapter 4. Most writers conclude that God used an already existent creature for Jonah's reansportation.
28. The Hebrew word conveys the idea of utter destruction. The LXX says three days.
29. Lewis Drummond, *Eight Keys to Biblical Revival* (Minneapolis, Minn.: Bethany House Publishers, 1994), 130.

Chapter 3

1. There is no consensus as to the exact date of this revival. Contemporary writers date the death of Solomon from about 936 B.C. to 931 B.C. Rehoboam ruled for seventeen years. Abijah ruled for almost three years. The revival occurred in the fifteenth year of the reighn of ASA. This would place

the date from 901 B.C. to 896 B.C., approximately forty years prior to the revival at Carmel.
2. Only three of Solomon's chidren are mentioned by name in Scripture: Rehoboam, Taphath, and Basemath.
3. Fifteen cities are listed in 2 Chron. 11:5-12.
4. On the bas-relief in the Karnak Temple in Thebes, Shishak inscribed that he had conquered 180 cities. Josephus wrote that he conqured 150 cities.
5. Rehoboam had twenty-eight sons and sixty daughters. Although Abijah was not the oldest son, he was Rehoboam's favorite and was appointed to be successor to the throne (see 2 Chron. 11:21).
6. Only Asa is known by name among the twenty-two sons and sixteen daughters of Abijah.
7. In 2 Chron. 14:5, he removed high places to pagan gods, but in 2 Chro. 15:17, he left the high places to God.
8. The Hebrew language describes the army of Zerah as a thousand thousand which was the largest number used in the Old Testament to count the size of a military force.
9. When Pharaoh Neco led his forces to Haran, Judah's army under Josiah met the Egyptian military at Megiddo in 609 B.C. Josiah was killed in that battle (see 2 Chron. 35:20-24).
10. For a discussion of some of the views, see Spence and Excell, *Pulpit Commentary,* 182. Also see Keil and Delitzch, *Commentary on the Old Testament vol.* 3, 365.
11. Kaiser, *The Quest for Renewal*, 82.
12. Ibid.
13. Cited in Pfieffer, *Old Testament History*, 337.
14. Ibid.,338.
15. Freedman, 4:497.
16: Buttrick, *Interpreter's Bible Dictionary*, vol. 2,991.
17. Ernest Baker, *The Revivals of the Bible* (London: The Kingsgate Press, 1906), 77. Under Ezra and Nehemiah, it took twenty-one hours of reading; however, there were explanations by the priests as the Law was read.
18. James Orr, ed., *The International Standard Bible Encyclopedia*, vol. 7 (Grand Rapids, Mich.: Wm. B. Eerdmans Publishing Company, 1939), 1752-53.
19. Kaiser, *The Quest for Renewal,* lll.
20. Baker, *Revivals of the Bible*, 81.
21. Portions of the decrees are recorded in 2 Chron. 36:23 and Ezra 1:2-4. The god of Cyrus was Marduk.
22. Josephus, *Antiquities*, XI, 1, 3.
23. A copy of the letter is found in Josephus, *Antiquities*, XI, 1, 3.
24. Pfieffer, *Old Testament History*, 530.
25. The New Year for the Hebrews started April 1.
26. Revival ignited in this observance. However, the revival that is covered in this section is the renewal that occurred in 444 B.C. under the combined leadership of Ezra and Nehemiah.
27. Friedman, vol. 2, 727.
28. Geoffrey Bromiley, ed., *The International Standard Bible Dictionary* (Grand Rapids: Eerdmans, 1988), 3:264.
29. Josephus, *Antiquities*, XI, 5, 1.
30. The two books of Ezra and Nehemiah have been closely linked throughout history. They were listed as one book in the Talmud. Josephus acknowledged them as one book. In the LXX they were combined into one book called Esdras B. In the Jewish Scriptures they were entered as one book and separated into two books in A.D. 1448. In the Christian Bible they were recognized as two books in early Christianity. Origen (about A.D. 185-254) and Jerome (about A.D. 420) were aware of two separate books. See Dockery, 287. Also see Buttrick, *Interpreter's Bible Dictionary,* vol. 2, 215.

31. Friedman, vol. 2, 726.
32. Josephus, *Antiquities*, XI, 1, 5.
33. In 2 Maccabees 1:18, 21, he is referred to as a priest and was involved in sacrificial activity. If this was the case, he was from the tribe of Levi (see Neh.10:1-8). There is no biblical evidence to support the view that he was an eunuch (see Friedman, vol. 4, 1069; also see Bromiley, vol.3, 513).
34. Cited in Bromiley, vol. 3,513.
35. Friedman, vol. 4,1069.
36. Ibid.
37. Walls and gates in Old Testament culture were for physical protection, demonstrations of prosperity, and city pride. Pfieffer wrote, "A city with no walls was not a city at all." Pfieffer, *Old Testament History*, 531.
38. Josephus, *Antiquities*; XI, 5, 8.
39. For the biblical account of this revival, see Neh. 8:1-11:2.
40. Since several revivals occurred during the Feast of the Tabernacles, this assessment intensifies the impact of this awakening.
41. Maccabean activities are considered reform and not revival
42. Abraham had numerous encounters with God and His representatives.
Under the classification of personal revival, the offering of Isaac must be considered as a significant encounter with God.
43. Although there is room for discussion, these five renewals listed during the days of the judges are termed revivals because the nation returned to God. They are classified as national based upon the assumption that the judges impacted the entire nation and not simply a particular tribe.
44. The entire book of Ezekiel is a record of his visions and their applications.

Chapter 4

1. Emil Schurer, *A History of the Jewish People in the Time of Jesus Christ* (Peabody, MA: Hendrickson Publishers, 1994), 1:197-202; F. F. Bruce, *New Testament History* (New York: Doubleday, 1980), 56-58.
2. Gratus was succeeded as procurator by Pontius Pilate (26-36).
3. Bruce, *New Testament History*, 77.
4. Ibid., 75-76.
5. Josephus, *Antiquities*, XVII, 2, 4.
6. Cited in Bruce, *New Testament History*, 83.
7. Ibid., 84.
8. For a detailed discussion of the Essenes, see Josephus, *Antiquities* XVIII, 1, 5.
9. Henk Jagersma, *A History of Israel from Alexander the Great to Bar Kochba* (Philadelphia: Fortress Press, 1986), 103.
10. In Mark 3:19 and Matt. 10:4, he is called the Cananaean.
11. Merrill Tenney, *New Testament Times* (Grand Rapids, Mich.: Wm. B. Eerdmans Publishing Company, 1965), 140. Also see Bruce, *New Testament History, 153.*
12. Josephus shared this interpretation of John's baptism. See Josephus, *Antiquites*, XVIII, 5, 2.
13. P. T. Forsyth, *The Soul of Prayer* (London: Independent Press, 1954) , 11.
14. Ibid., 12.
15. For a chronological sequence of events surrounding the resurrection, see John Wenham, *The Easter Enigma* (Exeter, England: The Paternoster Press, 1984). For a discussion on the evidences of the Resurrection, see Jonathan Dodson and Brad Watson, *Raised? Finding Jesus by Doubting the Resurrection* (Grand Rapids: Zondervan, 2014); Frank Morison, *Who Removed the Stone?* (Grand Rapids, Mich.: Zondervan Publishing House, 1930); Josh

McDowell, *The Resurrection Factor* (San Bernadino, Calif.: Here's Life Publishers, Inc., 1981); and Frank Harber, *Beyond a Reasonable Doubt* (Lynchburg, Va.: Liberty House Publishers, 1996).
16. John R. W. Stott, *The Spirit, the Church and the World* (Downers Grove: Intervarsity Press, 1990), 60.
17. Allen Myers, ed., *The Eerdmans Bible Dictionary* (Grand Rapids, Mich.: William B. Eerdmans Publishing Company, 1987), 1058.
18. Justin Martyr, *The First Apology in Saint Justin Martyr,* trans. Thomas Falls, *The Fathers of the Church* (Washington, D.C.: The Catholic University Press, 1948), 61. Some scholars believe that Justin confused Simon Magus with Semo Sanctus. See also Irenaeus, *Against Heresies in Five Books of Saint Irenaeus,* trans. John Keble (London:James Parker and Company, 1872), 203.
19. Stott, *The Spirit, the Church and the World,* 306.
20. Cited in Ivor Powell, *The Amazing Acts* (Grand Rapids, Mich.: Kregel Publications, 1987), 337.

Chapter 5
1. John Gillies, *Accounts of Revival* (1754; reprint Edinburgh: Banner of Truth, 1981), v.
2. Cited in Gillies, 9.
3. Alexander Roberts and James Donaldson, *Ante-Nicene Fathers*, vol. I (Peabody, Mass.: Hendricksen Publishers, 1994), 309.
4. Cited in Johannes Quasten, *Patrology*, vol. I(Westminster, Md.: Christian Classics, Inc., 1993), 287.
5. Roberts and Donaldson, *Ante-Nicene Fathers* 313. Gregory of Tours (d. 594) also mentioned that he was a martyr.
6.. Williston Walker, et al., *A History of the Christian Church*, 4th ed. (New York: Charles Scribner's Sons, 1985), 62.
7. Charles Kannengiesser, ed., Early Christian Spirituality, trans. Pamela Bright in *Sources of Christian Thought, ed. William G. Rusch (Philadelphia: For*tress Press, 1986), 5.
8. Eusebius, 202. The entire letter is contained in this source, 193-203.
9. Ibid., 199.
10. Roberts and Donaldson, *Ante-Nicene Fathers*, vol. 1, 310.
11. Ibid., vol. 6, 3. Some writers attempt to set his birth in 213.
12. Ibid., 4.
13. F. L. Cross, *The Early Christian Fathers* (London: Gerald Duckworth and Co., Ltd., 1960}, 175.
14. For a discussion of his ministry of miracles, see Roberts and Donaldson, *Ante-Nicene Fathers* vol. 6, 6.
15. W. H.C. Frend, *The Early Church* (London: SCM Press, 1982), 59-60.
16. V. Raymond Edman, *The Light in Dark Ages* (Wheaton, Ill.: Van Kamper Press, 1949), 97.
17. For a study of the legends of Patrick, see Ludwig Bieler, *The Life and Legends of St. Patrick* (Dublin: Clonmore and Reynolds, Ltd., 1949), 108-25.
18. Paul Gallico, *The Steadfast Man: A Biography of St. Patrick* (New York: Doubleday, 1958), 31.
19. Cited in Bieler, *Life and Legends*, 21.
20. Ibid., 25.
21. Mendell Taylor, *Exploring Evangelism* (Kansas City, Mo.: Beacon Hill Press, 1964), 93.
22. Bieler, *Life and Legends*, 28.

23. For a discussion of the rituals contained within Druid paganism, see Lucy Menzies, *Saint Columba of Iona* (London:]. M. Dent and Sons, Ltd., 1920), 84-100.
24. Gallico, 92.
25. Ibid., 92-95.
26. For a discussion of the miracles, see James O'Leary, *The Most Ancient Life of Saint Patrick* (New York: P.]. Kennedy, 1881), 135ff.
27. Taylor, *Exploring Evangelism*, 95. The most accepted date for his death was 461. Some date his death in 492.
28. Ibid.
29. Ian Finlay, *Columba* (London: Victor Gollancz, Ltd., 1979), 53. Other historians indicate uncertainty about the date of his birth.
30. Approximately a century after Columba's death, Adamnan, the ninth abbot of Iona, wrote a biography of his life that described numerous miracles he performed. Although the work is not considered reliable as a history in all areas, it does give many insights into the man and his ministry.
31. Taylor, *Exploring Evangelism*, 96. Columba died while on his knees in prayer.
32. Finlay, *Columba*, 123.
33. Ibid.
34. Cited in Finlay, *Columba*, 121.
35. Augustine of Canterbury is not to be confused with Augustine of Hippo (354-430).
36. Bede, *A History of the English Church and People*, translated by Leo Sherly-Price and revised by R. E. Latham (London: Penguin Books, 1965), 66.
37. Henry Howorth, Saint Augustine of Canterbury (London:]ohn Murray, 1913), 30.
38. Henry C. Sheldon, *History of the Christian Church* (5 vols.; New York:Thomas Y. Crowell, 1985), 2:29.
39. Bede, *Ecclesiastical History*, 88.
40. F. F Bruce, *The Spreading Flame* (Grand Rapids: Eerdmans, 1995), 404.
41. Ibid.
42. Howorth, *Saint Augustine*, 71.
43. Sheldon, *History*, 2:30-31. See Bruce, *The Spreading Flame*, 404-6.
44 .Bruce, *The Spreading Flame*, 406.
45. Sheldon, *History*, 2:32.
46. Kenneth Scott Latourette, *A History of the Expansion of Christianity* (7 vols; New York: Harper, 1937-45), 1:344-45.
47. Ibid.
48. Bruce, *The Spreading Flame*, 408.
49. Cairns, *Christianity Through the Centuries*, 177.
50. Sheldon, *History*, 2:38.
51. Christopher Dawson, ed., "Charles Martel Takes Boniface Under His protection," in *The Anglo-Saxon Missionaries in Germany*, trans. C. H. Talbot (New York: Sheedand Ward, 1954), 75.
52. Ibid., 61-62.
53. Sheldon, *History*, 2:41-41.
54. Latourette, *Expansion*, 1:349.

Chapter 6

1. For a discussion of his birth, see Emilio Comba, *History of the Waldenses of Italy* (London: Truslove and Shirley, 1889), 18-19.
2. Giorgio Toum, The *Waldensians* (Torino, Italy: Claudiana, 1980), 5. Also see Comba, *History of the Waldenses*; 20-21.

3. Cited in Tourn, *The Waldensians*, 6. Also see Comba, History of the Waldenses, 23-24.
4. Comba, *History of the Waldenses*, 28.
5. Ibid.
6. Ibid.,38.
7. Ibid.,36.
8. G. S. M. Walker, *The Growing Storm*, 143.
9. Phillip Schaff and David Schaff, *History of the Christian Church* (8 vols., 15th ed; Grand Rapids: Eerdmans, 1950), 6:512-14.
10. John Holland Smith, *Francis of Assisi* (New York: Charles Scribner's Sons,1972), 16,
11. Omer Englebert, *Saint Francis of Assissi* (London: Burn Gates, 1950), 56.
12. Ibid., 57.
13. Burns, *Revivals*, 90.
14. Ibid., 91-92. Peter Bernardone apparently died before 1212.
15. Bums, *Revivals*, 93.
16. Englebert, 75.
17. Bums, *Revivals*, 94.
18. Eric Doyle, *St. Francis and the Song of Brotherhood* (New York: The Seabury Press, 1981), 19.
19. G. S. M. Walker, *The Growing Storm*, 183.
20. The original words and musical score of this song are found in Doyle, 206-07.
21. Bums, *Revivals*, 108.
22. Ibid., 109.
23. Doyle, *Song of Brotherhood*, 26.
24. Ibid., 26-27.
25. Waldo Beach and H. Richard Niebuhr, *Christian Ethics: Sources of Christian Tradition* (New York: The Ronald Press Company, 1955), 162-63.
26. Marion A. Habig, ed., *Saint Francis of Assisi*: Writings and Early Biographies (Chicago: Franciscan Herald Press, 1973), xiv. For a discussion of the canonization, see Father Cuthbert, *Life of St. Francis of Assisi* (London: Longmans, Green and Co., 1956),464.
27. For a discussion of English mystics, see David Knowles, *The English Mystics* (New York: Benziger Brothers, 1927). Also of note is the mystic Gerhard Groote, (1340-84) founder of the Brothers of the Common Life. He, too, served as a revival leader. His spiritual diary is contained in the book Gerhard Groote, *The Following of Christ*, translated by Joseph Malaise (New York: American Press, 1937). This diary influenced Thomas a Kempis in his composition of Imitation of Christ.
28. James Clark, *The Great German Mystics* (Oxford: Basil Blackwell, 1949), 36.
29. Cited in Schaff and Schaff, *History*, 6:257.
30. Ibid.
31. G. S. M. Walker, *The Growing Storm*, 192. This pestilence broke out in 1345 in Asia, spread to Africa, and ultimately to Europe in 1348. It broke out in England in August 1348 at Dorchester. Also see Charles Webb La Bas, *The Life of Wiclif*(London: J. G. &: F. Rivington, 1832), 98.
32. Schaff and Schaff, *History*, 6:258.
33. Ibid., 258-59.
34. G. S. M. Walker, *The Growing Storm*, 212.
35. Roland Bainton, *The Medieval Church* (Malabar, Fla.: Robert E. Krieger Publishing Company, reprint, 1985), 175-76.
36. G. S. M. Walker, *The Growing Storm*, 212.
37. Schaffand Schaff, *History*, 6:260.

38. Ibid., 261.
39. Ibid.
40. Andrew Weeks, *German Mysticism from Hildebrand of Bingen to Ludwig Wittgenstein* (Albany, N. Y.: State University of New York Press, 1993), 98.
41. Warren Wiersbe and Lloyd Perry, *The Wycliffe Handbook of Preaching and Preachers* (Chicago: Moody Press, 1984), 174. "Wyclif" has been spelled in more than thirty different ways. See Joseph Dahmus, The Prosecution of John Wyclif (New Haven: Yale University Press, 1952), vii.
42. Le Bas, *Life of Wiclif*, 94.
43. Cited in ibid., 95-96.
44. Cited in ibid., 96.
45. Estep, *Renaissance and Reformation*, 64.
46. Dyson Hague, *The Life and Work of John Wycliffe* (London: The Church Book Room, 1935), 121.
47. Louis Brewer Hall, *The Perilous Vision of John Wyclif* (Chicago: Nelson-Hall, 1983), 261.
48. Henry Lucas, *The Renaissance and the Reformation*, 2nd ed. (New York: Harper and Row., Publishers, 1960), 119-122.
49. J. C. Carrick, Wycliffe and the Lollards (Edinburgh: T. &: T. Clark, 1908), 190.
50. For a detailed discussion of the Lollards and their ministry, see Anne Hudson, *The Premature Reformation: Wycliffe Texts and Lollard History* (Oxford:Clarendon Press, 1988).
51. Hague, *Life and Work*, 170. The term has also been defined as "mumblers of prayers," "mutterers," or "tares."
52. Carrick, *Wycliffe and the Lollards*, 199.
53. La Bas, *Life of Wiclif*, 385.
54. Ibid.,374. For a discussion of some of the names of the Lollards and their ministries, see La Bas, 369-406. Also see Carrick, *Wycliffe and the Lollards,* 199-300. Although some of the original Lollards recanted, the movement existed until the sixteenth century when they joined the reformers.
55. Lucas, *The Renaissance and the Reformation*, 122.
56. Estep, *Renaissance and Reformation*, 69.
57. Ibid.
58. Ibid., 71.
59. Piero Misciattelli, *Savonarola* (New York: D. Appleton and Company, 1930), 7.
60. Ibid., 8.
61. Pasquale Villari, *Life and Times of Girolamo Savonarola* (New York: Charles Scribner's Sons, 1888),14.
62. For a copy of the letter, see Misciattelli, *Savonarola*, 19-22. For a discussion of the conditions of the age, see Villari, *Life and Times*, 22-29.
63. Misciattelli, *Savonarola*, 46.
64. Ibid., 47.
65. Ibid.
66. Ibid., 50.
67. William H. Crawford, *Girolamo Savonarola: A Prophet of Righteousness* (New York: Eaton and Mains, 1907), 77.
68. Burns, *Revivals*, 138-39.
69. Misciattelli, *Savonarola*, 52-53.
70. Ibid., 53.
71. Ibid., 71-74.
n. Roberto Ridolfi, *The Life of Girolamo Savonarola* (Westport, Conn. : Greenwood Press,

1952),43.
73. Ibid., 71.
74. Pierre Van Passen, *A Crown of Fire: The Life and Times of Girolamo Savonarola* (New York: Charles Scribner's Sons, 1960), 180-81.
75. Ibid., 189.
76. Ibid., 190-91.
77. Michael de la Bedoyere, *The Meddlesome Friar* (London: Collins, 1958), 34.
78. Ridolfi, *Life of Girolamo Savonarola*, 98.
79. William Clark, *Savonarola: His Life and Times* (Chicago: A. C. McClurg and Company, 1890), 283-85.
80, Ibid., 286.
81. Ridolfi, *Life of Girolamo Savonarola*, 139. While the crowds gathered in the plaza, a thousand women who were members of his church gathered at San Marco to pray.
82. Ibid., 248.
83. Ibid., 270.
84. Ibid.
85. Burns, *Revivals*, 56.
86. Cited in Van Passen, *Crown of Fire*, xviii.

Chapter 7

1. *Here I Stand: A Life of Martin Luther* (Nashville: Abingdon Press, 1950), 185. Luther's famous "Here I stand, I can do no other" quote has been brought into serious disrepute by recent scholarship. His comment concerning his conscience being captive to the Word of God has far more substantive support.
See http://www.christianitytoday.com/ch/news/2002/apr12.html (accessed 4-22-2014).
2. Williston Walker and others, *A History of the Christian Church*, 4th edition (New York: Charles Scribner's Sons, 1985), 439.
3. Ibid, 458.
4. Cunliffe-Jones, Hubert, ed., *A History of Christian Doctrine* (Philadelphia:Fortress Press, 1978), 318.
5. Cunliffe-Jones, 318.
6. Alistair McGrath, *Reformation Thought* (Oxford: Blackwell, reprint, 1993), 103.
7. A list of the theses can be found in John Dillenberger,ed., *Martin Luther: Selections from His Writings* (New York: Doubleday and Company, Inc., 1961), 490-500.
8. For a detailed discussion of Luther's views on justification by faith, see McGrath, *Reformation Thought*, 87-119.
9. Ibid., 93-94.
10. McGrath, *Reformation Thought*, 137.
11. Geddes MacGregor, *A Literary History of the Bible* (Nashville: Abingdon Press, 1968), 68.
12. Margaret Deansley, *The Lollard Bible and Other Medieval Biblical Versions* (Cambridge: University Press, 1920), 18.
13. G. S. Wegner, *6000 Years of the Bible* (New York: Harper and Row, 1963), 184.
14. Ibid., 206.
15. Timothy George, *Theology of the Reformers* (Nashville: Broadman, 1988), 53.
16. Ibid., 156.
17. Schaff and Schaff,*History*, 7:495.
18. Luther published hymnals in 1524, 1529, 1542, and 1545.
19. Schaff and Schaff, *History*, 7:503.
20. Cited in M. Michelet, *The Life of Martin Luther* (New York: D. W. Evans &: Co., n.d.),

194.
21. Ibid., 195.
22. Estep, *Renaissance and Reformation*, 155.
23. Carter Lindberg, *The European Reformations* (Cambridge, Mass.: Blackwell Publishers, 1996), 169.
24. George, *Theology of the Reformers*, 114.
25. Cited in ibid.., 179.
26. Ibid., 124.
27. Ibid., 118.
28. Ibid., 158.
29. Cunliffe-]ones, *History of Christian Doctrine*, 368.
30. McGrath, *Reformation Thought*, 140.
31. George, *Theology of the Reformers*, 233.
32. John Calvin, *Institutes of the Christian Religion*, ed. Henry Beveridges (Grand Rapids: William B. Eerdmans, n.d.), 2:233.
33. Ibid., 180.
34. For discussions, see Daniel L. Akin, ed., *A Theology for the Church* (Nashville: Broadman & Holman, 2007); James Leo Garrett, *Systematic Theology: Biblical, Historical, and Evangelical*, vol. 1 (Grand Rapids, Mich.: William B. Eerdmans Publishing Company, 1990), 248-49; 513-14; Millard Erickson, *Christian Theology* (Grand Rapids, Mich.: Baker Book House, 1994), 354-55, 633-36, 907-21; John Wallace, *"The Evangelistic Expression of the Doctrine of Saving Faith within the Southern Baptist Heritage to 1925,"* (Ph.D. diss., Southwestern Baptist Theological Seminary, 1994). Also see Cunliffe-Jones, History of Christian Doctrine, 387-99.
35. Justo Gonzalez, *The Story of Christianity* (San Francisco: Harper Collins,1985), 2:56.
36. Lindberg, *European Refomations*, 199.
37. William Estep, *The Anabaptist Story*, 3rd ed. (Grand Rapids, Mich.: William B. Eerdmans Publishing Company, 1996), 15.
38. Ibid., 13-14.
39. Cited in Lindberg, *European Reformations*, 208.
40. Estep, *The Anabaptist Story*, 38.
41. Ibid., 39.
42. Gonzalez, vol. 2, 56.
43. Estep, *The Anabaptist Story*, 42.
44. Ibid., 52.
45. Estep, *Renaissance and Reformation*, 186-87.
46. Frank Harber, "An Examination of the Historical Development of the Ministry of the Evangelist within the Christian Church" (Ph.D. diss.: Southwestern Baptist Theological Seminary, 1994), 61.
47. Estep. *The Anabaptist Story*, 53.
48. Paulus Scharpff, *History of Evangelism* (Grand Rapids Mich.: William B. Eerdmans Publishing Company, 1964), 16-17. Estep noted that he baptized 10,252. See Estep, *The Anabaptist Story*, 175.
49. Ibid., 17.
50. Estep, *Renaissance and Reformation*, 207.
51. Ibid., 211-212.
52. John Allen Moore, *Anabaptist Portraits* (Scottsdale, Penn: Herald Press, 1984), 240-41.
53. Estep, *Renaissance and Reformation*, 216.
54. Moore, *Anabaptist Portraits*, 241.
55. Ibid., 57.
56. Moore, *Anabaptist Portraits*, 118-19.

57. Ibid.,119.
58. Quoted in Bainton, *The Reformation of the Sixteenth Century* (Boston: Beacon Press, 1952), 102.
59. For a discussion of the leaders, see Estep, *The Anabaptist Story.*
60. Estep, *Renaissance and Reformation*, 218.
61. Ibid.
62. Estep, *The Anabaptist Story*, 107-8.
63. Ibid, 108.
64. Ibid.
65. Roland Bainton, *Studies in the Reformation* (Boston: Beacon Press, 1963), 206,
66. John Knox extended Calvin's theology and reforms to Scotand.

Introduction to Part Two

1. Lauren Sandler, *Righteous: Dispatches from the Evangelical Youth Movement* (New York: Viking, 2006), 11.
2. Kenneth Scott Latourette, *Advance Through the Storm: AD 1914 and After, With Concluding Generalizations* (vol. 7 of A History of the Expansion of Christianity; New York: Harper & Brothers, 1945), 487.
3. Mark Shaw, Global Awakening: How 20th Century Revivals Triggered a Christian Revolution (Downers Grove: IVP, 2010), 27.
4. Sandler, *Righteous*, 12.
5. Timothy J. Keller, *Center Church: Doing Balanced, Gospel-Centered Ministry in Your City* (Grand Rapids: Zondervan, 2012), 54-55. Kindle Edition.
6. Jonathan Edwards, "Narrative of Surprising Conversions...." In *The Works of Jonathan Edwards*, ed. Sereno E. Dwight (1834, Reprint, Banner of Truth Trust, n.d.), I:347.
7. Michael Green, *Evangelism in the Early Church* (Grand Rapids: Eerdmans, 1970), 275.

Chapter 8

1. *The Autobiography of Richard Baxter*, ed. N.H. Keeble (London: Dent Pub lishers, 1974), 79.
2. Williston Walker, *A History of the Christian Church*, 4th edition (New York: Charles Scribner's Sons, 1985), 569.
3. Colin Brown, *Philosophy and the Christian Faith* (Downers Grove, Ill.: InterVarsity Press), 55.
4. Colin A. Russell, *Cross-Currents: Interactions between Science and Faith* (Grand Rapids: Eerdmans, 1985), 94.
5. Gonzalez, *The Story of Christianity*, 2:190. Source cited in Gonzalez, vol. 2. Italics added.
6. Gillies, *Accounts of Revival*. Gillies recorded example after example of men influenced by Perkins.
7. Cairns, *Christianity Through the Centuries*, 339. 8. *Gillies, Accounts of Revival*, 124.
9. Gillies, *Accounts of Revival*, 126.
10. William Estep, *Revolution Within the Revolution* (Grand Rapids, Mich.: William B. Eerdrnans Publishing Company, 1990), 62.
11. Gillies, *Accounts of Revival*, 157.
12. Philip Spener, *Pia Desideria* (Philadelphia: Fortress Press, 1964). This publication remains in print.
13. Shaw, *Global Awakening*, 27.
14. Lewis A. Drummond, "The Puritan-Pietist Tradition: Its Meaning, History, and Influence in Baptist Life," *Review and Expositor* 77 (1980): 485-86.
15. The fourfold categorization is adapted from "The Roots and Branches of Pietism," *Christian History* 5, no. 2:19.
16. Gillies, *Accounts of Revival*, 237.
17. Mendell Taylor, *Exploring Evangelism* (Kansas City: Beacon Hill Press, 1964), 228.

18. Cited in ibid.
19. Gillies, *Accounts of Revival*, 244.
20. Ernst Benz, "Pietist and Puritan Sources of Early Protestant World Missions (Cotton Mather and A.H. Francke)," *Church History* 20 June, 1951): 29.
21. Scharpff, *History of Evangelism*, 26.
22. Ibid., 27.
23. Ibid., 37.
24. W. R. Ward, "The Renewed Unity of the Brethren: Ancient Church, New Sect or Interconfessional Movement?" *Bulletin of the John Rylands University Library of Manchester* 70, no. 3 (autumn 1988): 77.
25. Jonathan Edwards, "Thoughts on the Revival of Religion," in *Complete Works*, I:135.
26. From "The Brotherly Agreement of the Brethren from Bohemia and Mora- via and Others, Binding Them to Walk According to the Apostolic Rule," in A. J. Lewis, *Zinzendorf the Ecumenical Pioneer* (London: SCM Press Ltd., 1962), 53.
27. "Did You Know?" *Christian History*, vol. 5, no. 2:6.
28. Arnold Dallimore, *George Whitefield: The Life and Times of the Great Evangelist of the Eighteenth Century Revival* (Edinburgh: Banner of Truth Trust, 1980), 2:325-332.
29. This unfortunate conclusion can be seen in the Pietist influence on Friedreich Schleiermacher. Schleiermacher considered himself to stand in the heritage of Pietism, yet his theological views led him to become dubbed the Father of Modern Liberalism. While Pietism began as an effort to complete the Reformation, adding orthopraxy to orthodoxy, it ultimately led many to an overemphasis on experience to the neglect of biblical conviction. See Bennie Dale Craver, "The Divine Govemment of the World: The Function of Providence in the Theology of Friedrich Schleiermacher" (Ph.D diss., Southwestern Baptist Theological Seminary, 1994), 80-138, for an elaboration of the influence of Pietism on Schleiermacher. Also Philip Jacob Spener, *Von der Wiedergeburt*, ed. Hans-Georg Feller (Stuttgart:]. F. Steinkopf Verlag, 1963).
30. J. M. Bumstead, ed., *The Great Awakening: The Beginnings of Evangelical Pietism in America* (Waltham, Mass.: Blaisdell Publishing Company, 1970), 1.

Chapter 9

1. From a letter of John Wesley responding to a critic of the awakening in 1749, in Arthur Skevington Wood *John Wesley: The Burning Heart* (Grand Rapids: William B. Eerdmans, 1967), 179.
2. W. H. Fitchett, *Wesley and His Century* (London: Smith, Elder &: Co., 1906), 139. For a detailed description of the deplorable conditions, see Dallimore, *George Whitefield*, 1:19-32.
3. Robert G. Tuttle, *John Wesley: His Life and Theology* (Grand Rapids: Zondervan Publishing House, 1978), 35-36.
4. J. W. Bready, *England Before and After Wesley* (New York: Harper Publishing Co.,
1938), 87.
5. Earle E. Cairns, *Christianity Through the Centuries* (Grand Rapids: Zondervan Publishing House, 1954), 416.
6. Percy Livingstone Parker, ed., *The Heart of John Wesley's Journal* (New York: Fleming H. Revell Co., 1903), 1.
7. John Drakeford, ed., *John Wesley* (Nashville: Broadman Press, 1979), 15.
8. Edwards, *Revival*, 60.
9. John Wesley, *The Journal of John Wesley*, ed. Nehemiah Curnock (London: The Epworth Press, 1938), 1:475- 76.
10. Wood, *John Wesley*, 74.
11. Dallimore, *George Whitefield*, 1:73. Whitefield's life has been greatly neglected compared to John Wesley. An older biography is Luke Tyerman, *The Life of the Rev. George Whitefield*; 2 vols. (London: Hodder and Stoughton, 1876-77).
12. Taken from *Christian History*, 12, no.2: 6, 28.

13. Ibid., 1:140.
14. Duewel, *Revival Fire*, 95.
15. George Whitefield, *The Journals of George Whitefield* (Edinburgh: Banner of Truth, Reprint, 1960), 216.
16. Gordon Langley Hall, *The Sawdust Trail: The Story of American Evangelism* (Philadelphia: MaCrae Smith Company, 1964), 39.
17. Wood, *The Burning Heart*, 97.
18. Wesley, *Journal*,11:121-22.
19. Taylor, *Exploring Evangelism*, 254-55.
20. Dallimore's biography, *George Whitefield*; contains the text to both documents.
21. Occasionally I meet people who question whether one can be a Calvinist and evangelistic. Whitefield is one of many Calvinists, including Jonathan Edwards and Charles Spurgeon, who were committed to evangelism. The two are not mutually exclusive, although hyper-Calvinism has injured evangelism at times.
22. Cited in *Christian History* 38, no. 2:2.
23. Duewel, *Revival Fire*, 64.
24. John Telford, ed., *The Letters of John Wesley* (London: The Epworth Press, 1931), 238-39.
25. Albert C. Outler, ed., *A Library of Protestant Thought* (New York: Oxford University Press, 1964), 178.
26. Ibid., 28.
27. Ibid., 178.
28. Drakeford, *John Wesley*, 347.
29. Cited in Ibid., 181.
30. Ibid., 328-29.
31. Wood, *John Wesley*, 154.
32. John S. Simon, *The Revival of Religion in England in the Eighteenth Century* (London: Robert Culley, n.d.), 136.
33. Edwards, *Revival*, II. Effion Evans said Rowland "was God's chief instrument of revival in Wales." In Evans, *Daniel Rowland and the Great Evangelical Awakening in Wales* (Edinburgh: Banner of Truth, 1985), xii.
34. Dallimore, *George Whitefield*, 1:239.
35. James Sallee, *A History of Evangelistic Hymnody* (Grand Rapids: Baker, 1978), 13.
36. Hugh McElrath, "Music in the History of the Church," *Review and Expositor* 69 (Spring 1972): 156.
37. Donald Paul Ellsworth, *Christian Music in Contemporary Witness* (Grand Rapids: Baker, 1979), 86.
38. Taylor, *Exploring Evangelism*, 284.
39. Cited in Beardsley, *Religious Progress through Religious Revivals*, 24-25.

Chapter 10

1. "An Humble Attempt to Promote Explicit Agreement and Visible Union of God's People in Extraordinary Prayer for the Revival of Religion and the Advancement of Christ's Kingdom on Earth," in *The Complete Works of Jonathan Edwards*, ed. Sereno Dwight (Edinburgh: The Banner of Truth Trust, Reprint: 1986), II:294.
2. Alan Heimert and Perry E. Miller, *The Great Awakening* (New York: The Bobbs-Merrill Company, 1967), xvii.
3. The author recognizes that to an extent dead orthodoxy or deviant orthodoxy are oxymorons — one cannot be a truly orthodox Christian and either deny the truth or live a spiritually dulled life. However, the terms are used to emphasize the essential and critical situation facing the American churches in the early 1705.

4. Perry E. Miller, *The New England Mind: From Colony to Province* (Cambridge, Mass.: Harvard University Press), 19.
5. A collection of fast day sermons in print is Richard Owen Roberts, ed., *Sanctify the Congregation. A Call to the Solemn Assembly and to Corporate Repentance* (Wheaton: International Awakening Press, 1994).
6. Mark A. Noll, ed., *Christianity in America* (Grand Rapids: Eerdrnans, 1983), 41.
7. Whitefield, *Journals*, 352.
8. Cited from a sermon in "Theodore Jacob Frelinghuysen in the Middle Colonies," *Christian History* no.23, 10.
9. Martin E. Lodge, "Great Awakening of the Middle Colonies" (Ph.D. diss., University of California, 1964),
10. Whitefield, *Journals*, 354.
11. Gary E. Schnittjer, "The Ingredient of Effective Mentoring: The Log College as a Model for Mentorship," *Christian Education Journal*, 15, no. 1 (fall 1994): 87.
12. "Frelinghuysen in the Middle Colonies," 11.
13. Joseph Tracy, *The Great Awakenin: A History of the Revival of Religion* (Boston: Tappan and Dennett, 1842), 53.
14. For more on the preaching of Tennent or the conflict among Presbyterians, see Sweet, *Colonial America*, 279; Trinterud, *American Tradition*, 59-60; and George M. Stephenson, *The Puritan Heritage* (New York: The Macmillan Co., 1952), 56.
15. Biographies of Edwards include George Marsden, *Jonathan Edwards: A Life* (New Haven: Yale University, 2003); Alexander V. G. Allen, *Jonathan Edwards* (Cambridge: The Riverside Press, 1889); Conrad Cherry, *The Theology of Jonathan Edwards: A Reappraisal* (Garden City: Doubleday and Company, Inc., 1966); and Perry E. Mille, *Jonathan Edwards* (New York: William Sloane Associates, 1949).
16. The writings of Edwards have extremely long titles, thus abbreviated names are used in the text.
17. Miller, *Jonathan Edwards*, 137.
18. Allen, *Jonathan Edwards* , 134.
19. Jonathan Edwards, "Faithful Narrative of Surprising Conversions…." in *Complete Works*, I: 349.
20. Ola Winslow, *Jonathan Edwards, 1703-.1758* (New York: Macmillan, 1941), 134.
21. Jonathan Edwards, "Sinners in the Hands of an Angry God," in *Complete Works*, I1: 10.
22. Alien, *Jonathan Edwards*, 127.
23. "Memoirs of Jonathan Edwards," in *Complete Works*, l: lix.
24. From "Distinguishing Marks," in *Complete Works*, II: 266-68.
25. Jonathan Edwards, "Some Thoughts," in *Complete Works*, 1: 366.
26. The minutes of the council's meeting made the point that the only issue was church membership, that Edwards was considered a fine Christian, and would be heartily recommended to any church with like sentiments on the issue. The account of his dismissal can be read in William J. Schiek, ed., *Critical Essays on Jonathan Edwards* (Boston: G. K. Hall and Company, 1980), 3-7.
27. Jonathan Edwards, ed. "The Life and Diary of the Rev. David Brainerd," in *Complete Works*, II:347.
28. An excellent assessment of these accounts is found in Michael Crawford, *Seasons of Grace: Colonial New England's Revival Tradition in Its British Context* (New York: Oxford Press, 1991).
29. Richard Warsh, "Introduction," in Charles Chauncy, *Seasonable Thoughts on the State of Religion in New England* (Reprint: Hicksville, N .Y.: Regina Press, 1975), 5.
30. John E. Smith, *Jonathan Edwards* (South Bend: University of Notre Dame Press, 1992), 9.
31. Edwin Scott Gaustad, *The Great Awakening in New England* (New York: Harper and Brothers, 1957), 26.
32. Benjamin Franklin, *The Works of Franklin* (Chicago: Townsend,1882), 138.
33. Nathan Cole's account of Whitefield's visit to Connecticut on October 23, 1740, from *Christian History*, 12, no.2: 12.

34. Edwin C. Dargan, *A History of Preaching* (Grand Rapids: Baker, 1954) II:307.
35. One should add the twentieth-century phenomena of Pentecostalism to the list.
36. See Roy J. Fish, "The Effect of Revivals on Baptist Growth in the South," in *The Lord's Free People in a Free Land,* ed. William R. Estep (Fort Worth: Evans Press, 1976),104-5.
37. Cited in Leon McBeth, *The Baptist Heritage* (Nashville: Broadman, 1987), 228.
38. Charles F. James, *Documentary History of the Struggle for Religious Liberty in Virginia* (Lynchburg:]; P. Bell Company, 1900), 75.
39. William Warren Sweet, *Methodism in American History* (New York: The Methodist Book Concern, 1933), 65-66.
40. Cited by Ibid., 59.
41. Jonathan Edwards, "Some Thoughts," in *Complete Works*, I: 424.
42. Ibid., 426.

Chapter 11

1. Quoted in Charles A. Johnson, *The Frontier Camp Meeting* (Dallas: Southern Methodist University Press, 1955), 11.
2. The focus of this chapter will be on the awakening on American soil.
3. For a summary of differing dates, see Munton, "The Contributions of J. Edwin Orr," 133-38. Historians who see the entire period as composing one awakening include Sydney A. Ahlstrom, *A Religious History of the American People* (New Haven: Yale University Press, 1972), 415-509; *Perry Miller, The Life of the Mind in America* (New York: Harcourt, Brace and World, 1965), 34ff; and Timothy L Smith, *Revivalism and Social Reform in Mid-Nineteenth Century America* (New York: Abingdon Press, 1957), 45-62.
4. Daniel Dorchester, *Christianity in the United States* (New York: Hunt and Eaton, 1895), 316.
5. Lyman Beecher, *Autobiography, Correspondence, etc.* (New York: Harper and Brothers, 1864), 1:43.
6. Bennett Tyler, ed., *New England Revivals, as They Existed at the Close of the Eighteenth Century, and the Beginning of the Nineteenth Centuries* (Wheaton: Richard Owen Roberts, reprint, 1980).
7. For more on the awakening in England near the turn of the nineteenth century, see]. Edwin Orr, *The Eager Feet: Evangelical Awakenings, 1790-1830* (Chicago: Moody Press, 1975),13-45.
8. Cited in Arthur B. Strickland, *The Great American Revival* (Cincinatti: Standard Press, 1934), 45.
9. Alvah Hovey, *A Memoir of the Life and Times of Isaac Backus* (Harrisonburg, Va.: Gano Books, 1991), 304.
10. Quoted in Beardsley, *Religious Progress through Religious Revivals*, 33.
11. Mark Galli, "Revival at Cane Ridge," *Christian History* 45:10.
12. Cited in John B. Boles, *The Great Revival1787-1805* (Lexington: The University of Kentucky Press, 1972), 42.
13. See Peter Cartwright, *Autobiography of Peter Cartwright: The Backwoods Preacher*, ed. W. P. Strickland (New York: Carlton and Porter, 1857), 24-27.
14. Boles, *Great Revival*. 49.
15. Galli, "Cane Ridge," 11.
16. Boles, *Great Revival*, 56-57.
17. Ibid., 68.
18. See Roy]. Fish, "How to Keep the Fire Going," in *Revival! The Story of the Current Awakening in Brownwood, Fort Worth, Wheaton, and Beyond*; ed. John Avant, Malcolm McDow, and Alvin Reid (Nashville: Broadman & Holman , 1996), 157.
19. Orr, *Eager Feet*, 63.
20. Bernard A. Weisberger, *They Gathered at the River: The Story of the Great Revivalists and Their Impact on Religion in America* (Boston: Little, Brown and Company, 1958), 45.
21. See Cartwright, *Autobiography*.

22. Ahlstrom, *Religious History*, 437.
23. Joshua Bradley, *Accounts of Religious Revivals in Many Parts of the United States from 1815 to 18.* (Wheaton: Richard Owen Roberts, 1980), passim.
24. Edwards, *Revival,* 117.
25. Beardsley, *Religious Progress*, 54.
26. Lewis A. Drummond, *The Life and Ministry of Charles G. Finney* (Minneapolis: Bethany House, 1983), 9.
27. Charles G. Finney, *The Autobiography of Charles G. Finney*, ed. Helen Wessel (Minneapolis: Bethany House Publishers, 1977), 21.
28. The Calvinism Finney faced was not the spiritually enriched type espoused by Edwards and Whitefield. For example, Drummond noted the preaching of the day was "plodding and pedantic; every word was first put on paper and then laboriously read." In *Charles G. Finney*, 67.
29. The following quotations, unless otherwise noted, come from Garth M. Rosell and Richard A. G. Dupuis, eds., *The Memoirs of Charles G. Finney* (Grand Rapids: Academic Books, 1989).
30. Ibid., 174.
31. Fish, 'The Effect of Revivals on Baptist Growth in the South," 110.
32. John F. Thornbury, *God Sent Revival* (Grand Rapids: Evangelical Press, 1977), 178.
33. Beecher, *Autobiography*, 11:94.
34. Drummond, *Charles G. Finney*, 139.
35. Quoted in Rosell and Dupuis, *Memoirs of Charles G. Finney*, 326.
36. Ibid., 307.
37. Ibid., 376.
38. This term has created confusion by some who fail to distinguish the significant difference between revival, which focuses on believers, and evangelism, which focuses on reaching the lost. A good example of confusion in terminology is William Mcloughlin, *Revivals, Awakenings, and Reform: An Essay on Religion and Social Change in America, 1607-1977* (Chicago: The University of Chicago Press, 1978), xiii.
39. One should note that there were yet many who opposed revival in general, especially as represented in the rising tide of Unitarianism.
40. J. Edwin Orr, "Revival and Evangelism," *World Evangelization* March 1985, 7. For a recent analysis of the views of Finney, see Daniel Bryant Forshee, "The Pastoral Evangelism of Charles Grandison Finney with Applications for Contemporary Pastoral Evangelists," (Ph.D. diss., Southwestern Baptist Theological Seminary, 1995), 166-204.
41. Winthrop Hudson, *Religion in America* (New York: Charles Scribner's Sons, 1981), 143.
42. Charles G. Finney, *Revival Fire* (Waukesha, Wis.: Metropolitan Church Association, n.d.), 10-11.
43. This extremely critical debate in the modem history of spiritual awakening bears further study than the present volume has space to give. The following can help to shed light on the subject. From the Calvinistic heritage see *Revival and Revivalism*, 163-274; Edwin Orr, "Revivals Can't Be Organized, . . . But If One Comes, Look Out!" *Moody Monthly*, July-August 1974, 28-29; Munton, "The Contributions of J. Edwin Orr," 87-113. From the perspective favoring Finney, see *Revival Lectures*; and Rosell and Dupuis, *Memoirs of Charles G. Finney*. In a recent book, Wesley Duewel demonstrates a bias toward Finney. In his history of revival he devotes half a page to Edwards and four chapters to Finney! See Duewel, *Revival Fire*, 63, 92-124.
44. John Wesley White, "The Influence of North American Evangelicalism in Great Britain between 1830 and 1914 on the Origin and Development of the Ecumenical Movement," (Unpublished Ph.D. diss., Mansfield College, Oxford University, 1963), 123.
45. For further comment about the absurdity of the usage of "revival" in the contemporary scene, see, J .Edwin Orr, *The Event of the Century* (Wheaton: International Awakening Press, 1989), xi-xvii . I propose a middle-ground understanding, using the expression "revival meeting" (a meeting focusing on revival) to refer to scheduled meetings designed to call the church back to God, and "evangelistic meeting" to refer to evangelistic crusades.

46. Orr, *The Fervent Prayer*, xx. (Italics added)
47. Benjamin Rice Lacy, *Revivals in the Midst of the Years* (Richmond: John Knox Press, 1943), 87 .
48. Weisberger, *They Gathered at the River*, 3.
49. Ellen Lorenz, *Glory Hallelujah! The Story of the Campmeeting Spiritual* (Nashville: Abingdon, 1978), 41.

Chapter 12

1. Beardsley, *Religious Progress through Revivals*, 40.
2. Roy J. Fish, "The Awakening of 1858 and Its Effects on Baptists in the United States," (Th.D. diss., Southwestern Baptist Theological Seminary, 1963), iii, said this was the least known of all evangelical awakenings. Fish's dissertatlon has recently been published as *When Heaven Touched the Earth*, (Azle, TX: Need of the Time, 1996).
3. Miller, *The Life of the Mind in America* (New York: Bobbs-Merrill, 1965), 88. Thus the inspiration for the title of a book by Orr cited elsewhere.
4. Orr, *Event of the Century*, 1.
5. Warren A. Candler, *Great Revivals and the Great Republic* (Nashville: Publishing House of the M.E. Church, South, 1904), 210.
6. Frank G. Beardsley, *A History of American Revivals* (New York: American .Tract Society, 1904), 216.
7. Orr, *The Fervent Prayer*, 5. William McLoughlin, *Modern Revivalism: Charles Grandison Finney to Billy Graham* (New York: Ronald, 1959), 163.
8. Samuel Irenaeus Prime, *The Power of Prayer, Illustrated in the Wonderful Displays of Divine Grace at the Fulton Street and Other Meetings in New York and Elsewhere,in 1857 and 1858* (New York: Charles Scribner, 1858), 14.
9. Weisberger, *They Gathered at the River*, 139.
10. "How to Have a Revival," *Independent*, 12 January 1854.
11. David N. Lord, ed., "Thoughts on the Revival of Eighteen-Hundred and Fifty-Eight," *The Theological and Literary Journal*, 11 July 1858-April1859): 197.
12. Orr, *Event of the Century*, 50.
13. Ibid., 25.
14. *Christian Advocate and Journal*, in J. Edwin Orr, *The Second Great Awakening in America* (London: Marshall, Morgan and Scott, 1952), 23.
15. Samuel Irenaeus Prime, *Prayer and Its Answer* (New York: Charles Scribner's Sons, 1882), 24.
16. Talbot W. Chambers, *The Noon Prayer Meeting of the North Dutch Reformed Church* (New York: Board of Publications of the Reformed Protestant Dutch Church, 1858), 42.
17. Prime, *Power of Prayer*, 22.
18. Chambers, *Noon Prayer Meeting*, 46-48.
19. Documented in Orr, *Fervent Prayer*, 9.
20. Prime, *Power of Prayer,* 77.
21. Ibid., 296.
22. Fish, "The Awakening of 1858," 60.
23. Finney, *Memoirs*, 443-44.
24. Chambers, *Noon Prayer Meeting*, 196-97.
25. Fred Hoffman, *Revival Times in America* (Boston: W. A. Wilde, 1956), 114.
26. From the pastor's biography as recorded in Lacy, *Revivals*, 114.
27. Orr, *Event of the Century*, 216.
28. Hoffman, *Revival Times in America*, 117.
29. J. William Jones, a chaplain in General Robert E. Lee's army, wrote *Christ in the Camp* (Atlanta: The Marin and Hoyt Company, 1887); also William w. Bennett, *A Narrative of the Great Revival Which Prevailed in the Southern Armies* (Philadelphia: Claxton, Remsen and Haffelfmger, 1877).

30. Fish, "The Awakening Revival of 1858," 259.
31. Jones, *Christ in the Camp*, 296.
32. John Pollock, *Moody: The Biography* (Chicago: Moody Press, 1983), 34.
33. Orr, "Revival and Evangelism," 6.
34. Orr, *Fervent Prayer*, 112.
35. Orr, *Event of the Century*, 313.
36. A. B. Earle, *Bringing in the Sheaves* (Boston: James H. Earle, 1868), 59.
37. John G. Lorimer, *The Recent Great Religious Awakening in America, and the Lessons Which It Suggests* (London: W. R. McPun, 1859), 1.
38. Thomas Phillips, *The Welsh Revival: Its Origin and Development* (Edinburgh: Banner of Truth, reprint, 1995), 1.
39. Ibid., 7.
40. Cairns, *Endless Line of Splendor*, 171.
41. Robert Shindler, *From the Usher's Desk to the Tabernacle Pulpit* (London: Passmore and Alabaster, 1892), 68-69.
42. Edwards, *Revival*, 78.
43. Fish, "The Awakening of 1858," 228-29.
44. Taylor, *Exploring Evangelism*, 326.
45. Ruth A. Tucker, *From Jerusalem to Irian Jaya* (Grand Rapids: Zondervan, 1983),261.
46. Beardsley, *History of American Revivals*, 238-39.

Chapter 13
1. Evan Roberts, in W. T. Stead, ed., *The Story of the Welsh Revival* (London: Fleming H. Revell, 1905), 6.
2. Orr, *Campus Aflame*, 111, said, "The fifteen years following 1899 proved to be years of great spiritual awakening around the world." The most detailed account of the awakening is J. Edwin Orr, *The Flaming Tongue* (Chicago: Moody, 1973). Also see Cairns, *Endless Line of Splendor*, 177-208. McLoughlin, *Revivals, Awakenings, and Reform*, 10, identified 1890-1920 as "the Third Great Awakening," ignoring the 1857-58 Prayer Revival. Further, see Philip Jenkins, *The Next Christendom: The Coming of Global Christianity* (New York: Oxford University Press, 2002); Shaw, *Global Awakening.*
3. Eifian Evans, *The Welsh Revival of 1904* (London: Evangelical Press, 1969), 46-47.
4. Jessie Penn-Lewis, *The Awakening in Wales and Some of the Hidden Springs* (New York: Fleming H. Revell, 1905), 28.
5. Ibid., 37.
6. Orr, *Flaming Tongue*, 3.
7. Ibid., 5. For a detailed account of Roberts' thoughts see H. Elvit Lewis, "With Christ among the Miners," in *Glory Filled the Land: A Trilogy on the Welsh Revival* (1904-05), ed. Richard Owen Roberts (Wheaton: International Awakening Press, 1989), 37-42.
8. James A. Stewart, *Invasion of Wales by the Spirit though Evan Roberts* (Ft. Washington, Penn.: Christian Literature Crusade, 1970), 28-29.
9. Cited in Arthur Goodrich and others, eds. *The Story of the Welsh Revival* (New York: Fleming H. Revell Company, 1905), 46. J. Edwin Orr examined the papers as seen in *The Flaming Tongue*, 15.
10. G. Campbell Morgan, "The Revival: Its Source and Power," in *Glory Filled the Lana: A Trilogy on the Welsh Revival* (1904-05), eq. Richard Owen Roberts (Wheaton: International Awakening Press, 1989), 170.
11. Penn-Lewis, *Awakening in Wales*, 69.
12. Stewart, *Invasion of Wales by the Spirit*, 52.
13. From J. Cynddylan Jones, "Introduction," in Penn-Lewis, *Awakening in Wales*, 8-9.
14. Orr, *Flaming Tongue*, 15.
15. Stewart, *1nvasion of Wales by the Spirit*, 15-17.

16. Darrell M. Robertson, *The Chicago Revival, 1876: Society and Revivalism in a Nineteenth-Century City* (London: Scarecrow Press, 1989), 2.
17. Beardsley, *History of American Revivals*, 309.
18. Penn-Lewis, *Awakening in Wales*, 17.
19. L. R. Scarborough, *A Modern School of the Prophets: A History of the Southwestern Baptist Theological Seminary* (Nashville: Broadman Press, 1939), 56.
20. Reports of Revival in America from Orr, *Flaming Tongue*, 67-80.
21. W.W. Hamilton, "The Baylor Revival," *Baptist Argus*, 13 April1905, 4.
22. J. Kennedy Maclean, *Torrey and Alexander* (London: S. W. Partridge and co., n.d.), 51.
23. R. A. Torrey, *How to Promote and Conduct a Successful Revival* (New York: Revell, 1901), 29.
24. J. Wilbur Chapman, *Revivals and Missions* (New York: Lentilhon and Company, 1900), 9.
25. Edward Everett Ham, *50 Years on the Battlefront with Christ; A Biography of Mordecai F. Ham* (Nashville: Hermitage Press, 1950), 26-27.
26. George Wheaton Taft, "The Pittsburgh Revival, 1904," *Watchman*, 31 March 1904, 14; George T. B. David, "The Great Philadelphia Awakening," *Baptist Argus*, 30 April1908, 5.
27. "The Present Revival," *Christian Observer*, 8 February 1905, 2.
28. M. A. M., "Revival in Denver," *Watchman*, 16 February 1905, 12.
29. B. F. Riley, "Great Revival in Houston, Texas," *Baptist Argus*, 25 May 1905, 7; other reports included Otis E. Carter, "The Austin Revival," *Baptist Standard*; 23 June 1904, 12; O.L Hailey, "A Texas Breeze and Revival Wave," *Baptist Argus*, 8 September 1904, 3; G. F. Robertson, "Spiritual Movement in Paris, Texas," *Christian Observer*, 1 March 1905, 10.
30. Donald W. Dayton, *Theological Roots of Pentecostalism* (Metuchen, N.J.: The Scarecrow Press, Inc., 1987), 65-66.
31. Klaude Kendrick, *The Promise Fulfilled; A History of the Modern Pentecostal Movement* (Springfield, Mo.: Gospel Publishing House, 1961), 31-32.
32. Orr, *Flaming Tongue*, 177.
33. Sarah E. Parham, *The Life of Charles F. Parham, Founder of the Apostolic Faith Movement* (New York: Garland Publishing, 1985), 52-53. Orr, *Flaming Tongue*, 178, said these "enthusiasts often naively thought that they had received a xenolalic manifestation."
34. Kendrick, *Promise fulfilled*, 54.
35. "When the Spirit Fell," *Pentecostal Evan*gel, 6 April1946, 6.
36. In Bartleman's own account of the revival, he spoke of hearing F. B. Meyer, in Los Angeles describe the Welsh revival. This and the tragic death of his daughter Esther caused him to seek God totally. See Frank Bartleman, "How Pentecost Came to Los Angeles," in *Witness to Pentecost; The Life of Frank Bartleman, The Higher Christian Life: Sources for the Study of the Holiness, Pentecostal, and Keswick Movements*, ed. Donald Dayton (New York: Garland Publishing, 1985), 11-12.
37. Charles Hummel, *Fire in the Fireplace: Contemporary Charismatic Renewal* (Downers Grove: IVP, 1978), 173.
38. Orr, *The Flaming Tongue*, 53ff.
39. Duewel, *Revival Fire*, 206.
40. Ibid., 241-52.
41. See Basil Miller, *Praying Hyde* (Grand Rapids: Zondervan, 1943), 29-39.
42. From Miller, *Praying Hyde*, 48-49.
43. Duewel, *Revival Fire*, 230. See also Orr, *Flaming Tongue*, 130-156.
44. For further study, see William Blair and Bruce Hunt, *The Korean Pentecost* (Edinburgh: Banner of Truth, 1977).
45. Jonathan Goforth, *By My Spirit* (Minneapolis: Bethany, 1964) , describes in detail Goforth's missionary work.

46. Orr, *Flaming Tongue*, 129.
47. *1905 Southern Baptist Convention Annual*, 36.

Chapter 14

1. This statement was made in a letter to the author in 1989 from Hogue concerning the growing signs of revival when he was pastor of the First Baptist Church of Ada, Oklahoma, in the late 1960s.
2. Read the fascinating account of the Shantung Revival by C.L. Culpepper here: http://www.gospeltruth.net/shantung.htm. See also Lewis Drummond, *Miss Bertha: Woman of Revival* (Nashville: Broadman & Holman, 1996). See also Wesley L. Handy, "An Historical Analysis of he North China Mission (SBC) and Kesweick Sanctification in the Shandong Revival, 1927-1937" (PhD. Diss., Southeastern Baptist Theological Seminary, 2012).
3. See J. Edwin Orr, *Good News in Bad Times* (Grand Rapids: Zondervan, 1953); Clifford Olmstead, *The History of Religion in the United States* (Englewood Cliffs, N.J.: Prentice-Hall, 1960), 589-91; Hoffman, *Revival Times in America*, 155-180; and Arthur Johnston, *The Battle for World Evangelism* (Wheaton: Tyndale, 1978), 126ff.
4. Orr, *Good News*, 254. One should note that these comments were made early in the decade.
5. Edward 1. R. Elson, "Evaluating Our Religious Revival," *The Journal of Religious Thought* 14 (Autumn-Winter 1956-57): 55.
6. Gerald Ira Gingrich, *Protestant Revival Yesterday and Today* (New York: Exposition Press, 1959), 9.
7. Billy Graham, "Our Greatest Secret Weapon," *The American Magazine*, 158 (November 1954), 19, as cited in Gingrich, *Protestant Revival Yesterday and Today*, 80.
8. Gingrich, *Protestant Revival Yesterday and Today*, 92.
9. Orr, *Good News*, 72. See Hoffman, *Revival Times in America*, 163-64.
10. Mary Dorsett, "Wheaton's Past Revivals," in *Accounts of a Campus Revival: Wheaton College* 1995, ed. by Timothy K. Beougher and Lyle Dorsett (Wheaton: Harold Shaw, 1995), 62.
11. Bill Bright, *The Coming Revival: America's Call to Fast, Pray, and Seek God's Face* (Orlando: Here's Life, 1995), 83.
12. Ibid.
13. David Lockard, *The Unheard Billy Graham* (Waco: Word Books, 1971), 13.
14. John Pollock, *To All the Nations* (San Francisco: Harper and Row, 1985), 41.
15. Richard Riss, *A Survey of Twentieth Century Revival Movements in North America* (Peabody, Mass.: Hendrickson, 1988), 143.
16. Ibid., 105.
17. David Edwin Harrell, Jr., *All Things Are Possible: The Healing and Charismatic Revivals in Modern America* (Bloomington: Indiana University Press, 1975) ,5-6.
18. Orr, *Campus A*flame, 195.
19. Edwards, *Revival*, 254. Ambassador Productions Ltd. of Belfast have a collection of Campbell's account on audiocassette entitled "Lewis-Land of Revival."
20. Duncan Campbell, *The Nature of God-Sent Revival* (Montvale, Va.: Christ Life Publications, n.d.), 9.
21. Ibid., 10.
22. N. Langford-Smith, "Revival in East Africa," *The International Review of Missions* 39 (Aprill1950): 72.
23. Collin Hansen and John Woodbridge *A God-Sized Vision: Revival Stories that Stretch and Stir*. Zondervan, 2010. Kindle Edition, Kindle Locations 1928-1930.
24. Ibid., Kindle Locations 2155-2158.
25. William E. Allen, *A History of Revivals of Religion* (Atrim, N. Ireland: Revival Publishing Co., 1951), 63.
26. Richard F. Loveless, *Dynamics of Spiritual Life: An Evangelical Theology of Renewal* (Downers Grove: InterVarsity Press, 1979), 11. See Alvin L Reid, "The Impact of the Jesus Movement on

Evangelism among Southern Baptists," (Ph.D diss., Southwestern Baptist Theological Seminary, 1991).

27. Richard Ostling, Mayo Hohs, and Margaret Boeth, "The New Rebel Cry: Jesus Is Coming!" *Time*, 21 June 1971, 59, 62.

28. "Street Christians: Jesus as the Ultimate Trip," *Time*, 03 August 1971, 31.

29. Don Williams, *Call to the Streets* (Minneapolis: Augsburg Publishing House, 1972).

30. See Reid, "Impact of the Jesus Movement," 52-60.

31. Southern Baptist leaders influenced by revival movements in the early 1970s, from Reid, "Impact of the Jesus Movement," 48-97.

32. Michael McFadden, *The Jesus Revolution* (New York: Harper and Row, 1972), 15.

33. Billy Graham, *The Jesus Generation* (Grand Rapids: Zondervan, 1971), 141.

34. Henry C. James, "Campus Demonstrations," in *One Divine Moment*, ed. Robert E. Coleman (Old Tappan: Fleming H. Revell, 1970), 55.

35. For more about the movement of God in Canada in 1970 see Henry T. Blackaby, *What the Spirit Is Saying to the Churches* (Atlanta: Home Mission Board, 1988).

36. The following statements can been found in the state convention annuals in the years mentioned.

37. *1971 Southern Baptist Convention Annual*, 141. Italics added.

38. For an overview of these and numerous other SBC churches, see Reid, "Impact of the Jesus Movement."

39. Dallas Lee, "The Electric Revival," *Home Missions*, June/July 1971, 32. 3

40. Reid, "Impact of the Jesus Movement," 70.

41. John Yeats, "Elliff Calls Southern Baptists to Prayer for Spiritual Awakening," *Indiana Bapt*ist, 30 July 1996, 1.

42. John W. Styli, "Sound and Vision: 15 Years of Music and Ministry," *Contemporary Christian Music*, July 1993, 42. By 1981 CCM was the fifth leading category of music, ahead of jazz or classical. In 1983 5 percent of all record sales were gospel music, the majority of which was CCM. Also, by the early 1980s there were over 300 exclusively Christian music radio stations.

43. Ibid. , 43. .

44. C. Peter Wagner, "The Prayer Movement and the Local Church," *Ministry Advantage*, 4, no.6 July-August 1993): 1.

45. Reid, "Impact of the Jesus Movement," 142.

46. Walker Knight, "Prelude to Spiritual Awakening," *Missions USA*, March- April1982, 19.

47. Nancy justice, "Jesus People: Where Are They Now*?" Charisma*, September 1993, 26.

48. Orr, *Campus Aflame*, 212.

Chapter 15

1. Taken from a letter from Fish inviting Fort Worth area churches to chapel on March 1, 1995, to hear John Avant's testimony of the Brownwood revival.

2. See Bill Bright, *The Coming Revival* (Orlando: NewLife Publications, 1995; and Robert E. Coleman, *The Coming World Revival* (Wheaton: Crossway Books, 1995).

3. The accounts in this chapter related to the Brownwood revival are adapted from Avant, McDow, and Reid, *Revival.*

4. See also Timothy Beougher and Lyle Dorsett, eds., *Accounts of a Campus Revival: Wheaton 1995.*

5. Arthur Wallis, *In the Day of Thy Power* (London: Christian Literature Crusade, 1956), 199. Italics added.

6. Interactive workbooks of *Experiencing God* and *Fresh Encounter* are available from LifeWay Press, Nashville, TN 37234. The trade book editions are *Experiencing God* (Nashville: Broadman & Holman, 1994) and *Fresh Encounter: Experiencing God in Revival and Spiritual Awakening* (Nashville: Broadman & Holman, 1996) .

7. Duewel, *Revival Fire*, 16.

8. Avant, McDow, and Reid, *Revival*, 2.
9. Bill McCartney, *From Ashes to Glory*, comp. Dave Diles (Nashville: Thomas Nelson, 1995), 285-86.
10. Ibid., 288.
11. http://www.huffingtonpost.com/2012/10/10/the-religious-none-a profile_n_1952794.html (Accessed 2-6-2013).

Page 26,

19346160R00195

Made in the USA
San Bernardino, CA
22 February 2015